A Lullaby of Flies

Kimberly Presa

Copyright © 2016 Presa, Kimberly
All rights reserved.
ISBN-13: 978-1532741890

DEDICATION

This book is dedicated to everyone who refuses to give in.

TABLE OF CONTENTS

Acknowledgements
Foreword

1. Lepidopteron
2. Rachel
3. Before the Flood
4. After the Flood
5. Role Reversal
6. A Troubled Place
7. Under and Ovary
8. Never a Tear, Baby of Mine
9. Sweet Fifteen
10. A Teenage Waste
11. Backseat Ashes
12. Out With the Old
13. In With the New
14. Don't Feed the Chickens
15. California is Burning
16. The Roadhouse
17. Heart of Clay
18. A Brief Homecoming
19. The Next Step
20. Recruiter's Block
21. Basic
22. Prue
23. Shady J
24. On Duty
25. Over the Pond
26. Mortar and Mettle
27. And Then There Were Two
28. Norah
29. By the Horns
30. Dollars to Doughnuts
31. Behavioral Commonwealth
32. Down at the Lodge
33. Twenty-one Guns
34. Sepsis and a Wedding
35. Land of Lincoln
36. Second Team
37. Not Really the End

Afterword

Acknowledgements

I find that some of the people I need to thank I have met only once; like catalysts, they came briefly into my life and changed everything: The Air Force recruiter and MEPS Captain, who fought to get a scrawny, puffy-face girl out of a tent and into the military. Anne, who took me to Victoria's Secret and helped me buy my first real bra. The Army MSgt in Afghanistan who could have ignored the figure sitting in the light, but decided, despite his exhaustion, to stop and see if she needed any help. I find my life is full of such precious, brief treasures- many of which are not mentioned in these memoirs- and to them I owe much of my current happiness.

And of course, there are those that I know, or have known, very well in my life, who have helped me make changes through their support, love, or other means: My unbelievable husband, Scott, who is more than I ever could have dreamed of. My mother and father-in-law, who have given their son and I so much love, encouragement, and support when we were at the edge of ruin. My cat Sandee-Claws, who, despite her horrid nature, always came to snuggle me when I needed it most. My co-workers at Lakenheath, for everything, and my co-workers at Seymour Johnson, for the same. To Yakita, for keeping my Warrior Letter after all those years. My first boyfriend, Miles, who stood up for me. My professors at Bradley, who understood that I was trying to build something on a broken foundation, and were wise enough to see that that was no easy task. The women at Timberline Knolls, who are stronger than I could ever wish to be, and who I will always look up to like big sisters. My therapist, who listened when it mattered most. My step-children who challenge me and stretch the limits of my heart everyday. Norah, who made me realize that I had a heart in the first place.

And Prue, who helped me to understand that friendship doesn't have to look just one way, to be real.

Thank you.

Bury her deep, down deep,
Safe in the earth's cold keep.
Bury her deep--

Excerpt from Cat's Funeral, by E.V. Rieu

Forward

Pure joy. When I think of what it might be like, I envision myself running through fields of grass, wearing a loose fitting dress, long and white and billowing in a soft breeze. I don't see anyone else, but I know I am not alone. The image is surreal, fuzzy at the edges, and incomplete. Where am I coming from? Where am I going? Or is it because I don't know these things that I am allowed to experience the lightness of heart that I feel? There are no shadows on the plain- the sun is bright, but not glaring, and with each step the light absorbs my footprints in the grass. In a lot of ways, it reminds me of the opening scene of The Sound of Music, except without the singing, or the dare-devil camera tactics. You, or I, the observer, are introduced to a woman, running and smiling; we know nothing about her, but are enchanted by her wholehearted joy and vitality. When people ask me, "Are you happy?" this is the standard I compare myself to, which is a ludicrous thing, indeed. Even the most satisfied person in the world cannot experience 'opening-scene-of-The-Sound-of-Music' happiness at all times, and logically, I know that. But somewhere along the line, I became an idealist. Despite my personal struggles, I keep striving for the kind of freedom where I'm sprinting in the sun, unhindered by my past and unconcerned where my footsteps might take me.

I'm acquainted with a lot of people that tend to say, when life go awry, 'Things could be worse,' and for the most part, I agree- things could *always* be worse. I have seen things worse; I have been places where people's lives are much, much worse than mine has ever been. But does that mean things can not be *better*? Think of it in a physical sense: does the pain of losing two arms make the loss of one any less of a tragedy, or is it, in itself, a struggle all its own? It is my belief that the larger evils of the world do not negate the lesser ones. All fights should be fought with passion, because to someone, that is the only fight they need to win in order to survive; it is their white whale- it is everything.

I want to make it clear that I don't believe my life has been harder than anyone else's. That's not what this story is about. But I do believe that I was not prepared for what eventually came my way, and that I handled things badly. Every human is raised- referencing their social environment, genetics, and existing (or non-existing) parental examples- with their own individual capacity to handle life's tests, and throughout life, as their environments change and experiences compound, those capacities are always changing. Some people, for example, may bounce back immediately from a difficult break up, while others may not recover for years- or not at all. There is no single guide that can teach someone to successfully react to and overcome something, since every person's tapestry is created from different material- even brother's and sister's.

Looking back on my early youth, there were so many chances for someone to step in and realize something was peculiar, or 'off' about me, and perhaps do some early intervention work. But life, the disinterestedness of others, and my own damned cleverness, kept that from happening. My family was distracted with their own troubles much of the time, and my depression, which had rooted itself deep inside me by the age of seven, covered itself with smiles, jokes, and erratic behavior. Despite my resolve to wear a mask, it slipped very easily; the smallest upset sent me into a storm of tears and self-hatred. I felt fractured and on-edge at all times, and when I fell, I fell *hard*.

Like many children with low self-esteem, I was friendless for many years. I had a few acquaintances that I played with as I grew, but they tended to make fun of my size, which was considerably large- and so I avoided becoming too close for fear of being hurt. As the years passed, I became a bit like the spider in Walt Whitman's famous poem- expending filament after filament, searching for an anchor. Unfortunately, it would be years until I found that anchor- a true companion, who, heart and soul, was what a friend should be- and then somehow find the courage to accept that person wholeheartedly into my life.

Reality is strange. When it first hits you, your first reaction is to deny it, and then to bargain with it; in a way it's almost like grief. It can hurt, and take a lot of time to recover from. It takes knowledge and experience to become accustomed- or one could say, numbed- to the constant blunting that the world sends. But once in a while- just every so often- it sends you the most real, most wonderful thing you never could have imagined, even if you had tried. And then you realize, with a shock, that reality had somehow surpassed fantasy, and that you wouldn't trade it; not for anything.

<u>Lepidopteron</u>
<u>(1)</u>

Memories for me have always been more difficult to deal with than the situations that caused them, because when I'm going through something, no matter how horrifying it is, I am somehow aware that the moment will pass. What I fear the most is looking back at that moment and wishing it had never happened the way it did, making it even worse than it was and reliving it with amplified emotions. Usually, there is really nothing I could have done differently, given the emotional tools I was armed with at the time. But that never made it easier. No one ever sees the worst memories of their lives coming.

My childhood is full of such memories; my sister's illnesses, my constant loneliness, my mother's depression, my father's absence; the list goes on. I don't know if I'm simply chemically inclined to retain the bad memories over the good, or if there genuinely are more of them- but certainly, when looking at my life before the age of nineteen, I am filled with a nameless anxiety and lack the ability to recall a happy thought on my own accord. When discussing memories with acquaintances in casual conversation, as normal people do, I feel adrift and unable to make a connection, because my youth was so unconventional. No, I didn't have sleepovers- I didn't have any friends for about a thousand reasons. No, my dad didn't get protective with me over my first boyfriend- he let me do whatever I wanted, with whomever I wanted, because he didn't know what to do with me. No, I actually didn't go to prom- or any school dance, ever- I dropped out of high school after limping through sophomore year. No, my mom didn't go to my wedding; either of them; she died when I was fifteen.

Many times I get frustrated: where are my good memories? Where are my happy moments to bring to the surface, to turn in the light and admire? And I get weighed down by my own darkness, and remain silent as those around me discuss the joys of visiting their grandparents when they were young, and how they played sports when they were teens and won such-and-such trophy, and all the mischief they got themselves into when they were in high school.

Sometimes, though- and though it's rare, it *does* happen- a sound or a smell will appear as if from nowhere, and I will begin to cry. The tears always shock me, because at first I don't understand where they are coming from. It can take many moments of quiet reflection for me to realize that I'm recalling, however vaguely, a happy memory. For example, the smell of a pine tree reminds me of my sister and I decorating our family Christmas tree while my mother watches, retelling us the stories behind each unique, precious ornament. The smell of leather reminds me of long car trips with my dad, where he would make up goofy stories to make us laugh and pass the time. These are the memories I wish I could call forth without assistance, but they move like fireflies in my mind, blinking in and out of existence. When called upon to make a comment on my past, I often attempt to shrug it away in hopes that the person querying will just move on. I never want to bring people down when they're having a good time, but I don't want to lie either; I have yet to master that strange social norm that requires a person to smile when they're hurting.

My name's Kimberly, and I'm an anti-social lepidopteron. I've never been one to float easily into a conversation or bob gracefully among the flowered conviviality's of strangers. I'm more of a house-fly, because whenever I find myself entrapped by a crowd I quickly become an observer rather than a participant. With the gleaming eyes of an insect, I see myself there, alone while among many, and I pity myself. I always look so cold and out-of-place among the chattering couples and dirt-dishing females who are so eager to share their filth. I watch myself fidget with my drink and fix my hair, and notice how I smile with tight, rusty lips at the people who endeavor to engage me in conversation. *I can't*, I try to say to them, I *can't because I'm broken; I'm a malfunctioning machine whose purpose is unknown*. But I am voiceless. All I can do is gaze at the other machines that are whirring and buzzing satisfactorily, and dream that things were different.

When I was very little, I used to talk a lot; not to people, though. As a young girl I used to discourse with my cats, and even further than that, I would create unique voices for each one of them and we'd hold entire conversations together. Once and a while, my elder sister Rachel would join in, and we'd sit there, in the living room or dining room, and converse with our furry family members as if we were equals. Talking to our pets didn't feel at all silly to me no matter how ridiculous the conversations became, and a small part of me even believed that the animal personas were real. *I'm the queen*, I made my fat orange cat Misty warble. *You must follow royal decree and lift me up on the counter to eat!*

It's not wrong to have an imagination, right? Surely that's the question my poor mother asked herself often, as she went about her household chores listening to her daughters squeal and create unique voices for each cat. My mother, who kept mostly to herself, never said anything against our antics, and once or twice I even caught her talking to her especial cat Shelly in one of our assumed voices.

Though I could perform an entire conversation between myself and my cats, I could barely squeak out a single word to the other kids at school. Maybe it's because I was afraid; afraid of being picked on, or mocked, because I was different. Because I was fat.

I don't know when I first became aware of my size, but by the time I was in kindergarten I knew it better than I knew anything else. Most of the other kids in my class called me fat, my elder sister called me fat- there was never any reason to doubt their sincerity. And when I entered first grade and was given the part of Jack Spratt's wife in our Mother Goose play ("his wife could eat no lean") it seemed my role was set: I was the 'fat kid'.

I hated it. Some people get a thick skin when they're taunted, but I never did. Instead, I let it eat me alive. Fat was ugly. Fat was unwanted. Fat had no friends. The few associations I remember from my early childhood ended up liking me despite how I looked, and I burned with that constant realization.

My young life was all about my size. I couldn't buy jeans like the other kids, my mom said, because they didn't sell them to kids my size. I couldn't run and play like everyone else because I had a big stomach and tired easily; I still remember every time I did run, I comically held out the front of my shirt like a sail so people couldn't see my stomach jiggle. By the time I was in second grade, everyone knew I was The Fat Kid, and treated me as such. I received the occasional teasing, but was generally ignored by everyone, which was almost as bad. It was a terribly lonely and confusing existence for small child with a naturally friendly nature.

The only way I felt I could connect with people of my own age was to make them laugh by pretending to be ridiculous, but secretly, it tore me apart, and often before school I would cry and beg my mother not to make me go and endure another day. She never gave in, of course, because it's normal for kids to cry and beg not to go to school. If all parents gave in, no one would ever attend. But for some reason, her simple act of good parenting made me feel betrayed by her, like she didn't care that I got picked on, was called names, and had no friends.

My grades were never stellar, except for in reading and writing. Reading was my only past-time; I absorbed words like a sponge, and taught myself how to use them. My mom was very proud of my compositions; she hung my stories on our refrigerator like other families hang up their children's art, and I gloried over my icy gallery.

"You are just like your dad and Rachel!" I remember my mother saying when I was in third grade, as she placed a banana magnet over the story I had written on the Donner Party. "You're my talented little baby!"

If popularity and friends could be won by writing interesting stories, perhaps I would not have had such a hard time fitting in, but such was not the case. Kids- especially the kids in the small town that I lived in- were not the most well behaved bunch. There was a definite anti-fat sentiment in my school, and I recall that third grade was the first time that the name calling started to progress into something more.

One day, while working on a papier mache craft, I turned to a fellow student who was struggling with his project, and I asked, in a small, shy voice, "Do you want help? I'm pretty good at faces. My sister taught me how to draw them."

He was a small boy with wide, brown eyes, and for everyone else he seemed to have a smile, but for me he had only a look of disgust.

"I don't need help from a stupid fat girl like you," he hollered into the silent room, causing the other children at our table to laugh uproariously.

Heartbroken, I ran from the room and locked myself into a bathroom stall until a teacher came to find me. That was only the first of many such incidents. Kids refused to stand next to me in line, and would hold their noses and make rude comments such as, 'Fat people stink.' They squinted their eyes and stuck their front teeth out and mimicked a rodent because I had large front teeth, 'like a fat beaver' (a nickname I had for a long time). When I read aloud in class, people would squish their skin under their necks, attempting to make a double chin in order to mock me. There were so many different ways that they found to hurt me that it would be impossible to list them all. I became afraid of people in crowds and avoided them as much as I could. I wandered alone at recess, sat alone at lunch, and was always the last one to have a partner in any class activity.

When I went home at the end of the day, the first thing I would do is go to the kitchen and eat a large, sugary snack- sometimes a package of frosted Pop-Tarts, sometimes a Little Debbie snack cake or two. That was my absolute most favorite thing to do in the whole world; it helped me forget my size, and my terrible days at school. Later on in the evening, I'd eat dinner with my family, because until I was ten or so all four of us sat together at the dinner table. Most of the time it was just my sister, my mom and I, but at times my father would join us, too. My mom was an excellent cook and she had a schedule of nightly meals planned out for every week. As time went on, however, and our lives became more complicated, the meals at the table languished, and we began to dine separately, and in consequence talk became scarce.

Despite being picked on, I never thought to lose weight, or avoid fattening food; actually, I had begun to use food more and more as a means to comfort myself. I ate second helpings at every meal simply because it made me feel better. Sometimes, in secrecy, I took seconds or third servings of dessert; I even stole my sister's Christmas, Easter, and Halloween candy. Eating junk food, especially sweets, was the only thing that seemed to make my stress subside. Even though I knew it was temporary, in the moment it felt like a panacea for all of life's difficulties at school and at home. I clung to food desperately, used it medicinally, and when I wasn't eating I dreamt about it constantly until it was time to eat again. I lived only for what I put into my mouth next, and consequently, I forgot how to live.

Rachel

(2)

It was a little cold in Brookings, Oregon when school started the fall of my thirteenth year. Not that it ever got excessively frigid there, on the coast; we were too close to the ocean for it to ever snow- so close we could hear seals barking in the morning- but all the same it was drizzly, and chilly, and encouraged one to constantly stare out the window and long for summer. And so, though it was a bit brisk that morning, one could easily get by with a long sleeved shirt and jeans. Knowing this, before school I chose a close-fitting, long sleeved top from my laundry and wriggled into it. It was my favorite shirt. It had been my big sister's, and now it was mine. I went to the mirror in my room and stared at myself. Brown hair, brown eyes. Plump, but passable. I was in a good mood and could look past all of what I thought was ugly about me. The magic of a favorite shirt, I suppose.

I walked down the stairs into the kitchen to grab some breakfast. My father was in the living room, which was a bit abnormal for him; he worked the graveyard shift as a correctional officer at the state prison, and tended to be dead to the world until about six pm. My mother was sitting at the dining room table, tinkering with her various craft projects which were her saving grace. They both ignored me, or just didn't see me, as I walked past them. I vaguely wondered what my mother was working on as I foraged in the cabinet for a package of strawberry Pop-Tarts.

"Kim. You should put on a jacket or something," said my sister's voice suddenly. I turned to look at her, and held my breath. Rachel. Very tall, slightly more overweight than me, and perpetually grumpy. She hated me, and everything she said and did lately showed it. Even still, it took a moment for me to register what she was saying.

"It leaves more to the imagination. Your stomach won't stick out so much that way," Rachel continued, opening the fridge to get something to eat.

It was her way of saying I looked fat. She was probably even being nice, in her own way, trying to give me advice- but we were not intimate. A word a criticism from her was as hurtful as one from a stranger. I felt hot tears at the back of my eyes, but I wouldn't let them fall. I hadn't even been thinking about my weight much that morning. I was having a *good* morning. I needed just one good morning.

"I just think... maybe if something is a little bit tighter no one will think I'm bigger than I am," I said in a whispered voice. I was afraid of Rachel.

There was nothing to be afraid of this time. Rachel stared at me briefly with her piercing, brilliant blue eyes, and then poured some milk into a bowl of cereal, and exited the kitchen to eat it alone in her room. I glanced at my mom, who was still engrossed in her crafting- she was making a doll out of felt, of all things. *What the hell is she going to do with that?* I thought. I could hear the sound of sports coming from the living room where my dad sat in his big chair, eating a giant bowl of white rice with sugar and butter. I looked at my Pop-Tart, and carried it back with me to my own room. Once there, I looked into the mirror again and felt more depressed than I had in days. Maybe the shirt was too tight for someone like me, and I was being foolish by thinking I could wear it. Rachel was large too, and must know what she's talking about. Believing this to be the truth, I slipped out of the shirt and put on a large oversized one instead, and then sat on my bed and ate my breakfast in silence.

*

"Kim," said Rachel, who was sitting on the couch a few feet from where I reclined in a chair, "*Cover your feet.*"

Those were words I had heard almost every day for as far back as I could remember. My feet were hideous. They distracted Rachel from her television watching. They annoyed her when they moved or did anything foot-like. It was only my feet, too, that caused this reaction in her. I knew it was because I was ugly and she couldn't stand the sight of me. This being the truth, the only way to avoid confrontation was to wrap my feet in a blanket and stay as still as a mummy. I proceeded to smother my feet with an afghan.

"Kim, you're breathing too loud," said Rachel, glaring in my direction.

That was another problem I had. If it was audibly evident I was in a room with Rachel in any way, which included breathing or sighing, it was unacceptable. This was one of the problems I was aware of that engulfed more than just me; my sister was also driven to madness by the sound of my father's breathing. He was a bigger man and tended to breathe like one, always as if he were little behind in his breath. This had helped cause a rift between Rachel and our father, who was hardly around due to his work and hermit-like nature. They practically never saw each other, and when they did it often ended with my sister heaving a dramatic, frustrated sigh and stalking from the room.

I adjusted my breathing accordingly.

Despite our issues, I loved my sister with a little sister's devotion. I wanted to be in the same room with her all the time, even if she didn't want me to be there. When we were little, about four and seven, we shared a room, but my breathing had driven her to near madness; she laid out her blankets in the hallway every night and slept there, on the hard floor; sometimes she even made up a bed in the bathtub rather than be forced to be anywhere near me. It hurt, and I cried about it often. I was angry at myself for making her go away so often, and angry at her, too, for not loving me.

I have so many memories of Rachel and me together that they practically crowd out every other memory I have just by the numbers alone. Many are filled with conflict, but others are a joy when I'm able to recall them, such as the time we built mazes out of Dr. Seuss books for our kittens to go through, or the time we went roller blading, and my sister lost one of her blades in a mud sinkhole and had to walk home in her socks. And of course, the countless times we drew cartoons together at our kitchen table.

Drawing was something my sister excelled at more than anything else. She always received straight A's in school, but to her that was almost a negligible skill. She wanted to be an artist, and so that's where she put in her real work.

Rachel was fascinated at an early age by paintings, and Japanese animation, and comic books. Bettie & Veronica was one of her favorite things, and she would read the digests out loud to me in moments of friendliness while I held my breath as long as I could, praying she wouldn't hear me exhale and send me out of the room. I loved those times, and in an effort to prolong them I did everything I could to please Rachel and find new ways to spend time with her. For a few years, every Saturday morning I would set my alarm to ten minutes before six. I would then dress myself in a fluffy robe, and knock on Rachel's bedroom door. There was never an answer, so I would always step inside and make my way to her bed in the dark.

"Rachel," I'd whisper, shaking her gently, "It's six, do you want to watch Anime with me?"

Rachel (never a morning person) would grunt and then tell me to go away. I would then dash gleefully into the living room, turn on the television to channel thirty-two, and wait. In a few minutes, I would be rewarded for my patience by the arrival of a vaguely human-like figure enshrouded in blankets, which would plop down on the carpet directly in front of the screen. And my sister and I would watch cartoons together, without a word.

Of course, with the combination of my being very young at the time, it being so early in the morning, and the content of Japanese animation sometimes being beyond me, I would sometimes fall asleep. And sleep-breathing was one of the many things that are like nails down a chalkboard to the sound-sensitive Rachel. Whenever I fell asleep, she would push me or snap at me, and I would jerk awake, ashamed of my tiredness and saddened at the loss of our companionability. It seemed like I was always ruining everything for Rachel.

When I became a teen, I developed a bad habit of going into her room and 'borrowing' her clothes even though I knew I would suffer terribly for it. When she inevitably found out, she would curse at me, scream at the top of her lungs and say what a miserable person I was. It was in my pattern, after that, to say how sorry I was and promise to never do it again... which was never true. For a long while, I never knew why I stole her clothes. We had grown further apart as the years progressed, and whenever I saw her the air seemed to be filled with strange electricity, one which made the hairs on the back of my neck stand up. My fear of Rachel was becoming a palpable thing, but for some reason that wasn't enough to stop my thieving. My mother, (after she suggested that I don't steal clothes), suggested that I did it because I wanted to be closer to Rachel, and that maybe a good way to stave off an argument would be to tell her exactly how I felt. It was a breakthrough idea, though I was terrified at the thought of ever putting it into practice.

But put it into practice is exactly what I did. I had gone into my sister's room one morning and grabbed a shirt of hers I knew she liked. I went to school wearing it and when I came home, I left it on, knowing she would see it on me. And of course, when she did, she exploded. In the middle of her tirade (because it was a breakthrough idea) I told her I loved her. I told her that I was sorry for making her mad all the time, and that I just wanted us to get along like real sisters did.

Her reaction was not what I had hoped for.

"You're an idiot! Do you think the families on T.V. are real or something? They're crap! I don't want to 'get along' with *you*!" she said, still fuming.

"But I love you," I said lamely.

"Yeah, well, I hate you to death," said Rachel, as she walked away from me.

That's the first time I recall telling my sister that I loved her. It would be years until the words passed my lips again.

Before the Flood
(3)

    I knew at an early age that there is a difference between being depressed and having depression. I knew this with the upmost surety, because I lived with my mother for almost fifteen years. Anyone who has ever had depression, or lived with anyone who has, knows and understands this distinction. Depression is a shell-like second skin. It settles onto you slowly, like dust over time when there is not enough spirit inside of you to shake it off. Its weight clouds your mind, it separates you from the world; it changes how you see life, how you see your family, and it can even alter what you see in the mirror every day. One of the most dangerous things about depression, in my opinion, is that it detracts you from your real problems, the ones that pushed you so far away from your real life in the first place.

To me, my mom was a quiet lady with very few friends. She detested crowds and conflicts, loved crafts, and hated to read anything thicker than a Woman's Health magazine. She married my dad at a young age and by the time I came along she had lived with him for nine years, birthed one living child, and lost three due to pregnancy complications. I don't know exactly when it was she discovered that my father wasn't romantically in love with her; perhaps she had known all along. Regardless of when she found out, it was evident in her actions that she loved her husband and her daughters, and she continued to play the part of housewife for almost twenty years, only occasionally (unsuccessfully) holding jobs after my sister and I were both in school.

My mother had a hard early life. She, like my father, came from a low income background, with divorced parents- actually, her mother had an entire separate family that her father knew nothing about, and that was what caused the rift. Her father quickly re-married, and she found herself the eldest of seven step-siblings, and the object of hatred and jealousy of her new step-mother. She was emotionally- and sometimes physically- abused, and when she became a teenager she was otherwise abused by men. When she met my father, she saw in his place a white knight, and she clung to him and their future together like a drowning woman. She told me once that she had proposed to him, and he initially declined, only to accept later because of guilt. Though my father denies this, now, my own observation of their love-life was that it was virtually non-existent. The most romantically charged I ever saw my parents was when my mother gave my father two pecks on the cheek instead of one before he left for work one night. My father even told me once that living with her was like living with a pal, who you were not sexually attracted to, that you saw everyday for twenty years.

My mother always wanted to own her own home. I believe she wanted it more than she wanted anything in the world- more than some people want fame or fortune, or world peace. Having her own home, to her, would validate her past pains and her passionless marriage; perhaps she even believed it would save her mind.

My mother got her wish when my sister was thirteen and I was nine.

It was a very small house on the edge of a cul-de-sac with not much to brag about except a huge, fenced backyard that my father filled with two big dogs. My mom, being more of a cat person, showed her loyalty to the feline species by adopting up to six cats at a time, which we all accepted was a normal number. All-in-all, it was a good situation for our family in the beginning. The neighborhood was prosperous and growing, with manicured lawns, low traffic and a mysterious lagoon-type enclave for kids to explore. My mom became a radiant being at the thought of no longer having to live in apartment complexes, and I was even able to attend a brand new school that had been constructed only the year before. It was a hopeful new world that we all stepped into when we took the keys to that small, gray house.

Then one day, after walking home from school I sensed something was very wrong with my mother. Her eyes were dry, but she wasn't talking to me like she usually did, and there was energy in the air that I couldn't find a source to. Without welcoming me home, my mother simply went to the kitchen, handed me a sugary after-school snack and went to sit at the kitchen table to stare out the window in silence. Her favorite cat, Shelly, even jumped on the table to be fondled but was ignored by her usually affectionate master. Watching her with wide, fearful eyes, I finished my snack and then went to sit by her side and hold her hand. I remember the chair made a loud, abrasive noise when I drew it back from the table.

My mother didn't tell me for quite some time, but our family had been dealt a crushing blow: the house that my parents had paid to have built had, unbeknownst to them, been constructed on pumped-out swamp land. Our basement was basically an indoor swimming pool, and cracks in the foundation the size of the Grand Canyon were quickly making their unwanted presence known. Nothing could stop it, because the very land we lived on was against us. My mom's dream house was sinking.

I was too young to understand lawsuits, but I knew that we were in one, that it involved our house, and that we were losing. My parents argued often and reconciled just as much, usually by dropping the subject at hand. I recall that my dad's face was very somber whenever I saw him, which was not often, as I learned that to pay for our attorney he was forced to work long, tortuous hours at the state prison. I made sure to hug him whenever I had the chance, hoping it would cheer him up, but it never really seemed to work. It was a hard time for my parents. Many days I'd come home from school and catch my mother sobbing over the phone as she spoke to her mother or sister-in-law, trying to find some comfort in a comfortless situation. *How could they do this to us,* my mom would ask brokenly. *Who would sell a family a house that would fall to pieces in a few years?*

At night, because my father worked the graveyard shift, my mother was alone. I knew how much she disliked having no one around, so there were many nights where I would make my way to her room in the dark. Once there, I would have to push the multiple sleeping cats aside in order to snuggle in next to her, the spot always still warm from their furry bodies. Sometimes my mom wouldn't wake up, but if she did, we would talk for hours. Or rather, she would talk to *me* for hours. While holding onto me, and stroking my arm, she would tell me her fears about bankruptcy, and her anger at my father and their situation. During those long nights, I learned about how delicate our situation was, and how financially unstable we really were. I learned that my mom felt sad a lot of the time, and that she felt that she couldn't bear the strain much longer (I never truly learned what she meant until years later). At the time, all I could do was nestle in to her as close as I could and tell her how much I loved her, and that everything was going to be okay- just like she had done to me countless times when I was younger. Inside I was tormented that I couldn't make anything better for her, and I was whole-heartedly ashamed that my parents had to spend so much money in order to feed and clothe me. I hated the thought that I was a burden, though my mother had never said so. But that's what I felt like.

My parent's fighting reached a breaking point one day while my sister and I were enjoying one of our truce moments by drawing together at the kitchen table. I remember I was trying to copy every curved line that Rachel made on her paper, because everything she did looked so graceful and magical to me. I was breathing as shallowly as I could, and releasing the air in my lungs slowly, with the deep control of long practice. Every time I accidentally made a small noise, she would glance up at me piercingly, with rage in her eyes; I would hold my breath until she relaxed, and then I would relax, and we'd return to our papers as if nothing had happened. Such was our sisterly companionship when I heard the sound of raised voices coming from my parent's bedroom. A door slammed loudly, once, twice; I was instantly frightened. I listened as thundery footsteps came towards us, and I turned to watch, my pencil forgotten.

"I can't do that!" my mother yelled as she rushed to keep up with my dad, who was storming away from her. "I won't! I'm too frightened! What about the kids?" Her eyes were wide, wet and begging.

"If you won't do it, Kathy, then I can't live here with you anymore!" screamed my dad, whirling to look her in the eye. I had never seen him look so alive before.

The moment hung in the air, and then my mom and dad turned to see us at the table, watching them. They spoke briefly together in low tones and my dad went to grab his coat. My mother stepped forward and spoke to Rachel.

"Can you be in charge for a few minutes? Dad and I are going to go for a quick drive. We'll be back in half an hour."

Rachel nodded mutely as Mom grabbed her coat and followed Dad out the door. In the silence they left behind them, we both heard the car's engine turn over, and then it pull away.

Only after they left did my eyes start to well up. I couldn't think, I was so scared, and I didn't even understand why. I felt confused and panicky. I looked at Rachel who had already resumed making the graceful curves I so admired.

"Why are they mad?" I begged Rachel to answer, "Are they going to get a divorce?"

Rachel glanced at me with little apparent concern on her face.

"No," she said, and turned over her sheet of paper to conserve our diminishing supply. She hesitated then, and quietly added, "Everything's fine. Finish your character. I want to see it."

The thought that my artistic sister would want to see something that I doodled thrilled me. I nodded happily and flipped over my own piece of paper, and we drew together until our parents came home- not half an hour, but three hours later.

Our parents didn't divorce then. In fact, they seemed to ban together for a time to make necessary decisions about the house, and the lawsuit. I knew my mom was scared- they were developing a plan to accept a settlement out of court at a significant loss, and then completely abandon the house. I had no idea how my father felt.

I remember a recurring dream I used to have during those difficult days. It always began with me waking up in a cold, dark room. I would then begin to walk towards my mother's bedroom, but the hallway seemed to stretch into eternity. Right when it seemed I would never reach my goal, I would suddenly be there. As I put my hand on the door knob I would hear a sportscaster's voice coming from inside, such as the kind that narrated the games my dad watched. I'd open the door to see an impossibly giant, glowing television; and there, lying on a bed in front of it, would be my dad, mom and sister, all cheering and whooping while watching whatever sport was on. I would then carefully make my way to the bed and try to crawl in, but there was never any room. I'd push and push at them so that I could fit, but in the end I would fall off and roll to the floor. And there is where I would curl up to sleep, shivering from the cold.

I hated this dream. Sometimes I would wake up with tears in my eyes because it had seemed so real, though I knew it wasn't. My mom and sister hated sports, so why would they cheer at a sports show on TV? Plus, my mom would always make room for me if she could, because she loved me. I comforted myself with these thoughts, though the dreams didn't stop for a long time.

We didn't move for a few years. Engaged in a messy lawsuit, my parents had some tough decisions to make before we could move on with our lives. To accept the settlement, or not? To abandon their dream home, or to fix it somehow? I did my best to be there for my parents, but the strain was starting to take a toll on us all. I specifically recall one incident where my sister and I went to a book fair at school while my mother waited in the car, and I suppose we took longer than we had promised. Angrier than I had ever seen her before, she barged in, grabbed Rachel and I by the hands and dragged us out to the car. Once there, she slapped Rachel across the face, turned to me and ripped up the Troll coloring book I had bought with my own money. I remember sobbing uncontrollably, terrified by the look of fury on my mother's face. It was a bad time for everyone. I was in a vacuum of emotion, and my grades were bad. Rachel was getting worse in her treatment of me, to the point where she threatened me with physical violence. My father was never there. My mother's depression reached such depths that she began to use me as her emotional squeak toy. And it was while we were still there, at that sinking house on the cul-de-sac, that I first encountered death.

*

My family was never big on friends. We never went over to neighbor's houses for barbecues, or attended Christmas parties, or anything like that. I have, in fact, no memories whatsoever of either of my parents being social, except for my mother's odd friendship with an old man and his wife across the street from our rapidly submerging home.

The first thing I recall about the old man, Al, is that he was probably in his late sixties, retired, and always sat in his garage chain smoking nasty smelling cigarettes and the occasional cigar. His wife, Margaret, tended to stay in the house and I rarely saw her, except when my mother and I were invited in a couple of times for cookies. Margaret was a kind, bright old lady with a pile of blue hair atop her head, and she liked to pinch my cheeks. She and my mom chatted a lot, and I remember being pretty bored as I mindlessly stuffed my face with treats. But I still liked being over at their house, because- well, cookies- and also because their house was nicer than ours- it was cleaner, and it didn't smell like dogs.

My mom had been a smoker earlier in her life, and I think her stress over the lawsuit and her need for friendship caused her to gravitate towards Al and his garage. I saw her smoking in there multiple times, laughing with him, a self-rolled cigarette in her hand, her pink face looking earnestly into his old wizened one. I didn't like the smell of smoke, and something about Al scared me. He had two giant yellow teeth that reminded me of a sewer rat, and he wheezed and coughed after every other word. Sometimes he would call out to me from his garage while I was playing outside, and ask me to walk to the postal box and check his mail, adding that he would give me a quarter if I did. I always complied because I wanted the money, but I still hated every moment of it that required me to be in his presence.

  One night, when my mother was venting to me as we lay in her bed, she told me that Al was in love with her, and that she had told my dad about Al's flirtations, but that my dad didn't care. What is a child supposed to do with that information? I told her, after a snuggle, that I was sorry, and that Al was gross and really old and creepy. My mother laughed and agreed, but I could tell she still wanted something I couldn't give her.

  One summer, Al bought his wife Margaret a bike to keep herself active, and also perhaps so he could slumber unbothered in his smoke-cave. It might have worked well if poor Margaret hadn't taken half a turn around the cul-de-sac and immediately broken her hip. She was confined to her bedroom after that, completely immobile, and my mom and I visited her once in a while with gifts of flowers and tea. On those visits, were no cookies or happy chats.

It was an early morning in the fall, and foggy, when the police showed up across the street. I alone of our household had been awake to hear the gun shot that ended Margaret's life- gun shots in that area were not normal, and it had frightened me, so I had awakened my mom. A little later, my family was gathered in front of our bay window and watching the flashing lights of the cop cars and ambulance, wondering what happened- but we weren't long in waiting to find out. Margaret had committed suicide with a handgun, one of Al's, and had left a short suicide note in near illegible handwriting saying she didn't want to live a bedridden life. I heard my mother whisper tearfully to my father,

"Al did it. Margaret didn't have a gun anywhere near her, she couldn't move. Al killed her so that he wouldn't have to take care of her anymore. And if she did shoot herself he must have handed the gun to her!"

After that, I was not allowed to check Al's mail for him anymore, or go anywhere near his garage, and I was not given a reason why. In my head, it was because Al was a murderer, and he had somehow gotten away with it. I avoided his house like the plague.

After the Flood
(4)

It was a big day for my family when my parents finally decided to abandon the old house in order to buy a new one that was half an hour away. In the end, they settled with the contractors who built their house for forty thousand dollars, twenty thousand of which went to pay the engineer who wrote the reports that had helped them in their suit. I was grumpy with everyone when we drove to go look at the new house, and very critical about the size of the bedrooms. I even complained about the mysterious 'smell' of the place. However, despite my churlish demeanor, I knew there was no good reason to give my parents such a difficult time about the move. I knew it was a better house (this one was on a hill, for instance, and not in a swamp), and that our moving meant an end to the lawsuit. What's more, it meant my mother could re-invest her dreams in this new ship, and let the other one drift, as it inevitably would, to the bottom of the sea.

Why then, did I feel so angry? I couldn't pin it down. My emotions were a storm even their originator daren't navigate. But I do recall, before we left for good, that I stopped to kiss the four walls of my bedroom and left behind my favorite Garfield Christmas ornament for the house to keep and remember me by.

By the time we had abandoned our sinking Titanic for the house on the hill, my parent's marriage was pretty much over, not that there had been much there to begin with- at least from what I had seen. My mother, who in the beginning had agreed to the abandonment of the old house, was fearful and regretful of the decision, and blamed my father for forcing it upon her. Additionally, with my sister and I getting older, we needed our mother around less, and whereas some women might enjoy the extra free time and spend it on a new hobby, it caused my mother to experience early empty nest syndrome. Where she was turning circles before, she was spiraling now. She tried throwing herself into her crafts, only to find herself losing interest in projects soon after she started them. She tried multiple times being employed, thinking it would pass the time, only to quit shortly after each venture because she felt inadequate in one way or another. She tried to reinvigorate her marriage, only to have it fall dismally back where it had been before.

Eventually, I had stopped sleeping in the same bed as my mother, as I began to realize the depth of the unhealthy relationship that had grown between us. I knew *everything* about her, and she knew absolutely nothing about me. It didn't feel right. I began to resent her as much as I loved her. I was becoming a preteen and starting to feel the strain of puberty, and having to be a bolster for someone three times my age was beyond me. I began to ignore her, and when I did feel the need for affection, my mother- who by that time had turned completely inward- wasn't always able to give it. My sister became a full-on teenager with a strange, alien social life of her own, and was never in the house anymore- sometimes I forgot I had a sister. My dad still worked nights and took on as many overtime shifts as he was allowed to support a single income family, and therefore he was a non-entity to me.

On the first day of fifth grade at my new school, I knew upon entering the classroom that the move had been a bad idea, after all. The looks on the other kids' faces brought tears to my eyes; looks of disgust, repulsion- some leaned over to each other, whispered and giggled, their eyes lingering over the soft curves of my stomach. I was mortified. I took in at a glance that I was the only large child in class, and I mourned it, because that meant I would be the only target. That morning I had tried hard to look my best and conceal my stomach; I had even asked my mom to curl my hair in an attempt to look nice. But none of it had worked, or mattered, because I was fat; that's all anyone would ever see.

That night when I went home, I ran my bath as I usually did- with one small difference. This time I brought a plastic bag into the bathroom with me, to place over my head while I was in the water, in hopes that it would make it easier to drown myself.

I don't remember where I got the idea from. But I do remember I felt very determined to die as I sank into the bath that night with the grocery bag clutched in my hand. It wasn't until I was lying back with my nose barely above the water with the bag over my head that I began to feel afraid, and started to cry. Sobs shook my plump little body, and I hiccupped repeatedly, desperately trying to silence myself so no one would hear and ask what was wrong. I was so confused, and lonely, and I hated myself so much; but in my mind, I was a coward- too cowardly to end it all. I ripped the bag off my head and remained in the tub for a long time, trying to cry myself into some semblance of sanity.

The school years passed the same as they always had; my strange sadness seemed to plateau for a time, and my grades remained mediocre; my only saving grace was my writing ability, which I attributed to my fondness for reading large, gothic novels. I loved learning anything that had to do with words, poems, or books; everything else I suffered through with almost physical pain. Words were without a doubt my secondary outlet, food being my first, though I tended to write stories and poems that included adult themes such as death and despair, as they were all that interested me. In sixth grade, I wrote two haiku's for a school contest, both of which disturbed my teacher with their subject matter:

Death Bells
Once upon a time,
A lion committed a crime,
He kidnapped old Kris Kringle,
And ran away with a jingle,
The meal was mighty fine.

Bly
I once had a brother named Bly,
I gave him a magic marker so he could Fly,
I knew it was fake,
But for Heaven's sake,
I didn't know he would die.

It wasn't that I was obsessed with death, exactly, but I found it a much more interesting theme than those that were often found in children's books. From an extremely young age, I had read novels written for adults, and watched R-rated horror films and mind-bending Japanese animation; plus, my neighbor has ostensibly killed herself; and so before I was ten I had already been introduced to a world that many children didn't know about until they were older. While still in sixth grade, I even started to use quotes from one of my favorite gory anime movies, *Vampire Hunter D*, to combat my bullies.

"Aren't you going to say anything back?" they would sneer, after mocking me for my size, or whatever else they found repugnant about me that day.

"There's nothing *worth* saying to you," I would reply quietly, with a slight overtone of menace. Oddly, it was during this strange time-period of death poems and anime quotes, that I had my first taste of romance.

His name was Miles, and he was a good-looking, slender boy with freckles who was always polite to everyone, which was strange because he was close friends with the worst bullies in school. When my attention was first drawn to him, I didn't know anything about him besides his name, and the fact that he sat somewhere behind me in class. One day, I was walking alone on the playground as usual after lunch, wearing an over-long Garfield the Cat shirt and black leggings (the kind that hoop over the ankle), when a boy that I'd never seen before ran up to me.

"Hey," he said to me, with a slight wild look in his eyes, "My friend Miles likes you."

I was shocked. "Who?"

"Miles. He wants to go out with you. Yes or no?"

"Um, how does he like me? He doesn't even know me."

"I don't know, he just likes you and I heard him say that he thinks you're cute."

A fugitive blush came to my cheeks, and I started to suspect that this was just another way for the boys in my class to make fun of me. "If he likes me he needs to talk to me himself. I don't know anything about him."

The boy hesitated, unsure what to do. "Ok," he said finally, and ran away without a backwards glance. I was left staring after him, my heart pounding. Who in their right mind would want to go out with me? I was overweight; I kept to myself, and had no friends. What was there for someone to possibly like about me?

I didn't have long to contemplate, because Miles was walking up to me with a red face. I looked him over; I recognized him now as the boy from my class. He had a bowl hair cut, and his clothes- covered as they were with holes and stains- looked like they had seen better days, but despite that I thought he was very good looking. He stopped in front of me, his hands fiddling incessantly with the pockets of his black, ripped sweatshirt.

"Hi," he mumbled nervously.

"Hi," I said, shy back.

"I'm not really sure what to say," he said, his gentle hazel eyes searching the ground. "Um, I like you… I have for a while."

I looked at him with surprise. "Why?"

"I don't know. I just like you, I think you're cool and nice and stuff."

"We've never even talked before."

"Does that matter? I still want to go out with you."

"What kind of stuff would we do?"

He shuffled his feet nervously. "I don't know. Like, hold hands, I guess."

I thought about it. "I've never held hands before."

"Neither have I."

I pursed my lips, not knowing how to proceed. This was the first time someone had spoken to me like this, and it felt rather nice. And he did look sweet, standing there, all shy. I made a sudden decision.

"We can go out."

He looked up at me, smiling happily. "We can write notes during class. I'll write you one when we get inside."

"Okay."

"I'll see you in class."

"Okay."

We stared at each other in silence for a moment, and then as Miles turned to go, the bell to go inside rang. We hesitated, the question on both our minds: should we hold hands as we went in? But we were both too embarrassed; it was too sudden. I followed him to class without either of us speaking a word.

Later, on the way to gym, Miles caught up to me in the hallway and slipped a well-folded note into my hand. Once I got into the girl's locker room, I sat in a bathroom stall for privacy to read it:

Kim,

I like you a lot; I think you are really pretty and cool. I thought your poems for the contest were neat. Did you win anything? What do you like to do in your free time? I like to read and skate board. I have a brother and two cats, do you have any brothers?

Miles

I couldn't help but smile as I read the words. Maybe this wasn't a big joke, after all, and he really did like me. I felt a thrill at the thought, and when we entered the gym and were instructed by the PE teacher to do self-stretches, I chose a spot across from Miles. He spent most of his time talking with his friends, one of whom I knew enough to absolutely detest. His name was Leonard, and he was loud, rude, and often made fun of me, but I wasn't the only one; he harassed everyone he could for the smallest faults he could invent. I watched out of the corner of my eye as he and Miles talked, wondering why a nice person like Miles was friends with a creep like Leonard.

"What?" said Leonard suddenly, his voice echoing in the gymnasium, "Why would you want to date that fat bitch?"

My face crimsoned, and I turned away as tears started in my eyes so that Miles wouldn't see them. I wanted to run and hide.

I heard the murmuring and giggling of my classmates, and then I heard Miles' voice say, "Shut up dude, she's not fat."

My heart leaped. No one had ever defended me before, and here was this boy, a near stranger, protecting me from one of his closest friends. I didn't know it then, but with that one sentence Miles had taught me my first lesson in love, and that was something that would stick with me for the rest of my life.

For the time being, Leonard seemed to drop the subject, but for the rest of the day Leonard often turned to glare at me, and I became afraid.

The next day, after lunch, Miles found me sitting on a bench, and he sat next to me.

"Can I hold your hand?" he asked softly. "I want to hold it and talk."

I nodded.

And for the first time, I held hands with a boy; but we had to hide them behind our backs, because the teachers roaming the school yard would have blown the whistle at us for inappropriate touching. We didn't say anything for a few minutes, and then in a quiet voice Miles said,

"I don't know how long we can go out."

I turned to him, my heart dropping. "What do you mean?"

"I got in a fight last night with some of my friends over going out with you. I got punched and everything." He turned to the side and showed me a large bruise across his jaw and neck. "So… I pretty much have to choose between my friends and you."

I swallowed nervously. "I'm sorry."

"It's not your fault. I want to go out with you but they're my only friends. I've known them since I was little. Our parents do everything together."

We were silent again, and giving his hand a gentle squeeze, I withdrew my hand from his. I felt I owed it to him to make this as easy on him as possible. I didn't want him to get hurt anymore. "Okay, we're not going out anymore. Thanks for a really good day."

He looked sad. "Maybe some other time."

I nodded, smiling. "Yeah, some other time."

He stood up, and as he started to walk away, turned and said, "See you inside."

"Okay," I said, trying to keep my eyes from welling up.

Thus ended my first romance; it had lasted a little less than twenty-four hours. I kept his note for a long time, and though we talked once in a while over the years, we never spoke again about dating. Perhaps we were both embarrassed at what had happened; I knew I was. I only threw his note away years later when I found out he had a new girlfriend, since by then I figured it was pathetic and weird for me to keep it.

Miles did tell me, however, years later, that his crush on me never went away, not until I disappeared from school and he was forced to forget me. If only I had known, maybe I wouldn't have felt so abandoned.

Seventh and eighth grade fell upon me as a great challenge. At some point, there had been a rumor spread that I was a lesbian, so the other girls avoided me as if I carried the plague. Angry at this mistreatment, I had started to snap back at their rudeness with bitter comments of my own, such as, "I would never date a bitch like you if I were a lesbian." They were pitiful retributions, and I knew it. Sometimes my use of language, colorful on an average day due to my large vocabulary, got me into trouble. And instead of deterring my bullies, my attempts to stand up for myself only solidified my loneliness and ostracization.

Though the rude commentary was constant even when I was placid, the physical abuses didn't start until I began to fight back. I had become tired with always being the punch-line of every joke, and on the receiving end of every verbal jab, so I started to hit back in whatever way I could. Unfortunately, this didn't go over as I had hoped, and every day as I walked home from school, it became a toss of the dice if it would end up being a race with my bullies or not. Armed with rocks, trash, clods of dirt, or whatever else they could find, they would start out by walking close behind me, laughing, and I always knew what was coming.

"Hey, you fat slut!" they would eventually call, meaning me, "Hey chubby, chubby, chubby!"

I never turned and gave them the satisfaction. Plus, I didn't want them to see that I was scared.

And then the rocks would come, or the trash, or the dirt-clods. Most of them missed me, or hit my backpack- but the others hit the back of my head and ached badly. *Fat-ass!* They would chant. *Run, Fat-ass, run!*

And I would; I would run as fast as I could to get away from them, and most of the time they wouldn't chase me, to my immense relief. I didn't know what I would do if they were really adamant about catching me. I was not a fast runner, and there were not many places to hide on my route home; most of the neighborhood had large, manicured lawns with little to no trees or bushes near the road. Plenty of adults, while out mowing their grass or weeding their gardens, saw how I was being treated, but not a single one of them ever felt the need to say something about it.

Some days I would come home from school with the back of my head covered with bruises and open sores, and at times I felt tempted to tell my mother about it, but in the end I felt that she would only make things worse. She would discuss things in her shy, ineffective manner with my teacher, the teacher would talk to my bullies, and then I'd face the repercussions, alone on the street, after school. It wasn't worth it- talking to my mother was never worth it. It was hammered into my brain at an early age that I would have to deal with the trials of life, alone.

<u>Role Reversal</u>

(5)

My mother was always on a diet. She was always doing something in an attempt to 'better her figure,' which usually had to do with altering what she ate rather than changing her exercise program. As a result, our house was full of magazines that promised to reveal secrets to desperate women who wanted to lose twenty pounds FAST and be purged of their mysterious bloat. I read them all, and as a curious pre-teen and then teen, I took especial care to re-read the articles on sex and how to be attractive to men. If it was good enough for adults, I reasoned, it was good enough for me.

My mother knew that my sister and I were overweight; had known about it since we were little, and had trouble finding cute clothing that fit us. Though I don't recall her saying a negative thing about our weight, neither do I remember her stopping us from eating entire pizzas by ourselves, or encouraging us to engage in exercise or play sports. She herself had weight that yo-yoed drastically, and would go through phases where she would eat a half a pizza, or just nibble on cheese sticks and insist she was full. Sometimes she would go running at the local track for hours, and I would go with her, watching her with curious eyes. There are many things that confused me about my mom, but I found that if placed her under the label 'erratic', everything she did suddenly appeared normal- for her, anyway. I didn't expect much from her as I reached my early teens; she had become sullen and distant; where she had once been avid about cleaning the house, she let it go weeks before vacuuming, mopping, or cleaning the bathroom. She stopped cooking meals for us, and instead bought dinners that we could fix ourselves without her intervention. What few house rules there had been became non-existent. I can see now, that in her own way, she was crying for help.

    I recall one night when I was thirteen, I emerged from my room and sat next to my mother on the living room floor as she watched the QVC shopping network (her favorite) and worked on one of her crafts- a dollhouse made out of plastic sewing mesh and rainbow yarn. As usual in my family, we didn't say a word to each other in greeting but sat there quietly, watching TV, until some kind of madness inspired me and I said,

"Mom, you're really pretty."

I don't remember a smile, but she must have done so- it would have been characteristic of her to smile self consciously. I wish I remembered that smile, if there was one. But what I remember is her flat denial, of *No, I'm not, I'm ugly.*

Of course I argued. "Why don't you ever shop for clothes for yourself? Or style your hair, or wear makeup? If you don't know how maybe you can learn. You really are pretty; I wish I had blonde hair like you do; mine is all brown and mousy."

My mom said something then that made me furious. "I don't have time."

I froze. Time? She didn't have *time*? This, from the woman who pined her days away, probably wishing for a better life than the one she was living. When she had complained before about having nothing to do, I had suggested that reading novels might be good for her; it was something the rest of our family enjoyed doing, it was something she could share with *me*. But she had demurred, saying they were too 'much' for her. What did that even mean? She couldn't hold a job, or keep up a steady work-out routine. She no longer cooked, or cleaned the house, or tried to do *anything* anymore, besides her ridiculous little crafts. What did she mean, she had 'no time?'

I remember standing up and flying back to my room, angry, no longer wanting to communicate. I was too frustrated with this woman who I loved so much; who for so many years had been my only support in the world. I felt like she was deteriorating, becoming a phantom of who she used to be, and I had no idea what to do.

It was a few months later that my mother surprised me by picking me up from school. I had been harassed every day that week by bullies, so it was especially pleasant for me when I spotted our junky, white ford truck waiting for me in the school parking lot. That is, it was pleasant until I saw my mom's face, all white and haggard, her eyes pink and puffy from crying. I knew something was very wrong, but she refused to speak to me until we went home and I had been ushered into my room.

My mother bid me to sit on my bed, and I did. After pacing a moment, my mother sat next to me, and looked at me in a strange, intense manner, as she grasped my hand in her tiny pink one.

"Kim," she said, her green eyes glassy, "I-I don't know if you know this, but I… I-I'm not happy."

I could only stare at her in silence. The statement she had made was such an anti-climax for me that I wasn't sure how to react. From the time I was little, she had whispered her dark secrets into my ear as I snuggled next to her in her empty marital bed. For years, she had told me about her passionless, sexless marriage to my father, and how she was lonely and desired friends, but felt that she didn't deserve them because she was dull and had few interests. It was I who knew the details of our house's lawsuit before I even knew what the term 'foreclosure' meant, me who knew about her abusive childhood, her step-mother who hated her, her first boyfriend who raped her. Did I know she was unhappy? Had she forgotten that I was her confident, and had been her only confident, since I was old enough to understand words? And lately, with her roaming about the house like a ghost, ignoring her family and barely brushing her hair, did she expect this to surprise me?

"Kim," she continued, crying now, "What would you say if I left? I mean- I mean, would it be okay if I w-went away, and moved to California? Please? Why are you just looking at me like that? Kim, please answer me."

I don't know how many other people in the world have had to deal with this situation before. I know I'm not the only one, and I won't be the last- but at the time, I was keenly aware that it was not normal for a parent to ask their child's permission to leave them. I remember being disgusted with her, and also feeling that I was being horribly wronged somehow. Why was it *my* decision? Why didn't she ask Dad, or Rachel, or *herself*?

But as I gazed at my mother, shaking and held captive by her own fears, I began to thaw. Despite everything- or maybe, partially because of it all- I loved my mom. She needed me; I didn't want her to be sad. I wanted her to be happy. In the end, I knew the formula was that easy, and the answer would be just as simple.

"I'll miss you, Mom, but I think it's a good idea for you to leave," I said. "I mean, it's been obvious to me that you're unhappy for a long time, and I want that to change, for you." I barely had time to finish my sentence before she enveloped me in her arms and sobbed like a child into my shoulder. I could only pat her on the back and let her know that I would be there to support her, no matter what.

I've always been a good liar.

*

 Divorce is an expensive thing, so it was decided that my mother would live with us for a few more months before she left in order to build up a small nest-egg. There was a time, in the beginning, where she thought that I might go with her when she moved, and it was with very little regret that I shut her down on that idea. As much as I cared for her, and wanted her to find peace- I felt intuitively that I could not find happiness for myself while living with her. And as little I knew of my father, I felt the opposite about the old saying: I'd rather, actually, the devil I didn't. So, my mother and father became legally separated, but still remained living together; therefore my mom's first few nights of freedom were spent sleeping in her husband's bed.

 After the separation, my mother began to change drastically, and I don't know who she tried to become. Something had broke free in her after I had given her my permission to leave, and different parts of her that none of us knew existed began taking control. She was a party animal. She liked to dance, so she went line dancing (she liked country music?) and flirted with older men. She started an internet relationship with her old boyfriend, Chuck, who had been the man who date-raped her when she was just a girl. She wore too much makeup. She dyed her hair. She lost thirty pounds. She went tanning; she tanned herself until she was as brown as a nut. She cursed, she drank fancy alcoholic drinks, and she ignored me.

During that short time when my mother and father were separated but living together, I don't recall having seen more than a few quick glimpses of my father. He still worked nights at Pelican Bay State Prison; he had ever since I could remember. It had gotten to the point where I sincerely didn't like seeing him, as he was practically a stranger living in our house- even though he was unarguably the sole reason we *had* a house. Even his face began to bother me, with its constant sleepy appearance and strange aloofness; but, loyally, I tried to find the good in him any chance I could. After all, he was the man who was to take charge of me when my mother left.

At some point during all this, my sister Rachel had started to prepare to move out. She was seventeen, had graduated high school with straight A's, and there was no way in hell she was living in a house without our mother in it, so she was working on a plan to leave as soon as possible. Though she made this clear to us, it took her a while to actually do it; for the time being, she was never home, but was out often with her boyfriend, Max. At the time, Rachel and I had come to our own tacit peace treaty, wherein we just didn't speak to each other at all. She invited Max over fairly often, and I grew to dislike him immensely; they would watch professional wrestling in the living room and I hated wrestling. Their conversation, at times sappy and at other times bickering, irritated the life out of me. A part of me was jealous that Rachel had someone to turn to during everything, but the majority of me a massive pit of smoldering angst.

It took about four months for my mom to leave for California. After she did left, in a flurry of kisses and tears, my dad announced his intentions to change from the night shift to the day shift at the prison. It was probably the proper thing for a parent to do, so that I wouldn't be in the house alone at night after Rachel moved out; but inside, I couldn't help but wonder, *Why couldn't you do that for my mom, who slept alone in your bed for so many years*? And despite his promise, it took a year or more for him to switch, and I was often alone in the house at night, anyway.

My father, for one reason or another, wasted no time in finding a girlfriend. Before meeting my mom, he had never dated anyone, and so it was the first time in his life he ever had an intimate relationship outside of his marriage. Her name was Samantha and she was a few years younger than him and overall appeared to be a very nice lady- but she was needy. She demanded a lot of his time, and slave-like, he gave it to her, spending all of his free moments at her apartment. Once in a while at Samantha's bidding he would invite me over as well, where he would let my fourteen year old self get buzzed on strawberry daiquiris in front of a rental movie while he and Samantha made out in her bedroom.

Looking back, I didn't mind that Samantha and my dad were dating; it seemed in everyone's best interest to learn to embrace their new life, if they could. But what I did mind was that their relationship began so soon after my mother left, and that it seemed like my dad could be a functioning, fully present romantic partner, after all, if he put his mind to it. The worst of it, however, was how my mother reacted. She knew immediately my dad had found someone, and in response she became a frantic, grasping creature, calling almost every day to talk to me; and not to discuss my day, or school, or anything about me, really; but to talk about Dad and Samantha. Did they hold hands in front of me? Was Samantha prettier than her? Did they have sex in the house, in their bed? Did I hear them do it?

I started screening my phone calls, and refused to answer when my mom called. My heart could handle a lot of things, but it could not handle the antics of my desperate mother. My sister, stronger than I in such matters, would often take the burden upon herself and answer the phone, and at the end of their conversations, when they had said all there was to be said, my mom would cry and beg Rachel to put me on the line, only to have Rachel refuse at my request.

"Mom," Rachel would explain patiently, "It's because you're always on her about Dad and Samantha. You need to stop. We love you, but…you just have to move on."

But our mom couldn't move on; she couldn't rid herself of her obsession with my father. Our poor mother, who had left her beloved daughters to search for greener pastures, had found only sticks and sand, and was parched with thirst.

A Troubled Place
(6)

So much happened during the fourteenth year of my life that it's hard to interpret where one event begins and the other ends. My mother had moved to California, leaving my sister and I behind. Rachel was never home; she was always off with her boyfriend, and was planning to move out as soon as she could. My father was still dating Samantha, but sometimes he forgot to come home, now, and left me and my sister small piles of money for groceries. School was Hell to me; I was still picked on, though thankfully, the rocks had stopped. I had a few acquaintances at school that I kept at a safe distance, because I trusted no one with my friendship. I was not cognizant that I was pushing anyone away, but looking back, it's obvious that I was. I was too afraid to let anyone in, lest they hurt me; I felt I couldn't bear any more disillusions in my life.

My mother had left many things behind her when she moved; her cat, for one, who had run away the very day she left. She also left some pairs of shoes, worn and stained; some craft items, mouse-eaten Christmas decorations, and in the bathroom, she had left tons of her Women's magazines. On a particularly lonely day, I picked one of them up and flipped through a few pages. 'How to Lose Ten Pounds in One Week!' screamed one article. 'Does He Still Find You Sexy?' queried another. Perusing the material with dull eyes, I came across an article that sparked my interest; it was about a woman who suffered from bulimia, and while in the throws of her illness had lost sixty pounds despite the fact that she ate thousands upon thousands of calories a day, because afterwards, she stuck her finger down her throat and rid herself of it all. When I read this, I felt a strange thrill go down my spine. It was possible to eat, and still lose weight? I quickly scanned the rest of the woman's story, and though she mentioned that she had almost died due to her disorder, she had overcome it, and was now healthy and happy. Despite the warning that bulimia brought with it many dangers, I quickly latched on to the idea of losing sixty pounds while eating whatever I wanted.

I was alone in the house, and so I went boldly into the kitchen and made myself four large servings of pancakes, with butter and syrup and powdered sugar and all, and devoured them with gusto. Afterwards, I tripped almost gleefully up the stairs, put my head into the toilet, stuck my pointer and middle finger down my throat, and threw up- or attempted to. It took a few tries, and with my head swimming, tears streaming down my face, I finally managed to activate my gag reflex and empty my engorged stomach. When I was done, I flushed the toilet with shaky, vomit covered fingers, and lay on the tiled floor of the bathroom, panting. It had hurt, a little. But I had done it; I had eaten what I wanted, and the calories were no longer inside of me to make me fatter. It felt like magic. Though I had vomit dribbling down my cheek and into my hair, and felt too dizzy to move, I felt like a superhero.

After a few more tries, I discovered that bulimia filled the void that was ever expanding in my life. At first, it was only once or twice a week, and I never thought much of it; it felt so innocent to me; it was just a way for me to indulge my food cravings without having to deal with the negative side effects. It's heartrending to look back at how wide-eyed and naive I was at the beginning of such a heinous, snake-in-the-grass disease.

Plus, I had to admit to myself, the very secrecy of the undertaking excited me. My dad didn't know about it, my sister didn't know about it; it was mine- only mine, and no one else's. As I had when I was younger, I began to hoard food, but instead of eating it at any free interval, I saved it for the times when I knew I would be alone and could binge and purge in peace. I began to lose weight, and people and school began to notice, and comment. I soaked it in, at first. They didn't know how I was doing it. They just thought I looked skinny and beautiful, and that's all they ever needed to know.

As a person whose heart had become bare and glacial, I was enticed by this dangerous venture that dragged me through fire.

*

It's hard to say when bulimia stopped being a hobby and became a desperate necessity to my everyday life. I believe, in retrospect, that it was due to a series of small, stressful events that I, failing to be aware of any other coping mechanism, turned to bulimia for assistance. And it was there for me, always; waiting for me to resent myself, so it could catch me in its black arms and tell me, ***There, there. I'm here for you. I'm all you need. Quiet, now.*** And child-like, I would obey every demand it made of me. I would hate myself bitterly when it told me to; I would punish myself with starvation until I was alone, and was able to binge and purge in secrecy. I began to stare into the bathroom mirror for hours at a time, picking my face until it bled, hating my reflection more than I had ever hated it before.

Despite this, I didn't realize the hold that bulimia had on me, until I tried to stop; my throat was raw and bloody, and I had started to feel dizzy during classes, and so reluctantly I decided to find another way to lose weight. And for a day or so, I managed to abstain- but then one night, I ate a slightly larger dinner than I had intended, and bulimia swooped down to me again, full of caresses and dulcet tones. ***Don't worry, dear, just get rid of it,*** it said cajolingly. ***You can try to be healthy again tomorrow, if you'd like, but if that doesn't work out, you'll always have me. I'm not going anywhere.*** And, desperate and half-panicked because of the amount of food I had eaten, I would feel grateful to bulimia for giving me recourse, and I'd vomit- sometimes over, and over again, the cycle never breaking, even on the days I cried and begged it to end. With a feeling of deep misgiving, I began to understand that I had trapped myself, and I was unsure how to become free again- or if I truly wanted to be free.

*

One afternoon, Rachel and I sat on her bedroom floor together, and I watched happily as she maneuvered her Final Fantasy VIII character around the screen. It had been a long time since she and I had video game time together, and I was very happy to be there next to her. Lately, my life had been nothing but binging and purging, and solitude. She was often out with friends or her boyfriend, so she was almost never home anymore. I was happy for her; she had changed a lot in just the last year. She had lost weight, and had started wearing her hair down, whereas before she has always pulled it up into an unappealing bun. She seemed more relaxed than I had ever seen her before. She still couldn't abide the sound of breathing, or eating, or the sight of my feet, but it seemed since our mother left Rachel had become a kinder, gentler version of herself, and I appreciated it.

"I have to find a frickin' save spot," Rachel said suddenly, "I have to get ready to meet with Max. Geez, where is it?"

My heart sunk. I didn't want her to go. "Where are you going?"

"Probably up-river," she responded vaguely.

Upon hearing this, I felt really sad, and my eyes welled with tears. When she left, I would be alone in the house. I would read my books, and try to distract myself, but it wouldn't work; in the end I would end up binging on the little food we had left in the cupboards, and then I would throw it up. Rachel seemed to sense I was upset and glanced at me, and upon seeing my tears she paused the game.

"Kim, what's wrong?" she asked, her voice soft and questioning. She had never spoken to me like that before.

"I have a secret," I told her, crying. "It's disgusting and I'm afraid to tell you."

"You can tell me anything. We might not always get along, but I am your sister."

This only made my tears flow more freely. "I-I do want to tell you, but please, please promise not to tell dad or mom. They will be mad, or blame themselves, and I really don't want that."

Rachel watched me cry for a moment, and then said, "Okay, I won't tell. Now what is it?"

I sniffled, unsure how to say it- but in the end I simply said, "Rachel, I'm bulimic."

Her eyes became soft and sad. "Kim, that's not good. That is very, very not good." She reached out to hug me, and drew me close. I almost lost it at that point. My sister was hugging me without being forced to! How many years had I waited for that moment? And I only had to become bulimic to get it.

"I noticed you were losing weight, but I never thought... I'm sorry Kim. I wish mom was here to help you. She shouldn't have left."

I gulped, waiting.

"You can die from that, you know," she continued, "It's not worth being skinny. Look, I only won't tell mom and dad if you promise to stop. Will you stop?"

I started to quiver. Would I stop? *Could* I stop? I had tried so many times before, only to fail. But I didn't want her to tell our parents more than anything, and now, my sister was here, worried about me, and I didn't want her to feel responsible for me now that we were getting along.

"I'll stop," I said.

"Please do," she said meaningfully. "It's an awful thing. Are you going to be okay?"

I nodded, forcing myself to smile weakly. "Yes, I feel better now that I told someone."

She smiled back. "Good. You can always talk to me about it, alright? I'm still here, no matter where mom and dad may be."

"Thanks."

With another quick hug, she turned back to her game, and continued looking for the elusive save spot that would set her free.

Despite her kind words, and despite my promise, she of course still went to the river that day with her boyfriend, as teenagers will do, and I, of course, still binged and purged.

While she lived in our house, I don't recall speaking to her about my eating disorder again, though she told our mother about it during one of their phone conversations. I don't know what made her break her promise; perhaps she had seen signs that I had not quit like I had said I would, and she was worried about me. I was shocked, however, when on one of the rare occasions I spoke to my mother on the phone, she brought it up as if it were a negligible issue, something to be swatted away like an annoying fly.

"Oh, well, we all have our issues, don't we?" said my mother, giggling. "You'll grow out of it. I remember when I was younger, I went a whole week eating nothing but carrots. Now that was tough! Women do stupid stuff to be pretty."

I listened to her voice on the other end of the line with my lips pressed tightly together. I wanted very badly to hang up on my mother at that moment. *This is my mother caring,* I thought.

"Oh, and I was going to ask- and Rachel told me I *shouldn't* ask, but you don't mind, do you? How-how has your dad been? Is he still bringing Samantha around, bringing her over for the night, or-?"

That was the last straw. "I have to go, Mom," I said bitingly, and slammed the phone onto the receiver.

Under and Ovary
(7)

My sister and her boyfriend were having loud sex again, and the noise was keeping me awake. *Goddammit.*

That night was nothing new. The noises of my sister moaning were annoyingly normal to me; she had been bringing Max around to spend the night increasingly often since our mother left, and since our dad worked at night, there was no one to stop them. At first I tried to block it out by shoving toilet paper in my ears and covering my head with pillows and blankets, but as nothing seemed to work I decided to give up on sleep just wait it out. But for some reason, the sounds didn't stop as they usually did, even though ten, twenty minutes passed. In fact, my sister's moaning seemed to get louder, longer and more intense.

"Holy crap," I thought, getting pissed, "When I have sex I will never fake it like that." I was, thanks to my mom's magazines, thoroughly informed about the difference between real and fake orgasms.

As more minutes went by with no decrease in sound, I gathered up my courage, and, throwing a robe of my sleep-shirt, went down the short hall to her door and knocked.

"Rachel," I said, raising my voice tentatively. "Can you keep it down, please?"

Mooaaaan.

"...Rachel?" I asked, opening the door a crack and peeking in.

I was confused by what I saw. There was my sister, alone in her bed, not having sex at all. In the slanting moonlight which poured through her window, I could see that she was on her side, cradling herself, half-sobbing and in obvious intense pain.

I came closer to her. "What's wrong?" I asked, instantly frightened.

"I don't know. My stomach," she mumbled, barely able to talk, and she moaned again.

I had never been in a situation like that before; where someone was in so much pain they couldn't communicate properly. I knew immediately, however, that she required more than a Pepto Bismol.

"What do you think it is?" I asked.

"…I don't know!"

"What do you want me to do?"

"'Don't know!"

I remember standing in her dark room, which was scattered with dirty clothes, and trying to make a decision.

"I'm going to call an ambulance," I told her.

Silence.

"Rachel, I'm going to call an ambulance, okay?" I said again, a little louder, making sure she heard me.

"FINE!" she yelled, and went back to moaning.

I ran out of her room and into my parent's empty bedroom, where we kept our second phone. I carefully dialed 911, and as the dispatcher asked what my emergency was, I froze for a second. What was our emergency?

"Hi, my sister is screaming and her stomach really hurts. She can barely talk," I ended up saying. I gave our address and was told help was coming. In relief, I hung up and went back to Rachel's room.

"Rachel, I called 911 and they're coming," I told her, raising my voice so she could hear me over her crying.

"Oh, God," she whimpered.

"Kim," she said abruptly, interrupting her own moans, "On the floor somewhere. My lip gloss. Find it for me."

I glanced around her messy bedroom, and replied slowly, "I don't think they're going to care what you look like..."

"Just... *get*... it," she seethed between clenched teeth.

So my next few minutes were spent digging amongst the dirty clothes on her floor, looking for lip gloss. I asked her if there was anything else I could do for her, but she was in so much pain words failed her, so I went to the living room to wait anxiously for the ambulance to arrive.

When it came, I led the EMT's to my sister room, and there she lie, still on her side, in terrible, agonizing pain but properly glossed. The medical technicians weren't long in deciding that whatever ailed my sister needed the attention of a hospital, so they brought in the stretcher and loaded her up, covering her shaking body with a blanket. On the way out, they told me what hospital they were headed to, and I assured them I would call my dad and let him know. And just like that, they were gone.

After watching the flashing lights of the ambulance pull away, I ran back into my parent's bedroom and picked up the phone again. This was my first and last time calling Pelican Bay State Prison. My call was transferred for what felt like a dozen times, the whole time my anxiety rising to peak levels, until I spoke to someone that at least *knew* my father, and promised to relay the message to him and have him call me, which he eventually did. I told him all I knew; Rachel was at a hospital (I gave him the name), something was wrong with her stomach, and I was the one who called the ambulance so if it cost a lot of money I was sorry but I didn't know what else to do.

After my dad and I hung up, I sat in the dark and listened to the silence of the house. It was hard to believe what had just happened, happened- but it had. I was not overly worried about my sister, as something inside of me was telling me that she would be okay; and I was weirdly relieved that the noises hadn't been my sister having sex. With that final thought, I collapsed onto my parent's bed, exhausted, and fell asleep.

The next day, after my dad came home from visiting the hospital, I learned what had happened. After arriving at the hospital my sister had been almost immediately been admitted to emergency surgery; a six-pound, cancerous tumor the size of a cantaloupe had attached itself to one of her ovaries, and had begun to rupture. If the ambulance had been any slower, or if I hadn't called them, the cancer cells would have spread throughout her entire body- but as it happened, the tumor was able to be removed in time and though she went through a lot of pain, she did not get cancer.

My sister and I never really talked about what happened. I was aware, and she was aware, that we had shared a strange, almost horrific experience, and that she and I together had survived it despite our missing parents. But in the pattern of our family we did not discuss it. And apparently, our father took not discussing things to the next level, because while Rachel was in the hospital he neglected to call and tell our mother that Rachel was ill at all. When my mother found out, she was frantic, and started crying uncontrollably while cursing my father for not telling her so that she could be there for Rachel. My sister, despite what she went through, had a level head, and asked our mother not to make the drive to come see her, because she knew that she had no money and couldn't afford to take time off of work. After some argument, our mom agreed, but she was still very resentful about the whole incident.

Never a Tear, Baby of Mine

(8)

It was the winter of my fourteenth year when my sister, her boyfriend Max and I decided to drive down to California and visit my mother to see how she was doing. I had really no interest in going, since I had started to feel guilty about ignoring my mother's calls, but Rachel had pressed the issue until I agreed. Maybe, I thought, she was doing better. I knew she had gotten an apartment, and had obtained a job as a pharmacist's assistant, something she had done in her early twenties. As we were driving, Rachel told me that mom had however found a boyfriend and that he was married, addicted to drugs, claimed to be a Mormon, and punished himself after making love to her because he felt that he had sinned. What hope I had that my mother was doing better was quickly dashed with that knowledge.

When we reached my mother's apartment, I remember feeling the most sad I had felt in a very long time. My mom had wanted a big family, she wanted love, she wanted to own a house- she wanted the American Dream. But there she was living alone in a tiny one bedroom apartment, divorced from the only man she had ever loved and separated from her children. My heart ached as we walked inside and I saw my mother. I could see with my own eyes that she was still broken. —Dad to (next paragraph)

She had gained back all the weight she had lost during the separation, and then some. Her hair was stringy and yellow; her skin hung off of her face in folds and her eyes were bloodshot as if she hadn't slept well in days. I instinctively recoiled from her when she came forward to hug me. *Is this what she was asking for when she asked my permission to leave?* I thought, fighting back tears. *Oh God, where is my mother?*

I could tell, that despite her misery in her current situation, she was overjoyed to see us and that she wanted to roll out the red carpet for her children. Her apartment, as small as it was, was spotless and smelled like cinnamon, and even had a tiny Christmas tree. Holiday decorations were strewn from wall to wall, and stocking were hung under the TV stand with our names carefully written in puff paint. She took our belongings and deposited them in the hall, and gave us a tour of her home, shyly showing off her new craft creations. When dinnertime came around, she quickly suggested that we should meet her boyfriend, and she pranced to her bedroom to call him on the phone. We ended up meeting him at a pizza restaurant, only to have his wife call his cell phone in the middle of dinner. My mom became upset after that, so we ditched him while he was chatting with his wife and made him pay the bill. I was glad, because he was creepy and looked like he hadn't eaten or slept for weeks. Both my sister and I told Mom she could do better. But she said she could handle her own relationship, so we stopped pushing. I wanted to crawl under a rock, or escape someplace far, far away- had I really just been sharing a dinner table with my mom's married, druggie boyfriend?

The next day, we went shopping for lack of anything else to do, and while we were browsing I saw a pair of boots that I really liked. My mom saw me staring at them, and ~~coming~~ as she came up from behind me, asked ~~me~~, "Do you want them?"

I paused, unsure how to answer. "Yes, but we don't have any money."

She smiled sadly. "No, *we* don't; but your dad does. All he does is spend it on his girlfriend, so let's make him spend it on you today." She giggled a little wildly, and then said, "I'm going to buy those boots with my credit card, and you make him write me a check when you get home, okay?"

I suddenly felt like crying ~~like a little girl again~~. My mom wanted so badly to buy something nice for me, to *do* something for me, and I somehow felt like it was the saddest thing in the world. I wanted to hug her, to shake her- tell her that boots weren't important to me, ~~that~~ *she* was, and that she needed to fix herself, and fast, because her youngest daughter needed her. I remembered when I was very little, ~~and~~ if I ever felt sad I would crawl into ~~my mom~~ her's lap and ~~snuggle there~~ curl up, and feel safe. Sometimes, When~~ever~~ I was especially upset, my mom and I would watch the movie Dumbo together, and she would stroke my arm and hum the tune to the song 'Baby Mine', and my anxiety would fade away. I loved that song ~~, and that part of the movie~~ as well. It belonged to us; that scene where Dumbo visits his poor mother in prison, and she rocks him gently with her trunk through the bars. To this day I cry whenever I hear the gentle melody and lyrics of that song.

(switch)

Baby mine, don't you cry
Baby mine, dry your eyes
Rest your head close to my heart
Never to part
Baby of mine

Little one when you play
Pay no heed to what they say
Let your eyes sparkle and shine
Never a tear
Baby of mine

      I wanted, right then, to go back to earlier days, and demand a do-over. *I'd be better to you, mom*, I thought. *I wouldn't let you stay in jail; I'd set you free before things got this bad. Please; let's just start over. Forget about California, about your crazy boyfriend- about all of this…!*

      But in our family we didn't talk about things- not things that mattered, anyway. So, instead of telling her what lay in the recesses my heart, I went with my mom to the cash register, and we bought the boots.

It was our last night in California, and the four of us; mom, Max, Rachel and I, decided to rent a movie. I was silent the entire time. I felt that something precious in me had died, that I had become an animated doll, eating and sleeping and not much else. I recall looking at a blonde, vaguely familiar stranger who was laughing with Max and Rachel as they perused movies, and wondering, *Who is that woman?*

"I know!" the creature cackled in my mother's voice, "Let's rent a porno! We can all agree on that!"

The joke rankled in me, but I remained silent, otherwise I felt I would surely scream. We did not end up renting a porno- I actually have no recollection of what we rented, because by the time we got back to my mother's apartment I was emotionally exhausted and wanted to do nothing but sleep. I felt I could sleep one hundred years if given the chance- but we were up early the next day, packed and ready for the long drive back to Oregon.

And so begins one of the hardest memories of my life.

One has heard of your own life flashing before your eyes- it is usually said to occur in moments of near death. But does it *have* to be in moments immediately before death? And what about someone *else*'s life flashing before your eyes? As I faced my mother, the car loaded and ready to take us away from her, it started to rain. She was trying her best to put on a brave face, but her eyes couldn't lie, and they glistened with unshed tears. I moved in for a quick, hard hug, and as we pulled apart and looked into each other's faces, she said,

"I love you Kim. Oh, I love you so much, Baby."

I started to tremble, and began to pull away a bit desperately. I felt I was going to break down completely. I needed to get away. Without another word I turned my back on her and ran to the car, slamming the door shut behind me.

Silence in the car, except for my breath coming in quick, struggling gasps. As we began to move away, the tires crunching on the gravel parking lot of her apartment complex, I felt a pull that I couldn't resist, and turned to the back window to wave- and I saw her there, drenched in the sudden down-pour, sobbing as I had never seen her sob before. I saw in that one glance, her years of abuse by her step-mother, her shame of her own body, her broken heart caused by her passionless marriage, her unutterable sense of heartbreak at having lost three children; I saw her struggle to make ends meet when we were poor, her comforting me when I was little, her fear of being alone, her pain when she discovered her dreams would never come true. In that one moment, I saw everything, felt everything; but most keenly, I felt her unutterable emptiness, and in response, my own grief at how the world had failed such a gentle creature.

The tears finally came, and they streamed unchecked down my cheeks. "Good-bye, Mom," I called, sobbing, waving- but the rain drops on the rear glass had started to distort our vision of each other, and she was soon lost from sight.

*

It was a few weeks later that my dad received the phone call reporting that my mother's body had been discovered by one of her co-workers after she had not appeared at work for three days. Apparently, she had stolen sleeping pills from the pharmacy, and one night, while drunk on an entire bottle of wine, she had swallowed over sixty of them, effectively ending her life. She was forty-three years old.

Upon receiving the news, my dad, large and stoic for as long as I had known him, broke down into convulsive sobs. He had, after all, lived with this woman for twenty-something years and fathered two children with her. It was normal for him to react that way. I hugged him because I felt that he needed it, but for myself, I felt no shock at what my mother had done. I don't know if I had exactly expected it- and perhaps I had never consciously thought of it- but I was not surprised that my mom had become a suicide.

My father and I went with pale faces to my sister's bedroom to tell her the news, but upon my father saying the words, she kicked us out, hysterical, refusing to hear more.

"No she's not! She's not dead!" Rachel cried, looking with rage and sorrow into my tearless eyes, "Stop it! What's wrong with you? Go away! GO AWAY!" She began to gesticulate violently towards the door, demanding our exit as she wept.

Upon shutting her door quietly behind us, my dad turned to me, zombie-like, and uttered:

"Baby, I-I think I need some time alone, too. Just…I just need some time. Do you understand?"

I looked him full in the face, saw his swimming, red-rimmed eyes, and nodded sagely. I gave him another quick hug which was weakly returned, and left him to face his grief.

Unsure of what else to do, I went for a walk, hoping it might stimulate thought, but my mind remained a complete blank. The air was crisp and cold; it had snowed three days previously, which was very rare in a coastal Oregonian town. No one was even able to recall the last time it had snowed there, before that. *Three days ago… it snowed.*

"It snowed on the day my mom died," I said out loud, coming to that realization. "The snow was falling, and we thought it was so neat because we had never seen it happen here, and I went outside and tried to catch some flurries on my tongue. I was goofing around, and had no idea she was lying there, dead."

I continued to walk, machine-like, one foot in front of the other, not caring in the least where I went. When I looked up at one point, I saw that I was near my high school. Classes had just been released a few hours earlier, and from the cheers I heard coming from the gymnasium I knew there was a basketball game going on. I never went to sports games, but something compelled me to peek in as I passed the school; and there, on the gym floor playing basketball, was Angela, a person who I might consider a friend, if I ever allowed myself to have one. Though we hadn't spoken in weeks, when I saw her I instantly felt the need to speak to her. Without waiting for the game to stop, I walked up to her, and took her aside. The whistle blew and their coach called a time out.

"Angela, I'm sorry… It's just- my mom died, she killed herself. I felt like I should tell someone, so I wanted to tell you. That's all."

I remember Angela gasping in horror, speechless- but then the game was trying to get started again, and she was needed, so I left without a backwards glance, forgetting Angela as soon as she was out of sight.

After having told Angela about my mother, I felt that a small weight had been lifted from inside me, though I wasn't sure why. Grief is an odd thing. As I walked home, I looked up into the dull, gray February sky, and whispered, "Good-bye, Mom," and this time, I knew it was the final good-bye she would ever receive from me.

*

When the time came, a few days later, to attend my mother's memorial in California, both my father and I declined to attend. I didn't know his reasoning, but I felt that I couldn't face her family, who I had been raised to believe had mistreated her since she was young. To think of them surrounding my mother's coffin, crying, to me was more than I could bear. Plus, the thought of seeing my mother's dead body freaked me out more than I cared to admit. I wanted to keep my mental picture of her as a living person, and not as a cold, rigid corpse. And so, I refused to go. My sister was livid with us both; she told us it was a mistake, and that we would regret it if we didn't go. I couldn't find the strength inside of myself to disagree with her, but neither could I muster the courage to face our estranged family or my mother's remains. I told myself that I had said good-bye to my mother's body when we drove away that last day of our visit, and that I had whispered good-bye to her spirit after being sent away by both my sister and father to face my own grief. Going back to the place of her death, I reasoned, would bring nothing to me but unnecessary pain. And so my sister went alone, without the support of her sister or father, to her mother's memorial.

My mother had written a suicide note, though she had torn it up and thrown it in the waste basket before succumbing to the sleeping pills. I was asked if I wanted to read it, but I found the very idea of a note repulsive. Why would I want to read a letter written by someone who pretended to be my mother? Because my mom was not that strange woman who had killed herself; my mother had loved me, and she would never have abandoned me for all eternity like this. Though I refused to read the note, my sister told me that it contained two things I should be aware of: the first was that my mother had left me her car, which astounded me, considering I didn't even have a permit yet. The other was that someday, she would like me or my sister to name one of our children after her. I laughed inside when Rachel told me this. *I'm never going to have kids*, I thought bitterly, *and even if I do, I would never ever name my little girl after a woman who committed suicide.*

Sweet Fifteen
(9)

Days passed, and I was generally ignored both my family and by my classmates; I don't think anyone knew what to do with me. Sometimes I would walk to school, and other times, if the weather was very poor, my father would stay up after he came home from working all night and drive me. Whenever that happened, he looked so exhausted that I felt unsafe being in the car with him. We rarely spoke on those morning car-rides, not that the drive was very long, only a few minutes- but sometimes they seemed to take forever. I think if he had tried to talk, we both would have been at a loss of what to say. What do you talk about when your mother and your ex-wife have just committed suicide, and you're tossed into each others sole company, for better or for worse? Do you say, 'Hi, how are you, how was your day?' No, because we both knew the answer would always be the same: our day was shitty. And it was true; every day really was.

School became a physical prison to compliment the mental one in which I languished. The classes meant nothing to me. I could not bring myself to care about history, math, science; everything that my teachers lectured about seemed pointless to me. It all felt like a waste of time, like there was always something else I should be doing.

I could admit to myself, at least in part, that it bothered me that none of my classmates or teachers had mentioned my mother's death after it had become known. No one had expressed their sympathy, or given me a chance to talk about it, and so I felt that no one cared. The few people that did speak to me could only say how 'wonderful' I was looking from my rapid weight loss, which only made me feel twisted and shameful inside. How could I tell them I had an eating disorder, that I was dying, and that their compliments were the last thing I wanted? Their sudden, unwanted compliments were often the only words people said to me all day; how could I refute them when I ached so badly for human contact?

In the first month after my mother's death, I went to all my classes without taking time off to grieve. I believe this was my way of reaching out, but, unfortunately, as I was unsure of how to ask for help, or even really what type of help I needed, I received nothing. As difficult as I found classes to be, lunch-time was the most challenging. I had never been one to eat in the cafeteria, because I was too embarrassed to be found sitting alone, and I also felt guilty when others saw me eat; it felt as if I was being 'caught'. It didn't matter to me that I had lost weight; I still felt like the fat little girl I had grown up as, and it was embarrassing to be seen adding to my girth by consuming lunch. So every day when the lunch bell rang, I would walk as quickly as I could to the library and spend my lunch hour there, reading books, or drawing in my binder, alone. It was the longest hour of my day. I was constantly distracted by the laughing, jovial voices from other students walking down the hallway, which filled me with jealousy and bitterness. Once in a while, someone who knew me would look in to the library and ask if I was in trouble, and I would be forced to lie and say I was catching up on my homework.

Afterawhile, The unchanging days became intolerable ~~to me~~, and I started to ditch school after the lunch bell rang. Every morning I would get dressed and feel myself start to crumble inside, ready to fall into the sea of misery that I surrounded myself with. I ached from the top of my throat to pit of my soul. I had divulged my darkest secret to both my sister and my mother, and my sister had ~~done nothin~~g; my mother was dead. I had become a burden. My very existence was a millstone around the neck of the last person in the world I had any feeling left for, my father. I ~~could not make~~ had a hard time making myself care to put on socks, or to brush my hair. The entity of Kim was no longer a person, but a substance, a shape of odium and mournfulness that moved and hungered without want or volition.

So instead of attending my afternoon classes, I started to make it a habit to walk to a grocery store across town and buy a pre-made birthday cake. I would shove it unceremoniously into my backpack, not caring if it became disheveled and unrecognizable. I was always vaguely aware of the cashier staring at me in bewilderment, but I never cared. And then I would walk home. Since my father was still working nights, he was always asleep during the day, so I had to be quiet when I crept into the near-empty house. I would slip quietly downstairs, throw a blanket over my shoulders to block out the cold, and binge in silence. While I was eating, I was numb; I felt nothing. For a few minutes, at least, I was free. But when my stomach felt near to the point of exploding, I would hobble to the kitchen to grab a trash bag, and make myself throw up into it, afterwards carrying it to the dumpster outside. After a quick wash, I would then go to my bedroom to lie down, thinking all the while that it was surely a mistake that I had been born a human, because no else could possibly be as broken and screwed up as I was.

Such was my everyday. Every night I cried when my father left for work, usually without saying good-bye, not suspecting that I had ditched school in order to feed my addiction. I could see no way to end the cycle. I felt so empty most of the time, and when I dared to feel anything the feelings were so painful and overwhelming I felt the compelling need to purge them away. I began to throw up in my room because I became paranoid that my sister or father would hear me in the bathroom; I would collect old popcorn cans, such as the kind you get at Christmas, and I would fill them with vomit and leave them to rot with their lids fastened until my room became filled with putridity and flies. Sometimes, the cans would spill when I tried to lift their heavy weight in order to dump them, and as a result my bedroom carpet became rancid with the scent of stomach acid and regurgitated food. Over time, my carpet began to rot, and I covered it with towels, hoping against hope that my Dad and sister never discovered how bad it had so suddenly become.

Life went on that way for a while, unchanging and bleak, and then one evening, something different happened. After my dad ~~had~~ left for work, there came a knock at the front door. That night I had neglected to wash myself after being sick, and my face was puffy, so I decided to pretend no one was home rather than answer the door smelling like vomit. But the knock did not repeat. After a few seconds I went into the dusty, cold living room and peeked through the blinds, but in the slanting lamp-light of the porch, I saw no one. Curious, I turned the (front door) handle and looked outside- and there, its furry face peering up at me, sat a little stuffed brown bear. I stared at it for a moment in perplexity before bending down to pick it up, dislodging a card that was stuck to it~~'~~s back in the process. After a quick glance around my empty front yard, I went back inside the house.

I sat down on the couch and ran my fingers lightly over the brown teddy's curly fur. I couldn't remember the last time someone had given me a stuffed animal… for it must have been meant for me; there was no one else home. Or, maybe someone had gotten the wrong house address? Eager to solve the mystery, I ripped open the envelope. I could feel my heart pounding.

The card was a simple one, with a picture of a bear holding a yellow heart balloon, and inside, it said something along the lines of:

"Dear Kim,

You might not know me, but I would really like to get to know you. I have seen you at school, I think you are pretty and I have heard about your recent loss and I would like to help you in any way I can. If you feel like it, please give me a call, and we can go out for ice cream or just have a chat. My phone number is -
Sincerely,

Preston Cory."

    My eyes were transfixed on the card before me, open but not seeing. In the temporary silence of my mind, a word or two floated into my consciousness. Call? …chat? Then my thoughts came all in a rush: a guy named Preston had just asked me on a date. I had no idea who he was; I didn't know who anyone was, besides the people who directly affected my every day life. I stared into the blank, shining eyes of the stuffed animal. It was cute. It would be nice to have someone to talk to, I reflected. But was I good enough for a boyfriend? The thought of me being close to a guy made my heart pound. I hadn't even thought about boys since I had dated Miles in sixth grade. Up until a few months ago I had still been heavy, and no one had noticed me at all. I was still that same person inside. I wondered if Preston, whoever he was, would have given even a second thought to either to me or my mother's death if I were still over two-hundred pounds.

The next morning at school I took a little extra time with my hair, which was not saying much, since no one had ever taught me how to style it, and attempted to do some sort of makeup effect on my eyes. I wanted to feel prepared to meet this Preston, just in case. My first class was history, and upon sitting down, I turned to a girl that I knew slightly, named Ashleigh. We were not friends, but she was one of those interesting girls that talks to everyone, be they princess, devil or slug.

"Ashleigh," I whispered, "Do you know a guy named Preston Cory?"

Ashleigh looked a little shocked that I was talking to her, but then replied, "Doesn't everyone? He's *so* hot! He's a senior, and a quarterback. He's got crazy muscles. Why?"

I was silent for a minute. I wasn't quite sure what to do with that information. "Well… um. I think he asked me out."

Ashleigh's eyes got wide. "No way! You are so lucky! Did you know that last I year I went out with Ira, and he…"

I shook my head in the negative; no, I didn't know that, because I didn't care. I turned back to the blank papers on my desk and pretended I was writing while her voice babbled on in the background.

So, Preston was a jock and 'hot.' Against my will, I felt extremely flattered that he had taken any notice of me at all; but I was also confused. Why me? There were much more beautiful girls that attended our high school. And if he was a senior, I was a lot younger than him, as well; I was just fifteen. My heart was pounding again, and my face flushed. Ashleigh was glancing at me surreptitiously from her desk, probably wondering the same things I was. What would I do if I ran into him? How would I even know if I did because I had no idea what he looked like—just be on the look out for muscles? With this thought, I stood up, packed up my binder and book, and walked out of the room and made a bee-line for home, and the safety of bed. School was too much for me that day.

That night, my sister came to visit. I don't know why she did, because we still didn't get along, and as far as I knew she still disliked my father. She may have just been there to grab some more of her items for all I knew, because she hardly spoke to me anymore. I sat on the floor of the living room and tried to watch television and keep my brain empty, but was shocked when the doorbell rang. With my heart in my throat, I went to the front door, paused for a moment to straighten my hair, and then opened it.

On my front porch was a tall, muscular, Greek-looking young man with white teeth and ruffled black hair. My voice caught in my throat. I didn't know what to do or what to say. I was frozen.

"Kim?" he asked politely, his voice deep and quiet, "I'm Preston. Did you get the bear I left for you yesterday?"

I opened my mouth to speak but the voice inside refused to work. I had never spoken to a person like him before; he was so pretty. In the end I just nodded.

He seemed to expect my speechlessness and his smile widened. "Would you mind if we talked outside for a moment? I would really like us to get to know each other, if that's okay. I don't think you know me, do you?"

"N-no..." I stammered, "Well, I don't know *much* about you." *Only that you're muscley and god-like.* I followed him out the front door and walked down the slope of my driveway and sat down on the curb, with my feet in the road. The night was cool, and clear, and the stars glittered above us in a seemingly endless expanse. He sat next to me, so close our hips were almost touching. His presence filled my senses completely. He smelled like pine and gasoline, and I could see in the pale light that his hands were covered in grease. To this day, because of him I still can't stand the scent of car lubricants, or oil.

"Well, I'm just going to come right out and say it... I have seen you around school and I think you are the most beautiful girl I have ever seen. Now, I never have any luck with beautiful girls, so you'll probably turn me down..."

I let out a shocked, graceless snort. "That's ridiculous!"

"It's true!" he said with a gleaming look in his eyes. "No pretty girl ever wants anything to do with me. But I just had to take a chance with you. I think you're special. I would really like to take you on a date, to get to know each other. And I heard about your mom. Maybe I can be there for you if you ever need someone to talk to. My grandma died last year and I know what it's like to lose someone you love. Maybe, you know, if you like me, I could end up being… your rock."

I could only hold my breath and stare at him while the crickets chirped. Everything he said sounded perfect, but I wanted it so badly to be yes. I had never met a guy like him before; true, I had not met many guys, at all; but he seemed so solid and capable that I felt I could trust anything he said. If only I had known.

"Well," I said shyly, "I don't think I'm pretty, but I would like to go on a date with you. It sounds like fun. And thank you for the bear. It was… very nice." I smiled at him and tried to look appealing, even though I knew it must have been horribly unattractive that I was wearing flannel Christmas jammies in the middle of May.

He smiled anew. "Awesome! How about this Saturday? Twelve? We can go for a drive."

"Sure," I said, looking at his hands. They were so greasy that I wondered if he worked on cars for fun or for necessity.

"Ok then," said Preston, and walked me back to my front door, "I will see you Saturday then, Kim. Have a good night! "

"Mm-hmm, Bye," I returned awkwardly, and watched him as he walked swiftly down the driveway and jumped into the old Chevy truck he had parked on the street, and drive off.

When I eventually turned back to the house, Rachel was there, with an impish grin on her face.

"Who was that?" she asked.

"His name's Preston. We have a date on Saturday," I said, embarrassed.

"Oh. Well, don't have sex!" she advised ominously, and then left without another word. I was alone in the house once more.

*

From the time Preston left that night until noon on Saturday, I refused to eat a single thing. I was much, much too anxious. Instead, I used Kool-Aid sweetened with Splenda as filler to trick my stomach into thinking it wasn't hungry, though in reality I felt like I was dying. I was tired and dizzy, and I was constantly having to sit down lest I pass out. I must have drunk at least two gallons of Kool-aid a day, but I was so nervous and focused on my upcoming date that I didn't care. What would I wear, what would I say? Those were the important things. I mean, what could I *possibly* have to talk about with a high school football player who was three years older than me? The only answer that floated back to me was: *nothing*. Believing myself boring, I was determined to look my best; I bought a new shirt, which, although it was tight on me, I felt it looked decent; anyway, it made it appear as if I boasted some cleavage (even though I was an A cup at the time, if that). So for the rest of the week, I continued to drink my Kool-aid and ignore my light-headedness. If I couldn't be interesting, I swore to myself, I was at least going to try and be pretty.

When Saturday came, I was dressed and ready an hour early, but Preston was half an hour late. I stood waiting for him by the front door, pacing nervously, peeking through the blinds, checking my hair, smelling my breath, looking at the clock. My muscles were all tense. As the half-hour passed, I thought, *He stood me up. He saw when he came here that I'm actually a fat slob who wears Christmas pajamas and he wants nothing to do with me.* It was only after I began to truly despair that I heard his truck pull up in front of my house, and suddenly I was the happiest girl in the world.

I stepped away from the door, determined that he not suspect that I had been eagerly waiting for him- I even let him ring the bell, and let two or three seconds pass before I opened the door.

And then there he was, just as fit as when I last saw him, just as tall and tan. I smiled with my lips closed tightly together, since I hated my teeth as much as I did the rest of my body, and didn't want him to think I looked like a beaver.

"Hi, ready to go?" Preston asked, echoing my smile with a much, much more brilliant one.

"Mm-hmm," I said, and walked out the door, shutting and locking it behind me.

He was a little surprised.

"Is no one home?"

"Oh, no, no one's ever home. My dad works nights, and then he goes out on the weekends, so… I lock up when I leave," I said matter-of-factly.

He laughed as got into his truck. "You never get into trouble while he's out, do you? Invite anyone over for some fun?"

I glanced at him to see if he was joking and decided that he was. "Oh, haha. No, not me. I never do anything like that."

"Aw, that's too bad," he said, and we drove off together towards town.

"I thought we might grab some ice cream and then head to the beach, if that's okay?" asked Preston, "We can do a lot of good talking there, and it's a nice day."

The thought of ice cream made me cringe, but I wanted to please him, so I said, "That sounds great!" In my head I was figuring how I would to punish myself later for the additional calories.

We ended up going through the drive-through at Dairy Queen, where one of his friends was working- a girl named Tabby.

"Hi Preston, whatcha… oh, who's that?" Tabby asked, leaning out her little window to look at me.

"This is Kim. We're just hanging out today," he replied.

Tabby stared at him unbelievingly. "Uh-huh, okay. Don't be stupid, Preston. I know you."

He scoffed. "Just give us our ice cream, Tabby."

She frowned at him. "What happened to Tiffany?"

"It didn't work out."

Tabby looked at me. "How old are you… Kim, right?"

I nodded shyly. "I'm fifteen."

Tabby glared at Preston, but before she could say anything else, he said,

"Our ice cream, Tabby. *Now.*"

As we drove away, I asked, "So that was your friend?"

"Kind of. That was Tabby, she's in my class. She never likes it when I'm with other girls, because she has a crush on me. She's just jealous. Don't let what she said get to you."

"I wasn't going to," I said. I licked my ice cream delicately, careful not to make a sound, and watched him. He was driving with one hand, the other holding his ice cream cone. He would periodically bring it to his lips, and lick it with a thick pink tongue, or bite into it. I was fascinated. He caught me looking at him, and he smirked.

"What?"

I turned beat red. "Nothing. I've just never ridden in a car with a guy before, or eaten ice cream with a guy before… or been on a date before..." I finished lamely.

"Well, if it's okay with you, I would like to ride in cars with you more often. What do you think?"

The thought made my body go warm. "I think I might like that."

By the time we arrive at the beach our ice cream cones were gone, and Preston made use of his free hands to help me climb a few large rocks so that we could have a good view of the ocean. His hands were so big that they seemed unreal, and though he had obviously tried to clean them, they still retained hints of grease around the nails and knuckles. I mentioned the stains to him, and he looked at his hands.

"Yeah, I am always working on my car, or someone else's car. It's my favorite thing to do. I love to figure out what makes stuff go, y'know?"

I didn't know, but I nodded. We were both standing on the rock outcropping, staring at the ocean, and Preston sat down and indicated the rock next to him, inviting me to sit. I sat.

"I like to figure out what makes people go, too," he said, "I like complicated people, because they give me something to try to figure out. I think that's what drew me to you. You seem like you have a lot going on. You're not simple."

If he knew how complicated I really am, he'd run away screaming, I thought to myself, recalling my bedroom which its cans of vomit and surrogate flies.

"I like you, Kim. How would you feel about us becoming boyfriend and girlfriend?" he asked suddenly, turning his brown eyes to mine.

I pursed my lips. "We don't know anything about each other. Plus, I'm such a boring girl, and you're so popular and everything."

He shook his head, and reached out to grabbed a hold of my hand.

"You're not boring to me," he whispered, and with that, he leaned over so close that our faces were almost touching. My heart was pounding so hard I was positive that he must have been able to hear it. *Oh my God.*

"Can I kiss you?" he asked huskily, his breath hot on my lips.

I couldn't speak. I had never kissed anyone. I thought maybe I should get it over with. "Mm-hmm," I whimpered.

And he kissed me. His lips were very soft at first, closed, testing to see how I would react. My blood was rushing in my ears. I didn't have a single thought in my head. I was trying not to panic at the suddenness of this development and just experience every sensation of the kiss, imprint it on my memory so I could revisit the details later when I was by myself. Trapped in the moment, I was as still as a piece of stone as his mouth touched mine, and I was aware that I should probably do something, but I did not know what; I had never really thought about kissing a man before. Preston pulled back, smiling, his arm suddenly around me and his body nestled close.

"That's not how you kiss," he chuckled softly, and leaned in again, harder this time, pressing into me until my lips ached. And suddenly, I felt something small and wet slither its way into my mouth, and it took me a second to realize it was his tongue. It pushed its way past the barriers of my closed lips and forced itself towards the back of my throat. My eyes opened wide. It was gross.

I jerked away and rubbed my sore mouth with the back of my hand. With his eyes sparkling, he asked, "How was that?"

I wasn't sure how to respond. His tongue had made me want to gag- I hadn't been prepared for anything like it. But he was more experienced than I was- maybe that was just how people kissed. If I told him it made me uncomfortable, there was the possibility that he might see me as too much of a kid to be his girlfriend. Maybe I could get used to it.

"I liked it," I said, forcing a smile.

He leaned back on the rocks. "Yup, I knew you would!" We stayed at the beach for another few minutes, not talking, until he said he should get back to work and that he would drop me back off at my house. I was a little disappointed that we hadn't gotten to know each other better, but I agreed. We were quiet on the drive back, and when we reached my house, he put his truck in park and turned to me.

"Are you my girlfriend?"

"Yes, I'm your girlfriend. If you want me."

Preston smirked. "Good, I'm glad. Come here." I tensed as he drew me towards him and kissed me on the lips, but to my relief he was just as gentle as he had been the first time. My body relaxed.

He pulled back. "I would like to see you again soon. Give me your phone number."

I gave it to him, and crawled out of his truck and watched him drive away. When he was gone I went inside the house, locking the door behind me, and sat down on the couch. In the dead silence of my empty home, I touched my mouth, remembering the feel of his full lips on mine, and I shivered. *Did that really happen?* I thought. *Do I really have a boyfriend? I can't believe I kissed someone- and he thinks I'm pretty!* And *interesting!* And then I recalled that I had eaten an ice cream cone, an *entire* ice cream cone, and I was immediately filled with shame. I would get fatter, and Preston wouldn't like me anymore- he would dump me and I would be all alone again. With these horrific thoughts floating in my mind, I determined not to eat a single thing for the next three days.

Preston didn't call until the next Friday, asking if he could come over later that night, so that we could relax, eat, and watch a movie together- he would bring the dinner and the movie. Of course, I agreed; and so the second date was made. I didn't think to mention to him again that my dad would be working, and in my naiveté, I hoped he wouldn't mind the fact that it would be just us alone. I was, after all, boring. I could think of absolutely nothing to say to this older, more experienced guy. I didn't know what he was getting out of dating me- on my part, I just wanted to be in his presence, talked to, and maybe even held a little.

He arrived forty-five minutes late, but I hardly noticed, because I was so happy to see him when he did come. He gave me a quick, soft kiss in greeting, and I knew I was beaming because my cheeks hurt from smiling so much. For dinner, he went into my kitchen and made Campbell's vegetable soup mixed with Ramen noodles, and we sat down on the dingy couch in the living room to eat and watch the movie he had rented, Jay and Silent Bob. I had seen it before, but I told him I hadn't, because I thought it would be more special if he thought we were having a new experience together.

As the movie started, he wolfed down his food, and when he was done I put my bowl aside, untouched, even though I was starving. He scooted closer and put his arm around me.

"Mm, wow, you smell good," Preston said, his face buried in my hair. I giggled nervously.

"Um, thank you." I said, turning to look him in the eyes.

The movie played on, unheeded. Preston took a small lock of my hair and started playing with it, almost idly, as he looked my body up and down. "You really are beautiful," he whispered, his eyes piercing mine, "but I don't know if it's right that I asked you to be my girlfriend."

I froze. "Why?"

He sighed, dropping my hair. "I forgot how young you are. I've thought about it all week, how I'm two years older than you. I'm used to being in a physical relationship, and that's probably not something you're ready for."

I began to panic; I saw my hopes of having a boyfriend being dashed before I had barely known I had them.

"I'm not too young, I'm fifteen."

"That's still very young. I bet you're a virgin," he said.

I replied slowly. "Y-yes, I am."

He continued: "I'm not- and when I care about someone I need to show it in a physical way. And I'd feel bad if you felt I forced it on you."

I shook my head emphatically. "You wouldn't force anything on me!" *What was I doing?*

"Oh, yeah? So you'd lose your virginity to me?"

I started trembling, just a little, because I was still determined not to lose him so soon. I would have agreed to anything he asked of me at that moment. "Yes."

He leaned closer, his breath hot on my face. "Right now?"

I nodded very slightly, and sat still as he reached a hand towards my ~~breast~~ chest and whispered, "I hoped you would. I've wanted to do this since the first time I saw you."

I was a statue as he stroked my breast, toyed with it, and drew circles around my nipple. Suddenly he commanded, "Take off your clothes."

I was hesitant. "I don't know if I look… no one has ever seen…"

"Take them off," he growled, reaching for the hem of my shirt and pulling upwards. Not knowing what else to do, I complied, quickly removing my garments and pushing them away.

I was naked for the first time, then, in front of a man. I watched his eyes rove over me, exploring every inch of my skin, pausing to appreciate my erect nipples and the space between my legs. I wondered if I looked like other women, or if I was disappointing. I was afraid to ask.

"Get up and spin around for me, I want to see your ass."

Shivering, I obeyed and turned my back to him. I felt cold, and uncomfortable. From behind me, I heard him give a soft moan, and I glanced back to see what he was doing- and there, in his hand, was the first penis I had ever seen, hard and small. He toyed with it with is car-greased fingers, and he looked me in the eye and asked, "What do you think?"

I felt like I couldn't respond. I didn't think anything about it; it was a penis, and I had never seen one before, not even on a baby. It was just new.

He instructed me to lie down on the couch, and like an automaton, I did as I was commanded. He unbuckled his pants, and climbed on top of me, and began kissing my breasts. I watched him as he did this, and I was fascinated despite my fear that I was doing something that normal people did all of the time. This was how babies were made; *this*, my mind interjected from somewhere far away, *is what my father is terrible at.*

He brought his face up to mine, and said "This might hurt."

I gulped, and nodded and he pushed himself inside of me. I was taken aback at first by the odd feeling, but, despite what he had said, it didn't hurt. He started thrusting, at first slow, and then more quickly, and- still not knowing how to react- I lay still and let him do everything for fear of doing something wrong.

"I'm gonna come," he announced abruptly, and he quickly reared back, pulling himself out of me. I screamed in shock as liquid shot all over my chest, warm and then instantly cold; I had not expected that.

The whole event was over in less than twenty seconds, from start to finish.

He rolled off of me, sighing, and I remained on my back with my limbs sticking in the air like road-kill. I tried to disguise it, but I was disgusted- semen was disgusting. It smelled bad. I didn't know what to do with it. It was rapidly starting to run down the sides of my body and I was afraid it was going to stain the couch.

"Where are your towels?" he asked.

"Um… in the hall closet, up the stairs. Can you bring me one, please?" I asked, refusing to look at his naked body as he stood up and stretched languidly.

He went up the few stairs to our hall closet and came back with two towels. He tossed one at me and cleaned himself with the other, then proceeded to get dressed. I tried my best to clean myself off with the towel, but I felt as if I would never be clean again. I got dressed, and then we sat on the couch next to each other.

"How was it?" he asked, glancing at me.

"It was…nice," I replied, lying. It was awful.

He was silent for a moment, then said, "Are you sure you're a virgin?"

I stared at him. "What do you mean? Of course I'm- was a virgin. Why?"

He shrugged. "Well, you didn't bleed or anything and you didn't feel like a virgin to me. But, if you say you're a virgin then that's what we'll go with."

My lips flattened into a thin line. What the hell did he mean, 'that's what we'll go with'? I was fifteen years old. How much sex did he think I'd had before him? It wasn't my fault if I didn't bleed. Had he *wanted* me to bleed? If I had avoided it, to me that was a good thing. And what did a virgin 'feel like?'

I was about to tell him that I didn't appreciate what he was implying, but he stood up and said abruptly, "Well, I should get going."

Instantly my anger turned to hurt. "But we haven't finished the movie yet. You just got here like half an hour ago."

He smiled at me, and my heart ached with how cold and perfunctory it was. "I've actually seen the movie, and it's really not that good. Maybe we can do a different movie next weekend, how does that sound?"

"Why do you need to go?" I persisted.

"I need to get cleaned up, and I figure you do too," he said, coming forward and giving me a kiss on the forehead. "I will give you a call soon."

I bit my lip, but nodded, and watched as he left. As he walked down the driveway he turned and called, "See you soon, beautiful," and then he was gone.

I stood at the open door for quite a while after he left. I could feel the residue of his semen on my chest and stomach, and a slight soreness between my legs, and I felt disgusting. Was this sex? Was this love? I shut the door and leaned my back against it, stifling a sudden sob with my hand. What the hell was I so sad about it? I had agreed to do it, after all. So what if I was no longer a virgin; it wasn't as if my virginity was something I had been proud of, or felt like I was saving for 'that special someone'… but in that moment I still felt like I had been cheated. I wanted Preston to come back, to kiss me, to hold me, to tell me how much it meant to him that I had given myself to him. But I knew he wouldn't. A tear trickled down my chin and dropped to the floor.

I walked slowly to the living room and picked up the towels from the floor. Putting on a pair of slippers, I went outside and tossed them into the dumpster, closing the lids with a loud slam. I never wanted to see or use those particular towels ever again. Then, taking a deep, shuddering breath to rid myself of his scent, I lifted my face to gaze up at the stars; they were especially beautiful that night, and seemed to sparkle like jewels crowning a full, yellow moon. *The stars were like this the night Preston came to my house to ask me on a date*, I recalled. *He told me he liked me, and that he could be my rock.* The once pleasant memory made me bitter.

Romance is for idiots, I thought coldly, and went inside.

A Teenage Waste
(10)

Preston never called again. I tried to call him, a few times; once I begged him to tell me what I had done wrong, why he didn't want to date me anymore, but he always refused to speak on the subject. "You wouldn't like the answer," he said once. I was crushed, of course; and from those feeling of rejection came feelings of obsession. He was a baseball player, so I went, uninvited, to all of his baseball games, and cheered him on. If I knew he would be at a place, I would be sure to be there, too. I even got a job at an espresso stand just because his mother worked as a clerk in the store where it was located; so I further made her acquaintance, and found some comfort when she said how disappointed she was that her son had treated me so shamefully.

But those silly games can never last long. He soon found another girlfriend, and though I was filled with jealousy at first, I mostly blamed myself. I was not girlfriend material; I was not attractive enough. I was uninteresting. My clothes were not fashionable. I didn't know how to style my hair, or put on makeup. I wasn't popular.

After that, I dropped out of school entirely. I couldn't find the energy to do anything anymore, besides eat and vomit. My dad was never home, so I had plenty of time to dive into my sickness and find refuge from my emotions in my addiction. I felt less sick at heart when I was binging. All I could feel while eating was numbness and some slight satisfaction when I chewed and swallowed something as if it was going to stay down forever. But it wasn't. I would always end the cycle by sticking my fingers down my throat and purging as much out of my stomach as possible. Sometime my throat would bleed, and I would cry and my body would spasm because the pain was so acute. Afterwards, I was so exhausted that it was all I could do to walk to my bed and collapse. I'd sleep for hours, then, only waking up in a drugged stupor after it was dark.

Though I was skipping school, I still maintained my job on weekends at the espresso stand in the grocery store where I bought most of my binge food. I was terrible at my job, and I knew it, but something kept me coming back. Perhaps I didn't want to disappoint my boss, who seemed to have taken a chance on hiring a fifteen year old, or maybe I enjoyed having tip money to buy binge food with. Either way, it was there at my espresso stand when I first saw the Stock Boy.

He was tall, and as skinny as a pole; but he had gorgeous brown [hazel] eyes and Crest commercial teeth which widened into a smile whenever someone greeted him. I didn't know his name, and had never spoken to him, but in my head I thought, *He looks nice. He doesn't look like someone who would sleep with me and then dump me.*

Eventually I couldn't handle the mystery, and I asked one of my coworkers, Kelly, who the stock boy was.

"That's Ian," answered Kelly. "He just broke up with his long-time girlfriend, and he's really good friends with my friend Sam. Why? Do you like him?"

"I think he's pretty cute," I said.

"We should all do something together!" said Kelly, getting really excited all of a sudden, "Sam is always saying we should get together. It's Friday night, I bet we can figure out something to do. What do you think?"

I hesitated. "Would Ian come?"

"They're always together, I don't see why not. But I'll ask. Hey, give me your phone number, and I'll call you after I get off work. I'll let you know what we come up with."

That night would be the first time I had ever gone out with friends, and also the first time I had ever spent an evening with people of both genders. Kelly called my cell phone later that day, and informed me that Sam's older brother was out of town, and that he was house-sitting, so he was offering to drive us up to the house and we could have a little house party with just the four of us: Kelly, me, Sam, and Ian. I agreed, eager to learn more about Ian the Stock Boy.

At about eight o'clock, a small silver Mazda drove up to my house, and I walked outside to meet it. Inside was Ian, and Kelly, and Sam. Sam was a tall, slender boy of about eighteen, with a plain face and sandy blonde hair that hung limply past his shoulders. I was not favorable impressed with his looks, but he made up for it with his humor, and he made all of us laugh with his quick wit. He and Ian talked and joked like they had been friends forever, and it made me smile to listen to them. I watched Ian closely from the back seat, and wondered if he had even noticed me.

"So, I have Everclear up at my brother's house," said Sam. "I mixed it with punch so you can't even taste it. It's freakin' delicious."

Kelly frowned. "I really don't want to drink."

Sam uttered a theatrical gasp. "What? No drinking? Why not?"

"I don't want to get in trouble? I don't like being drunk? Are those enough for you?"

"Geez, you don't have to get drunk, you lush! And no one is going to find out, you know my brother lives way up on a mountain, right? The cops aren't going to just waltz in there screaming 'Put your hands up!'"

Kelly was adamant. "No drinking for me, but you guys knock yourselves out."

Sam pouted. "Party pooper. What about you, Kim? You going to drink?"

I thought about the strawberry daiquiri's my dad had made for me at his girlfriend's house, and I figured if he didn't care if I drank, I didn't either.

"Sure," I said, "I'll drink a little."

"It's good shit. You won't regret it!" said Sam.

It took about fifteen minutes for Sam's silver car to crawl up the side of the mountain, and then pull into a heavily wooded driveway in front of a small house that resembled a shabby hunter's cottage. Upon entering, I felt that my initial observation had been correct, as the walls inside were covered with pictures of cougars, quail, elk, and other forest animals, as well as a complete fishing tackle and even the skull of a bear.

"Let's drink!" said Sam, pulling out a large drink dispenser from the shabby fridge and grabbing some red Solo cups from a cabinet. Falling in with his enthusiasm, I accepted a drink, and endeavored to sip it; indeed, it was hard to believe it contained alcohol at all- it tasted just like fruit punch.

The four of us conversed late into the night, but what struck me most was how bright and funny Sam was, and how quiet and restrained Ian seemed by comparison. I wondered if he was as shy, so I tried to ask him a few questions, but he could never quite meet my eyes, and only responded with single word sentences. After a while, Kelly and I went outside, ostensibly for a moment of fresh air, but in reality I wanted to ask her about Ian's standoffish behavior.

"Is he shy? He doesn't talk to me." I said.

She shook her head. "No, I don't think he's shy. He's just a little weird. Uh, I don't know if I should tell you this... but his dad committed suicide when he was little. Shot himself. Awful, huh?"

I stood there silently, stunned. So he was just like me. Had I seen that in him, somehow? Had I recognized that he was abnormal, like myself?

When we went back inside, I watched Ian's face. He had beautiful dark eyes, and I thought I saw a depth there that I felt could only be obtained one way. I found myself wanting to explore that depth.

The night didn't last long, because the more Sam drank the more rowdy he became, and Kelly decided that she had better head home. She said that she could take his car, drive me home, and then return the car in the morning. Sam seemed disappointed, but he agreed. I was tired and a bit dehydrated, but I also felt let down. Ian and I had hardly exchanged more than two all night. Before climbing in the car to leave, I turned to him, and said,

"It was nice spending time with you. I think we have a lot in common."

To my mortification, Ian just shrugged.

"If you say so," he said shortly, and turned to go back into the house. Sam, on the other hand, remained outside as we pulled away, waving energetically, and shouting,

"Thanks for coming! It was fucking awesome!"

Two weeks passed, I had heard nothing from Kelly, Sam, or Ian, and I figured it was because I had been a boring companion, and therefore I held no hope of ever being asked out again. During that time, things got even more uncomfortable at home. Rachel had completely disappeared by that point. No one was taking care of our dogs or cats anymore- one time, they went two days without food- so one day, my dad packed them up and gave them away. When I found out, I sobbed like a little girl, even though I knew it was probably a wise decision, since I was not able to take care of six cats and two dogs by myself the way I was. But the memories of the years that my furry family and I spent together consumed me until I felt I would be eaten alive by them. My pets had been my only friends and confidents, and I had abandoned them like they didn't matter- and now they were gone forever.

A couple of nights later, I was laying awake in my dark room, listening to the buzz of dozens of flies as they fed on my open cans of vomit. *Well, at least I'm not completely alone*, I thought bitterly. *As long as I feed them, they'll be here to keep me company.* I was just about to shut my eyes when I heard loud voices from outside, and the front door slam. I sat up quickly, my heart pounding.

"Make yourselves at home!" came my father's booming voice from the living room, and then I heard a chatter of male and female voices, and laughter, and then after a moment loud rock music began to play. I sat there on my bed, confused and tired, and now a little frightened. What was going on?

I stood up and turned on my bedroom light, and slipped on a robe. Opening my door, I peeked down the hallway- and saw that our living room was filled to the brim with people who looked like they had just spilled out of the bar, drinks in some hands, cigarettes in others. In the center, I saw my dad, laughing with a tall dark haired man with a goatee. I stepped into the hallway and quickly shit the door behind me, and began to make my way towards the crowd, almost running into a drunken man making his own way towards the bathroom as I did so.

"Sawree, Sweetheart," said the man, bumping into the wall and spilling his drink a little. "This the restroom?"

I looked at him, emotionless. "Yes."

"Thanks!" and the gentleman turned and slammed his way into our bathroom where I had thrown up one hour previously, and where orange vomit splatters still decorated the wall in a depressing fresco.

I went quickly up to my dad, and tapped him hard on the arm.

"Dad," I said loudly to be heard over the music. "*Dad!*" He turned and looked at me, his eyes red-rimmed and hazy.

"Hi, Honey!" he said, smiling and giving me a big hug. He smelled like beer.

"Dad, who are these people?" I asked.

My father looked around the room slowly with a dumb grin on his face, and then laughed. "I have no idea, Baby!"

I stared at him for a moment, and then asked slowly, "Are they from the bar?"

My dad nodded. "Yup! We shut it down. I invited 'em all over."

"Dad, I really want to sleep."

"Go ahead, Baby."

I bit my lip, and glanced around the room at all the strangers. A couple was sitting on our couch and kissing, the woman's legs wrapped around the man's body, and I looked away quickly, embarrassed. I turned back to my dad to ask him if they could keep it down, but he was already on the other side of the room, chatting to a busty woman with mischievous eyes. The man with dark hair and goatee that my dad had been talking to previously was looking at me, and he leaned into me suddenly, and asked,

"You're really, really sexy, do you know that?"

I backed away, and ran through the crowd up the stairs to my room, shutting the door heavily behind me. *I want to go home, I want to go home,* I thought desperately as tears spilled down my cheeks. But it was a pointless wish, and I knew it even then. For better or worse, I was already home.

Since my door didn't have a lock on it, I found different items to wedge in the crack to hold it fast in case someone tried to open it: I rolled three socks, hard and tight, and pressed them under the door, and also a large book, and hoped that they would work to keep out any intruders. Maybe I was paranoid, but I was fifteen, and I was alone, and scared. After a while, I lied on my bed, leaving the light on, and slipped a five pound hand weight that my mother had left behind under my pillow, so I could use it to attack someone if they broke through my barrier. After that, I felt relatively safe enough to close my eyes and try to sleep- but the noise was so great from the living room that in the end I grabbed a book from my book shelf, and read until my body, exhausted and weak, couldn't remain awake any longer- and I fell asleep to the sound of a bar in my living room and a lullaby of flies.

*

It was a Friday afternoon that Kelly called me out of the blue.

"Hey, Kim, what's up? So, I'm calling to tell you that Sam is crazy about you. Like, madly in love with you."

"…what?"

"He's fallen for you, you harlot! He wanted me to call you and ask if you want to go upriver with him."

"I don't like him like that."

"Well, this wouldn't be a date, really. Ian would be there and one of their other friends, I think."

I perked up. Ian would be there?

"If it's not a date I don't mind. When are they going?"

"Tomorrow like around noonish. I'll give him your phone number if that's okay. He can call and you guys can set up a time."

"Who, me and Ian?"

"No, idiot- Sam!"

"Oh… okay."

Kelly laughed. "Be nice to Sam. He's my friend and he's a nice guy."

"I think he's very nice, and very funny," I agreed. "I'll be nice. Thanks, bye."

"Bye!"

After hanging up the phone, I felt a little guilty. I had absolutely no interest in Sam in a romantic way. When I pictured his face in my mind, I felt nothing. When I pictured Ian, on the other hand, my heart skipped a beat, and I started to daydream about impossible things. I felt hampered by my insecurities; I wanted to walk directly up to Ian, tell him I thought he was gorgeous, and that I wanted to spend some time alone with him. But I was terrified of how he might react. Maybe he thought I was ugly, or fat, or just looked funny. Sam, according to Kelly, liked me, but maybe that was because Sam looked funny, too, and he felt I was low hanging fruit. I was besieged with those thoughts when the time came the next day to go to the river. Though the afternoon was warm and sunny, I wore jeans and a T-shirt; I didn't own shorts, or even a bathing suit, so neither of those was an option for me. Even if I had owned a suit, I doubt I could have found the courage to wear it. I did, however, spend time straightening my wavy hair which came down to my mid back, and I was pleased with the effect it made when the wind blew through it.

Sam and Ian came to pick me up in the silver car, and this time I was given the passenger's seat next to Sam. I frowned.

"Oh, no, it's okay, I can sit in the back," I said to Ian, as he began to climb out of the front seat.

"It's cool," Ian said, and buckled up in back. *Damn it,* I thought.

So I sat in the front with Sam, and he and I chatted, laughing periodically, as he was truly a very entertaining guy. He had the car windows wide open, and my long hair kept blowing across his face, and I apologized so many times that he finally said, "No, I like it. You have sexy hair, and you smell *awesome*." I flushed uncomfortably; it reminded me of what Preston had said to me the night I lost my virginity.

When we got to the river, there were two other guys there I had never seen before, but they were apparently good friends of Sam and Ian. Sam left the stereo playing in his Mazda, so that we could listen to NOFX while we 'partied', though I had a hard time associating the term with that we ended up doing. Everyone started talking about nonsensical things, laughing at unfunny jokes, and Ian brought out a cooler from the trunk and started to drink copious amounts of Mickey's which they had coerced a homeless man to purchase for them. One of the guys I didn't know lit up a bowl; I was offered it, but I refused. I found the whole thing a bit ridiculous.

After a bit, everyone decided it was time to get in the water, and stripping to their shorts, they jumped in with shouts and playful screams like little children. I watched Ian. He was so thin, and so pale, but I didn't care. To me, with his long limbs, and wide, hazel eyes, he was a moving piece of art.

Since I couldn't get into the water without stripping naked, Sam stayed with me. I insisted that I was fine by myself, but he refused to leave me alone as I was 'his guest'. He had taken off his shirt, and though he was also pale, and slender, he was covered with acne, and his limbs were shorter than Ian's and corded with muscle. After glancing at him once, I looked away. I couldn't help it; there was nothing about him that attracted me.

"I was going to ask you, do you have a boyfriend, or something?" Sam asked after a few moments.

I bit my lip, thinking of Ian and how much I wished I was talking to him instead of Sam. "No," I replied slowly, in a tone that did not encourage further questioning, "No boyfriend."

"Oh. Cool," he said, and then went on to talk about how he had broken up with a girl recently because she had cheated on him. Against my will I became sympathetic, and I told him that I was sorry that had happened. He seemed to feel encouraged by this, because he said, "We should hang out more often."

I remained silent. I didn't know enough about the relations between men and women to know if that meant 'hang out' as in 'date' or 'hang out' as in just 'hang out'. I knew nothing. I was inclined to think the former, but I wasn't sure. I liked Sam as a person, and I had no other friends that I could go and do things with. Plus, he was friends with Ian, so potentially if I spent time with Sam I would also be spending time with him.

"You don't have to, but everyone's coming to my house tonight," he continued. "I live in Smith River, on a farm, even though the only animals we have are an old horse with a bowed back and a dog. I don't know exactly what we're going to do… but I'm pretty sure it involves getting drunk and going cow tipping."

I lifted my eyebrows. "Cow tipping?"

He laughed. "Yeah. My neighbor owns a shit-ton of cows and they're always in the pasture next to my house. We always joke about doing it, because it's such a hick thing to do and we live way out in the boondocks, but I think we're actually going to do it tonight, just to say we did. Plus, you know, I want to see if they actually fall over if you push them hard enough."

"That doesn't sound very nice for the cow."

"Oh, it's asleep- it doesn't care."

I smiled. "There's no way you can possibly know that."

"I do know that! I've always felt a very strong cow connection."

I laughed. "Okay," I said, relenting, "I'd like to go."

"Great! You can spend the night, if you want. It's probably easier. I'll be doing the driving so you don't have to worry about that. I'll drive you home in the morning whenever you like."

I nodded, and as I did so I wondered what I was doing. Was I leading him on? I wasn't trying to. He was the only one who was talking to me, so I was talking back. Should I be rude? Should I say bluntly, 'I don't want to date you, by the way'? Why couldn't we just be friends? We could try, at least, and if he ever came right out and asked me on a date, I would refuse politely, and see if he would still consent to spend time with me. In the meantime, I would just fervently hope he would never ask me.

Night came on quickly; when it was time to go to Sam's house, Ian was already tipsy, if not drunk. He seemed to be in very good spirits, and laughed nonsensically at just about everything, but still paid absolutely no attention to me. Hurt, I decided to ignore him right back. The drive to the farm was quiet, and when we got there we had to wake Ian up. The night was warm and the stars were out, and Sam, Ian, and I, along with their two friends, stalked through the dark fields on our covert mission. Ian and one other boy couldn't stop giggling, and we kept having to shush them fiercely, for fear of being caught.

"Guys, shut up," hissed Sam, "I don't want the farmer to hear us. In case you town-dwellers don't know, farmers *shoot* trespassers."

That sobered everyone, and all became quiet again. We continued to make our way through a field until we reached a fence.

"This is it," said Sam, "Climb over. Who's coming?"

We all hesitated.

"Dammit, I'm not going by myself!" Sam said irately.

Ian suddenly staggered forward and started to climb the fence. "Then come on, ya pussy!" he said, his words slightly slurred. Sam hooted like an owl and followed him, and on some crazy impulse, I came behind them.

The three of us soon found ourselves standing in the pitch-black cow field. We could see the shadows of the sleeping beasts around us, and hear their deep breathing and soft moaning. My heart was pounding in my chest. I had never seen a cow up close before in the daylight, let alone in the dark.

"Come on," whispered Sam, "Let's pick a heifer. Remember to push hard, near the top, on three."

We walked forward for about twenty steps, but then Ian fell hard onto the ground, making a loud 'Oof!' as he hit the earth. We each held our breath, and in the silence we heard a cow low, then another, then another.

"They're awake!" shouted Sam. "Let's get out of here!"

Suddenly, all the cows were lowing, and their dark shadows seemed to surround us in an attempt to block our exit. The ground became alive with the sound of hooves. We were screaming with fright and stupidity and we ran forward, hoping that an opening might show itself. In the cacophony of animal noises, a louder, more irate sound made itself heard.

"FUCK!" yelled Sam, "I think the bull's in here!"

We ran, narrowly avoiding the giant shadows in the dark, and when we reached the fence, our friends were shouting our names, encouraging us, and they helped hoist us over to safety. All we could do for a few moments was lay there on the other side of the barrier, panting from exertion, and attempt to keep our hearts from bursting through our ribcages. The cows were still lowing, louder now, trying to alert their master that danger was near. Sam was the first stand up, his eyes wild and a large grin slapped across his plain face.

"Let's get the hell out of here before the farmer comes and fills us full o' lead," said Sam in a perfect John Wayne impersonation- though I don't think John Wayne ever said that- and he began to jog the distance back to his house.

*

Though Ian and his friends returned home the day after the cow-tipping incident, for some reason I remained at Sam's house for many days afterward, sleeping on his top bunk, and spending the long days outside on his farm, brushing his ancient horse and playing with his dog. Though the night with the cows had been frightening, I found myself attracted to the excitement that it had offered, and to the boy whose idea it had been. Despite my misgivings, Sam and I became good friends, and I discovered that we could talk about everything, as long as it wasn't serious- Sam had a definite inability to talk about anything 'real', which at that time in my life was fine with me. I discovered he was a bit of a rebel; he fancied himself a drum player, and had dropped out of school when he was my age because he believed school was stupid; but he did eventually earn his high school degree through home-schooling, and so he was much farther along than I was. He wasn't sure what he wanted to do with his life, but he was in no rush to find out. For the time being, he was content living with his parents on their little farm, helping his dad with odd construction jobs, and loafing around the house whenever he had a chance.

Though a part of me still wanted Ian to notice me, so that I could have someone to talk about my mother's death, I realized that Sam had something that Ian didn't- spirit. True, Sam and I had very little in common, but when I was with him I didn't binge and purge as much as I did when I was alone. I also didn't have to deal with my father ignoring me, because I wasn't around to be ignored. Sam's parents, hippy-like, loved that I was bunking with him in his room, and made no fuss about my moving in, though the whole thing had been very unofficial. Before I knew it, I had lived with Sam for a month, but nothing romantic had happened between us.

One night, however, after bailing hay for his horse, Sam sat next to me on his bed, shirtless and sweating, and asked if he could give me a back rub.

"You're probably sore," he said, putting his hands on the back of my neck and squeezing gently.

Guessing with what little female intuition I possessed that he was presenting me with a sexual overture, I hesitated, thinking of Ian and his long, pale limbs- and I turned to look at Sam. Where Ian was handsome and tragic, Sam was available and plain- but maybe he was what I needed. Why hold out for someone that could obviously do so much better than me? Though I wasn't attracted to Sam, he at least desired me- and after all, what else did I have the right to ask for? Preston and his false affections were fresh in my mind, and I still keenly felt the wound he had left behind him. Looking at Sam, with his simple face looking a question into mine, I knew I could only give him one answer.

By the time the sun rose the next morning, Sam and I were boyfriend and girlfriend.

We had a strange relationship from the very beginning; we were both young and sexually inexperienced, but we suddenly found ourselves living together like a married couple at the tender ages of sixteen and eighteen. We fought often over the smallest, most ridiculous things, and sometimes I would leave his house and try to return to my dad's, only to find it abandoned except for the flies I had left behind in my room. Eventually, unable to face the mess I had left behind, I would swallow my pride and go back to Sam, apologetic and desperate for affection, and he would always accept me with open arms.

Another thing that confused my inexperienced mind was Sam's relationship with pornography. I had had no encounters with it before meeting him, but now that I lived with him I was forced to accept it as a part of his daily process; he would sleep, wake up, eat, and masturbate to porn- repeat. I was always very uncomfortable around it- in fact, I couldn't look at it without gagging- but I felt there was nothing I could say; I didn't understand it, and that's all there was to it. Though I never instigated it, sometimes we would have sex because, 1.) He wanted it and 2.) I felt it was the rent I had to pay to be in a relationship. He often attempted to act out something that he had seen in his pornography, and like a doll, I let him do whatever he wanted. When I mentioned to him that I felt inferior to the women in his films, he attempted to make it clear to me that our sex life had nothing to do with his porn habit- those were just his 'other girls', and they meant nothing. I didn't believe him.

Because I was extremely self-conscious, I would obsess over the videos he watched, wondering why I didn't look the women who starred in them, with their large breasts and tiny waists. I believed I wasn't enough for him sexually, despite my giving in to his every desire; I felt like a failure. When I asked him one day, tentatively, if he would give his habit up for me if I tried harder in bed, he started yelling as if I had threatened his family; he even overturned a desk chair in his rage, and threw a cup of coffee across the room. Frightened, I curled up on his bed and sobbed miserably until he calmed down, and came to my side to comfort me.

"I'm sorry, Kim," he said softly, "It's just... I've told you what that stuff means to me. I'm not going to give it up. Okay? Stop asking about it."

I still didn't understand, and I turned to look at him with tears in my eyes.

"Can you at least wait until I'm out of the house when you do it, so I don't have to see it?" I asked.

He sat up, his face becoming stormy again. "You're never out of the house for very long. The coffee shop only gives you like ten hours a week."

"I'll get another job," I said. "I just turned sixteen, so there shouldn't be a problem finding one, like there was when I was fifteen."

He seemed to think about it, and then nodded slowly. "Okay. If you do that, I can do it when you're gone."

I reached out to grab his hand, and held it tightly. "Thank you," I whispered, honestly grateful.

He grinned down at me. "Don't cry, hot stuff," he said. "It's just porn. Don't let it ruin your day."

It only took me a week to find a second job at a pizza restaurant, and additionally, I requested more hours at the espresso stand, so that in total I was working over forty hours a week. After a while, Sam began to complain of my constant absence from the house, but all I could do was shrug regretfully; work distracted me, and that way, at least, I didn't bother him while he was spending time with his 'other girls'.

Backseat Ashes
(11)

I watched the sea gulls dance across the sky in a natural ballet, their only music the sound of the ocean's waves flowing back and forth upon the shore. They were so graceful that it was a shame that I was their only audience. I glanced around the rocky sand bar- yes, I was alone. It was miraculous that I was alone. How could it be, that a child of sixteen could set up a tent in a cave near the sea, and no would come to look for her, or send out a search party? Every time I went to work at the espresso stand, there were pictures on the wall of missing children, some of which were my age. Someone was looking for them, missed them, and wanted them to return. I envied them as much as I feared for them. I hoped they were okay.

I knew as far as homelessness went, to a certain extent, I had made a choice of it. After a large fight with Sam three months previous, I had run away from him just as I had run away from my father, taking all of my clothes and books with me. Since I had nowhere to go, I had spent almost all of my available funds for the month on camping gear, and set myself up there, in a sandy cave overlooking the beach.

But I could return to Sam at any moment, and I knew he would accept me; I could go back to my dad, if I didn't mind the steep price of both of our happiness, because I knew he didn't want me around the way I was as much as I didn't want to be around him the way he was. I could even potentially impose upon my sister, but I was not prepared to burden her with my problems. I had recently acquired a small red car which I used to get to and from work, and store most of my belongings. Sometimes I even slept in it if I felt like a change. I felt lucky, in a way, because I had work, I had a car0 I even had a cell-phone, which my father paid for no matter where I lived. The only part that made living alone difficult was the fact that, despite my belief that I was doing the right thing, I was sill sad that no one demanded my return or fought for me. Sometimes when I awoke at night shivering from the cold, I would wish that my dad would find me and say, 'Kim, all of this isn't your fault. I'm going to change; you can change; we can change together. It's you and me kid, for better or worse.' But I knew it was never going to happen.

As I watched the seagulls, the mist in the air began to thicken, and it grew colder. I gathered my sleeping bag around myself with a shudder. I glanced around my little cave; it was very small, and every inch of it encompassed my tent which was set up to capture body heat, keep my blankets dry, and protect my store of food. My collection of blankets had grown over the last few months; I had even started bringing all of my coats out from my car when I set it up, so I could make a sort of mattress out of them over the hard-packed sand. I could have brought more things to the cave to make it more home-like, but I liked the thought that I could clear out quickly in case a police officer came by and asked me to leave. As it was, with just a few things, I could pass as a kid camping out for the night, and if I needed to I could always sleep in my car until suspicion faded. But stuff like that never happened, not really. I had been out there in the cave for months now with no incident. Sometimes, pedestrians would walk by and ask what I was doing, and I would reply that my sister and I were camping out, but that she was at the store buying marshmallows for our fire later that night. I took it for granted that they always believed me; I suppose I was a good liar, even then.

My stomach began to growl, and so I crawled back into the tent and unzipped my large blue backpack which I had bought to keep my food safe from bugs and animals. Inside were nuts, a few water bottles, protein bars, and a couple of apples. I grabbed the bag of mixed nuts and went back to my post to watch the sea gulls. Most of them had landed and were attacking the seaweed closest to the shore. *Well, I guess it's time for everyone to eat*, I thought, stuffing a few almonds into my salivating mouth.

Warmth spread throughout my body as all my thoughts suspended themselves and a rush of endorphins and other chemicals filled my brain. I no longer lamented being alone; I didn't lament anything, because time ceased to exist. I wasn't aware of any disappointment, or the chill in the air- all I felt was the pleasure of the *crunch, crunch* of the nuts against my teeth, and the satisfaction of feeling them slide down my throat. My eyes kept watching the birds, my body was still on the beach, but my mind was soaring in a place that only exists for those who have experienced 'the high'. For, like a drug-addict, I was indeed high; and my world at that moment was slightly salty, nutty, with just the right amount of sweetness.

And then my hand hit the bottom of the bag. I swallowed my last mouthful of nuts. With a resounding crash, I came down to earth. *Shit.*

I sat in silence after that, watching the birds at their meal, but not really seeing them. I still felt hungry; at least, I thought maybe I was hungry, but also perhaps I wasn't. I wasn't good at reading my own hunger cues anymore. *I can eat an apple from my bag.* No, those were for my breakfasts before work. *I can have a bar.* No, those were for my lunch. **You can go to the grocery store and use the rest of your tip money to buy binge food**, suggested the oily voice in my mind. I shook my head: No! But... *maybe, I can go to the grocery store and buy some more nuts.* It seemed like such an enlightened idea that I immediately stood up, wiped some sand off my jeans, shouldered my backpack and headed up the beach towards the parking lot where my car was stored. I usually moved it every other day, but lately I had been lazy, and luckily it had never been booted or ticketed. When I got there, I shoved my belongings in the trunk, put my key in the ignition and took off towards town.

The road to town was covered in trees, so I made sure to drive at a safe pace to avoid elk, because an accident was the last thing I needed. Even as I took such precautions, I felt like I was functioning on automatic- I was driving into town to buy food with money I didn't really have. *Don't think, don't think, don't think.* Every time my brain tried to warn me it wasn't a good idea to go to the grocery store, I had to shake my head in rage and keep driving. What was my alternative? Sitting there on the beach, hungry and cold, bored, hopeless. All of this flashed through my skull in a moment, and I suddenly felt a great, groaning need to feel alive, even if it was just for a while.

When I pulled into the grocery store parking lot, I sat in my car, taking deep breaths. *I can still turn around and go back to the beach. I can take a nap.* Goodness knew I was tired enough. I didn't have to work at the pizza place until five o'clock that night, which was more than four hours away. I had already showered at the gym the day before, and I didn't smell that bad. I had nothing on my to-do list. Why not rest a little?

Against my will, my entire body began to shake. My eyes saw it before I felt it- my hands shivering like leaves in a light breeze on the steering wheel. In frustration, I clenched them tightly. *Stop it, stop it, stop it,* I willed them. *You're tougher than that.* After a moment, I slowly opened them, but they still shook. My eyes started to tear up. *Why am I not stronger than this? Where do other people get their strength from?* I remained seated, refusing to get out of the car, but not courageous enough to drive away.

I watched families come and go from the grocery store, some smiling and laughing, carts full of food to be eaten together around the dinner table. I especially took notice of the mothers and children, because to me, they were alien, and mystifying. One mother looked like she was scolding her very young daughter, but then she laughed as if it had all been a joke, and hugged her close to her chest. My heart ached at the sight.

Sitting there, I began to feel an urge to use the restroom. *Well*, I thought, *since I'm here, I should use the store's, instead of going in the sand where someone might see me. Plus, going inside doesn't mean that I have to buy anything.* I leaned over to the backseat, grabbed a well-used hair brush, and ran it through my long brown hair a few times, and then exited the car.

"Hi!" said the little girl who had been scolded by her mother, waving at me from her perch in the cart where she was kicking her tiny, sausage-like legs and waiting for her mom to finish loading their groceries.

I started, uncertain if I should reply or not. I didn't know anything about kids. "Oh, hello," I said timidly, while continuing towards the store.

The little girl giggled, and kept waving at me as I walked away. I glanced back a few times, and watched as her mother lifted her out of the seat and into the back of their luxury SUV. Had I ever been that little, and that open to smiling at strangers? It was depressing how the passing of time and the trials of life could change people.

Inside, I was assaulted by the tempting smells of the bakery. My head reeled with the aroma of sweets, but I made a bee-line for the restroom, refusing to look around. After I was done, I glanced at my reflection in the mirror, meaning it to be only perfunctory, but remained standing there staring at myself for a very long time. I looked like shit. My hair, though I had washed it the day before, was already showing signs of greasiness. My skin was utterly bloodless, and my eyes were red-rimmed and one had a broken vessel. My cheeks were puffy from misused salivary glands, and I was covered absolutely everywhere with sand; it was even caked into my nostrils. I peeled off the layers of my clothing one by one and shook them vigorously, creating a beachy mess on the restroom floor. I washed my face in the sink with hand soap, and pinched my cheeks, trying to get some color into them with no success. After I was done, I analyzed myself, hoping to see some improvement, but in my eyes I was still a monster. I leaned my forehead against the mirror.

"You are so ugly," I said to myself quietly, gazing into my own eyes. They stared back at me, dull and unresponsive.

By the time I left the restroom, my brain had shut itself off, as it usually did when I suffered an emotional overload. I went straight to the discount section of bakery aisle, knowing that I only had six dollars in my pocket. I gazed over the marked-down treats. A normally five dollar apple pie was on its last sell-by date, and it could now be bought for two dollars. I grabbed it and slid it under my arm. I also spotted a dozen questionable looking donuts, far from being fresh: three dollars and twenty cents. I grabbed it as well, and then headed to the register.

"Good afternoon," said the cheerful, elderly female cashier, "Did you find everything alright today?"

I couldn't look her in the eye. "Yes."

"Oh, good. Isn't it cold out there today? Brrr! That mist is awful!"

I watched her scan the items impatiently. "Mm-hm."

She glanced at the total. "Okay, dear, that's five-twenty."

I dug into my coat pocket and handed her a five dollar bill, horribly crumpled, and a quarter.

"Thanks so... oh!" she ejaculated, bewildered. She had uncrumpled the five dollar bill, and from its folds had spilled a seemingly impossible amount of sand which dispersed itself all over her scanner. The customer behind me in line stared at the mess blankly.

Without pausing, I grabbed my bag of pastries, and blurted, "No change, thanks." I ran for the door as quickly as I could, my pale face afire with embarrassment and shame.

*

"Kim, we need to get together soon."

"Hello? Helloooo? Call me."

"Kim? Are you there? Well, let me know when you're in town because I think we should…"

"Call me. We should really spread Mom's ashes."

I don't know exactly why it took me over two years to agree to scatter my mother's ashes, but it did. I'm sure for most dutiful children it is considered a filial obligation, the disposition of your loved one's remains. But not for me. Whatever had happened with my mother's physical body after she gorged herself with sleeping pills had never mattered to me. Maybe I was broken in my brain, somehow, and that's why I couldn't find it inside of me to care. And it's not that my sister didn't try to get a hold of me and *make* me care. She called me repeatedly on my cell-phone, trying to locate me, to get us together so that we could find a resting place for the fine dust that was once our mother. But she could hardly ever reach me, because by then I was just…well, gone.

And so it was a few years after her death that I finally drove to my sister's house. After a short visit with my infant nephew, Mason, whom I had only seen a handful of times, my sister said,

"What do you say we go spread mom's ashes? I think I found a good spot."

No, I don't want to. You do it. I don't care. That's what I wanted to say. But when I glanced at Rachel and saw she was looking at me with a pleading look in her bright blue eyes, I knew I was caught.

"Where are her ashes now?" I asked.

My sister hesitated. "In my car. Actually, they've been in the backseat since I picked them up."

I stared in disbelief for a second, and then laughed bitingly. That was so like our family that it was as humorous as it was depressing.

"So your son's been riding in the back seat with his dead grandma since you took him home from the hospital? What's it been, two years?"

Rachel sighed. "Well, I just keep thinking I'll see a place that she'd really like her ashes to be scattered. I just never saw the right place, and even if I thought I did, you weren't there, so..."

I nodded. I didn't want or need any further explanation. I knew I was never there; I was away with Sam, or in my cave, or off being sick, or working. It was me who had held up everything. Well, I was there now- for the next hour, at least- and I was eager to get it over with.

We drove five minutes north along the coast of southern Oregon, until we reached an area with a gorgeous view of a natural land bridge reaching into the sea. My mother had always admired the ocean and its beaches, even if she couldn't spend much time there due to an extreme wind sensitivity that left her prostrated with headaches. I was happy with Rachel's choice, until we learned that the land bridge was off limits to all foot traffic due to it being extremely slippery and prone to rockslides.

So there we were, standing by the side of a busy highway with our box of ashes, overlooking the land bridge and the ocean, considering what to do next. I don't recall who came up with the idea, but eventually, while looking out at the bridge, we decided that the view that beautiful enough, and that the wind was strong enough and could carry Mom's ashes out to the water.

With the sun setting over the land bridge, we readied ourselves. With the busy highway zooming behind us, we carefully opened the box of ashes. With the wind swirling around us, we waiting until it felt just right, so that it was blowing towards the ocean. And with a deep breath, and a whispered, "Here you go, Mom," we tossed what was left of our mother's body high into the air so it would catch the breeze and fly…but the wind suddenly died, and my mother's ashes fell heavily and hard, straight down into the ditch by the side of the road.

My sister and I had waited over two years to toss my mother's remains into a ditch. Well, surely, for my sister's sake, it was the thought that mattered.

Out With the Old
(12)

Tired, filthy, I entered my dad's house wanting nothing but to lie down and get some rest. My throat was burning from indigestion and my first thought was to go to the bathroom in hopes of finding some medicine under the sink- but the moment I opened the front door, I knew that wasn't going to happen. The house was ice cold, and empty- our furniture was gone, the television was missing- even the rug that used to be on the living room floor was absent. There were no cats, no dogs, and no sounds; just me and my bag of unwashed clothes. *How long have I been gone?* I wondered. I tried calculating the months I had been off with Sam, and then staying the tent, but I had lost count. I glanced around the empty walls and dusty corners, and tried to feel nothing, but failed.

"Hi, house," I whispered sadly.

I walked through the kitchen, which was mostly empty- there were a few blocks of cheese in the fridge and hot sauce- evidence of my dad's existence. The bedrooms were cleared out as well, except for a couple of empty mattresses up against the wall, and to my surprise the walls had all been re-painted- and in the room where I had been so sick, the carpet had been pulled up and new wood planks laid down to replace the rotting ones. Gone was the smell, the flies- everything looked neat and new; it had survived living with me and became habitable once again.

"I don't belong here," I said aloud, and thought of returning to my tent; but instead my feet carried me into my parent's room. Their bed was still there, where it had always been; the coverlet was tossed, the pillow skewed as if my dad had gotten up in a hurry, or slept badly. Most of his clothes still hung in the closet, and his sock drawer was wide open, full of socks, all neatly rolled. He had an ironing board out, and I recalled how my mother had done all of his ironing for him when they were married, and I wondered how he was getting on doing it all by himself. I stepped into his bathroom, and saw there were cigarette ashes in the sink and toilet. His toiletries were spread around haphazardly, caps open, and I spotted two bottles of Viagra amongst them. Fighting back emotions, I went into his shower and took out his bottle of Head & Shoulders, and shuffled to the bathroom that I had formerly used when I lived there. I undressed while I ran my bath water, waited until it to become scalding, and then stepped in, letting the sand that had been trapped against my body scatter unheeded all over the linoleum. Though the water burned, I reveled in its heat, and turned my thoughts inward. Evidently, my mind ran, my dad was alive and functioning; at least, he ironed his clothes, rolled his socks, smoked, and went to work. The house was doing better; I wondered if he had been forced to clean it all by himself or if he had hired someone else to do it.

After my bath, I put my clothes back on and went downstairs to put my dirty laundry into the washing machine. After starting it and double checking to ensure it was running well, I climbed, completely exhausted, into my parent's bed. Though I had taken such a hot bath and was wearing all of my clean clothes, I still felt as if my body were a hunk of ice. I covered my shivering, malnourished self with blankets, and fell asleep in seconds.

*

At some point the next morning, my father came home and nudged me awake, and asked how I was doing, as if I were a visitor. I told him I was fine; that I was staying with Sam (a lie) and working, still. Despite his casual speech, his attitude reminded me of a beaten dog; weary, heart-sore, but eager for signs of affection. In the state I was in, I could offer him none. He seemed to sense my distance and so didn't encourage much conversation, and whatever response I gave to his questions he replied with short nods and systematic responses.

"Now that I know you're not dead," he said, "and that the house is cleared up- I don't know if you've noticed- I've sold it, and we're moving," he said. "I have the place all ready to go; most of our stuff is already at the new place. It's smaller, but it's cheaper. We'll be moving in there soon. Until then I have your bed stuff still, just have to put it together."

I looked at him, my eyes cool, unemotional. "Are we poor?"

He shook his head. "We're not rich," he responded, "but we need a cheaper place, and selling this house is good for us. There are too many memories here for me- for us."

I shrugged. What did I care? It was just a cold, empty tomb filled with mice. Let them have it. My stomach rumbled.

"Dad," I said, "Can we get some groceries?"

He looked at me and smirked, and I quailed inside. "What's the point?" he asked sarcastically. I hung my head.

He stood up. "Let's go out to eat."

As we stepped outside, I saw that my dad had purchased a new vehicle; a Nissan 350Z. It looked as expensive as it was useless, but I said nothing as I climbed into the passenger seat. We ended up going to a small restaurant where all the cute waitresses knew his name; evidently he was a regular. We found a booth by the window, and while looking around, my dad said, "I bet people think I'm an old creep. An old dog like me, sitting with a pretty young girl. They probably think we're dating."

Over the tip of the menu, I stared at him in disbelief. It was probably his idea of lightening the mood, but for some reason his comment sent chills of disgust down my spine. *No, Dad*, I thought, *there is no way anyone would think we are dating. There is obviously no chemistry between us.*

My dad ordered a steak with cottage cheese; he had started the Atkins diet after my mom left, and had managed to lose a few pounds. He looked as if he had been working out, as well. *It's amazing what cutting carbs and popping Viagra can do for a person,* I thought coldly. Keeping my opinions to myself, I ordered a salad from the salad bar, and we ate without speaking again.

My dad drove by the place where we would be moving on the way back; it was one of those manufactured houses with rusted tin siding and no foundation, and located near a busy highway, and was within walking distance from my dad's favorite bar. It was surely more than a lot of families had, and I knew I should be grateful that I still had a place to go if I ever tired of the tent, or of Sam. But at the time I felt cheated, and angry. My mother had wanted a nice house for me to grow up in, to feel safe in, and had fought, in her own weak way, for that to become a reality. It was a tragedy that in the end she lacked the strength to face her demons, and that her ex husband had sold our family home in order to purchase a forty-thousand dollar sports car. But there was no point in reflecting on the past. Life and death had visited my family, and all I could do was survive as best as I could until it was my turn to become dust.

In With the New
(13)

    Before I knew it, a year and half had passed since I had stepped foot inside my high school. I had managed to keep my part-time jobs, once in a while taking on one or two small ones on the side, but unfortunately, I was not smart enough to save money- I spent all I earned, which wasn't much, on binge food… or on feeding and caring for Sam. He was still very much a part of my life, even when we weren't actively living together. He had fought with his dad, and had a hard time finding and keeping a job, and I sympathized with him by giving him money to live on while he applied for unemployment. I felt I owed him that for letting me live with him for all those months.

    My living conditions remained extremely erratic. For a few weeks at a time, I would return to live with Sam at his mother's farm in Smith River; then we would fight, and I would move back to my cave on the beach, telling Sam I was with my dad, and telling my dad that I was with Sam. Sometimes I slept in my car, and showered at a co-workers house, or at a local gym. For a few months, I even took a job at a seaside hotel, and broke into a room every night, only to clean it in the morning before I left as if I had never been there. I felt like I belonged nowhere, and I though I always gave my home address as the manufactured home that my father had rented, I tried my best to stay away from it as long as I could- until the day I decided to go back to school and get my high school degree.

I don't know what made me want to go back; perhaps it was because I could no longer hide from the fact that I had dropped out, or the feeling of failure that came along with it. Small towns are interesting because you can never avoid the people you want to; I was always surrounded by my old classmates. I served them coffee at the espresso stand, and pizza at the restaurant, and often I would be recognized and asked why I wasn't at school anymore. I never had a good answer for them.

I learned after inquiring at my high school that if I chose to go back I would graduate two years after I normally would have. This depressed me thoroughly. I had known I had fallen drastically behind, but the fact that time had marched on without even so much as a backwards glance really hurt. Frustrated but determined, I investigated my other options: I could go to the local community college and get my GED, or attend a new charter school that was close to my dad's new house. I could potentially catch up on what I had missed there, if I worked hard enough. To me, that seemed like the best option because I didn't want a GED, I wanted a diploma like a normal teenager. My dad and I discussed it, and after I enrolled in the charter school I started sleeping in his house again.

I entered the small alternative school feeling prepared for anything. There were always six or seven other students of varying ages in attendance in the school at a time. After sitting down at large table that served as our desks and listening to them for an hour or so, I discovered that everyone was enrolled in the charter school for very different reasons that I was; some were there because they had been arrested for drug-use; one female had become a prostitute at the age of fourteen in order to financially support herself and her mother. Two of my classmates were dropped off every morning in handcuffs by the police, and then picked up in the same manner at the end of the day. It was a side of life I had never seen before, and I tried to look at it unflinchingly, but it was hard- I couldn't help but take in everyone else's emotions as if they were my own. I had an antenna for sudden changes in mental states, and I didn't know how to turn it off, even though I wanted to.

As far as the school-work went, it was very DIY; everyone had their own workbooks to complete by the end of each week, or sooner. I found the books simple despite my missing the last year of school; I imagined it was because I read a lot in my free time, and was consequently a self-educated person. On breaks, I would go to the small art room and paint pictures while some of the other students watched.

"Where did you learn to draw?" someone asked one day, staring at my pencil work with awe.

"My sister used to make me sit me down at the table and draw with her for hours," I said. "She's very good, much better than me. She's actually trying to become a comic book artist."

"That's awesome," said the student, who was a small-boned boy with unwashed hair and a lisp.

"I guess so," I said dubiously.

"I wish I knew how to draw," mourned the boy.

"You can. Everyone can draw; it just takes practice."

"I don't think my mom would like it if I started drawing," said the boy. "All she does is sell dust all day, and she wants me to be there to help her. She hates that I even come here."

I lifted my eyes to his for a moment to see if he was serious, because it was such a weird sentence to hear come out of a little boy's mouth- but I quickly saw that he was. I kept drawing, but said, "You're mom doesn't own you, you know. You can do whatever you want. You don't have to sell anything if you don't want to."

"Yeah, I know. But we need the money," he said. "She's gotten busted by the cops so many times… she can't keep a job for shit. So she needs help."

"Well, I'm glad you're still in school," I said, unsure what to say.

"I might quit," he said. "My mom says this isn't even a real school, so it's a waste of time."

I remained silent. I felt angry at this boy's mother for treating her son that way. What kind of parent would do that to her kid? My heart ached for him, but I felt powerless to help.

"I can teach you how to draw a face if you want," I offered.

"I suck," he warned.

"It's okay, I still kind of suck. I'll just show you some basic stuff."

He thought about it for a minute, and then shrugged. "Okay, sure. Why not. Just don't make fun of me."

I smiled, and slid a sheet of paper in front of him.

A week passed, and the boy stopped showing up to school. I asked about him at the front desk, and learned that his mom had called and disenrolled him, using the excuse that they were moving soon. The school sent police to check up on him, but they found his house abandoned, their car gone. I felt sad for the kid, but there was nothing I could do about it.

*

"Why do you think the youth in Brookings turns to drugs and sex?" asked the little woman in front of the classroom, her eyes stopping briefly to rest of each of us. "I would honestly like to hear your opinions- that's why I'm here. I can't help if no one talks."

Everyone remained silent; some doodled in their notepads, one of two toyed with their fingernails, ignoring her. I felt embarrassed for the woman, as I could tell that she really did want to help. But the truth was, they themselves didn't know why they did those things. Teenagers were ruled by emotions, not logic. I ventured to raise my hand, and the woman brightened as she saw that someone wanted to speak.

"Yes?" she said eagerly, pointing at me.

"Um. I just wanted to say, that I don't think most people know why they do bad or illegal things, so that's a hard question for anyone to answer."

The woman nodded. "Yes, yes; I agree. I suppose I could have phrased my question differently. Hmm. Okay, how about this question; what can the adults of Brookings do to help turn the youth from potentially dangerous and self destructive paths?"

Once again, silence. I raised my hand.

"What have the adults done so far?" I asked curiously.

"Well, hmm. We could do more, that's for sure, and that's why I'm here. I've always believed, as a senior member of the chamber of commerce, that we can do more. Me and a couple of others fought pretty hard to have this charter school opened, and we had the skate-park built two years ago, since children loitering on skateboards became an issue with the elderly. But our town's drop-out rate is sky-rocketing, as is our teen pregnancy rate. I *know* we have more to offer- I just don't know what."

I sat for a moment, hand on my chin, contemplating. I was remembering the young boy whose mother had taken him out of school to help her sell drugs, when all he wanted to do was get out of the house, to be with friends, and learn to draw. I tried to think of what might have helped him- he certainly had had enough adults in life - the police, the school- but they had taken on the image of villains after a while, bad-guys trying to take him away from his helpless mother. The best way to get someone to make the right decision in something is to get them to think they made the decision on their own. How could the town convince kids to not do drugs without actually convincing them?

"What if…" I said slowly, "There was a program available that was run by teenagers, for teenagers. But it had nothing to do with 'staying clean', per se, but… had to do with enjoying life."

The little woman's eyes widened and she came a little closer, and asked, "What do you mean?"

"Like… I don't know- drugs and whatnot fill a void in life, don't they? What if there was something else to fill it? Something that THEY wanted, that adults weren't trying to shove down their throats? I know I'm a teenager, but even I know that teens can't stand it when adults think they know what it's like to be our age."

"Very interesting. What kind of stuff would this club-er, program, do?"

"I'm not sure. People could suggest things, maybe, in an open forum. Like, horseback riding, art classes, skateboarding classes. I don't know. But I think teens should mostly run it, with adults helping with the classes as needed. I'm just thinking out loud, though, there could be other things."

The woman came closer to me, pulled up a seat, and sat down. "I'm Mary. What's your name?"

"Kim," I said.

"Kim," she repeated, staring at me as if I was lunch. "You have some good ideas there, Kim. Would you be interested, in- hmm- maybe talking more on this subject with me?"

I shook my head. "I work a lot, and when I'm not working, I'm here-"

"But, Kim, don't you think your idea could really do some good?" Mary asked. "How about this: you write down your ideas, and I come by again next week and we talk about them together? Would that be okay?"

I hesitated, and then nodded. It couldn't hurt. Mary smiled brightly, and stood up.

"Great!" she said, "I will be back Wednesday… oh, no, sorry- Thursday! I so very much look forward to hearing more ideas from you, Kim!"

I smiled briefly, but then frowned. I didn't think my idea was very good, really. What did I know about keeping kids off of drugs? I had never touched the stuff. But…I knew what it was like to be addicted. And I knew that there was only one thing that could take the place of my addiction, and that was happiness.

*

    I shuffled my papers in my hands nervously, and looked out over the crowd of old people, and breathed a shuddering sigh. I had practiced my speech three times at home in front of Sam, and though I knew I was a terrible public speaker, I felt that this, at least, was something I should put my own voice to in support of.

    Mary had come by every week for the last three weeks, and we had gone over plans for the program I had brain-stormed, which we named Teens-to-Teens. We had written down a plan of action, and then discovered how much funding we would need to get it started, and so on, and now it was time to speak before the city council and see how the plan would be received. I sat next to Mary, and I glanced at her; she smiled at me. She was a nice lady, though a bit bird-brained. Her husband was helping us out on the project as well; his name was Mike, and he sat on the other side of Mary, and was shuffling papers of his own. Mike was a large, elderly gentleman with a booming voice; the kind of man who you could never see as feeble, no matter how old he became. He had a certain, indefinable power about him. I liked Mike. I was glad he was on our side.

My time to present came up, and I began to stand, but Mike turned to me quickly, and said, "I got it, sweetheart," and walked to the center of the room. After clearing his throat repeatedly, he began to talk about the dropout rate among teenagers, and how it was unfair to expect every child to fit into the mold that society had cast for them- I could hardly believe what I was hearing. The bastard was giving *my speech*.

I watched with narrowed eyes as he went through topic after topic, and I gloated inside when he forgot the details of a key topic- which I supplied to him with a smirk- and as he finished, I glanced around the room to see how the members of the council were taking it. Two were asleep. Some were looking at their phones. Others, though they were watching Mike speak, looked bored or restless. My heart was pounding with rage; if only they had let me speak!

After the meeting was over, I stood up as soon as I was able, and began to leave, but Mary caught me.

"I think it went well, don't you?" she asked.

My lips flattened into a thin line. "I thought I was going to give the proposal since it was my idea."

Mary looked flustered. "Oh, I did too- but when Mike stood up I figured maybe it was a good idea since he is a council member, and all."

I looked away. "I hope it works out, but I'm done with it," I said. "Thanks for working with me."

"Oh, but Kim!" said Mary, catching my arm as I began to walk away, "I didn't mean to offend you. We need movers and shakers like you; real determined teenagers who want to see a difference. You're important."

I turned to her coldly. "I didn't feel important. I was the only one in there under fifty, and I think out of everyone in that room I was the best person to talk about 'troubled teens'. I wanted to help, but no one wanted to hear me talk. So, yeah, I'm done." And with that, I turned and walked out of the building. This time, she didn't try to stop me.

*

Months passed, and I continued to go to the charter school, and steadfastly ignored Mary whenever I saw her. After a while, the behavior of the students in the school began to grate on me; they were hard for the grown-ups in charge to control; a few began to have sex in the bathroom, and other did drugs in the janitor's closet. At least twice a month, someone was violently hauled away in handcuffs never to be seen again. The environment became intolerable to me, mostly because I felt so hopeless about helping any of them, and I had trouble separating their emotions from mine. Frustrated and anxiety-riddled, I asked one day to speak to the director of the school.

"I have two jobs," I told him. "I don't do drugs or drink; I do my work. Is there any way I can just come in, get my books, and bring them in when I'm finished? I want my diploma, but I can't focus in here. It-it's too much for me."

The director considered it. "I suppose that's alright. This school is very new, and all the little rules about enrollment aren't well established yet. As long as you are constantly turning in work, I don't see a problem."

"Thank you," I said, "Is every two weeks okay? Two books at a time, turning them in, that's two weeks."

He shrugged. "If that's the time-frame you complete them in. If you get them done sooner, come in sooner. A little later, come in later."

And so I began to do my school work at home, and when I wasn't doing that I was working at the pizza restaurant or at the espresso stand. I continued to give Sam money to live, until one day, unable to pay his rent any further, I suggested he just move in with me and my father, which he quickly agreed to. I hardly consulted my dad on the matter; he had let me live with Sam for so long that I didn't think he cared about his underage daughter rooming with a man. I wasn't overly enthused to have him stay with me, but I was too soft-hearted to leave him penniless. Plus, that way, I figured I saved money, as he did not need to borrow money for rent, though he continued to sponge off me for food and gas.

About two and a half weeks after speaking to the director of the charter school, I walked down the road with my books in hand, ready to turn them in and pick up the next few weeks' worth of work. When I entered the front door, the plump lady at the front desk gawked at me when I greeted her, and as I handed her the books and told her I was finished, she turned positively green.

"Oh, God. Oh, no," she said, biting her lip.

I stared at her. "What's wrong?" I asked.

"I thought someone called you. I was so sure of it. I don't know how to say this, but- when you stopped showing up we had to drop you from the school."

I gaped at her. "But I had a deal with the director."

"He didn't say anything about that before he left; he quit at the beginning of last week, right before we had the meeting to see if we could renew our contact with the state to get more funding. He left us in a bit of a pickle! We couldn't have any loose ends, so we had to drop you. I'm so sorry."

I started to quiver with rage and sorrow. I picked up the books I had placed on her desk. "So, this- all this? All this work I did, it was for nothing?"

"I can take it for you, dear, but I can't give you any credit for it," she said apologetically.

"This is bullshit!" I yelled, tossing the books on the floor with a loud 'thud'. I hadn't exploded like that before in my life, and it felt good- *cathartic*. "You're supposed to help kids who are in trouble! *What the fuck*! You didn't even make sure someone called me! Thanks, thanks, just SO fucking much." I stormed out of the building and ran all the way home, angry tears standing in my eyes. When I got there, I opened the front door and walked in on Sam watching porn on his computer, his penis in his right hand. After a moment of shocked embarrassment, my anger rekindled itself.

"What the *actual fuck*? I'm gone for ten minutes and you whip your dick out? Were you just waiting there, holding your breath until I left so you can spend some time with 'your girls'? This is my dad's house! Go get a job, you fucking perverted moocher, because I'm not paying for your shit anymore!"

I ran into the bathroom, slamming the door behind me and locking myself in. Sam knocked at the door, trying to get me to come out, but I refused. He raised his voice, at first angry, then pleading. I sat on the toilet seat, hugging my legs to my chest, ignoring his entreaties.

I'm going to kick him out, I said to myself. *This asshole has always been all wrong for me. Why did I have to take him in? I'm too nice. I just need to be brave enough to be alone, to be by myself again.*

I felt a quiver of fear at the thought. Sam had always been there for me, even though he always took my money, and treated me like an object. He still cared for me in his own way- didn't he? Tears slid down my cheeks. I didn't know what to do. *Who do you run to if your confidant turns out to be a disappointment?* I wondered.

*

"Kim," my dad said through my bedroom door, "Come out for a minute, Baby, I want you to meet someone."

It was two days after I learned that I had been dropped from the charter school, and I had already divulged to my dad what had happened. He was inclined to think I was at fault, and I didn't argue with him; I probably was, somehow. I tended to be in the wrong most of the time. Sam, at the moment, was out looking for a job in order to conciliate me, and so it was just my dad and I in the house. Slipping on a robe, I opened my bedroom door and looked at my dad.

He looked sprightly, and tan, and slender. I hadn't seen him looking so fit and happy before. I smiled gently at him.

"Hi, Dad," I said.

"Hey, Baby. Come out here for a sec, I want you to meet Tammie."

Tammie was his new girlfriend, who I had seen from a distance once or twice before. I walked into our tiny living room, and on our couch sat a blonde, well-built Italian woman with a smile on her face.

"Hi, kiddo," she said in a husky voice. "Nice to meet ya, I've heard a lot about you."

"Hi," I said, instantly distrustful. In general, I had never liked my dad's girlfriends, besides Samantha, and this woman felt no different. However, this was only the second one I was meeting face-to-face in even a semi-official manner. I sensed something new in the air that I couldn't put my finger on.

"So, Baby," my dad said, addressing me as he sat down on the couch next to Tammie, "I'm been trying to get a hold of you for a while to tell you, but…Tammie and I are getting pretty serious. We're thinking about getting married."

The world spun a little, but I controlled myself and kept my feet firmly on the ground. "Okay," I said, unsure how to respond.

They looked at each other for a moment, and Tammie nodded to my father encouragingly. "We're going to move into Tammie's house as soon as possible- since it's a whole Hell of a lot nicer than this dump- but we have been working out what to do with you, and we think we got it figured out. We can set you and Sam up in a little apartment…"

I was floored. "Wait, you're getting married *now*? I mean, do I have an option to come with you? I just turned seventeen."

My dad looked uncomfortable. "Well, we figured this would be best. You've been living with Sam for so long, and well- he would be with you."

I stared at him in shock. I had just been about to kick Sam out of the house; as soon as he found a job and could provide for himself I had planned to never see him again. And now they wanted me to live with him, alone? Hated tears sprang to my eyes.

"Can't you wait?" I begged, "Just a bit, until I'm eighteen?"

They looked at each other again. "It's pretty much settled, Baby," my dad said apologetically. "I've already talked to the manager of your apartment building. If you both help pay rent, you can afford it just fine. I'll help a little, too, like I do with your car."

I sat down on the dilapidated couch, thinking hard. "Why do you guys want to get married so quickly?" I asked.

"It just feels right," answered my dad lamely, gazing lovingly at Tammie. She smiled in return.

I watched the two of them in silence. He did, indeed, look healthier and happier than I had ever seen him before. I liked to see him like that, but a large part of me was bitter, and jealous. All I had ever done was add to my father's misery, and Tammie had swooped in like an angel and magically made everything better.

"When do I move out?" I asked quietly, staring at the floor.

My dad smiled and moved over to where I sat, and hugged me.

"This will be for the best, Baby," he said, squeezing me tight. "And you'll love your apartment. It's even right by the grocery store. You'll see."

Don't Feed the Chickens
(14)

Sam and I moved in to our small apartment a week later, taking with us a meager amount of furniture, his coveted computer, and my large pile of books. Apparently, my dad had greased the palm of the owner of the apartment, telling him to keep a blind eye to the fact that I was underage, and also to keep an eye on me in case I ran into any trouble. Despite this, I never saw the owner except a few inches of him through the slot of his front door when I gave him the monthly rent.

Sam had found a job installing home satellite systems, and for the first few weeks he was triumphant in his victory over the working world. The job was something he was well-paid for, and he got to drive around his own truck and keep his own hours. But after a short while, the veneer of something new started to fade for him, and he began to hate his work in a very vocal manner.

"I'm too smart for this shit," he would often say, "I need a job where I can work with computers, like, at a desk, in an office. I'm going to quit as soon as I can find something better."

I begged him to try to see the bright side; he was getting a steady pay-check for the first time in a very long time, he held decent hours, he could even take a college course to finish his associate's degree if he wanted to eventually obtain the type of job he described. He quickly nixed that idea.

"School's not for me, you know that," he'd scoff.

Since my second attempt at getting my high school diploma had failed miserably, I signed up at the local community college to take my GED test, and I passed it without studying, almost as if it were an afterthought. When I eventually held the GED certificate in my hand, I didn't feel a rush of joy, or accomplishment- I felt trapped.

As far as my days went, I continued to work at the espresso stand and pizza restaurant, and despite my dual jobs I would often find myself alone for many hours before Sam got off of work. Sometimes, I would just fall asleep, miserable in my existence, but mostly I would use my time alone and binge and purge so that I forget my life for a while.

The apartment my father had found for us was one block away from the grocery store, which made it very convenient for me to walk to, and buy whatever sweet or salty treat I desired, then return home and ravenously consume it all in the privacy of my own four walls. I was ashamed of myself after every event; always. It was disgusting, exhausting, and a waste of money. *I should be saving money to get out of here,* I thought miserably. But what did it matter, when I had nowhere to go?

My romantic relationship with Sam was basically non-existent. We depended on each other for what company we could offer one another, and I gave him my body whenever he wanted it, but whatever connection we might have had once was gone. The exciting, cow-tipping rebel than had won me had faded into a long-haired, apathetic pervert. Perhaps I was partially to blame; he knew about my binging and purging, and distanced himself from me for lack of knowing what to do with me. He was tired of my nagging him, urging him to make something more of himself, to pursue an education. On my part, I could barely stand to look at him. I believed him to be a laggard, a sex addict, and most disappointingly, uncaring of my illness. I could understand many people in my life not caring about my bulimia, or failing to educate themselves about it; but in a love partner, I had begun to desire someone who would fight harder, care more. Sometimes I remembered Miles, my first boyfriend, and how he had stood up to his friends for me. Sure- he had been forced to give in- but he had still fought for me, and that meant something. I wasn't completely sure what I wanted in an adult relationship, exactly, but I knew that Sam was not it.

    And so we two lived together, each paying our part of the rent, my dad supplementing the rest, and waited, and hoped, for something to change.

    A few months after moving into the apartment, my dad called out of the blue and asked if I wanted to go to his wedding. I was surprised at this, but I was even more astounded when he told me it would be held in Hawaii.

"Wow, Dad," I said, amazed, "Where did the money come from?" I was forever asking him where he got his money from, since he has made it clear to me a year earlier, when I had been attending the charter school, that even if I got my high school degree, he was too poor to afford college for me.

"We pooled our funds together, don't worry about it," he said, "So, are you in? I can pay for you and Rachel to come. I want you both to be there. Come on, Baby. Please? It will be so much fun. And you will be able to meet your new step-sister, Jamie, and her husband, since they're coming, too."

Though I felt no sentiment at the prospect of seeing my father get married, the thought of escaping the small, backwoods town I lived in, escaping Sam, sent thrills of yearning down my spine.

"I would love to go, Dad," I said. "Thank you for inviting me. That's really nice."

"Sure, Baby, I wouldn't get married without you," he said. "We'll probably be leaving in just a week or so- sorry for the short notice. I'll be calling you in a day or so with the details, but you should start packing for warm weather. I figure we'll be there for about seven days."

"That sounds amazing! Okay- talk to you soon." I hung up, my heart pounding at the thought of travel.

Later that night, when I told Sam about the trip, he became enraged. How could I just up and leave him like that, as if he didn't matter? With his face flushed with unjust jealousy, he grabbed my hand, and said,

"If you're going, I'm going. I'm almost a member of the family, aren't I? We can probably afford a ticket for me, too, even if we have to be late on the rent."

I withdrew my hand in horror. "No! We can't be 'late on the rent'. What the hell? You're just not going, okay? I'm sorry, but you're not invited."

He turned a shade redder. "Only because your dad's a cheap bastard!" he growled.

It was my turn to flush in anger. "*Cheap*? He's buying me and my sister tickets to *Hawaii*! Plus, he pays for my car, my phone, and a part of our rent every single month, *not* to mention the fact that he fed and housed you for months under his own roof. How is *that* being a 'cheap bastard'? I can't even talk about this with you. You're not making any sense." Though everything I said was true, I wasn't sure why I was defending my father so passionately.

"*You're* the one not making any sense!" Sam raged. "Why would you want to go to this guy's wedding, anyway? He kicked you out! For years he acts like he doesn't care that you're killing yourself, for the most part acts like you don't exist, and all of a sudden he calls out of nowhere and is all, 'oh, that never happened, let's just celebrate my new life.' That doesn't sound like you, Kim."

I pursed my lips, clasping my hands together to steady their shaking. He was right, in a way; my dad had made a lot of mistakes after my mother left. But I had a hard time blaming him; after all, I hadn't made it easy. Who knew how to deal with a strong willed, bulimic daughter? In my heart, I was disappointed, hurt, and bitter; but logically I knew my father had been through his own hell, and had done the best he could with the tools he had at his disposal. I looked Sam in the eye and placed my tremulous hands in my lap to hide them.

"I can't say I'm not mad at him, because a part of me is," I said more calmly, "I mean, I lived with you on the farm, and then in a stupid tent for like a year and he didn't try to get me back. But right now, for this occasion, I feel like I need to go. If I don't go, what chance will we have to get along as a family? Plus, Rachel is going, and I want to spend time with her, both of us as adults, and that's something I haven't done before. Please understand. We can't afford a ticket for you to go and keep up with our bills. This isn't about you; this about me and my family. I will only be gone a week."

Sam looked at me for a moment, and then sighed, giving in. He came forward and hugged me.

"I'll miss you," he said. "Sorry I yelled."

I buried my head into his shoulder, and enjoyed the comfort that one human being feels when enveloped with another; such was the simple basis of our entire relationship. Together, at least, we didn't have to face the void alone.

*

The first thing I noticed about Hawaii wasn't the verdant green of the grass or the cool, clear water- though both of those were displayed in glorious abundance- what struck me first was the air, which was humid, and alive, and seemed to be seasoned with just a pinch of zest, as if some great chef had flavored it to let vacationers experience something unique, something one could only experience on those magical, mystic isles.

As I stepped off of the plane, I inhaled a deep breath of that tangy, energizing air, and smiled with delight as a woman in a grass skirt placed a lei around my neck, and said, 'Aloha.' I touched the lei gently, and admired it brilliant purples and pinks. The colors there looked nothing like the colors in Oregon; everything there was brighter; everything had spirit.

My sister Rachel got off the plane behind me and donned her own lei, and grinned as she glanced around with wide blue eyes.

"This is so amazing," she said, indicating the great expanse of greenery and beautifully cultivated flora around us. "It's so pretty I could cry."

"Dad chose a good place to get married," I agreed.

"They're meeting us at baggage claim," said Peal, checking her cell-phone. "Let's go, I can't wait to see where we're staying! Dad said it's near the beach, though I suppose on an island most everything is near the beach. What island are we on again? This is the smallest one- Kalui?"

"I think its Kauai. They filmed parts of Jurassic Park here."

"Oh, trust me; I remembered *that* part," said Rachel, smiling, "They also filmed Raider's of the Lost Ark here. I just didn't remember the name of the island. I keep wanting to say Maui, but I know that's not right." I smiled at my sister's nerdiness; the name of the island was way, way less important than what movies had been filmed on it.

We headed inside the small airport, and instantly spotted my dad, looking tan and brilliant in a Hawaiian print top and board shorts. He greeted us with a big bear hug, inquired about our flight, and then helped us pick up our luggage.

"Tammie's in the car," he said, "She can't wait to see you both."

Rachel and I glanced at each other, but continued to smile. We both had a theory that Tammie, perhaps, would have been happier if our father had been childless. Privately, I thought my father would have preferred it, too.

As we went out to the car, Tammie stepped out, her blonde hair shining, and offered both Rachel and I embraces and tender words of greeting, which we accepted nonchalantly.

"We're so glad you're here," she said, looking us both in the eyes, "You're going to love it here; it really is paradise. And the condo is so fabulous. Can't wait for you to see it. Jamie has her own, but it's right next to ours- oh, there's Jamie now."

A low red corvette pulled up next to my father's rented Sebring, and out stepped a petite brunette with a deep tan and giant sunglasses. She wore heels and a low-cut pink dress, and behind her was her husband, blonde and buff, who looked to be as much of an accessory to her as her Balenciaga bag.

Tammie turned to introduce her. "This is my daughter, Jamie and her husband Will; they live in Redding, California. Have you ever been there? No? You should visit sometime; it's a cute little city that sits under Mount Shasta. Anyway, we're so happy for you guys to finally meet."

Though Jamie was kindness itself, I couldn't help but notice that next to her, Rachel and I looked like giant walking thrift store advertisements. Everything she said and did was classy; her nails were perfectly manicured, her hair was faultlessly curled, and even her laugh, low and burbling, somehow sounded charming. Rachel and I both wore clothes that were at least three years old and somewhat stained; our hair, though we had tried our best, did not possess the Hollywood level of glamour that Jamie's had. I had never had my nails painted before or worn heels; both Rachel and I were shod in well-used flip-flops. I felt a little embarrassed at my own inadequacy, and moved away a little to hide myself.

Jamie offered to drive Rachel in her car back to the condo, and, after waiting a moment for my invite which was not forthcoming, I climbed into the backseat of my dad's car. The drive to the condo was brilliant; it seemed, somehow, that we had traveled through time. The leaves on the plants were larger than any I had imagined, despite my having grown up among the Redwood trees; the mud was a dark, earthy red, and the road we drove on was low and winding and mostly unpaved. The sounds of odd-looking birds and other strange animals filled the air; my dad pushed a button and the top of the car folded down, and my hair blew freely in the wind. I felt like an adventurer.

The condominium was lovelier than I had expected; it looked like a large indigenous hut that had been modernized on the inside. It had three bedrooms and three bathrooms, with the master bedroom having its own veranda looking out to the ocean. Everything had recently been renovated, and it showed- from the gleaming marble countertops to the plush, cream carpet and opulent furniture; I had never set foot in such an elegant place before.

Upon discovering that my sister and I would share a room, I felt a shadow of unease pass over me; it would be the first time she and I had shared a room since we were little, and with her intense sensitivity to sounds, that had not gone well. When we entered our room, which was just as lavish as the rest of the house, I placed my luggage on one of the full-sized beds, and turned to my sister, who was already unpacking.

"Rachel, are you going to be okay sleeping in here with me?" I asked nervously. "I don't snore, or anything, but I don't want to bother you with my breathing…"

"I should be fine," Rachel said, "I brought ear-plugs! Lots, and lots of earplugs." She turned and grinned at me, holding aloft a brand new package of green earplugs. "If I have trouble, though, I'll let you know." Suddenly, she sighed. "I miss Mason," she said.

I started. I had almost forgotten, in the turmoil of my life, that Rachel had a son, and I, a nephew. With a surge of guilt I said, "It must be hard, being away from him like this for the first time."

She nodded. "It is! I almost didn't come because I couldn't imagine leaving him for a week. He's my little angel. I know he has his dad, but still…" She shrugged. "It's not the same."

"Is Max good with him?" I asked.

"He's alright," Rachel evaded, then, changing the subject: "Hey, let's go out and look at the porch."

I followed her out onto the veranda, and together, we stared out at the glory that was the Pacific Ocean at sunset. I glanced over at my sister, and watched her as she changed colors with the sky, first pink, then orange, then purple. I thought she looked beautiful; tired, and older than when I had seen her last, but beautiful. I wondered how life was treating her at home. I knew almost nothing about her anymore.

"Are you and Max going to get married?" I asked.

"No… probably not," Rachel replied slowly, "He's asked me a few times, but I've said no. I don't want to marry him just because we have a baby together. But it's a long story. We're fine where we are right now."

"Okay," I said, sensing a sensitive topic and choosing to drop the matter.

There was a knock on the bedroom door behind us, and our dad entered, wearing a goofy, lop-sided grin that told of many alcoholic beverages already consumed.

"You girls wanna go to a luau?" he asked, hanging on to the door-knob for balance. Looking into his luminous eyes, brimming with excitement and life, my sister and I could only smile and nod in assent.

*

That night, I saw many things I never thought I would see: I saw my dad wear a coconut bra, and get up on stage and attempt the dance the hula; I saw a half-naked Hawaiian native breath fire into the air like a dragon; I saw my sister laugh and hug my dad as I had never seen her do before. But mostly, I saw myself sitting on the outside of it all, too timid to join in the laughing, the festivities, and the overall good humor. Whenever I thought I might say something, my throat closed up, and I ended up holding my breath instead, and sat in silence as the conversation continued to flow around me as if I were a stone in a river. What could I say that would interest these witty, happy people? Despite the party atmosphere, I couldn't escape from the reality of my situation- I was a drain on my family. I was a failure. I was the malfunctioning cog, and they included me here because it was their duty to do so. At least, that was how I felt.

After everyone had indulged their stomachs with roasted pig and copious amounts of fresh fruit, (I nibbled on pineapple), Jamie and my sister began to discuss going to a dance club. My ear pricked up at this. Were they leaving me?

"Can I come?" I asked, though I didn't want to dance, I didn't want to be alone, either. I had come there to spend time with my family, after all.

Jamie frowned. "Sorry, Kim, you have to be twenty-one and over for this club. You coming, mom?" she asked, turning to Tammie.

"Definitely!" she replied, grabbing on to my dad's arm.

I bit my lip. They were all going.

"What about me?" I asked in a hushed voice.

"We'll drop you off first, kiddo," said Tammie, not looking at me. "Plus I want to freshen up, anyway." She drained her pina colada, and then turned to Jamie and Will. "We'll meet you guys there if you want to head out."

As everyone climbed into their respective cars, I found myself packed away in the backseat, looking at the stars. Why the hell was I sad? It was just one night alone. I should be able to handle it. But... I didn't feel like I could. I wanted to be with everyone; I wanted to feel included. I ran my hands through my hair, frustrated with myself; why couldn't I connect?

When we reached the condo, I took a shower and went to bed, afraid that if I stayed awake I would end up binging on the food in the kitchen and throwing it up. Goodness knows, I wanted to; the pineapple I had eaten felt like a sack of rocks in the pit of my stomach, and I began to take deep breaths, trying to calm myself so that I could fall asleep. I rolled to my side, staring out the sliding glass door to the terrace, and thought,

Tomorrow I will try harder to fit in. I'll try to be someone that they actually want to be around. I curled my legs up to my chest, and sighed. *I wonder how the hell I'll pull that off, when I don't even want to be around myself.*

*

"What the heck is this?" came Tammie's voice from the condo kitchen, loud and irate. "Who did this?"

It was the morning after the luau, and I had awoken only a few minutes earlier to use the restroom. Coming out with a feeling of trepidation, I went to see what the problem was, and saw Tammie staring in disgusted disbelief at a bag of macadamia nuts with the corner ripped open. I waited, still uncomprehending.

"These things are expensive!" she stormed, "It wasn't open correctly; it's rude! Its bad manners, that's what it is. They lose their freshness this way. It's not one person's personal bag of nuts." She turned to me. "Did you do this?"

I shook my head. "N-no…" I said.

Rachel came in then, makeup smeared across her face from a hard sleep. "I did it, sorry about that," she said with a small smile.

"You know it's not *your* bag, right?" asked Tammie angrily, grabbing the bag and rolling it up. "Look, it doesn't roll up properly because you opened it wrong. And you left it open so that they'll lose their freshness. It's rude."

Rachel's eyes opened a little wider, but she maintained her poise. "I said I'm sorry," she said, glancing at our dad, who had watched the whole interchange with an impassive face.

Tammie sighed in frustration, and lifted the bag of macadamias. "I'll have to find another bag for them now," she muttered, moving into the kitchen.

Rachel and I looked at each other briefly, and then went back into our bedroom, nonplussed.

"What the hell was that?" asked Rachel, getting a little pissed. "It's just a bag of nuts."

I lay down on my bed, and stared at the ceiling. "She's just a really high-strung person," I said in a quiet voice, "I don't think she likes us very much, either."

"Well, whatever," said Rachel, who began to dig in her suitcase for the day's clothes.

I watched her for a moment, and then asked, "Did you have fun last night?"

Rachel shrugged. "It was alright. Jamie and Will have a lot more experience dancing than I do so I felt a little weird. And Tammie and Dad were wasted."

"I wish I could have gone," I said meaningfully.

"You didn't really miss anything," said my sister as she grabbed her clothes and walked to the bathroom.

Still reclined on my bed, I wondered if that was true, and if Tammie was only mad about the macadamia nuts because of something that had happened last night. Maybe she just had a hangover? I smirked. No, that was ridiculous; I didn't need to give her an excuse. I could admit it to myself, at least: Tammie was just a bitch.

*

Despite my feelings towards Tammie, I felt grateful that she had adopted my dad and for some reason, decided to marry him, as well. The day after they were married in a small, sweet ceremony on the beach, we all went out to eat at a restaurant which boasted a large buffet and a giant, cascading waterfall right in the center of the room. Steadfastly ignoring the pastries, I placed a few slices of honeydew melon on my plate, and found a spot next to my sister at the long, white-clothed table that had been reserved for us. Tammie frowned when she saw my plate.

"That's it? You should eat more, kiddo. We pay for each plate- it's a *buffet*," she said, as if I didn't know.

I stared at her uneasily. I wasn't sure how to respond.

"Oh, look at that funny sign!" Jamie said suddenly, pointing with a manicured nail out the window. We all turned our heads to look at a small wooden sign that had been tacked into a flower garden that read 'Please, do not feed the chickens.'

I grinned. There were a ton of feral chickens on Kauai, which had been brought over by the Polynesians thousand of years ago, which I thought was hilarious. They were treated as rats on the island and though they preyed on the poisonous centipede native to the island, they were still looked upon as a menace. I took out my disposable camera and took a picture of the sign so that I could show Sam when I got home.

"That *is* funny," agreed Tammie, taking a bite of sausage and chewing, "Kim, are you a chicken? If you are we could have saved ourselves twenty bucks."

I raised my eyes to hers, and she stared right back, eventually forcing a sweet, innocent little smile as if she had been only playing. But I knew she hadn't been.

"Where do you live, Kim?" asked Jamie suddenly, taking a large bite of her omelet.

I looked up at her, surprised she was talking to me. "Oh, I live in an apartment with my boyfriend. But I'm looking for a different place, kind of. I don't really want to live with him anymore."

"Aw, that sucks," said Jamie, "I hope you find a place."

"Thanks," I said, smiling at her. I glanced over at Tammie and my dad, but they didn't seem to be paying attention to anything but their plates.

Later on, as the sun was setting, I sat outside on the veranda to watch the sky change colors, and say my goodbyes to a paradise I never thought I'd see again. It was my last night in Hawaii, and though my family and I were no closer than we had been when we first arrived, I was still glad that I had been invited. I heard a noise behind me, and I turned to see my dad walking up to me. I smiled at him; he smiled back, and took a seat next to me on the ground.

"Kim, you know that Jamie and Will are separated, right?"

I shook my head. "I knew they were having trouble and that this trip was supposed to be a last ditch effort to save their marriage, or something… but no, I didn't know they were actually separated."

"Well, they are. And- keep this between us- Jamie doesn't want him back. It's over, she just has to get up the bravery to let him know. But anyway... what would you say to moving in with Jamie, down in California?"

My jaw dropped. "What? Did she offer that?"

My dad nodded. "She did. She would like to have someone help with the rent, and she just bought a Doberman puppy, so she needs someone to help watch her during the day. I told her I'd tell you about it, and then you can think a bit and let me know when you make a decision. I know it won't be easy for you to leave Sam."

I almost broke down in tears right then. "It'll be easier than you think," I said, "I want to go. Of course I want to go."

My dad smiled again, and put his arm around my shoulders and gave me a little squeeze. "I think this will be good for you, Baby," he said. "I never thought Sam was good for you- he seems to be controlling, and to want to keep you all to himself."

Then why did you send me off with him without a word? I wondered, but then I shook the thought away. The past was the past. I could escape him now. Or at least, I could have a few hundred miles head start.

California is Burning
(15)

"Jamie," I said, "I'm so thankful to be here. Thank you for letting me stay with you."

Jamie smiled, and made a vague gesture in the air. "Don't worry about it!" she said, "Since the divorce, the house is too empty for me and Chanel. Plus I need someone to help me watch this little trouble-maker."

We turned our attention to the half-grown Doberman puppy lying on the floor, who rolled over onto her back as if to say, 'Who, me? A trouble-maker? You must be joking!'

Jamie sighed dramatically. "She has torn up throw pillows, blankets, the other side of that couch cushion there…" she indicated where I was sitting. "I flipped it over for now, but if she gets this side I don't know what to do. I adopted her because she's adorable and so that I won't be lonely, but she's pissing me off more than anything right now."

I got down on my knees and started to rub Chanel's tummy, and she responded with happy air kicks. "Aww, I'll help watch her for sure. I love dogs. I always had them growing up," I said.

"Good. You watch her. She's a pain my ass. I'm having a friend make her a dog-run outside so she's not stuck in here all the time while I'm at work, ruining my furniture, but he's taking his sweet time."

"Why can't you put her in the back yard?"

"I don't want dog crap everywhere in my back yard! Plus, she'd probably chew a whole in my fence and escape."

"Oh."

We sat in silence for a minute.

"Well, if there's ever something you need to know, ask," said Jamie. "I don't know if there's anything else I need to tell you. I get hair supplies at crazy good prices so feel free to use them whenever. I don't mind sharing food once and a while, as long as you buy stuff too, once in a while. I have tons of alcohol in the freezer. I have friends over sometimes, and well… we smoke weed, but you're okay with that, right?"

"Yeah, I mean, I have never smoked personally, but it's none of my business." "Alright, nice. Well, I've got to go to work, I'll be home in the evening sometime. My hours are weird- hair dressers life, I guess. Make yourself at home!" She bent down to give Chanel a couple of pets.

"See you later, you big baby!" she said, and left the house.

When the door closed behind her, I felt a pang of anxiety. I wanted her to stay so badly, but I knew I had no right to ask. I had made a big choice, moving here, into a strangers house; I had taken a gamble that she and I would get along, and I wanted to bond with her. But something inside of me kept whispering, in a dark, slithering voice, ***Why would she want to be friends with you? You sick, grotesque, uninteresting person. She's successful, she's beautiful. What do you have to offer her?***

I walked to window and watched as she got into her yellow Lexus, slip on a pair of giant pink sunglasses, and pull out of her driveway while blasting hip-hop music. She was certainly very different from me, that much could not be disputed; but what did that matter? Rachel and I were very similar, and we did not get along, so maybe sisters needed to be different in order to be close. But I knew nothing about Jamie, either, besides the fact that was cooler than me. She had friends; she was a successful hair-dresser, went dancing, smoked weed- she *did* things. What did I do*?*

I decided to roam the house to get a better picture of the girl who would be my sister; I had spent so little time with her in Hawaii. I went into the bathroom I would be using, and explored the cabinets. She had tons of hair care products, which I spent half an hour reading the backs of. I was fascinated that there were so many different ways to wash and moisturize your hair; I hadn't realized fully until that moment what a true novice I was at being 'feminine'. Curling? Volumizing? Clarifying? What kind did I need? Unsure, I picked two out at random and placed them by the bathtub for later use, then went into Jamie's workout room which doubled as her wardrobe.

Opening her closet, my jaw dropped; inside were countless beautiful, expensive items of clothing, hanging elegantly and sorted by hue. I had never seen anything like it outside of a store. I genuinely had had no idea that there were people in existence that were so organized, so tasteful. I thought back to my and Rachel's old bedrooms, with our clothes all over the floor, never knowing what was clean and what was dirty, and I grimaced. *Why are we like that, when other people are like this?* It wasn't fair. I made my way into her private bathroom, and glanced into her makeup box, and confirmed what I suspected I would see: rows upon rows of organized, clean makeup containers. I reflected on my own makeup experiences; broken bottles, smeared eye shadow, missing brushes. I was a mess. No one had ever taught me how to put on makeup or take care of the different cosmetics, so when I started wearing them I just did the best I could. Looking at Jamie's treasure trove, though, I knew I had failed, and failed miserably. *This* was what being a girl was supposed to look like. I clenched my fists with emotion. *I want to be just like Jamie.* I closed her makeup box and went back to her closet and took down a pink shirt with a very low, risqué neckline. I had never worn anything even close to it before.

Going into her bathroom, I put it on and looked at myself in the mirror. It seemed to fit, but my sports bra came out of the top and ruined the effect of the shirt. When I turned to the side, I gasped in horror. *My stomach is so huge and puffy!* I thought. Upset, I tore it off, and hung it back up in her closet, probably not as nicely as it had been before. I had next to no practice hanging things up.

I told you, Little Girl; you're ugly, said the dark voice inside of me, chuckling dryly. *Nice try, though.*

I had shamelessly walked through most of the house, but for some reason when it came to entering her bedroom I became shy; I didn't want to. I was curious about what a normal adult female's room looked like, but I felt that perhaps there were especially private items in there that she wouldn't want me to see, and so while I glanced in, I did not enter.

I went back into the living room and sat down on the couch, contemplating what to do next. Chanel jumped up on the couch and put her head on my lap and I scratched behind her ears her absently. I needed a job, I knew; it would do me good to get out of the house, plus my mother's death benefits wouldn't last much longer, especially at the rate I had used them for binge food the previous few years. Jamie had told me, upon my moving down there, that she had a friend who was a manager at a local restaurant, and that she could put in a word for me. Though grateful, I was not keen on working in a restaurant again because of my eating disorder. My time at the pizza place in Brookings had only given me a healthy fear of all the free food that came along with working in such an establishment. The temptation would be too great for me, and I worried about making a bad start in California. But in reality, what other choices did I have? I was eighteen and had no high school diploma; no one was going to hand me a desk job.

I didn't want to start out my new living arrangement on uneven terms, so I decided to go out and hunt for jobs on my own. Looking down at myself, however, I knew I would not get a job looking the way I did; I needed new clothes, and possibly a hair cut. Though I was low on money, I decided a good use for some of my remaining funds would be to go to the mall and buy more professional clothes. I sighed. I didn't want to go out in public, but I didn't have a choice. Moving to California had been a step in a new direction for me, and I needed to keep moving forward. I could no longer afford to avoid people like I used to.

Suddenly, Jamie's house phone rang, and I started. I got up, unsure if I should answer it or not, but after a few more rings I decided that I could at least take a message.

"Hello?" I asked.

"Kim?" asked Jamie's voice. "Good, you answered. You can answer the phone, you know! Anyway, I wanted to let you know that I'm coming home real quick to grab something I forgot, so can you unlock the door?"

"Oh, sure!"

"Thanks!"

We hung up, and a few minutes later Jamie pulled into the driveway, and ran inside. She went into the kitchen first to grab a drink of water, and asked, "How you doing?"

"Good. I think I might go to mall and get some new clothes to wear while I go on interviews and stuff."

"Awesome. I'd go with you if I could. Hey! I have a friend who needs to go to the mall. Want to go with her?"

I paused. "Who is she?"

"Anne. She's a school teacher, she's my bestie. She's needs to pick up some sun-glasses she ordered- she's been putting it off for *weeks*, but she has the day off today. I'll give her a call and have her come pick you up, or meet you there."

"We can meet there," I said quickly, "I don't want to bother her by taking a long time looking at clothes. I'm sure what my sizes are or anything."

Jamie looked at me oddly. "Uh-huh, okay, let me call her while I go grab that crap I forgot." And she went off to her bedroom, to emerge a few minutes later with a large box.

"Shampoo. My whole life is shampoo," she said, smiling. "Anne said she'll meet you there in an hour. Food court?"

"Yeah, that sounds great. Thank you for asking her to go with me, it will be nice going with someone."

"Oh sure, Anne's the best. Here, do you have your cell-phone? I'll give you her number."

"Yeah."

A moment later, she was turning to leave when a question popped into my mind.

"Jamie, what's clarifying shampoo?"

She giggled. "You're cute. Alright, babe, see you later."

And she was gone.

Half an hour later I was walking in the food court of the mall, and my cell-phone rang. I jumped at the sound, because it so seldom rang that I was unaccustomed to it. Looking at the caller ID, I saw that it was from Anne, and I quickly answered it.

"Hello?'

"Kim? Hi, this is Anne. Where are you?"

"I'm in front of the... the, um, pretzel place."

"Okay, I'll be there in a minute."

I was nervous; I felt like I was being set up on a blind date. I didn't know much about Jamie, but I knew nothing about Anne, and here we were at the mall together. What if she didn't like me?

"Kim?" asked a voice, and turning, I saw that it belonged to a short, stocky blonde with bright blue eyes. She was wearing a tank top and jeans, but what struck me about her the most was the fact that she had an extremely deep tan.

"Yes, hi!" I said.

"Jamie told me about you. Oh, look at you, you're so cute!" she said brashly, smiling with perfect teeth. I blushed.

"C'mon honey, I have to pick up some glasses I ordered, but after that we can do *whatever* you want to do. What *do* you want to do?"

"I'd like to buy a few clothes to go to work in when I get a new job. All I really have are two or three pairs of jeans that don't fit well, and a few old tops. It just doesn't seem very professional."

"Okay, well how about we pick up my sunglasses and then we take a look around? There are *so many* cute stores here, you'll *definitely* find something."

"Oh, good! It's been a long time since I went shopping in a big mall like this. I'm glad to have someone with me."

We walked through the mall, which, due to it being the middle of a workday, wasn't very crowded. Anne pointed out a few stores that she liked to shop at, most of which I had never heard of before. Buckle. Forever21. I nodded, trying to retain them in my memory. When we reach the Sunglass Hut, Anne waltzed straight up to the counter to inquire about her order, which the helpful clerk presented to her immediately. She looked the glasses over, tried them on, and turned to me, asking, "How do I look?"

"You look great," I said, inwardly feeling that I was the worst possible person to ask that question to.

She turned to the clerk. "Okay, what's the damage?"

"Two-hundred and forty dollars and sixty-eight cents," replied the man, and Anne nodded and took out a payment card from her stylish purse.

Ohmygod! My mind reeled, T*wo-hundred and fifty buck for sunglasses? That's crazy*! Then the voice in my head interrupted, laughing drily. **You think you have a right to think that, you who have spent thousands of dollars on food that you eat only to throw up**, it said. **Who's the crazy one?**

When she was done, I asked her where she suggested I should shop first.

"Oooh, Buckle!" she said, "They have *such* cute tops and shoes."

Once inside the store, I did not find myself overly impressed with the selection as it seemed that much of their line was directed to very thin, or very young persons. I did, however, decide that I wanted to buy a pair of jeans.

"I'll help! I love jeans shopping. Hmm…what size do you wear?" asked Anne.

"Um. I'm not sure. I guess I'll grab some and try them on."

Anne shook her head emphatically. "No, no, that's ridiculous. Let's ask this lady. Miss? Excuse me, Miss?"

A small, dark woman who was folding clothes twisted around to gaze at us with heavy-lidded, disinterested eyes. "Yes?"

"What size of your brand of jeans would you recommend for her?" Anne asked, indicating me. Red faced, I suddenly realized how Julia Robert's character must have felt in Pretty Woman.

The woman eyed me up and down, sizing me up with professional coolness. "A 27 would probably do, but could probably go up one size, or down one. Are you having trouble with our sizes? Are they different than what you're used to?"

"Oh, no, she just didn't know what size to try on. Thanks."

Pulling down four pairs of pants off the shelf, Anne handed them to me, and then said, "You *have* to try on a few new tops with them," and handed me two shirts with low cut necklines, similar to what Jamie owned. "I'll come in too! I have to try on this top, it's so ridiculously *cute!*"

I had never gotten undressed in front of another girl before, but I was too shy and too grateful to her to argue. We went into the large changing stall, and tried on our shirts. I tried not to look, but it was difficult; Anne had extremely large breasts, and she almost spilled out of the top she had picked out.

"*Oh my God*, I love this!" she gushed. She glimpsed at me. "Yours is cute, too, but it will look better when you change your bra," she giggled. I was still wearing my tattered green sports bra, and it was peaking out of the top of the shirt.

"I don't have anything but sports bras."

Anne looked at me in surprise. "What do you mean? Don't you have bras with cups?"

"No."

"Why not?"

I looked at her self-consciously. "I don't know, I just never got around to it. My dad bought me my first bra, which was a sports bra, and I've been buying the same kind ever since."

Anne regarded me in disbelief, and then said, "Well, *that's* going to change! You can't wear your new shirts with a sports bra. After this we're going to Victoria's Secret, and you're buying a real bra!"

"Aren't they really expensive?"

"No! Well, sometimes- but they're not *too* bad. But c'mon, you need a real bra! We'll get you one that you can wear with a lot of different types of clothes. It's worth the investment. Trust me."

"Okay," I said, smiling at her enthusiasm. With our new goal in mind, I quickly tried on the pairs of jeans, and ended up leaving Buckle with two pairs of pants and two shirts. From there, Anne and I made a bee-line to Victoria's Secret, which I entered with a slight feeling of trepidation. I stood for a moment in the middle of the store, overwhelmed by the sheer amount of lingerie. I found myself staring at one of the mannequins who was outfitted in a teddy and a thong that looked like someone could floss their teeth with it. *How do people wear those?*

"May I help you ladies?" asked a tall woman, who was re-stocking panties by size and color into a drawer.

"Yes, you can," said Anne. "My friend here needs a bra, one she can wear with most everyday clothes; like a beige one, probably. She's never been sized, though."

"I don't own any bras with cups or anything," I added, trying unnecessarily to explain my situation. "All I have are sports bras, and all you have to know for those are small, medium or large."

"Oh!" said the lady, "We can definitely help with that. Here, let's head back to the dressing rooms and we'll get you started. My name's Leah!"

I followed her into the back while Anne browsed around, and when asked, I took off my shirt so that I could be measured. Leah regarded my sports bra with its numerous holes and rips with concern.

"Oh, wow, is this what you've been wearing?" she asked. "Sweetie, that's not very supportive!"

I hung my head in shame.

She placed the tape measure around my rip cage. "About a thirty-three, so let's say thirty-four. And I would say cup size you're about a B. So, you're bra size is thirty-four B! See how that works? I can bring you a few day-to-day options to try on; you can just stay here, alright?"

"Okay. Thank you."

While she whisked away to grab the lingerie, I was left alone with my reflection. My joy and good humor faded away as I gazed into the mirror, and I despaired at everything that I saw. I hated my tired face, my lanky hair which fell in lifeless ripples over my shoulders; my teeth were uneven and unattractive to look at, and I resolved once again to keep my mouth shut every time I felt like smiling. I hated my thighs, which despite the agony I went through with food and exercise, remained stubbornly large and saggy. I wanted to stop looking at myself, but I couldn't. I got closer to the mirror, and began to pick obsessively at my face, especially at my moles, which I wanted to tear off. *Monster,* I thought, looking into my own bloodshot eyes.

"Kim?" asked Leah's voice from outside the stall, startling me. "I have some brassieres for you to try! Let me know if you need more help, okay?" She handed me three beige bras over the door, and I took them, and began analyzing them instead of the mirror, steadfastly refusing to pick myself apart any further.

The first one that caught my eye was a dark tan affair that seemed to be made entirely of lace. It was, by far, the most girly thing I had ever seen, and the thought of me trying it on seemed ridiculous. I held it up, and squeezed the cups, which were slightly padded. Who would want to make their breasts look *bigger*? I hated that I had any at all. I knew that men liked big breasts, but I could not bring myself to agree with them. I liked being small-chested; it made me feel safe, somehow. But then I recalled I had made a determination to change, and with a sigh, I pulled off my sports bra and put on the lacy one, with the cups place over my breasts and the back pieces hanging open, un-clasped. I tried reaching behind me to close them, but failed. *How the hell…?* I considered calling for help, but then I came up with an idea. Taking the bra off, I closed the clasps, then slipped the bra over my head as if it were a sports bra. It was a little difficult, as the material wasn't very stretchy, but it worked. Turning to the mirror to view the effect of such a contraption, I gasped. *Boobs!*

The monster in the mirror I had seen moments before seemed to have somehow transformed into a human girl. Who the hell was I looking at? I placed my hands on my breasts, pushed them together, lifted then, and dropped them; I had never seen my body act like that before. I smiled a goofy little smile, ignoring my crooked teeth, and started to jump up and down to watch my chest move, knowing all the while I was acting like an idiot and would die of embarrassment if anyone saw me. After a moment I sat down on the small seat, and against my will two large tears rolled down my cheeks. It felt so good to be wearing something so beautiful, something I never thought I could wear, something that *real* women wore. Maybe it was a little late, but now that I knew my size I could buy a bra at any store I wanted. That silly torch that had been passed down, woman to woman, for centuries, had finally made its way to me; I could wear adult undergarments. I don't know why I cried; perhaps because I was sad it had taken me so long, or that it had taken the promptings of a stranger to get me through the threshold of a lingerie store. How long would I have gone on just wearing sports bras- my whole life? I rubbed my eyes, grateful for the kindness of strangers.

I ended up buying that lace bra, and as we left the store Anne announced that she needed to go as she required rest before going out later that night. I turned to her, my heart in my eyes.

"Thank you so, so much. I don't think you know how much you helped."

"No problem!" Anne said, shrugging off my thanks, "Everyone needs a good bra! I hope it works for you with those new tops! I'll see you around!" And with that simple parting line she sauntered away, placing her new sunglasses over her eyes as she did so.

I felt that there was probably no way to make her understand what she had done for me. How can you express to someone the impact they have had on your life, when to them it was a negligible, everyday act? Was it worth it to try and let them know? I wasn't wise enough to know the answer. I knew that I had felt a small change in my heart, and though I still felt badly about my looks, I also felt that there was potential inside of me to be much more than I was; I had the potential to become a woman.

The Roadhouse
(16)

I had imagined a lot of things for my life in California, but something I had hoped and prayed (in my own way) that wouldn't happen, was that I end up bringing my baggage with me. But that is exactly what I ended up doing. I had over-estimated the influence of my surroundings on my mental state. I had left everyone and everything I knew behind, but I still felt like the same person inside; a woman at a new airport, stuck in baggage claim, waiting for the same old suitcase.

I had to find a job. Sitting at home was not going well for me; I focused too much on my body and its many imperfections. After only a few days, I had begun to use the food in Jamie's kitchen as binge material, and made pathetic attempts at replacing it. I knew that she noticed, but I was too frightened to talk to her about it. We hardly saw each other, and her house, which at first had felt warm and welcoming, started to feel cold and empty, just like my old house, and I knew it was because of what I had done to it. I had altered it from a place of comfort to a place of secrecy and ritual. I wondered if Jamie felt it, too, and was avoiding coming home because I was there.

In an effort to get myself out of the house, I had submitted multiple resumes, only to run into failure again and again. My lack of education hindered me from finding jobs outside of the food business, so I decided to try to find work as a hostess at higher-end restaurants where I would not have to actually touch the meals, thus keeping my disordered appetite at bay.

Out of the many establishments I applied at, I received only one interview. I was so nervous beforehand that I tried on at least ten different outfits, casting off each one immediately, deeming myself not professional looking enough, or too fat, or too young-looking. Eventually I settled on black slacks and a fitted blazer I borrowed from Jamie, and a low pair of heels, which I had never worn before. I practiced walking around the living room a few times, and decided that though I was a bit awkward, I would be passable for a short period of time. With a deep breath I gathered my resume and application and drove to the interview.

The interviewer was the owner of the restaurant; an elderly man with a stiff jaw and a high, buttoned-up collar. When I entered the room, he looked me up and down with cold, calculating eyes, and then extended his hand in greeting.

"Good afternoon," he said in a gravelly voice, sitting behind a large oak desk after we shook hands, "So you want to work here, do you?"

"Yes, I would, very much," I replied nervously, sitting. I had never been looked at so brazenly before.

"You don't have any hostessing experience, do you?"

"No, I don't, but I'm a fast learner."

He looked at my resume, which was lying before him. "This doesn't mention if you have a high school diploma."

"I... don't have one."

"Why the heck not?"

"Um. I had a family tragedy a few years ago, and it kind of threw me off..."

His eyes slithered over my face, and then to my chest, and the shadow there that suggested a hint of cleavage. He put my resume down.

"Do you have any experience that would make me want to hire you?" he asked.

"I'm great with customers," I stumbled. "I worked as a barista for many years."

The old man settled back in his chair, sighing, making a teepee with his hands.

"I see. Good with customers. Well. I'm not sure that'll be enough to get you a place here."

"I also have a great memory," I added, desperate.

"Sorry, girl, this isn't going to happen. You did know, coming in here, that good looks wouldn't get you hired, right?" he asked, squinting at me boldly.

I flushed in embarrassment and anger. "I didn't even think of that."

He continued as if I hadn't said anything. "And you're cute enough, but your eyes are kind of droopy. Did you know that?"

I stared at him, shocked. He continued:

"This is what I suggest to you, girl. Go back and get your high school diploma and go to college. You can't live life off of your sex appeal."

And with that, he stood up, went to the door, and opened it, indicating that it was time for me to go.

I stood awkwardly in my heels, avoiding his gaze, and then with quick steps I left the restaurant and made for my car. I fumbled to unlock it; my hands were trembling so hard I could barely hold my keys. Once inside, I ripped off my blazer and flung it angrily into the backseat. Reaching into the glove compartment, I pulled out a napkin, and spitting into it, I dabbed at my face vigorously, removing as much makeup as I could. After I was done, I sat there, staring at my small reflection in the review mirror, thinking, *Monster, monster. You can't escape, no matter where you go, you will always be a failure.* And then the sobs came; deep, gasping sobs that made my chest spasm and my head ache. With a floundering hand, I reclined the seat and lay back, trying to catch my breath and wanting more than anything to rewind my life back to the very beginning, where I knew nothing about the ruthlessness of the world.

*

I slammed the car door, staring at the low, red and tan building in front of me: *'Logan's Roadhouse'*, the sign read in large scarlet letters. The sound of country music drifted outside from the open front door as a small family exited, clutching to-go boxes in their hands and wearing smiles on their satisfied faces. If I got this job, it would be only because Jamie put in a good word for me; not because I deserved it. And why had she even recommended me? What did I do for her, besides use her shampoo, borrow her clothes and binge on her food? I was a terrible house-guest, and a shitty, shitty step-sister. My heart felt heavy in my chest. Well, that was why I was there; to make an active change- to get out of the house and meet people. I breathed deeply, and went inside.

The moment I entered the door, I was assaulted by the smell of cooking steak, and my mouth watered so suddenly and so fiercely that my salivary glands began to ache. A petite blonde with kohl-lined eyes came up to me with menus in her hand and a smile on her sprightly, perfect countenance.

"Good afternoon," she said sweetly, raising her voice a little to be heard over the country music. "How many today?"

"I'm here for an interview with… Stuart?" I said, unsure if I remembered the name correctly.

"Oh, sure! Follow me, I'll take you back and tell him you're here."

I followed her through the restaurant, and became aware that under my feet, there was an audible 'crunch, crunch'. I looked down, and saw that the floor was absolutely littered with peanut shells, from the front door to the back windows.

"Why are there peanut shells on the ground?" I asked.

The pretty girl giggled as she seated me at a medium-sized booth. "Stupid, isn't it? We have these buckets of peanuts everywhere-" she indicated a small silver bucket on a table next to the one I was sitting "-and customers snack on them and dump their shells on the floor. At the end of the night we have to sweep them up. It's a big mess more than anything. I hate it, it's so nasty! I'll go get Stuart."

"Okay, thank you," I said, gazing uneasily at the buckets of nuts.

A moment later, a short, sleepy-eyed of about twenty-five years of age emerged from the kitchen, holding a clipboard. His eyes were red-rimmed and he introduced himself with a slight slur, so I quickly changed my impression of him from 'very tired' to 'very hung-over'.

"Jamie told me about you," he said, rubbing his eyes as he sat across from me. "Really, I got nothing to say, as long as you can make it work on time, you got the job. Jamie's a good friend of mine. How many hours were you expecting, though? Can't give you too many to begin with; the girls with seniority here get the most."

I told him I would be happy with any amount of hours he could afford to give me, and maybe as time went on and I proved myself he could assign me more. This was agreed, and I signed my tax form, shook his hand, and told him I would see him the next day at ten o'clock for training. I tried not the think about how I would deal being surrounded by peanuts all day, and focus on my one small victory; I had a job. That was something.

Over the next few days, I learned the basics of what it meant to be a hostess at a family restaurant. My trainer turned out to be that tiny blonde that had I first met; her name was Sheila, and she had been a hostess at Logan's for two years. She was hoping that my being hired meant she would be promoted to waitress, so she put extra effort into making sure I knew how to fill her position. From her, I learned how to sequence the timing of the seating with the servers, and I became an expert on the menu. I answered all phone calls, and shined and rolled in papers napkins all the silverware that passed into the mouths of our hungry customers. I programmed the country music that played in the jukebox, filled the buckets of peanuts at each table, changed the special board, and served drinks to tables when the servers were swamped. It wasn't long before I started working by myself during the day when it wasn't very busy. I was excited at first because I had progressed so quickly, but I soon realized that my enthusiasm was premature.

My first day by myself was slow; I seated a handful of customers, programmed the jukebox, and spent the rest of the time standing behind the hostess' podium. I watched a few families at their meal, and because I was interested, I paid close attention to what they ate; the husband ordered a steak- the kids both ate cheeseburgers, and the wife had a salad with no cheese or croutons. This started me on a new project where I observed what many people ate, and while doing so took note of their physical size and disposition. I don't know what inspired me to do it; there was just something hypnotizing about watching normal people, especially women, eat their meals. I began to notice that not all thin women ate salads, and not all thick women ate fattening meals, even though Logan's had a plethora of such things available of their menu. Whenever I witnessed a slender woman bite down on a burger, I always thought in the back of my mind, *Does she keep that down? There's no way she keeps that down.* I hated myself for those thoughts.

My time at home was spent avoiding conversation with Jamie, since I dreaded retribution from my binging on her food, which had not stopped since I had obtained work like I had hoped. While I was being trained, I ate nothing all day, and when I came home at night I was famished. At first I would try to eat something light, like a salad, but eventually the same old hunger would take control, and I'd eat everything I could get my hands on. Finding the privacy at home to purge was difficult; except on weekend, Jamie was often home after seven o'clock, so I knew that if I went into the bathroom to get sick I would be discovered. So for a few weeks, I would come home in the evenings, binge on food that I had secreted into my room, and then go on a walk to a forested area about a quarter mile from her house. There, I would throw up into a ditch. I perhaps should have felt more disgusted with myself than I did for the way I behaved, but by that point, such actions were as familiar to me as the back of my hand: I had been throwing up outside for years and it felt almost natural. As I wiped my face on a pile of leaves, I could only ponder if my tomorrow would always continue to be the same as my today, and what it would take to eventually stop it.

One afternoon, when I should have been taking my break, one of the waitresses came up to me and asked if I was hungry, as there were some extra French fries in the kitchen that were up for grabs. I quickly told her I wasn't- not really- and that I was on a diet anyway and cutting carbs.

"Oh, well eat some of these, then! Low carbs!" she said, handing me a bucket of peanuts.

I looked at the bucket with trepidation. "Won't I get in trouble for eating at the podium?"

The waitress waved her hand in negation. "Absolutely not. The other hostesses eat up there all the time. Just keep it under the podium out of sight, and you're good."

"Thank you," I said, taking them from her.

I knew, looking at that bucket, that resistance was futile. I had always had an issue managing myself around nuts, and now here was a whole bucket just for me, with as many refills as I wanted all day. I started to tremble a little. I felt like an alcoholic that had been offered a lifetime supply of alcohol, and told, 'just keep it hidden, you'll be alright.'

Over the next few hours, I learned how to crack a peanut as quietly as a mouse, and to sneak the salty morsels to my lips and chew in such a way that someone could hardly tell my mouth was moving. I became a ninja of binging at work. Every day, while at Logan's, I consumed countless peanuts to the point where my tongue and lips were sore from excessive contact with salt. And after work, lethargic and depressed, I would drive my aching stomach home and throw up in the woods behind Jamie's house. I became so dehydrated and constipated and I started taking laxatives that I found in Jamie's bathroom, hoping that they would help, but they only made me feel worse. Despite how terrible I felt, I stopped eating any other food, and only ate peanuts. I became obsessed, and bought bags of shelled peanuts and hid them under my bed. Despite my constant snacking, I lost ten pounds, and though I stood five feet, eight inches tall and had a large build, I weighed one hundred and eighteen pounds.

I was sitting on the couch with Chanel one night after work, exhausted from being sick, and Jamie walked in and paused the TV. I sat up, alert. I knew what was coming; I had been dreading it for weeks.

"Kim, we have to talk," she said.

I watched her, one hand gripping the arm of the couch, the other petting Chanel absently.

"I know you've been having a hard time," she said, "And I'm sorry for that. But you need to work with me if you want to stay. You know I don't mind you borrowing my clothes, but you need to wash them and hang them up right away, just as neatly as you got them, do you understand? Because that's the right thing to do. It's polite."

I nodded, and tears sprang to my eyes. I knew there was more.

She took a deep breath and sat next to me. "And you eating my food- I don't mind sharing, but you need to replace everything you use. And I want to know that you're actually eating it, not using it to-to be bulimic with. Do you understand? I don't want that going on in my house."

Silence.

"Why do you do it? You are so pretty, do you know that? And you don't need to lose any weight. I'm at the salon all day long, and I listen to women complain about their looks all the time and believe me, some would kill to have a face like yours."

I fought back tears as I continued to stroke Chanel's short fur. "I don't know why I do it. I'm sorry."

"I don't want you to be sorry, I want you to not do it anymore," Jamie said, her eyes hooded and sad.

"It's been so long at this point… I don't know how to not do it."

She looked at me, and pursed her lips. "Try harder," she said. "I know you've had a tough life, but you're not the only one who has, okay? And you're not the only one who's had an eating disorder. You can stop."

I hung my head.

Jamie stood up, and after clearing her throat, changed her tone.

"I also wanted to tell you that a couple of my friends and I are going to the lake this weekend, if you want to come," she said, suddenly smiling. "We're going to go out on a boat, and drink a little and relax. Does that sound like something you'd want to do? It'll get you out of the house and you can meet some people."

I lifted my face to hers, and said distressingly, "I don't own a bathing suit."

"That's okay, I have tons. You can borrow one… just wash it afterwards." She grinned, and then turning to go back to her room, added, "Cheer up, Kim. Everything's fine."

I sat on the couch for a while after she left, thinking. I was living by an erratic flurry of impulses which were so all-consuming that they cancelled out any good intentions that I might possess. Very often I would emerge from a fog, and realize that I had, in a manner, tied myself to the train tracks, and was only waiting for the train to end it all. While I struggled feebly in my bonds, questions would rush at me in a frenzy from bystanders: How had I managed to tie the ropes so tight? Where had I purchased the rope? What crime had I committed that I so desperately wanted to die? And I could only flounder and insist that I knew nothing, that I was a victim! But the evidence so overwhelmingly pointed to my own culpability, my own desire for death, that my accusers could only shake their heads in pity as the sound of a whistle blowing in the distance intensified.

*

On Saturday morning, I woke up early, excited and nervous about going to the lake with Jamie. I had tried on a few of her bathing suits the day before, and though they were all bikinis (I had never worn one before) I had chosen one with boy-cut shorts so I didn't feel like I was completely naked. I felt very self conscious in the swimsuit, but I figured I could wear jeans or a T-Shirt over everything when I was not in the water.

I was just coming back from taking Chanel on a walk when Jamie came out of the house, dressed, with her cars keys in her hand.

"There you are," she said, sounding relieved. "I left you a note; I can't make it to the lake today because I have to work. Important clients; you understand. But you're more than welcome to go, still."

My face fell. "But I don't know any of them."

"You know Will," she said, "My ex-husband? You met him in Hawaii. He'll be there. And I think your boss will be there, too- Stuart. Everyone's really nice, believe me. Come on, please go- for me? Take my place- everyone's pissed I'm not going."

I bit my lip, contemplating. "How would I get there?"

"Will can stop by- he needs to pick up some stuff anyway- and you can follow him in your car. It's a little bit of a drive, but it's not that bad. Whattya say?"

After a moment, I agreed, though I felt sad that she wasn't going. I had been looking forward to spending time with her and getting to know her better, and for her to get to know me as something besides a vomiting, stealing entity that resided in her house. At my reply, she smiled her brilliant smile and headed to her car, saying, "Great! I'll give Will a call. He'll probably be by in an hour or two, so just be ready, okay? Have a great time!"

Chanel and I went inside, and after unhooking her leash, I sat down on the sofa with a deep sigh. I was already dressed to go; I was already wearing the wretched bikini under my clothes, and had put on sunscreen hours ago. I hadn't been sure when we were leaving so I had wanted to be prepared. I didn't know what to do to distract myself until Will came over to collect his things. My mind wandered to the peanuts I had stashed under my bed, but I shook my head furiously. There was no time for that.

Instead, I tried to recall what I knew of Will. From what Jamie had said of him, I gathered that he had not wanted the divorce, and that he had become very depressed after their parting and was going through some emotional issues. I found it strange that they would hang out together considering their past, but what did I know? All I knew about relationships and divorces was what I had witnessed with my mother and father, and they had hardly given the best example.

I spread my body out on the couch, closed my eyes, and waited.

The doorbell woke me, and I sat up with a jerk and rushed to open the front door. Will poured into the room, blonde and smiling, though his eyes seemed veiled in a deep shadow which I didn't recall being there when I had seen him in Hawaii.

"Hey, Kim, good to see you again," he said. "Coming to the lake with us?"

"I'd like to, if that's okay? If you'd rather me not I understand," I said lamely.

"Of course you can come! We'd be glad to have you. Though you might be bored; right now it's just me and Stuart. We're probably just going go out on the boat and have a few beers, maybe swim a bit."

"That sounds fun," I said. "I haven't gone swimming in a long time. I'm ready to go, actually. Jamie said I could just follow you in your car."

"Yeah, absolutely. Let me grab some buds real quick." He turned to a side-board and opened a drawer, and pulled out a sandwich bag filled with weed. He looked at it and shrugged. "This looks about right," he said, and pocketed it.

"Was that the stuff you came to get?" I asked, wondering if I call Jamie to make sure he wasn't stealing her stash.

"Yup. Alright, let's go!"

I grabbed a towel and a couple of water bottles and followed him outside, locking the door behind me. As I put the towel in the trunk of my car, I thought I saw Will check me out, and I felt a shiver of repulsion; but then I quickly berated myself. I must have been mistaken; I was just nervous because I hadn't hung around people in a very long time. It was egotistical to think a guy was checking me out just because I saw him looking at me like that.

It took about fifteen minutes to drive to Shasta Lake, and though I had been there before, I had never been swimming in it. It was a beautiful area, surrounded by trees and walking paths- the lake itself was a cool azure, and reflected the white snowy peak of the mountain atop its inviting waters.

Stuart, the man who had hired me at Logan's Roadhouse, greeted me with a noncommittal, "Sup," and then heaved a giant cooler in his arms and walked it awkwardly down towards the water's edge.

Will had already removed his shirt, and I saw in a glance that he was pale and a bit overweight, though he seemed to carry himself well. We followed Stuart to the boat, which turned out to be a flat-bottom paddleboat, and Will held it still as his friend hopped in with the cooler.

"Your turn," Will said then, turning to me with a smile.

Once we were all in, Stuart shoved off from the shore, and we were drifting out towards the middle of a small part of the lake. Both of the men I was with had stripped themselves nearly naked, and I was the only one who still wore jeans and a shirt. Will commented on this, and embarrassed, and I told him I didn't like the way I looked in a suit, and that I thought I was fat. He appeared shocked.

"That's ridiculous! You're like a model or something, right?" he said, and then he looked down at his own body and pulled at the flaps of his skin unbecomingly. "I'm the only ugly one in this boat." And though he said it with a smile, the shadow in his eyes reminded me that he was still depressed over his divorce with Jamie. I sympathized with him. I knew what it was like to feel unattractive and unwanted.

"You're not ugly, Will," I argued. "You're a very good looking guy."

He perked up. "You think so? Thank you, I appreciate that very much."

Stuart had settled back into a reclined position and lit a bowl, and was apparently ignoring us as he soaked up the sun like a lizard. I began to think that maybe it was kind of silly that I was wearing so many clothes, after all. After another moment of hesitation, I grabbed the hem of my shirt and pulled it over my head, and then slipped out of my jeans, and before I knew it I was sitting in a bikini, in a boat, with two half-naked men. A year prior I wouldn't have recognized myself.

Will smiled at me, and, reaching into the cooler, pulled out a beer and opened it.

"That wasn't so hard, was it? And you look amazing," he said, handing me the beer.

I hesitated only a moment before taking the drink from him. The only beer I had ever tasted was the slightly sweet, grassy Mickeys, and that was when I was fifteen; this was a Budweiser. I sipped at it gingerly, and it was so bitter that I regretted for a moment that I had taste buds. My displeasure must have been apparent on my face because Will laughed at me.

"Is it bitter?" he asked, "You don't have to drink it."

I shook my head, stubborn. "No, I'll drink it. It just might take me a while to finish. People say it takes a bit to get used to the taste of beer, right?" I took another sip, and grimaced.

"Don't torture yourself," he said.

"I can torture myself if I want," I replied with a rare smile.

*

Ten hours later, I found myself at a house party; I didn't know where I was, or how I got there, or why I was still in my bikini even though it was dark and everyone else, all of whom were strangers, were properly dressed. With a start of self-awareness, I realized I was extremely drunk. I had no idea how many beers I had consumed; it seemed like I couldn't remember anything after the second or third had passed my lips. I seemed to come to myself all at once, and I started to shiver. Where the hell were my clothes? *Wasn't I just on a goddamn boat?*

"Come here, girl," said Will suddenly from my side, and he put his arm around me and drew me closer. "You're freezing. I'll warm you up."

I sat there dumbly, my mind fuzzy, hardly aware of what was going on. I started to stand up, but only fell gracelessly back onto his lap, and he held me close to him, inhaling the scent of my hair.

"You smell so fucking good," he said, and the hackles rose at the back of my neck. I *hated* being smelled.

"I'm r-really tired," I slurred.

"You want to go to bed? My bedroom is right back there." The invitation was obvious.

I shook my head, trying to clear the thick fog which clouded my mind. I didn't feel right. I felt like something was very wrong, and I wanted to leave.

"Can someone drive me home?" I asked Will.

He opened his mouth to say something, but then Stuart came forward and slapped Will on the back. They were both obviously the worse for drink.

"Hey!" said Stuart, "Getting lucky tonight, or what?"

Will smiled stupidly, shaking his head, and shrugged.

"Can anyone drive me home?" I asked again, looking at them both desperately. My head was pounding and I was having a hard time concentrating.

"We are wasted, honey; we can't drive. You should to stay here tonight," said Will, "Sit down and relax."

"No, I need to go," I replied almost hysterically.

Will stood up and put his arms around me. "Calm down. Why do you want to go? We were having so much fun."

I tried to step back, but his arms held on. I tried to look him in the face but all I could make out was a vague outline, it made me feel nauseous. "Jamie..."

This seemed to anger him, and in a raised voice said, "Jamie can't keep me from being happy forever. She's not even your real sister."

"I know that. I just- I don't feel well. I just want to leave, please."

He let go of me, apparently disgusted. "Fine, go ahead."

"Is my car here? Where are my keys?"

"Yeah, it is. Your keys are probably over on the counter. Come here-" and he leaned over and kissed me on the brow. "Thanks for coming out today, I had a great time. You made me feel like a man again."

I nodded dumbly, and quickly grabbed my keys from the counter before someone stopped me. Stumbling barefoot and wearing only my bikini, I made my way outside, and looked up and down the street for my small red car. I eventually found it parked crookedly at the far corner, and with quivering fingers I finally managed to unlock the door and sit inside. For a while, all I could do was sit there, my heart pounding, and try to recall what had happened after the boat; but for some reason it was all a blank. I ran my fingers through my hair and let out a small scream of frustration. Why did I get myself into these messes?

Taking a deep breath, I started the engine and turned on the heater, letting it's warmth revive me for a few moments. I wasn't quite sure where I was; I hadn't asked anyone, and so I didn't know how to get home. I knew, also, that I was in no way fit to drive. But I was terrified at what might happen if I stayed; I figured if I took it slowly, I would be okay. So, turning the wheel, I pulled slowly away from the curb, and with drunkenly exaggerated caution I made my way through a few neighborhood streets, which were thankfully abandoned, it being so late at night, looking for signs to the highway that would lead me home.

I eventually found the road I needed, and somehow managed to make my way back to Jamie's house without getting pulled over. I parked in the driveway, and as I stood up to go inside the house I suddenly doubled over and vomited everything I had in my stomach into the bushes in front of her house. It hurt so bad I thought I would pass out, and just when I thought I was done I heaved again, though by that point I had nothing left and I just dry-heaved. After a little while I sat down on the ground outside, trying to make the world stop spinning.

Well, I thought bitterly, *this is different. Throwing up, but not on purpose. Can't say I'm a fan.*

I stood up cautiously and went inside, first stopping by the bathroom to wash my face and hands with hot water. Afterwards I shuffled pitifully into my bedroom, and, closing the door softly behind me, I collapsed onto my bed and passed out almost as soon as my head hit the pillow.

*

I didn't wake up until late afternoon the next day, and the first thing I remembered was what had happened with Will the previous night. My chest squeezed with anxiety, and I folded my body in on itself until I lay in fetal position. My temples were throbbing, and though I wanted desperately to fall asleep again I couldn't quiet my mind. *What the hell happened last night?* I was in no way interested in Will. I felt bad for Will. Had I been too nice? Had he misconstrued my friendliness for something else? Why had I let myself get so drunk? I didn't even remember drinking more than a few beers. Was I really that much of a lightweight? I swore at that moment I would never drink beer again.

I could hear the television from the living room, and I knew Jamie was out there, and I dreaded seeing her that morning. Should I tell her that her ex husband and I… no. We hadn't done anything serious, I was sure, and for what we had done, I was as much at fault as he was, wasn't I? I shouldn't have let myself drink so much. I shouldn't have been wearing such a stupid, tiny bikini. I shouldn't have been so nice to him. I tried to tell myself it could have been worse. I thought of the conversation Jamie and I had had the other day about my eating her food and borrowing her clothes, and I realized how much worse this was than that. *I really am a terrible sister,* I thought miserably.

I grabbed a bathrobe and went into the bathroom for a shower, and when I emerged Jamie was on the couch, cell phone in her hand, her eyes looking flat and expressionless at the television. She didn't even glance up as I entered.

"Good morning," I said.

"Morning," she replied. "Did you have a good time? You were out really late."

I hesitated. "The boat was nice. Then we went to Will's house with some friends of his, but I honestly don't remember a lot of it. I guess I was really drunk."

She nodded and continued to watch TV. I sat near her for a moment, and then, my conscience getting the best of me, I turned to her and said:

"Jamie," I said, "I should tell you that Will was kind of… handsy? I guess the word is…"

Jamie stood up, not looking at me. "I don't want to talk about it. My friends already texted me and let me know what you guys were up to. And really, whatever. You two are free to do whatever you want."

I gaped at her. "We didn't do anything. I was so drunk I didn't even realize where I was… but we didn't! And then when I did realize things were getting weird I drove home drunk to get away from him. I don't like Will, Jamie."

"I don't want to hear it, and I don't want to be lied to," said Jamie, walking calmly towards her bedroom. "You're both adults. Like I said; do whatever the hell you want." She shut the door firmly behind her.

I stared at the closed door, and my eyes filled with tears. I blinked them away angrily. She didn't believe me. And after all, why should she? I was a liar and a thief; I stole her food and borrowed her clothes without asking, so why wouldn't I be deceitful about this?

Later that day, feeling hopeless, I called my dad and asked him to speak to Jamie for me. I told him briefly what had happened, and his response was not what I had hoped for.

"Well, Baby, when we were Hawaii you did say that he was attractive, and all that."

I paused in horror on my end of the line.

"Dad," I said, my voice dropping an octave, "*If* I ever said that it was because I was being nice, because I knew he and Jamie were having problems."

"You seemed to have meant it, Baby," my father said.

I felt rage build inside of me. "Dad, do you think I slept with Will?"

"Well... Jamie called Tammie and told her everything, and it sure sounds like you did."

"You think I would do that!" I yelled.

"You've been known to lie before, Kim," my dad said somberly.

"Dad, I drove home, drunk off of my ass, to escape a situation I didn't understand. Because I care about Jamie. Because I'm not the type of girl to sleep with her sister's ex-husband. And now there are rumors that we had sex, and everyone, even my DAD believes it. Thanks a lot for the support."

My father was silent for a moment, and then he cleared his throat.

"Aside from all of this, I was going to call you later today, anyway, Kim," he said, "Tammie and I think we found a place where we can get you some help for the- um, the bulimia problem, but you would have to go right away. It's an in-patient place in Los Angeles."

Holy crap! "How can we pay for it?"

"Insurance will cover it," he said. "They took some convincing, but they finally agreed. I need to know if you'll go, Baby. Just say the word, and I'll drive you down there in a few days. The downside is, you'd have to quit your job, and all that."

"I want to go," I blurted, not even thinking about it. "I'll give my notice tomorrow."

"Okay," said my dad, sounding relieved. "I will get things started then. Sorry things had to work out this way, Baby."

I remained silent as he said goodbye, and then hung up. Despite the situation I found myself in with Jamie and her ex-husband, my entire existence seemed to have just been changed for the better. I was going to get help, from people who knew- people who had seen monsters like the one that lived inside of me, and could possibly help me get exorcise it. I clutched my chest, and sat down on the ground, overwhelmed. It didn't matter that no one believed me, because they didn't know me. How could they, while I was like this? But I could show them. I'd show them who I was when I wasn't ill; and then they would understand that I never would have done something so horrible to Jamie, no matter what frame of mind I was in.

The next day at work, I gave my notice, telling them I had to leave in just two days to go to the hospital because I was unwell, but I left the details of my illness vague. Everyone seemed indifferent, except for the girl who had trained me, Sheila; she seemed genuinely sad to see me go.

"I don't want you to leave!" she said, holding my hand. "You're the only one who does things the right way around here!"

I laughed. "You'll just have to train someone else, I guess."

Sheila was about to reply when two customers walked in the door, a black man and woman, and we both immediately put on our hostess masks.

"Good afternoon, Sir," I said, "Two today?"

"Yep," said the man, who appeared to be about middle aged. He had his arm around the woman, who appeared so painfully thin that I wondered how his arm could possibly be comfortable.

As I sat them, the waitress came forward to great them, grinning from ear to ear. I made my way back to the podium.

"So," said Sheila, "That was Sir Mix-a lot."

My eyes bulged. "What?"

She nodded. "He comes here every week, sometimes twice. He lives in town."

I peered at the couple who I had seated.

"But… is that his wife?" I asked.

Sheila shrugged. "I don't know. He doesn't always bring her, sometimes it's a different lady."

"Isn't he famous for a song about women with big butts?" I asked, slightly outraged. "That woman weighs about as much as my left thigh."

Sheila giggled. "You're ridiculous! But that's so true about the lady! That's hilarious. Do you want to get his autograph? Most everyone here has it already."

I shook my head. "No thanks. I feel let down. I used to listen to that song, sometimes. Now I just feel like it was a dirty lie."

Sheila turned to the hostess counter and started to polish the silverware.

"I used to be as skinny as her," said Sheila.

"Really?" I asked.

She nodded. "Yeah, I haven't told anyone else here this, but… I've had anorexia since I was little. I've gained back some weight though, thank goodness. I was freaky looking, just like that lady, for a while."

"You look beautiful," I told her honestly.

"Thank you."

I bit my lip. "I have bulimia. That's why I'm going to the hospital; it's actually an inpatient clinic in LA."

Sheila turned to me, and held my hand again. "Oh, Kim, I had no idea. I'm sorry."

"It's okay. I'm getting help now, so things should work out, right? It's been… really hard, so I look forward to a change."

"I've been to a few of those places," said Sheila, turning back to the silverware, "They're not easy, but they're the best thing to do if you're really sick. You learn a lot. I'm glad you're getting the help you need."

"Thank you, Sheila," I said. "I'll miss you, you know."

Sheila grinned, and passed me some silverware to polish. "Just think of me anytime you hear 'I Like Big Butts', okay? And write me once in a while. And I'll be happy."

We laughed, and side by side, we worked until it was time to go home.

I never did write her a letter.

Heart of Clay
(17)

My dad apologized to me again that he had to 'do this' to me, but I had left him no choice. I could only nod stoically in response. My dad believed that my going to the inpatient clinic for would be a punishment to me, and that I would be mad at him for bringing it down upon me.

If only he knew, I thought, *how relieved I am that I am actually getting help like I am a valid human being that mattered.* How many years had he known, now? It didn't matter. He had seen me so little during those years, I'm sure it was easy for him to forget I was there, let alone sick. Hell, the only reason I was getting help now was probably because his new wife was making him do it for Jamie's sake. My eating disorder had begun to disturb the peace of her precious daughter's life to the point where something just had to be done.

So there we were my dad and I, driving south to Los Angeles with a small bag full of my clothes, and not much else.

"And one more thing," my dad said, hesitating, "When you get out, whenever that is, you won't be able to live with Jamie anymore. She won't have you."

This saddened me. Once again, my eating disorder had lost me a home. Or was it because she still thought I had slept with Will? Either way, I was not surprised, so I merely remained quiet.

It was a long drive from Redding to LA, but my dad and I didn't talk the entire way, except for that small exchange of words. When we reached the hospital where I would be staying, my dad stood around the white pristine front desk looking uncomfortable. Pitying him, I gave him a hug and told him I'd be fine, and that he should probably begin his drive back. He gave me a small smile of relief, waved, and with a quick, "Good luck, Baby," he was gone.

Being an inpatient in an eating disorder clinic can be surreal, and the experience differs for every individual who enters one. Every one has their own illness, their own story, and individual personality; these factors made it obvious to me that there is no way that a group of people can have the same experience even if they are put into a controlled environment like one I was in. My own experience was eye-opening, in a good way, whereas I know others had a horrible time. I can only hope that the people I met in that clinic have since found their path to healing.

There were strict rules. There were cameras everywhere, even in the bedrooms and wardrobes. You could not use the restroom without someone watching you, in case you tried to purge your meals. No exercising was allowed, whatsoever. You had to eat three meals a day, everything on the plate, plus two snacks. It was mandatory to attend all individual therapy and group therapy sessions. All prescribed medication was also compulsory, and could be force-fed if necessary. A person's weight and vitals were taken every day, but the patient was not allowed to know their weight.

For some of the other patients, the bathroom rule was more than enough to make them hate the clinic- they felt it was too far beneath their dignity to have someone watch them defecate- but for some reason I didn't mind having someone watch me. I would usually try to make a joke about it; this was probably a nervous tick left over from when I was a child; and the nurse would laugh, and then it would be over. It even created a weird kind of bond between me and one of the nurses; there was the nurse that gave me meds, the nurse that took my vitals, and the nurse that watched me poop. After a few days it became normal to me, and I didn't think anything of it.

When I entered the hospital, my vitals were a mess; I was anemic, had drastically low pressure, and a slew of other issues. It was decided that I needed depression medication, vitamins, and most importantly, nutrition. For the first few days, my body didn't know how to handle the sudden intake of regular food- I was constantly in pain. Before arriving there, I couldn't remember the last time I had eaten a normal meal, and my stomach was eager to let me know how pissed off it was. After a while, however, things settled, and for the first time in years, I felt proper hunger pangs, and was able to satiate them.

The best thing about being a patient in the Los Angeles facility was meeting the other patients, and learning that I was not alone. Though I had known, logically, there were others like me, seeing them up close and becoming companions with them made it so much more real to me. There were two other bulimics, three anorexics, and one binge eater with multiple personality disorder. I adored them all almost immediately; I even treasured the separate personalities of the woman who suffered from MPD; and as the youngest patient there they adopted me as their mascot. The bulimics and I talked about the painful cycle of binging and purging; the anorexics and I discoursed on our theories of what 'skinny' truly meant to Western cultures, and the binge eater and I talked about our complicated, emotional relationship with food. It was a new undertaking for me, speaking with someone about these issues that been a hidden, and yet so prominent a part of my existence, and I found it the most freeing experience in my life.

Unfortunately, despite the greatness of the team I worked with and my fellow patients, the few therapy sessions I attended were forgettable- all except one. It was a group therapy session, and the whole motley crew of us was led into a brightly lighted room supported on one side by a big, filthy-looking wall. The rest of the space was filled with chairs, all of which faced the wall in a semi-circle. The experiment was explained to us by our group counselor, Dr. Hun- while recounting a memory to the group, and focusing on memories that made us angry, we would throw large balls of clay at the wall. This, Dr. Hun said, could potentially help us express some of our repressed anger. He then asked for a volunteer to go first, and unsurprisingly, no one raised their hand. Dr. Hun looked at me, who had found a seat in the back of the room, and he cocked an eyebrow.

"Miss Kim? Will you go first?"

I took a deep breath and stood up. There was no reason to argue with the doctors; you never won. But though I didn't fight, I really didn't want to do the experiment, as it sounded cruel and sort of violent. And so it was with apprehensive feet that I shuffled to stand before the wall.

"Okay," said the therapist, "As you communicate your memory aloud, and throw the clay, I will be standing by to immediately hand you another. Throw the clay after each sentence, do you understand? Even if the sentence you spoke did not stir in you feelings of anxiety, or anger. I will push you only if you need it; otherwise this is your story, and you can feel free to say whatever comes to mind. Are you ready?"

I nodded, uncertain what memory to relate; what was I mad about? I couldn't think of anything. And then all of a sudden I recalled something that I thought had only slightly irritated me as a child, but as the first sentence passed my lips, the words began to fly, and I was throwing clay like I'd been waiting to do it for years.

"I used to play with my sister." THUD.

"She always got to pick what games we played, or if we played at all." THUD.

"When we played Barbies, she was always Barbie. I was the monster." THUD.

"Why was I always the monster?" THUD.

"She always hated me." THUD.

"She hated to see me." THUD.

"She hated to hear me breathe." THUD.

"I loved her." THUD.

"I didn't understand." THUD.

"I was just a little girl." THUD.

"Why didn't she love me?" THUD.

"Why can't I breathe?" THUD.

"Why couldn't she be nice to me?" THUD.

"I wanted to be Barbie." THUD.

"I" THUD.

"WANTED." THUD.

"TO." THUD.

"BE."THUD.

"BARBIE!" THUD!

With the last word spoken, I threw my ball of clay so hard that my shoulder ached, and the ball actually managed to cling to the wall, hanging there, as my words echoed in the minds of the listeners. Dr. Han took hold of my arm and said I did a good job, but I could barely hear him. Tears were somehow streaming down my face, and I was lost in contemplation, trying to recall what had just happened. What was that? Had I been in some kind of trance? My fellow patients were staring at me in awe, a few were even in tears; the woman with MPD was rocking herself in her chair in an attempt to self soothe. *That was so intense,* one of them whispered to another. *I* really *don't want to do it, now*.

"Kim, you can sit down now," said the counselor. And so I sat.

My mind was whirling. *This is what it feels like to heal,* I thought. *I am doing to right thing by being here.* In that moment, I was so thankful to my dad for sending me to LA that I forgot he had done so simply because he had no other recourse.

It was on our way back from that session that a nurse asked me to stop by the nurse's station, and so while the other patients went in to lunch I halted in front of the small glass window where we received our medication each morning. The nurse led me into the back room, where I found my primary therapist sitting with a bunch of papers in front of him. He looked grimly into my face.

"Kim, do you feel that you have made any progress here the last week?" he asked.

I was surprised by the question, but answered. "Yes, I think so, but everyone says it will take a while for me to get all the way better."

The doctor sighed and rubbed his temples. "Yes, well. We got a call today from your insurance. One of the stipulations of them covering your inpatient care was that they continuously receive your vitals information, and of course since you have been eating a normal diet the last two weeks your body is responding positively. Your vitals by themselves are healthy; you don't have arrhythmia, your electrolytes are pretty well balanced- and your insurance does not see a reason for you to be here anymore."

My heart went cold. *No!* "B-but I'm not ready! Don't they know that's not how eating disorders work?" I said, tears forming, hands shaking. *Please let it not be true!*

"I know, and I have told them that- repeatedly," said the doctor. "But they are adamant. They aren't interested in the relapse rate, or anything I have to say, really. I'm sorry, young lady, but you are to be discharged immediately. There is nothing I can do that I haven't tried already."

The words damned me. I crumpled on the floor, overwhelmed. I was so close! So close to learning what was wrong with my head, and possibly becoming a real person- I had been so close to *living!*

"GOD DAMN IT!" I screamed, lost again.

*

    I ended up leaving the next morning, since my dad had to drive the entirety of California to pick me up. I found out later he paid out of pocket for that last full day, and it made me feel very guilty- all I seemed to do lately was sponge his money. During the drive back, we were just as quiet as we had been on the way down; I was morose, and didn't want to talk about treatment or insurance, or anything else that mattered. I just wanted to go to bed. As we drove up to my step-sisters house, I started in shock- all of my bedroom furniture was out on the lawn.

    "What the hell is this?" I said.

    I thought I told you that wouldn't be able to stay with Jamie anymore…" my father began.

    "Yeah! And I can find a new place! But for God's sake I just got out of the hospital and my crap is on the lawn! Can't she give me a day or two? JESUS! And for fuck's sake, I didn't sleep with her goddamn ex-husband!"

    My dad looked sad. "Sorry, Baby."

    I covered my face with my hands. "I have nowhere to go. I will have to sell my shit."

    "We got a storage unit for your stuff. You can stay with me and Tammie for a little bit," my dad said quietly.

    I laughed deliriously. "Yeah, and I'm sure she is thrilled with that idea!"

    My dad looked at me somberly. "Just for a while. She's fine with it."

I glared back at him, challenging. "Fine," I said, trying to call his bluff, "Let's load up my stuff and you can drive me all the way back to Oregon with you and I'll sleep on Tammie's two-thousand dollar couch from now until the end of time."

Instead of rebutting, all he did was get out of the truck and begin to load my mattresses. I was almost touched.

A Brief Homecoming
(18)

When we arrived at my dad's house I could tell that I was thoroughly unwanted. Even when I had slept in the tent, or the nights I was squished bonelessly in my frigid car, I had never felt as uncomfortable as I did under the hawk-gaze of my stepmother. She watched me with fiery eyes, and lectured me endlessly about how I was killing myself just to get attention. She told me, more times than I can recall, that I was being selfish by having an eating disorder, that I had treated Jamie shamefully by being sick in her house after she had opened her doors to me. It was unforgiveable how I had betrayed her, that my childish 'stuff' had gone on long enough.

After a stressful encounter, not that I needed much hedging, I binged on some of the food in their cabinets, and purged in their small, elegantly decorated bathroom. Though I carefully cleaned their toilet afterwards, Tammie still found out, and verbally attacked me to the point I couldn't do anything but stare at the wall in response. After I couldn't respond anymore, she then continued to have an argument with my dad about what to do with me, and it went badly. He eventually said something to the extent that he would rather leave Tammie than put me out of the house again.

Though I appreciated what he threatened to do, though I doubted it would ever come to pass- I knew that if I stayed, his unhappiness would be my fault. I had always known it was that way, ever since my mother died- known that my presence did not factor into my dad's vision of a joyful life. I was a responsibility that he wanted to forget, but- if given the choices plainly- he would stand by me, just like he had worked for over twenty years at a job he detested so that our family might live. I was a selfish, half-crazy ass, but damned if I would let anyone say I didn't love my dad. *The fire or the flame*, I pondered.

I woke up early the next day, packed up some clothes, and told my dad I had found a place to stay, and so I didn't need to stay with him and Tammie anymore. He seemed concerned, surprised; and then relieved.

"Well, as long as you will be okay, Baby…" he started.

"Yeah, I'm fine. I can stay with friends." I said.

And with that I drove off in my little Chevy Prism. He may or may not have known I was lying about having a place to stay, and was only leaving to save his marriage. For despite our differences and issues, I just wanted him to be happy. He was, after all, my dad.

The Next Step
(19)

Lying on the ground in my sleeping bag, I stared with unfocused eyes at the tent's ceiling and wished I would die. *Just stop breathing*, I begged my malnourished body, *Pass away into nothing*. If I would just die, it would solve so many problems. Not only would I not have to live with the darkness in my mind anymore, but I would also no longer be a drain on my father, and I wouldn't be forced to stay in my loveless relationship with Sam, who I had stupidly run back to as soon as I left my father's house. Why did I hold on to him so tightly? Did I hate him, or love him? Most of the time I wanted nothing to do with him- I couldn't even stand to even look at him- but I also felt I couldn't survive a day without him. So why survive? I put my hands on my head, my fingers grasping my hair in painful hunks, and I curled into a ball. I was crazy. I was crazy, just like my mother, and I knew it; I needed to get away from myself.

I was too cowardly to commit suicide. Memories of trying to go to sleep in the bathtub with a bag over my face when I was ten surfaced in my mind, and tears spilled down my cheeks. How unfortunate, looking back, that I had tried unsuccessfully to die at such a young age. What had time brought me since then? Loss. Illness. Endless confusion and self-doubt. I felt at my core that something bigger than just bulimia was wrong with me, but I couldn't put a name to it. My memories had begun to slip away from me like I was senile. I couldn't recall what had happened the week before, where I had slept, what I had eaten, how many times I had thrown up. I tried to recall the last time I had talked to someone besides Sam, but came up with nothing. Even when I asked myself questions such as, 'What day of the week is it? What month is it?' my mind could only return blanks.

At that point I had been bulimic for four years. Why was I still alive? Why hadn't my stomach exploded, or my heart given out, like all the books I read about bulimia said they would? It wasn't that death had not always been in the forefront of my plans all those years- it had not been something I pined for every time I went to the store for binge food, or bent over my knees to purge- but now, as I lay there alone and friendless in a tent on the side of a mountain, I felt like I had been duped. What had the whole thing been about, then, if not my eventual demise?

I tossed and turned in my sleeping bag. Sam would be home from work in a few hours, and the same pattern we had lived before I left for California would continue, except now we didn't have an apartment. I hadn't gotten another job since I came back to Brookings- I had been too depressed to even get dressed; anyway, none of my clothes fit anymore because I had gone up two sizes due to my constant binging. Currently, my days consisted of lying in bed and sobbing in self-pity. At night, Sam would return with fast food of some sort, and we'd eat in the tent in silence, and then go to sleep. That was my life and future for as far as I could see, and would continue to be until I found a way to end it somehow.

I had to end it. Only I could end it- no one else could end it for me.

THUD.

I sat up suddenly, as if shocked by electricity.

THUD. THUD.

In my mind, I saw the wall from the clinic in LA. I stood before it, a ball of clay in my hand. Get angry, I willed myself. Get mad! Get motivated.!

THUD.

"No one can end it for me," I whispered into the silence of the tent, my heart pounding.

THUD. THUD. THUD.

If I remained like this my entire life, whose fault would it be, except my own? Thoughts of my sister, Jamie, my mom, my dad- the joke that had become my entire existence, assaulted me all at once and squeezed my chest, turned my stomach, and flushed my pale skin with shame. When I was younger, I must have had a dream, a desire to be become something. After all, didn't everyone dream, at least once in their lives? I racked my memory, desperate for an answer, but there was none forthcoming. Had I always been this hopeless?

"No one can end it but me," I repeated, taking strength from my own words.

I stood up, tossed my blankets aside, and without a thought to what I was doing I began grabbing everything that I owned and shoving it into a large backpack. Clothes, food, water bottles, they all went, and after my pack was full I grabbed empty grocery bags and started to stuff them with my books and blankets. Once that was complete, I hesitated on the threshold of the tent, thinking of Sam. How many times must I abandon him until we become free of each other, I wondered. I grabbed a pen from my backpack, and on the back of a grocery receipt, wrote, 'Staying elsewhere tonight. Will call. Kim,' and placed it on top of my sleeping bag for Sam to find. And with that, I grabbed my keys, hefted my bags, and exited the tent for the last time.

I fought tears while I drove down the mountain, because I had no idea where I was going and I was still afraid of being alone. I couldn't go back to my dad's. I daren't go to my sister's- she had Mason, and from what I had learned from her in Hawaii, possibly a troubled relationship as well, and I couldn't add to her worries without hating myself even more. I had some money left over- not enough to get an apartment, definitely not enough to go to college- just enough to keep buying binge food to kill myself with. Oh, how badly I wanted to throw up right then! To fill up my stomach until it was round and gorged, to feel nothing but the simplicity and joy of eating for an hour, and then purge it all away into oblivion along with whatever remained of my heart. Use me, said the same old voice. Use me the way you've always done. Why give up on it, now?

With these words echoing in my mind, I quickly pulled over to the side of the road, nearly blind with tears at that point, and put my hands to the sides of my head in a desperate effort to block the horrible thoughts.

"STOP IT!" I screamed to myself. "This is not normal! Why can't you be normal? Why are you such a freak? Who thinks like this? Stop it, stop it, stop it!" But the desire to binge didn't fade- it actually seemed to grow stronger. I could just stop by a grocery store in town, and drive to a quiet spot on the beach where no one would pay attention to me… No! Taking a deep breath, I lifted my hand, and slapped myself sharply across the face- again, and again, and again, desperately trying to erase the thoughts that drew me closer and closer to complete ruin.

My head reeled from the pain, and panting, shaking, I collapsed across the center console of my car, and for a while, I knew no more.

It was much later when I awoke. My head ached, and my back was bent in an uncomfortable position and was spasming periodically. Still, for a moment after I opened my eyes, I didn't move, but lay there and stared out the window. The sun was sitting low over the mountain, its golden rays shining through the green boughs of the trees until they came to lie gently on my face. The sky above me began to turn a softly bruised color as the seconds ticked by, casting new shades upon the earth, and worked in conjunction with the rays of light to cast crystalline rainbows across my skin.

I sat up slowly, and groaned as my back muscles convulsed painfully. My entire body ached, and my head was throbbing. I licked my lips tentatively to find they were cracked and bleeding. I reached into my backpack and pulled out a water bottle and drained it, then turned the car over to check the time; it was six-thirty. Sam could drive by any minute on his way home from work, and the thought sent shivers down my spine. I immediately started the car and began to drive down the mountain again. I didn't want to run into Sam. If I saw him, I would talk to him- and if I talked to him, I would probably stay with him, because I was weak, pathetic, and didn't want to be alone. My lower lip trembled. Better to be alone, I thought, than to stay in whatever kind of relationship we had haphazardly remained in over the years.

There still remained the mystery of what I was going to do next. My head was pounding, and I was cold- I began to imagine about how pleasurable it would be to sleep in a soft bed and sink into a warm bath. Could I, perhaps, get a hotel room for the night? The sick part of my mind recoiled from the thought; why spend all that money on a hotel room when I could use it on binge food? Wasn't it a waste? But I shook my head angrily, arguing with myself; I needed to lie down and rest. I was tired, dehydrated and unwell. I would get a hotel room, just for one night, and then figure out what I was going to do with the rest of my life tomorrow.

I drove to the center of town and checked into a cheap hotel. Sore and fatigued, I carried my bags up the stairs to my room, unlocked the door, and once inside I collapsed onto the bed. My senses vaguely noted my new surroundings; the bed was soft and large- so large I could stretch full length and still not touch the edge. The air inside the room was still and deliciously quiet. I sighed, and rolled onto my back to look at the ceiling. There were multiple water stains, but I welcomed them, because they meant there was a roof over my head. I reached my arms above me, grabbed a pillow and pulled it over my eyes.

Relax, I told myself. *Be at peace, God damn you- peace.*

I fell asleep.

I awoke in the dark. I was shivering with cold, so I turned the heater in the room to seventy-three degrees just because I could. I went into the bathroom, which was small and tidy, and saw that it had one of those ill-placed mirrors situated so that you had to look at your reflection while you sat on the toilet. So, sitting, I stared at myself while I peed. I was hideous. My hair looked like it hadn't been washed or brushed in weeks. I had a large puffy face from repeated vomiting, dark shadows under my eyes, and large bruises were starting to show where I had hit myself. I pulled down the skin under my eyes and saw how cloudy and blood-shot the whites of my scleras were. I let the skin go, and chuckled a little madly.

"Oh, my God," I said, laughing quietly, looking into my own eyes mockingly, "You look so awful. You look like you've been abused."

My laughter died in my throat, and I looked at myself with fresh eyes. It felt just like that; that I had been abused. But if I was a victim of abuse, who had abused me? Myself? Maybe. No, I thought sternly, not me- bulimia. Bulimia promised that it would always be there for me, take care of me, and give me everything I needed to survive- but all it does is take, take, take. It estranges me from people, and leaves me looking and feeling like a stranger to myself. I hated and loved it more than I had ever hated and loved anything or anyone in my entire life. The thought of living in a world without it scared me into madness, but living in a world with it destroyed me, incrementally, body and soul.

As I ran my bathwater I tried to recall the last time I had had a bath, and I couldn't recall. I decided to make the most of it, and dumped a whole container of complementary shampoo and conditioner into the running water, and watched with a smirk as a few pathetic bubbles made attempts to form.

"Ooh, look at all that luxury," I cooed to myself mockingly, as I took off my clothes and climbed in. The water was very hot, but I embraced it, sinking in until my face was completely covered except for the tip of my nose.

I lay in the tub until the water grew cold, and then I washed, rinsed, and ran naked towards the bed, diving in under a small pile of blankets. Getting under the covers directly after a bath was always one of my favorite things to do. The air in the room by then was hot, and I lay there for a minute, my naked body warm and dozing, until I decided to stay awake for a bit longer, and watch some television for the first time in months. I wondered if there were any new good cartoons on that I had been missing the last few years. I grabbed the remote from the end table and clicked on the small TV at the other end of the room.

What I saw on the screen was a raging storm- water swirling everywhere, over homes, cars, and trees, and at first I thought it was a movie, but I soon saw that it was a CNN news clip of something called 'Hurricane Katrina.' I was horrified. I had never heard of it.

The screen went to a reel of a white-haired anchor sitting at his desk with a melancholy look on his face, and he said, "…Coverage continues tonight in this special edition of 360. Shocking images from New Orleans. What is happening there is an outrage. We are going to go in-depth on that tonight, as well as what is happening here in Waveland, Mississippi, and all these neighboring communities."

The screen showed images of flooding, of people trudging through water up to their chest- children floundering in filthy pools.

Another correspondent continued in a voiceover as the video footage of the destruction of New Orleans continued: "This is America? Chaos, anger, a desperate city feeling abandoned. Violence, gunfire, looting, and starvation."

Three children came onto the screen, yelling into the camera with tears in their eyes, "We want help! We want help!"

"Mothers, children, the elderly, hurricane survivors still waiting for help," the anchor continued. "They are marching in search of food, water and relief. They're surrounded by a crumbling city and dead bodies. Infants have no formula, the children no food, nothing for adults, no medical help. They're burning with frustration, and sure they have been forgotten."

My heart started pounding; at some point during the broadcast, I had sat up and clutched one of the pillows to my bare chest. The images on the screen frightened me, but more than that, they tugged at something deep within me, something I was not familiar with, and couldn't put a name to. Tears fell from my eyes as I watched images of children suffering, dying, looting and starving. I felt guilty that this horrendous, unspeakable event had been going on for days, in my own country, and I had known nothing about it. What kind of small, backwoods life was I living, that people were dying like this and I still languished on the coast, totally unaware of everything? Maybe... maybe I couldn't be there; maybe I couldn't help with my own hands, but wasn't it the least I could do to be aware of their pain? To remain ignorant of it all seemed to me the greatest sin I had committed, an affront to human life.

I turned off the television after a while, and lay back, contemplating. I wanted to know things; to help those who needed it- and why couldn't I help? What was stopping me? I had tried to help, once- but I had given up. I always gave up. What made me different from everyone else in the world- my bulimia? I raged silently. I could conquer it; I didn't know how, but I knew I could overcome it, and live my life as a true member of society. I wanted to take an active part in the world, instead of playing the role a vagrant, only ever traversing the outside of life. *Somehow...*

I got dressed and went down to the hotel's main office where I knew there was a computer set up for guest use. I typed, 'military recruiter Brookings, Oregon' into a search engine, and scoured over the results. The closest recruitment office for all branches was in Coos Bay, which was about two hours away. Without hesitating, I went to MapQuest, entered in the address, copied down the driving directions on a blank piece of paper, and went back to my room to solidify my plans for the next day. I would wake up early, shower, and drive to Coos Bay and join a branch of the military, because it was my last option to get out into the world and become somebody that mattered. I knew of some classmates from my high school that had joined the Coast Guard, but I didn't feel that it was for me. As far as I knew, they did not travel much (I later learned I was wrong), and traveling was something I was very interested in now that I had begun to think about it as a possibility. I didn't care where I went, as long as I got as far away from where I was as soon as humanly possible.

Recruiter's Block
(20)

The next morning I showered and went down to the free continental breakfast held in reception. Instead of sitting to eat, I grabbed five apples and shoved them into my backpack, made a coffee with three sweeteners, and headed out the door to begin my long drive north. The road to Coos Bay was gorgeous; it was surrounded by tall, majestic trees on one side, and the wild, glistening blue ocean on the other. I thought about the people in New Orleans, and wondered if they would ever find the sight of water beautiful again. As I drove, I saw the land bridge where my sister and I had spread my mother's ashes, and I smiled sadly.

Coos Bay was a lumber town with a community college thrown in for color; it was ugly, and sloping, and had very little in the way of entertainment to offer its citizens. I made my way directly to the recruiter's offices via my written directions, and I soon found myself standing in the middle of a tiny, unimpressive mall called Pony Village with four doors facing me: the Navy, Army, Marines, and Air Force recruitment centers.

I had driven the entire way without giving it much thought, but now that I was there, I contemplated; what branch should I join? It was a big decision. I looked at the Navy sign; an eagle in flight grasping an anchor. I didn't know anything about the Navy except that they went out on boats and submarines, and the thought of being trapped at sea made me feel claustrophobic, so I decided against them, and turned to the Marines.

Their insignia was the most beautiful; bright red and black, it depicted an eagle in flight perched atop the world, with an anchor crossing behind. What did I know about the Marines? *Full Metal Jacket*, my brain answered. *A Few Good Men. Born on the Fourth of July.* I took a deep breath, visualizing myself getting hit with socks full of soap. Maybe, I thought, the Marines weren't for me, either. It wasn't that I didn't like the idea of a challenge, but I didn't feel up to brutality, either. I turned to the Army door. An eagle in flight on a field of green; *E pluribus unum*, the ribbon in the eagle's mouth read. I knew enough Latin from reading novels to know it translated to, 'out of many, one'. It was a good motto, and it drew me in. I was almost going to step into the office when the face of a short, muscular man in Army fatigues poked out the door.

"Howdy!" he said in a loud southern twang, "Looking for somethin'?"

"I-I am looking to join the military but I don't know what branch to join."

"Well you've come to the right place!" said the Army man, opening the glass door wide for me, "Come on in, little sweetheart! I can help you see if you don't think the Army is the right choice for you."

Instead of coming closer, I backed up a little. The man had a weird sparkle in his eye that reminded me of a used car salesman, and something in his manner made me instinctively distrust him, like he would say anything to get me to join the Army. Looking for a way out, I glanced up at the last sign, the Air Force sign- an eagle in flight on a field of azure blue- and I made my choice.

"I'll stop by after I go into the Air Force recruiters'," I said, "I have an appointment with him."

The Army recruiter pulled a face. "Air Force? Don't let him get to you. The Army is the way to go, believe me. We take the best care of our people."

"Well, my dad was in the Air Force," I said, pulling that out of my memory, "I want to give it a shot first."

The recruiter smirked, giving in, and gave a little wave of dismissal. "Alright, but when you're done, come on over. I'm here till four."

"Thank you," I said, and walked quickly through the Air Force door.

I entered a small office which contained nothing but a man in uniform behind a desk, who at the moment was writing absorbedly into a large, open ledger. When I opened the door, a tiny bell jingled and he glanced up, analyzing me quickly with cool blue eyes. He glanced from my ratty jeans to the backpack in my hand, and I could see his gears turning, trying to categorize me in his head.

"Be with you in a second," he said in a soft voice, indicating a chair opposite his desk for me to sit, and he continued to work. I sat there nervously and began to wonder what an Air Force recruit should do with their hands when they sit. I ended up putting them in my coat pockets.

"Okay, sorry about that," he said, closing his ledger after a few moments, and raising his eyes to mine again. "How can I help you?"

"I, um…I want to join the Air Force. If it's right for me, that is." I bit my lip. I didn't want to seem too eager.

He gave me a friendly smile. "Alright. Well, that's what I'm here for, after all, five days a week, hour after hour…"

He turned and pulled out some papers from a drawer, and laid them neatly in a pile in front of him. He clicked his pen loudly and said, "The best way to go about this is to ask you a few questions about yourself, and see if *you're* right for Air Force. Joining the military is a big decision, a big step to take, and actually a lot of people want in, especially into the Air Force, because it's the best branch- but not everyone is fit for it. What do you say to me taking notes and filling out some papers while we talk?"

I nodded. "Okay."

"Alright then. Full name."

"Kimberly Sarah Presa."

"Age."

"Nineteen."

"Just graduated, right? Straight from high school? What school? Marshfield? Bend?" he asked, checking a box.

"Um, no. I didn't graduate from high school," I said.

He paused, looking up at me. "GED?"

I nodded.

He looked mildly disappointed. "We usually don't accept non high-school grads."

I deflated. "What? So I can't join?"

He sucked the side of his cheek and turned to his computer. "Well, just a minute… I think maybe we started letting in something like one or two of you a year, but I don't know all the details. Let me see."

I waited in suspense while he tapped through a few screens, grunted, and then turned back to me.

"I think we can accept a GED if they have a good ASVAB score. But it's got to be good. Have you ever taken a practice ASVAB?"

I shook my head, still upset. "I don't even know what an ASVAB is."

"Well, if you do join the Air Force, you will have to get used to our acronyms, and ASVAB is the first you'll come across- it stands for the Armed Forces Vocational Aptitude Battery. It's a test that potential new recruits for all branches take to see where their strengths and weaknesses lie. You can take a practice test here, in a little room I have in the back, and if all else goes well and you still want to join, you get sent to MEPS- another acronym, Military Entrance Processing Station- in Portland, where you take the real ASVAB. Does that make sense?"

"So you want me to take a test?"

"In a little bit. Let's finish filling out some information first. Address?"

I stared at him. "I don't have one."

He returned my stare. "You're shitting me."

"No."

"Where do you get mail?"

"I don't get mail anymore."

He sighed. "Where do you sleep?"

"In a tent or in my car. Sometimes with a friend. And hotels."

"You're homeless?"

"No!" I argued. "I just don't have an apartment or house."

"Where are your parents?"

I turned my face away. "My mom's passed, but my dad lives in a nice house in Brookings, which is about two hours away from here."

"Okay, why don't you stay with him?"

I played with the frayed edges of my coat, and answered, "Because it would make him unhappy."

The recruiter was silent for a moment, and began to tap the desk with his pen in evident frustration.

"How did you get here?"

"I drove. I have a car. My dad pays for it. He pays for my phone, too."

He shook his head in confusion. "Okay, well what's your phone number?"

I gave it to him, and after he copied it down, he said, "So he pays for your stuff but won't let you live with him?"

"I don't want to talk about it, please," I told him, "It's hard to explain."

"I can imagine," the recruiter said, looking at me. "Well, I need an address to put down, but I don't have to use it for anything that I know of. How about we use this recruiter's office for now? Is that okay?"

"That would be very nice, thank you."

"Done. Moving on. I need your social, and a copy of your GED."

I frowned. "I don't have those with me. I have my driver's license, though."

He sighed, exasperated. "You are going to be a handful, aren't you?" Then he sat up, stretched, and cracked his knuckles. "Alright, I'm up for the challenge. Where and when did you get your GED from?"

"In Brookings, Southwestern Oregon Community College- I got it a few months ago, I don't know the exact date. I do have the diploma somewhere in my dad's garage. He can send it…"

"How about I just give the college a call. They should be able to send me a copy. Just wait a few minutes."

And he called them, and in ten minutes he had a faxed copy of my GED in hand, as well as my social security number, which he re-wrote on a sticky note and handed over to me.

"Keep this safe, put it somewhere or better yet- memorize it and shred this thing. Everyone should know their social security number by heart, okay? You will be asked for it a lot in your lifetime."

"Thank you, I will memorize it."

"Alright, now- where were we? US citizen?"

"Yes."

"Any criminal charges, outstanding traffic tickets, anything like that?"

"No."

"Have you ever done drugs?"

"No."

"Do you drink alcohol?"

"Not really. I have before and didn't like it very much."

"Any hospitalizations?"

I paused, unsure of how to answer. "What do you mean?"

"Have you had surgeries or illnesses that have caused you to be hospitalized?"

I hesitated again, and decided to answer truthfully. "I haven't had any surgeries, but I have been an inpatient for a mental illness. It was in LA."

The recruiter leaned back in his chair, and eyed me calmly, judging. He evidently came to a decision and when he began to speak again his voice was measured and succinct. "That was my next question, don't jump ahead. This one only deals with *physical* illness. So, that answer was 'No'." He swiftly checked a box, then leaned forward, and looked me in the eyes. "Listen, alright? This next question I am going to ask deals with mental illnesses. It boils down to, Have you ever had a mental illness or suffered from severe anxiety and/or depression? And you have a choice. You can say 'Yes', or you can say 'No'. If you say 'Yes', I will check that box and will detail whatever mental illness you may have had. But I'm telling you right now, if that happens, there is a good chance you will not be joining the Air Force, even if you have a perfect ASVAB score. If you answer 'No', then I will check 'No', and we will carry on to the next question. I am laying these options before you openly, and honestly, because I think you are a good kid, and I think if you had a chance, you could make something of yourself. Do you agree?"

My eyes watered. "Yes."

He sat back. "So. Here we go. Have you ever had a mental illness or suffered from severe anxiety or depression?"

My brain was screaming, *Yes, yes, just look at me! I have bruises all over my face, my eyes are bloodshot, I'm a mess! No one after seeing me will be fooled by this stupid questionnaire!* But out loud, I replied calmly, "No."

"Okay then," he said, and checked the box. I took a deep breath.

After a few more questions, he escorted me into a tiny room, furnished only with a small desk and a computer. He bade me to sit.

"You will take the practice ASVAB here, and I'll send the results and your paperwork to headquarters in Portland," he said. "...and from there, we'll see what happens, okay?"

"Okay," I replied, watching him leave the room. What was I feeling? Fear? Excitement? Both? I turned to the computer screen, which was alight with a giant idiot-proof 'click here' button, and I took a deep breath. I could do this. If I could pass the stupid GED, I could pass the ASVAB.

After the test was over, I went back to the front room, and the recruiter was printing out my results. He sat down at his desk with the printouts, perused them for a moment, and then smiled.

"You did great," he said, congratulating me. "And I ran your social- you have no criminal record- not that I thought you were lying to me, but I had to check to make it official. Things are looking alright. I think, if you decide to continue, and barring any unforeseen circumstances, that we can get you a place in the Air Force within a few months."

My heart, which had jumped at his praise of my scores, fell upon hearing his last words. "Months?" I asked. "Why can't I can join now?"

He seemed to have expected this from me, and replied, "Don't you want to read over the job options, pamphlets, take some time talking things over with your dad, just to make sure? Plus, even if you were one-hundred percent positive, it would take time to get you a guaranteed job and get you on a flight to Portland MEPS. And then to secure you a place in basic training…"

"I'm sure!" I said, panicking, "I'm very sure that I want to join! Don't make me go, *please*! I don't care what job I have!"

"Look, Kimberly…I don't know what I can do besides send off your paperwork and test results to MEPS. This stuff takes time. It's a- well, it's a giant bureaucracy."

The tears that I had fought against started to fall, and I wiped them away fiercely. "Well, how long then?"

He thought about it. "Two, three months to get into MEPS? And I'm not sure how long until you'll be able to actually enter basic- it depends on a lot of things, like when your guaranteed job becomes available."

"I already told you, I don't care what job I have. I'll clean toilets if I have to. Please, is there any way I can get in sooner? Please?" I was begging, and I hated the sound of my voice as I said the words. It was not my proudest moment among many, many not proud moments.

We sat in silence as the seconds passed, neither of us looking each other in the face any longer. I knew I was pitiable and had nothing to offer, but I didn't want to give up. I feared going back to Brookings, where something could occur that would again change the direction of my life, and cause me to never join the Air Force. Eventually, the recruiter sighed, and said,

"Here, let me make a few phone calls. Don't get me wrong; I promise nothing," he said sternly, looking at me, "Come back in half an hour, and we should know by then if I can do anything for you."

I stood up and thanked him profusely. As I left I turned and saw him pick up his phone and start to dial, a serious and determined look on his face.

"Thank you," I whispered.

After a half-hour of impatient pacing back and forth outside of his office, I opened his door again, feeling more nervous than I had been when I had first entered, and I found him sitting at his desk with a self-satisfied smile on his face.

"Well, I have some news, and you can tell me how you feel about it. Tonight, instead of going back to your tent, you'll stay in a nice hotel here in Coos Bay, and tomorrow morning at six am you'll take a taxi to the airport here in town and fly to Portland MEPS for processing. All paid for by us, of course- that's what we do. I have all the instructions printed out right here," he patted a large packet on his desk.

I bowed my head, overcome, feeling as if the wind had been knocked out of me. "Thank you so much! Oh, my God!"

Grinning, he once again indicated the chair across from him. "You're very welcome. This is why I became a recruiter, after all."

I was truly speechless, so I just sat and stared at him stupidly, vibrating with excitement.

"Now, when you get there, you're going to undergo a lot more questioning and probing than what you went through here, okay? Just keep your answers the same, and there should be no problems. They're also going to do a physical, which everyone has to go through, so just go with the flow. Judging by your test ASVAB score, you shouldn't have any trouble with the real ASVAB, but here is a pamphlet with some website info that can help you study if you feel inclined. We will eventually need more paperwork from you, but for now, don't worry about it; just go relax for the night, and prepare yourself to fly tomorrow."

I pressed my hands over my mouth. "I am so grateful to you," I muttered through my fingers. "I don't know how to ever thank you. You don't know what this means to me."

His eyes were soft as he said, "You can repay me by doing well in the Air Force. Do that, and every bit of trouble, every favor that I pulled in, was worth it. Sound good?"

I removed my hands, and nodded, smiling through my tears. He handed me a sealed packet which he ordered me to not open, but to hand directly to MEPS when I arrived, and also printed directions which I would need to get there. I accepted it all gratefully, and left the office with a ridiculous wave and an extraordinary feeling of hope.

As I walked by the Army recruiter's office, I poked my head in the door. The recruiter looked up from his desk in surprise, and smiled when he saw me.

"Hi!" I said, nervous, but still happy. "Sorry; I can't join the Army because I just joined the Air Force."

"Aw, dang," smiled the recruiter good-naturedly, "Well, good luck to you, darlin'."

"Thank you!" I said, and swept out the door with a grin.

*

When I flew in to Portland, I had nothing with me but two shirts, an extra pair of pants, and the clothes on my back. I had left everything else behind, even my car, and I had no interest in reclaiming any of it because they were all pieces of a past I sorely wanted to forget. In my mind, the only way to forget painful memories was to build newer, happier recollections, and I was dead-set on doing that as a member of the US Air Force.

I walked into the Military Entrance Processing Station, or MEPS, with a nervous grimace on my face, lips closed tight. It was a large, low building built of white mortar, and was filled with men and women bustling about in uniform. I felt extremely safe there, for some reason; like if the world fell apart I'd be able to crawl out of the rubble unscathed. I walked directly up to the counter where a man in fatigues sat, typing abstractedly at a computer.

"Can I help you, Ma'am?" he asked, seeing me.

"Hi, I was sent from the Air Force recruiter's office in Coos Bay. He told me to hand this to someone at the front desk when I got here. Am I supposed to give this to you, or someone else?" I asked, holding up the sealed folder the recruiter had entrusted to me.

"I'll take it, Ma'am, thanks. I'll need a moment to look over everything, so if you'd like, feel free to take a seat in the waiting area, where the others are sitting. I will call you over when I'm done. Should be just a few minutes. There's snacks in the machines right around the corner if you get hungry, and the restrooms are back there as well."

"Thank you," I said, and went to sit down with the other recruits. I studied with open curiosity the other entrants to the US military. Everyone seemed so different from each other; it seemed incredible that we all were headed to the same place with similar goals. There were some who dressed like hipsters, cowboys, rap-stars, and even one guy that looked like he might have been a sumo wrestler at one point in his life. I couldn't help but grin. It didn't matter what I looked like, here; I felt like a fish that had finally found the stream it was meant to swim in.

Around us there were many offices with the doors constantly opening and closing, phones ringing, papers shuffling. People dressed in all sorts of uniforms were walking around, speaking in low tones; I recognized the Navy, Army, and Air Force uniforms, but there were a few I could not identify. There was one uniform I saw that looked like it had been designed to emulate cat-puke, and I wondered what natural or unnatural background it could have possibly been created to blend in with. I learned later that it was the Australian camouflage, and as I knew nothing about the Land Down Under, I kept my potentially embarrassing questions and comments to myself.

In front of the waiting area where I sat hung a large flat-screen television playing the film We Were Soldiers, which I thought to be a rather cliché choice. I had thought that people in service looked down on films about the military, much the way real doctors and nurses had made fun of the show ER (which I had learned while eaves-dropping on the nurses who used to burn my warts when I was little). But what did I know, really? I watched the movie with half an eye, keeping most of my attention on the man who was handling my papers. He had opened the parcel and was flipping through my information, entering data into his computer. He made one phone call, and then another. I wondered if he was calling the recruiter back in Coos Bay. When he hung up, the man looked up at me at called,

"Kimberly Presa."

I stood up immediately and walked to his counter. He tapped a few keys and turned to me.

"Okay, you need to take the ASVAB. The next one is in three hours, so you need to be in this room by one o'clock sharp and someone will call you into the room to take the test. It's all done on computer now, so you won't need any writing materials, though a pencil and a piece of scratch paper will be provided for you when you enter the room, and must be turned in to the proctor before you leave.

As you'll be staying next door in the hotel for the night, I'll be giving you the information you need to check in after the test has been taken. Tomorrow you will start the physical examination process, which pretty much takes all day; I have some papers here for you that describe what is included in that process, if you'd like to read it. We have a doctor here that's about one-hundred years old, that's been doing these same examinations since WWII, and he's pretty efficient, so though it's a long process he'll do his best to get you out of here as quick as he can."

"Okay," I said, ready for anything. He handed me a few sheets of paper containing information about the ASVAB, the hotel, and MEPS in general.

"These are for you to keep," he said. "You're free to go and come back when it's time to take the test, or you can wait here- it doesn't matter to us. We don't own you quite yet."

"Thank you," I said, laughing a little, and I went to sit down for a long wait. There was no reason for me to leave the MEPS building. I didn't know much about Portland; the few times I had visited the area had been brief and in the company of Sam, who knew more about the geography than I did. I didn't want to risk getting lost, so I settled in and tried to enjoy the movie, but for some reason Mel Gibson's face started to bother me, so I tried to take a nap instead.

An hour passed, and when We Were Soldiers ended another film took its place, although I no longer recall what it was. My mind had begun to wander. *By now, Sam has for sure received my phone message, and he's probably freaking out.* Like the coward I was, I had kept my phone turned off, fearing his intrusion on my plans. I didn't want anything to ruin the day, or deter me from moving forward from a place I viewed as purgatory. He would try to keep me there with him, selfishly, despite my illness and despite my wishes for a better future. Even though I knew what I was doing was right, my heart felt ill when I thought of him, because I did believe that he cared for me, and that I owed him for taking me in. I shook my head, trying to clear his face from my mind. That was the past now- he was the past. He would never leave that town, had said he wouldn't, and I needed more than anything to never set foot in that place again.

It was a few minutes before one o'clock, and my stomach felt like it had begun to consume itself. I was so hungry that I felt faint, but I refused to go find an ATM and pull cash out in order to use the snack machine. I'd just throw it up anyway, I thought bitterly. So I sat and waited, my stomach growling angrily.

One o'clock came, and a man in Army fatigues came towards the group of us who were sitting, and holding up a piece of paper, began to call out a list of names in alphabetical order, and instructed those he named to go into the room behind him and pick a computer, but not to touch anything.

"Presa, Kimberly," he called, and I stood up and went into the room.

I took an empty seat, and was surprised to find that the computers were sunk into the desks so that they were completely hidden from the neighboring desk's view. *Wow*, I thought, *they really nailed this anti-cheating thing.*

When everyone was seated, the man in fatigues cleared his throat. "I'm Sgt Walters, I'll be your tests administrator for your CAT-ASVAB. You shouldn't need anything from me, but if your computer has problems, raise your hand quietly and I'll come take a look. Now, a few things about the test: read all of the direction carefully, as well as the answers, before picking one, because once you submit an answer you may not go back. I'll repeat that: you *may not* go back. Do not attempt to leave any questions blank- this test won't allow you to- so guess if you need to. My advice to you is to go with your gut, because changing your answer again and again is never a good idea. Any questions before you all log in and begin?"

No one raised their hands.

"You will have three hours to complete the test, though most of you will finish earlier. When you finish, stand up, hand me your writing materials, exit the room and go back to the waiting area."

He roved around the room, checking our computers briefly, and then cleared his throat.

"To log in, who knows what they click? That's right; you click the 'Log In' button..."

He told on how enter the testing site, using our names and social security numbers, and with the beep of a timer, the assessment was underway.

I found the real test no more difficult than the practice one I had taken at the recruiter's office, though there were many more questions, some of which I found to be ridiculously easy, while others were far beyond my comprehension. For example, I did not know much about mechanical or electrical principles, which seemed to make up about a tenth part of the test, so I was forced to guess. After an hour and a half, much to the relief of my aching head, I was done, and I had used the scratch paper only for the math portion, which I felt I had blundered horribly on. I stood up and brought my papers to Sgt Walters, and then left the room.

I sat down in the same seat I had waited in before, and nodded in a half-slumber for another hour before my name was called by the same man behind the counter. When I stood before him, he pointed to a female in army fatigues.

"Sgt Dower will be taking you and a few other recruits over to the hotel to check you in," he said. "She'll also give you the information you need for tomorrow, and about getting a meal ticket. Go ahead and wait over there with her."

"Okay," I said. I grabbed my backpack and went to stand next to the sergeant, eyeing her. She was small, but seemed very solid, and her hair was pulled into a tight bun that looked almost painful. She also did not look friendly, so I remained quiet.

She led me and a group of ten others across the street to a large Embassy Suites by Hilton Hotel, and it was so beautiful I gaped like a simpleton. Though it was not as glamorous as the condo in Hawaii had been, it was the closest thing to luxury that I thought I would ever see again. The inside of the hotel was a wide open area, with all the rooms facing each other over an exquisitely outfitted atrium. Everywhere I looked was pleasant greenery and cascading fountains, and I could almost imagine that I had gone back in time only to find myself promenading through a Grecian garden. Despite the fact I was joining the military, I felt spoiled, and I couldn't stop smiling.

We followed Sgt Dower up to the front desk, and she as passed out room keys, she said, "Most of your are shipping out tomorrow, but the rules for everyone are the same; no one but you and your assigned room mate are allowed in your room. If you're married, or have kids, I'm sorry but they're not allowed up there. Everyone needs to be in their rooms by ten o'clock, and may not leave again- even if you are not shipping out tomorrow. It makes it easier to keep track of people."

One tall boy with dreadlocks raised his hand, and asked, "Ma'am, I'm supposed to meet my family for dinner at seven. Will they be able to ask for me at the front desk?"

Sgt Dower shook her head. "I'm sorry, someone should have told you before, or maybe you could have read the pamphlet- but you are not to leave this hotel until tomorrow. You can call your family and tell them that you'll see them tomorrow when you swear in at MEPS."

The tall boy looked nonplussed, but remained silent.

The sergeant turned back to the rest of us. "I will be handing out your meal tickets for dinner, which you will eat down here in the restaurant. And don't worry; they have great food. Dinner is served from six o'clock until nine, so you have plenty of time to eat before curfew. You have free run of the hotel; they have a gym and a swimming pool you can use that are pretty nice. Just use your room key card to access those areas, and seriously- don't lose your damn key cards, because I don't have time for that nonsense."

We all nodded, and there were a few 'Yes, Ma'ams' among us, and she continued: "Everyone will receive a wake up call at four am. When you're ready, come downstairs, *bringing all of your items*, and grab something to eat; there'll be a buffet ready for you. Around five thirty we'll head over to MEPS where some of you will prepare to swear in and the rest of you will start your physicals.

One more thing; while you are here, even though none of you are sworn in yet, you are representing the United States Military. Do *not* act like idiots. The hotel is nice enough to let us use their facilities, so let's treat them with respect so we can *keep* using them. You are all adults, so I highly suggest you act like it. Take care of your belongings. Take care of each other. I also suggest that you not imbibe in alcohol or try to get lucky, because now is not the time for a party. Now is the time to buckle down and work. Got it?"

This time we all replied, "Yes, Ma'am."

"Alright, come here and get your meal tickets. They have information on them, a lot of which I just said. I'm also giving you each my personal card in case you have any questions and need to call me. But here's a word of advice- don't call me unless it's an emergency. I am *not* a babysitter."

When we each had our tickets and her card, Sgt Dower turned and pointed to a room. "Behind that door is sort of a lounge for you guys that we've set up. Movies will be on, there are board games- I think- and you can ask questions to the NCO on duty there. NCO- that's non-commissioned officer to you unenlightened ones.

But he's not your baby-sitter either, okay? Alright, then. See you guys tomorrow." And she turned and left the hotel.

Left to our own devices, the group of us looked at each other for a moment, and then dispersed to go put our luggage into our rooms. A few people had started chatting and laughing boisterously, commenting on how ridiculous it was that they couldn't leave the hotel and wasn't Sgt Dower *fine*? I frowned. *I suppose boys are boys everywhere,* I thought.

The rest of the night passed quickly. I went up to my room after we were released to put my backpack on my bed, and found that I was sharing a room with a small, thin girl who had already collapsed for the night, and so I left her to her sleep in peace and went downstairs to the lounge Sgt Dower had mentioned. There were about twenty people sitting in rows of chairs facing a television, but no one was watching whatever was on- they were all laughing and talking boisterously. I quickly decided that it was too crowded and loud for me, and I left to go sit in the restaurant and get something light to eat.

I used my meal ticket to purchase a salad, and as I hadn't eaten since the day before I ate the entire thing, croutons and all. Afterwards, I felt bloated and disgusting, and wanted nothing more than to throw up, but I didn't know where I could go to do it, because as far as I had seen there was no private place to escape to. I shivered. This was what I was signing up for. I would have no more privacy to practice my disgusting rituals, and maybe that was for the best- even if it felt a little bit like dying.

I went back to my room, and after an indulgent shower that lasted about half an hour, I laid in bed and began to re-read, for the millionth time, Alice Through the Looking Glass, trying to keep my mind blank except for the sentences in front of me.

I remind myself of something, I thought, as I flipped through the dog-eared pages of the heavy novel, scanning the familiar words. Suddenly it hit me- everything fit; the lying, the guilt, the gorging- I was the Walrus. I laughed to myself quietly, bitterly. *'Of shoes, and ships, and sealing wax; of cabbages, and kings. And why the sea is boiling hot, and whether pigs have wings.'* Surely, if I had a spirit animal, the Walrus was it; he who held a handkerchief in front of his meal so no one could see how many oysters he consumed; he, who betrayed his friends; he, the least likable character of them all.

I wish I were Alice, I thought, rolling to my side and sliding the implicating book underneath my pillow. *I'd wake up and realize that all this has just been a strange, horrible dream...*

I slowly shut my eyes, laying the book aside. I was worried that my brain would be too full of bulimia, of the Walrus and the Carpenter, or whatever was coming next to allow me to fall asleep, but before I realized it the phone was ringing: it was the four am wake up call. I had slept the night through and hadn't dreamed a single dream.

*

I was dressed and downstairs by four-twenty, and the breakfast bar was nearly deserted. An NCO sat at one of the large, empty tables that been set up for the recruits, and after he took a sip of his coffee, he glanced at me and sleepily muttered,

"G'morning."

"Good morning," I replied, looking over the huge quantities of food that been laid out for our consumption.

On the table there was every type of fruit, bread, and sweet I could imagine, all laid out in a delicious juxtaposition with flowers interspersing each course. My mouth began to water. *If this was binge food*, I thought, trying to retain my self control, *I would destroy the living shit out this table.*

As it was, though, I got a plate, and grabbed two slices of pineapple and a scoop of cottage cheese, and placed it on a table, then went and poured myself some coffee and orange juice. The NCO was watching me with half an eye, and when I sat down, he asked, "You know this is free, right?"

I smiled self consciously. "Yeah, I'm just on a diet, is all." *And if I eat more than this I will barf all over the place, and probably on you*, I added inwardly.

"It doesn't look like you need to be on a diet," the man said.

I shrugged, not feeling the need to respond to him, cut up my pineapple, and took a bite.

Time passed and more people gathered to eat. I was shocked at the amount of food some of the other recruits ate. I specifically recall one young man stacked his plate until it resembled a small mountain, devoured it in what must have been less than a minute, and then went back for seconds and thirds. I was no stranger to large amounts of food, but the thought of keeping it all inside… the thought made me queasy, and I started to feel that perhaps the pineapple I had eaten might have been a bit too much for me, after all.

At five thirty we were walked back to MEPS, and asked to sit in the same waiting area where I had sat the previous day, and there I remained for a long time, waiting for something to happen. (I didn't know it then, but that was my first introduction to that famous military past-time, the 'hurry-up-and-wait').

Around seven-thirty, I and many other recruits were taken to the medical section of the building and underwent many physical examinations, including blood tests, eye tests, and hearing tests. Once we were even asked to strip to our waist so that a tiny, elderly man could check our spinal cords for abnormalities. Lastly, we women were sent to a separate room from the men and told to disrobe to our undergarments and perform strange physical maneuvers, including the duck-walk, so that doctors could discern if our joints were working properly.

After all tests were complete, we were ushered to the waiting area once again, and lunch was given to us- a prepackaged affair such as you might give to an elementary school student, except larger. I ate only the apple and a few potato chips, finding myself not brave enough to consume the cookies, candy, or large sub sandwich. After lunch I was called into one of the back offices, and lifting my backpack to my shoulder, I followed a man into the room and then took a seat in front of a desk with a dignified woman sitting behind it. She had an insignia on her collar that I had never seen before, and I examined it curiously.

"Hi, Miss Presa, I'm Captain Averly," said the woman. "This is Sgt Villenueva, and we'll be working with you on your job selection." She indicated the man in fatigues who had led me into her office.

My heart leapt, and I waited.

"Based on your ASVAB score…" she said, looking at a sheet of paper, "You scored most highly in the general knowledge area with a ninety four percent, second in the electrical with an eighty-three percent."

I was surprised at that, since I knew next to nothing about electricity, except that it shocked you.

"Your physical came back just about perfect. No past hospitalizations, or breaks- your dental is great- about as clean as you can ask for." She flipped to a new sheet of paper. "Your weight is a little low- you're actually *at* out minimum weight for someone your height joining the Air Force, but it's passable. Nothing to worry about. Hmm... everything else looks good. No criminal record, clean fingerprints. No debt. How about we look at a few jobs that I think might interest you?"

I nodded eagerly. For the next fifteen minutes we went through a packet that she provided, and discussed many different options which dealt specifically with recruits who scored highest in general knowledge. The Captain seemed to think I should go in for Intelligence, as she seemed impressed with my scores and my maturity.

"You don't have to decide this now," she said, circling a few job descriptions and highlighting them, "You can go home, talk to your family, talk to your recruiter- take this packet, of course- and then let your recruiter know what works for you, and then he'll get in touch with us. When that happens, you will be entered into the delayed entry program, or DEP... what's wrong?"

At her words, my face had fallen. Delayed entry program- *go home?* Go to *what* home, exactly? Why did they keep trying to send me away as a civilian when all I wanted was to sign the dotted line and march off into the sunset?

"I don't need to ask anyone else," I said, controlling my voice, "I would like to join now. Please."

The Captain stared at me. "These jobs are not available right now. There is a wait-list, and when you choose one and are accepted, you will be put on that wait-list, and then when the time comes we'll fly you back here..."

"Then give me a different job!" I said, unable to bear it any longer. My eyes started to glisten. Why was I always crying? "I have no place to go. Please, I don't care what job I have, I'll do anything."

She exchanged a look with the sergeant, and then said, "You could come in 'open general', but even then it could take a few weeks to find you a place."

My tears started to flow freely. "I'm begging you. I really have nowhere to go. Please don't send me back."

"What did you mean, you have nowhere to go?"

"I've been living in a tent in southern Oregon. The only things I own are the shirts and pants I'm wearing and one change of clothes in my backpack."

"Where are your parents?"

"My mom died a few years ago, and my dad is remarried. I can't live with him."

The Captain's eyes softened. "Well, shit. I can't send you back to live in a tent." She turned to Villanueva. "I'll be back in a minute." And she left the room.

I waited with the sergeant for about half an hour, looking over the various jobs. I tried my best not to think of what would happen if they sent me back to Brookings; it was too horrible for me to imagine.

When Captain Averly came back, she sat behind her desk, and locked her powerful eyes with my weak ones.

"I found you a job," she said succinctly, "You're shipping out tomorrow."

Thank God! My eyes started to water, but I refused to let the tears fall. "Thank you. Thank you so much for doing that."

She smiled, taking the pamphlet full of the job descriptions, and circled one. "Here's what I found. Tell me what you think."

I wiped my eyes, and read, 'Maintenance Management Analysis.'

"As far as coming in open general, and so quickly, it was either this or Security Forces. I thought this would be better, because I believe it to be a better use of your knowledge. It is somewhat similar to the Intel job we were looking at, but instead of Secret Squirrel stuff, it deals with the maintenance of aircraft."

"I'll do it!" I said immediately, "It sounds very interesting- does that say, 'statistics?'- I'm so happy. Thank you."

"You will have to stay here again tonight, so you'll be going back to the hotel. It will be the same deal as last night, except tomorrow when you come in you'll only undergo a drug test, and then swear into the armed forces, and sign a lot- A LOT- of paperwork. Afterwards, you'll be shuttled to the airport with other new members of the Air Force, and you will all fly to basic training together. Our basic training is in San Antonio, Texas. You will briefed again tomorrow with more details, but really, that's about it."

My head was swimming; I felt like I was drunk. The Captain stood up and extended her hand. "Good luck to you, Miss Presa."

I stood up, and shook her hand. I was so touched by the kindness of this woman, this stranger, and I was frustrated that I didn't know how to properly express it. I owed so much to strangers- to Anne, to the recruiter in Coos Bay, to this woman- without them, where would I be? *People*, I thought, *are not all bad. Some are very, very good.*

"I'll never forget this," I said.

"This is why I'm here," she said, almost echoing the words my recruiter had spoken two days before. "You're going to do great. I wish you all the best."

I nodded, thankful beyond words, and left to go back to the waiting area, where many people were already gathering together to go to the hotel. How would they know that I was going to spend another night ~~at the hotel~~? Was I supposed to tell someone? As I contemplated what to do, I saw Sgt Villanueva hurry out the room from which I had just come, and hand the sergeant in charge ~~of the recruits~~ a sheet of paper. The sergeant nodded, and called out,

"Kimberly Presa, grab your stuff."

Relieved, I came forward, and as Sgt Villanueva walked away, he turned and winked at me, and I beamed at him in reply. Everything was going to be okay.

Basic

(21)

    Nestled amongst the sobs and moans of misery of others, I smiled.

    What was there to be miserable about? I had a roof over my head. I was warm, fed and generally more looked-after than I had been in years. The screaming and push-ups weren't so bad, really. They were a bit of a joke, actually, which is something I had to work on- giggling while the training instructors, or TI's, were trying to be serious. But it was hard for me to take them at face value. They couldn't hurt me, after all. And oh, how funny it all was, how much they frightened the other girls! It almost seemed like there was a large age gap between me and the rest of my flight, though I was only maybe a year older than the average.

    It was the second night of the rigorous and demanding basic training to become a full-fledged member of the United States Air Force, and I was as happy as an oyster.

It had been a long day which started with the ~~playing~~ sounding of Reveille, and then didn't stop for fourteen hours full of yelling, physical exertion, and tears, until Retreat was played. My relatively small flight (which was what they called the gaggle of girls I ate, showered and suffered with) was made up of about thirty girls, and I don't think I ever knew all of their names. We were so busy all of the time that there was no room to socialize, except for a quick minute in the showers, or a few stolen moments after lights out. We slept in a long room made up of beds arranged perpendicularly like a WW2 hospital ward. Along the wall there were lockers, not for personal belongings, but for our military clothing and minutiae. We weren't allowed personal anything, which was fine with me, since I didn't have any, though some girls had cried over the fact they couldn't have their makeup or family photos with them.

    I loved working hard during the day, and then finding my pillow the most beautiful thing in the world when it came time to lay my head on it. I didn't mind the tough mattress, or rough blankets that so many of the other girls complained about- all I could think of was how different I felt inside, how peaceful. I couldn't recall a time when I felt such weightlessness upon me. I felt no sense of failure, or disappointment- only eagerness and joy. I could make something of myself here. I could pave my own way in the world now, without being a liability to anyone.

Every morning was a revelation to me in how strong I could become. I was always the first out of bed when the TI came in the room; the first to be dressed; the first to make my bed; the first to help others when they needed it. We were told at every moment what it was that we were supposed to do, but it was solely up to our own strength and determination if we were successful or not.

Not that the entirety of my basic training experience was all sunshine and rabbits. The thing I found the most difficult about those two months had nothing to do with the drills, the technical instructors, or the constant mind-games; it was the other women in my flight. I had never been in such close quarters with other females before, and here I was forced to sleep, shower, exercise, and eat with them, twenty-four hours a day, seven days a week. I found some of them to be very kind, but others were vicious, and seemed to live by the motto 'every woman for herself'. Against women like that, I felt like I had no defense. If I was ever brought to tears, it was only after I had gotten into a fight with someone I had viewed as a comrade, a sister.

This peculiar dynamic in female flights was commented upon by my TI one day, when he found me crying alone on fire-guard duty.

"What's the matter, Trainee Presa?" he asked.

I stood to attention immediately, and sniffling, said, "Trainee Presa reports as ordered. N-nothing Sir."

He raised his eyebrow almost comically. "Well, something's wrong. This is the first time I've seen you cry."

"Trainee Presa reports as ordered. I just… I don't have a problem with the yelling, or the pushups, or anything you or the other TIs do. But when the other females in this flight attack each other, and refuse to work together, I don't know what it is- it *destroys* me."

He watched me for a moment as I sniffled pathetically, my back still as straight as a ruler, and then he asked me to step into his office. I was nervous. TI's didn't act like that; they hollered, or they told you to get on your face until you threw up, and then told you clean up your mess with a soft bristle toothbrush. But they were never *nice*. But here was my TI, with his ass-hole switch apparently switched to the 'off' position, inviting me to take a seat in his office. I complied.

"Trainee Presa reports as…"

"Relax." He said, indicating a seat. I sat.

"You know, you're one of the brightest airmen in the flight. You have a lot of potential," he said. "You came in here, and you seemed to realize right away that all this was just a big game. Because that's what it is. I'm not really this guy. Do you think I act like this at home with my wife and kids? Of course not. I'd be sent to social services."

I nodded, unsure if I should say something.

"I've always said how difficult it is to be a TI for a female flight, because of how different they are than men in large groups. With male flights, they tend to start out a complete mess, and then gradually- after a ton of errors and a few bloody noses, they figure things out and work alright as a team. Female flights, on the other hand," he said, gazing out into our spotless dorm room, "They tend to start out great, as far as teamwork goes. They ban together and accomplish a lot… for the first few weeks. And then things start to fall a part. There tends to be a lot of in-fighting, and jealousy. Things can get better at the very end, but very often, they don't. So, anyway, I guess what I'm saying is; continue not to play the game. Don't get caught up in everyone's little pettiness, or whatever it is they're doing that upsets you. You do your best, be a good wingman on your own account, and when you get out of here you will probably never see any of these women ever again."

My tears had dried themselves as he spoke, and I looked at him with gratitude. He had said exactly what I needed to hear. I had gotten caught up in this little world, had forgotten that the whole thing was a farce. True, I had always remembered that the TIs were putting on a show, but when it came to the behaviors of my flight I had assumed that that, at least, was real. In what reality, however, would I be forced to work in conditions like these, where I was constantly being hollered at for a spec on my uniform with thirty other women straining beside me, and all of us unable to speak to friends or family for weeks? Everyone was stressed and wasn't acting how they normally would. Or, even if they honestly had bad characters, I would never usually associate with them outside of basic training.

"Thank you, Sir," I said.

"You're welcome. Now, get out of here, I'm going to tear apart the dorm room and pretend to go ape-shit."

I smiled at the mental image of him dancing around the dorm, ripping apart our well-made beds. "Yes, Sir," I said, and performing an about-face, left him alone.

Every day after that in basic training I felt was better than the last. I believed nothing could faze me. Even when a big, scary ex-Marine TI came and made me perform pushups until I felt ill, I still carried a smile in my heart. It was a game. I was being paid. I was making a life for myself. It was through these means that I could stand out and become a genuine human being.

Towards the middle of Basic, we were able to make phone calls to friends and family at designated times, and send letters. I puzzled for a while over who I should send my first letter to, but I finally settled on my step-sister, Jamie. I wanted her to know that I was sorry for breaking her trust and that I was truly thankful for her opening her home to me. I also promised her, at the end of the letter, that I had not slept with Will despite what everyone believed, but that I understood if she didn't believe me. I told her I cared for her, and that I wished her well. Though she never wrote back, I felt better after writing her, like I was closing a chapter of my life, and moving on; which made me recall other parts of my life that still stood open, unhealed, and needing attention.

The only phone call I ever made from basic training was to Sam, and when he realized it was me on the phone he swung between fits of rage and fits of joy. He informed me that he had gotten an apartment since I left, and a new job at a furniture warehouse; he had gotten his life together, he insisted. He wanted me to come back to him, or let him come be with me, somehow. *You're my entire life*, he pleaded. With misty eyes, I told him that is wasn't even possible anymore now that I was in the Air Force; that we were moving in two different directions and that I didn't see a future for us anymore. When my time on the phone was running out, he asked desperately when I was graduating from basic training, and when I gave him the date he declared that he would be there to support me. I hung up the phone, unsure of how I felt about that. I had invited my dad to my graduation as well by sending him an invite in the mail, but I knew he wasn't coming; he had other things on his mind, like his new wife, and the last thing he needed to focus on was his wayward daughter. I supposed that having Sam come to my graduation might be a good way to say goodbye to him for good, for I knew, that no matter what happened, I was never going back to Oregon as long as I lived.

*

Graduation day came swiftly, and my flight and I, by then a well-oiled machine, became very emotional about leaving the place where we had been molded into something grander than just ourselves. We each truly felt, and believed, that we were an irreplaceable member of a special, elite team called the US Air Force, and when we marched in the graduation parade that day, in front of the crowd full of our friends and family, our hearts were full to the point of bursting, and many shed tears openly.

For the parade, our flight had been chosen to carry the state flags, and we practiced for hours each day, learning how to carry the long rods and to turn gracefully while holding them aloft. When the time came to actually fit us with the flags, I had to laugh to myself, because the flag in front of me was none other than the Oregon state flag. As we marched, the image of a golden beaver waved in my vision, and I had a hard time keeping my military poise, especially when the flag, caught in the thralls of the wind, whipped out at me suddenly and took off my cap, dropping it to the green grass at my feet. I panicked for a moment, but then remembered that no matter what, it was my duty to maintain my bearing and pretend that nothing had happened; but inside I was seething. *You stupid goddamned beaver*, I raged. *I'm going to set you on fire the first chance I get.*

After the parade and ceremony was over, I searched the marching ground, and though I didn't find my own hat, I found plenty of lost and found ones to choose from. Placing a random cap on my head, I turned and began to search for Sam, who had sent me a letter assuring me that he had arranged to be there. I hardly needed to look, because Sam came quickly through the crowd, smiling at me.

"I saw you right away," he said, a bit breathlessly, "You did amazing out there. You look great. You cut your hair… it's nice."

I smiled back at him. "I'm glad you're here, Sam. Thank you for coming. How was your flight, and getting here? Was everything okay?"

"Yeah, I mean, it was expensive, but… it was alright. I got a hotel room and I rented a car. When can we get out of here?" he asked a bit nervously, looking around.

I grinned at his discomfiture. The base was a little imposing if you weren't used to it. "We can leave right now, if you want. I'm on leave until tomorrow noon, so I need to be back here a little before then. Do you have any plans, or something you want to do?"

Sam moved forward as if he wanted to wrap his arms around me, but I stepped back. "I'm in uniform," I warned him, "No public displays of affection."

He frowned. "That's ridiculous."

"It's just the way it is, Sam."

"Then let's get the hell out of here. I want to touch you. I haven't touched you in months; I miss you, Kim," he said, looking into my eyes passionately.

"I look forward to relaxing a bit," I said, avoiding his gaze, "It's been a very tough few weeks, and I'm very tired. Where did you park?"

We walked in silence to the vehicle he had rented, a silver Jeep Liberty, and when we got inside he sat there for a moment, his hands on the wheel.

"Kim," he said finally, his eyes focused on his hands, "Do you love me?"

"I will always care about you," I answered hesitantly. "You're the only friend I've had for years; you've always been there for me, and now you're the only one who cared enough to make it all the way to Texas to see me graduate, even though you were against me coming here to begin with. I-I can't say that I'm in love with you, though, in that way, Sam. We've been through too much. I can't feel the same way that I used to."

"I was worried you might say that," he said glumly. "But I came out here because I wanted to prove to you that I'm a changed man. I'm going to keep this job I have; I'm done relying on you and your dad for money. And I'm going to appreciate you more."

I shook my head. "That has nothing to do with how I feel; not really. We've just reached a point where we have gotten all we can from each other. I needed to get out of Oregon, and you want to stay."

Sam was silent. "Can we talk about this later? I mean, no matter what, I want to show you a good time; I spent a lot of money coming here, and I want to take you to dinner, and then to Six Flags, and just have some fun, you know? Can we do that, please?"

"I would like that... and thank you."

"Okay then," he said, starting the Jeep's engine, "Let's go. I have everything mapped out. First, we go eat. Then, we go to Six Flags; unless you'd like to go change first?"

"I need to stay in my Blue's," I said, "It's the rule for new graduates. Sorry."

He looked downcast at this. "Well, let's go, anyway."

Sam and I avoided talking about anything serious for the rest of the day, and despite the heavy subject that hung over us, we ended up having a nice time at dinner and at Six Flags. I told him all about my experiences at basic training, and though I could tell he felt left out, I couldn't stop myself; it was all I had known day and night for the last two months. He told me about his new job at the furniture warehouse, and I expressed my happiness for him, and that I hoped he continued to like it and stick with it, as it sounded like it paid well and that they treated him nicely.

It was night, and Sam and I drove to the hotel room he had rented. I was very tired by then- having been up since five in the morning- and so when he opened the door I was rubbing my eyes and thus missed the initial romantic effect he had tried to produce by revealing a bed covered in rose petals, and lamps shaded with red cloths to turn the light inside rosy and warm. Electric candles were scattered about, their fake little fires wavering gently against the shadows. My heart dropped into my stomach, and I turned to Sam to beg him not to do whatever it was he was going to do, but he commanded me to sit down on the bed, and let him talk. With deep misgivings, I complied.

Reaching into a nightstand, he pulled out a small black box, and then turned to me. My heart was pounding. Looking into my eyes, he dropped to one knee, and opened the box, revealing a golden ring scattered with tiny green jewels. It was beautiful; I was speechless.

"Kim," he said, taking my hand in his, "We haven't always been the best to each other, but we have been through everything, *everything*, side by side. I love you more than life itself, and when I try to imagine living without you, I realize that I simply *can't*. You are my best friend, and I want to grow old with you. Kimberly Presa, will you marry me?"

Moisture came to my eyes. What was I to do? I didn't want to marry him; I knew that positively, even affected as I was by the sweetness of his speech, and the beauty of the ring he had chosen for me. I bit my lip and held his hand tightly.

"Sam," I said, "I can't marry you. I'm sorry. I don't know what's going on in my life right now, and we just don't fit together anymore. Don't you feel it? If I hadn't left Oregon, we would be in the same rut we were in before. It's only because I left that you got a new job, and are making these changes, and want to marry me. This, all this-" I indicated the room, "is because you don't want to break up with your girlfriend, because it's hard. But in this case, it's the right thing to do."

He stood up and ran his fingers through his hair. "Kim, that's not true. I want to marry you because I love you. I'm changing because I realized what a little kid I was being. How can I prove that to you? What do I need to do to not lose you?"

I looked at him sadly from the edge of the bed, and whispered, "It's not losing me, really. You haven't lost anything. We just grew apart, the way young people do sometime."

He crossed his arms, and for a moment I thought he was going to yell at me, and I braced myself for it; but in the end, he took a deep breath and sat down on the bed next to me.

"Listen," he said, "I want you to keep the ring, because I love you, and maybe someday I can prove to you that what I feel is real, and not something that just came about because you decided to leave all of a sudden. Can you do that for me? Can you hang on to the ring?"

I hesitated. "I don't think its right…"

"Just take the ring, Kim!" he demanded, his voice going up an octave.

"Okay, I'll keep it. But when you want it back, let me know, and I'll send it to you," I said, taking the box from him, and setting it on the nightstand. Sam never did ask for it back.

We sat together for a moment, and then I stood up, and glanced around the room.

"I really think this is the most romantic thing you have ever done," I told him softly. "And I want you to know that I appreciate it with all of my heart, just like I appreciate you coming to see me. Even though things are the way they are between us, you have still been a very good friend to me, Sam. So thank you."

He looked away from me, not answering. After a large, heavy silence, I told him I was going to shower and get ready for bed. When I came back out, the rose petals were gone, the lights were out, and he was under the blankets, apparently asleep. I climbed into bed next to him, and watched his outline for a few moments in the dark, thinking to myself, *this will be the last time I ever lay in the same bed as Sam, after nearly four years together. Good-bye, Sam.* I sighed, turned my back to him, and fell fast asleep.

The next morning, Sam drove me back to the base, and while we were still in the car, we gave each other one last, lingering hug, and a final kiss good-bye,

"You know, I can send you some of your things that I still have, when you settle wherever it is you're settling. I'll miss you, Kim," he said, trying to hold back tears.

"I'll miss you too," I replied, giving his hand a squeeze. "I'll call you when I figure out where I'm going, and let you know how things are. Take care of yourself."

I slid out of the Jeep and shut the door behind me. As I walked into the processing building which would direct me to the next leg of my journey, I turned to wave to him, but he was gone.

Prue
(22)

    I hadn't thought Texas could get any uglier than the base in San Antonio, but Shepphard AFB proved me wrong. It was, to my west-coast accustomed eye, utterly dead. What grass there was, was short and yellow, and the few bushes which lined the roads were scraggly and unkempt. There were a couple dozen trees, but they were all short and sparse, and were absolutely covered in bird droppings, since the base had an infestation of starlings and grackles. The buildings were mostly uniform and grey, like the sky, except for a few buildings off in the distance that appeared to be built of red brick, most likely left over from WWII.

I glanced around the open area where I stood with my fellow Airmen. It was a large space, most likely a drill field, and at one side stood the US and Air Force flags. We were all freshly arrived on base, dressed in our battle dress uniforms, or BDUs, hurrying-up-and-waiting for something to happen; some spoke together in low tones while others stood alone, like me, contemplating their surroundings quietly. I didn't recognize anyone, but then again, I hadn't expected to; it would have been strange if someone from my basic training flight had the same career field I did. But this was my new unit, now, and this was where we were to remain the next few months, learning our military trade. We had all survived basic, only to come here, and whereas technical school was supposed to be more lax than the rigid, tense atmosphere we had come from, we were still unsure what to expect. Our duffle bags other luggage were heaped into piles on one side of the court where we stood, and I did not look forward to sorting through the massive pile to find my own.

Suddenly, a strong, deep voice broke the stillness:

"Squadron! Atten-TION! Present, ARMS!"

The groups quickly broke up, came to attention, and saluted in the direction of the flags. Towards the open area, there walked a pretty, petite Asian woman bearing lieutenant rank. Some of the boys around me snickered under their breath as she took a place near the flags.

"Or-DER, ARMS!"

As one animal, we dropped our salute, and the lieutenant lifted her small face in the air so that her voice could carry over the crowd.

"At ease," she called. We relaxed our stances.

"Welcome to Sheppard!" she said, pacing, her eyes scouring over us, "And welcome to the 364th Maintenance Training Squadron!" Applause.

"Things will be different here than at Basic- you may feel like the rules are more relaxed- but don't get complacent. I say it again, DO NOT GET COMPLACENT. Learning a new job is challenging and you each have a duty to learn it quick, learn it right, and aptly apply what you learn. Wherever you go in the Air Force, remember that the Core Values are always the same."

She continued pacing in front of the flags, eyeing us all as if we were mice and she a hungry hawk. I watched her, entranced. "I'm sure all of you know the Values: Integrity First. Service before self. Excellence in all we do. But how many of us apply them, every day of our lives? These values are not something we learn about cursorily in basic training so we can brain dump them once we get to our first duty station. What is integrity to you? What does it mean put service before self? How about striving for excellence in everything that you do? What do these things mean to you? The next few days, as you are adjusting to the many changes you will experience here, I want you to think about these questions, and find how you can apply the Values to your life here at Sheppard.

I don't want to make this a long speech, but I do want to impart to you how important it is you all act like the professionals you are while you are here. Your MTL's and teachers are not your babysitters- they are here for your professional development. Make the most of them.

I'd like to finish up with reciting the Code of Conduct. You should all have this memorized from Basic Training. If you have already forgotten it, I suggest you re-learn it, immediately."

The lieutenant stopped in the center of the flags, and began to recite the Code- and a dull roar of voices echoed hers:

"I am an American, fighting in the forces which guard my country and our way of life. I am prepared to give my life in their defense.

I will never surrender of my own free will. If in command, I will never surrender the members of my command while they still have the means to resist.

If I am captured I will continue to resist by all means available. I will make every effort to escape and aid others to escape. I will accept neither parole nor special favors from the enemy.

If I become a prisoner of war, I will keep faith with my fellow prisoners. I will give no information or take part in any action which might be harmful to my comrades. If I am senior, I will take command. If not, I will obey the lawful orders of those appointed over me and will back them up in every way.

When questioned, should I become a prisoner of war, I am required to give name, rank, service number and date of birth. I will evade answering further questions to the utmost of my ability. I will make no oral or written statements disloyal to my country and its allies or harmful to their cause.

I will never forget that I am an American, fighting for freedom, responsible for my actions, and dedicated to the principles which made my country free. I will trust in my God and in the United States of America."

As the voices of the crowd faded away the lieutenant turned to go, and a voice from an invisible throat called out,

"Present, ARMS!"

At attention again, we saluted; this time, no one sniggered.

"Order, ARMS!"

As the Lieutenant exited, she was replaced by a slightly overweight, frumpy middle aged man who looked like he would rather be fishing. My trained eye crawled reproachfully over his uniform, which appeared to be wrinkled and stained. *Is he really a MSgt?* Things really were different at tech school. He cleared his throat a few times, and called out in a deep, bored-sounding voice,

"As the Lieutenant said, welcome to Sheppard. We're happy to have you. Now, let's get this mess started. Each of you will be called by name and sorted into groups- group alpha, bravo, etc. As your name is called, head to the group you belong to and listen to the instructions of your respective Military Training Leader, otherwise known as an MTL. Do this in absolutely silence, and move quickly, and no funny business. We have a lot to do today."

And so we were sorted, and each group collected its baggage and marched to the buildings where they would be living for the next couple of months. The building that my group was led to happened to be one of the newer ones, conveniently placed a few blocks away from the chow hall. I was pleased that I did not have to live in one of the older brick buildings, which looked like they might have rats in them.

The males of our dorm were to reside in the three above floors, while the females were situated in a single hallway on the bottom floor, locked with a secure key-card entry. The rooms themselves were nice, like college dorms- and amazingly, perhaps because we were females and there weren't many of us, we only had to share with one other person. Each room had a desk, two beds, two closets, and a shower.

Every morning began as everything had in my Air Force career thus far, with a march. While it was still dark outside, my fellow Analysts and I marched to the flight line with the rest of the maintenance squadron, and then turned off early at a large hanger while the rest went further on down the line. Inside were classrooms, one room assigned for each 'block', the blocks being the level of learning you were designated. As the new Analysts, we were told to enter 'block one' and take a seat. There were four of us, two females including myself, and two males. It felt strange being in a classroom for the first time in five years. I looked around at the students who were to be my classmates for the next few months. They all seemed to be about my age; all were slim and wiry from basic training, and the males had barely any visible hair on their heads. I caught one of the males' eye, and I gave him a small smile, but he quickly turned away. Frowning, and feeling a little out of place, I faced towards the front of the class, and we continued to sit together in silence.

An instructor came in shortly and introduced himself as SSgt Ksanochka, and without much preamble got down to the business of educating us on documentary side of aircraft maintenance. It was incredibly tedious, and I had to fight hard to keep myself awake; I knew nothing about jets and was confused how I could be expected to learn the acronyms and terms regarding their upkeep; my brain after a few minutes started to feel fuzzy and dim, and time passed slowly.

About mid-morning, the door opened and a sandy-haired female Airman entered, approached the instructor, and with a pouted lower lip, handed him a slip of paper. She was fair skinned with freckles, slender, and tall, with a pretty face.

"Here I am," she said, sighing dramatically, "Dang test was nothing like the flippin' study material. You're so mean, Sgt K."

The instructor smiled indulgently, took the paper from her and placed it on his cluttered desk. "You'll do better next time, Airman Katrickson."

She sighed again, rolling her eyes. "Yeah, yeah." She turned, eyed the class, and without hesitation took a seat next to me.

I didn't realize I was staring at her until she turned to look me full in the face. Her eyes were a pale, grayish blue, and they contained a mischievous sparkle that flashed when she saw me looking at her. Instead of being indignant, she gave me a cheesy grin, and she said, "Hey! I'm Prue. I got washed back because I failed this block's dang test."

"Oh," I said, instantly shy in the face of her honesty, "That sucks."

"Um, yeah, it sucks! I don't get to graduate with the rest of my class, and I'm stuck here a week longer. Lameness."

I didn't know how to respond. There was a strange energy about this girl that I couldn't quite figure out, but I liked it- and it was not usual for me to like someone right away. I decided to introduce myself.

"I'm Airman Presa..." I started.

"Durr, yeah okay, I can see that on your name tag-thingy, but what's your real name?" she asked, making a face.

I was nonplussed. "Kimberly."

"Oh. I might end up calling you Kimmy. Sorry."

I laughed a little. "That's okay."

She smiled again turned to introduce herself to the other people in the class. They were as drawn to her as I was- it was not because she was pretty, exactly, even though she was- but she had such a magnetic personality. When she spoke, you wanted to listen because you just *knew* whatever she was saying was interesting, or amusing, and you somehow knew it all came from her heart. I had never met a person like that before.

"Hey!" she said suddenly, turning to us all, "Let's have lunch together today."

Everyone hesitated, not wanting to seem too eager.

"We march there together anyway, people!" Prue said, exasperated at the silence, "And we're stuck together for months, so you might as well learn to get used to me. Oh, whatever. If you don't sit with me, I'll just sit my ass right next to you anyway, whether you like it or not."

And so it was agreed we would all have lunch together that day- and every day after that- and thus began the first real friendship of my life.

*

With Prue by my side, the days at tech school passed quickly. Everything became less about the information I was learning in the classroom and more about the education in friendship I received at her hands. I had neglected the part of me that craved human interaction for so long, that seeing her every morning, cantankerous but jolly, became the highlight of my day. She had, for some reason, developed an attachment to me, and insisted on my going everywhere with her despite my awkwardness. We would often spend hours together studying, or at the gym (though she was not a fan), and because I was a little nervous around her at first, she was often the one who did most of the talking. I was completely fascinated by her; where everyone and everything around her was grey, she was a fierce, brilliant purple. She got along with absolutely everyone; and if by some chance someone did rub her the wrong way, she told them exactly what she thought of them, and then afterwards somehow managed to become friends with them, too. All the males loved her, and all the females wanted to be her best friend.

I didn't feel for one moment that I deserved Prue's time or attention. I knew I was dull to be around, and it confused me why she would want to spend her days with someone like me. I had very few interests due to my years of absorption with bulimia; to my knowledge, I didn't even have a favorite color, song, or film. My secret, which I kept covetously hidden from the military world I had entered, kept me so consumed that all of my energy went towards maintaining it. I was terrified to let it become known, but felt too far gone into the abyss to climb out. I felt trapped; and so, with both feet planted firmly inside my boundaries, it was all I could do to stretch out my hands occasionally to let Prue know that I was there and that in my own way, I appreciated her. I couldn't commit to a friendship that I felt I didn't deserve and couldn't uphold, no matter how much I wanted to.

One Friday afternoon after class, Prue asked me if I wanted to go to an under twenty-one dance club with her and a couple of her friends. I recall not even thinking about it, as I answered No, I don't feel like going, thanks. I had nothing to do otherwise, but the prospect of letting go was too frightening for me- I didn't trust myself in social situations anymore, especially after California. This was only one the many times that Prue had asked me to leave the base with her and socialize, only to have me refuse point blank, and I could tell she was getting exasperated.

"Kimmy, why don't you go *do* stuff?" she asked, locking me with her steel gray eyes and not letting me look away.

"I-I don't know," I said dumbly.

"Yes, you do. Tell me!" she insisted. I remained still, keeping my countenance blank. After a moment she rolled her eyes skyward, at her wit's end. "That's it, I've had enough! You're going to tell me right now what's up, Missy!" She grabbed a hold of my arm and dragged me to a bench in the common area of our dorms, and pushed me into it. She sat down next to me, and with crossed arms and glaring eyes, waiting in silence for me to speak, tapping her petite foot on the ground.

I didn't know what lie to tell her, because I surely couldn't divulge to her the truth. *Maybe I can tell her I'm just extremely shy...?* But, looking at her, all irate and concerned, my heart throbbed with affection; she was my only friend, and she was waiting for an answer. She deserved something more than lies.

"I'm... sick," I said finally.

"How are you sick?" she asked.

"I don't know how to explain it."

"Dammit Kimmy, just tell me," she said, frustrated. "I can't be there for you if you don't tell me what's going on!"

"It's gross," I said finally, nervously.

"Everyone's gross. Tell me."

I hesitated, then throwing caution to the wind, said, all in a rush: "I've been bulimic for five years and it's all I ever think about. I lied to get into the service, but the recruiter let me lie because I was so pathetic. I hurt all the time. My throat bleeds, my stomach aches; I even pass out sometimes. I don't know why I started doing it, but I've read lots of articles and books and they all say it probably has something to do with my mom dying. But when I think about it, I don't feel sad about my mom dying, so I don't know how they can be related."

I took a deep breath, and continued. "As far as going out, people bother me- it doesn't matter who they are, because almost everyone bothers the living shit out of me, except you, and I don't understand it. Going out in public scares me more than anything else in the world, because everyone is normal, and happy; and I'm crazy, ugly, and can't stop thinking shitty thoughts about myself. It makes me... feel worse than bad. A bit like dying while being alive, I guess. But, like I said, I don't know how to explain it. "

Prue looked at me in silence, digesting this sudden influx of information. As far as I knew, Prue was a regular girl, who had lived a normal life with an average amount of sorrow and joy. I didn't expect her to understand; and who knows, maybe she didn't- not really. But what she did then was something that no one else had done before, and something that I had always wished someone would do once they discovered the truth; she stayed with me.

"I'm sorry, Kimmy," she said, and leaned in to hug me tightly. I blinked, fighting tears, and failing miserably. She sat back.

"Now that you told me, you don't hide it that well, you know," she said. "You don't eat anything at lunch but sometimes you take huge containers back to your room. I always wondered what you did with them."

I remained silent.

"You know… you don't have to be someone your not to hang out with me," she said suddenly, looking at me, "Now that I know…if you don't feel like talking, don't freakin' talk. If you don't want to go to Olive Garden, even though they have sweet breadsticks, then don't. I get it, and its fine. But I mean, you don't have to hide shit from me."

My heart swelled. I didn't know what to say.

"I never really get to talk about how I feel," I told her. "And I just kind of unloaded on you. It feels weird. Sorry."

She shook her head. "That's what friends are for. Unload on me. I can take it, yo."

I smiled, touched to my very core. "Anytime you want to talk about anything, I'm here, too. And… maybe I can go and do something with you, off base, sometime."

She smiled back. "You better, or I'll punch you in the face."

*

    I cried like a baby when we graduated from Tech School three months later, and learned that Prue and I were to be shipped off to separate bases. In just a few weeks, I felt like I had gained a sister- the kind of sister I always dreamed of having- and I never wanted to let her go. There was one small consolation; I was going to a base in North Carolina, while she went to one in South Carolina, so we could conceivably visit each other once every so often. I reminded myself of this during the last few days of school, and it helped my depression a little. When the time came to pack up and leave, however, I was a mess; I felt like I was having my arm ripped from my body. Prue took my blubbering well; she always seemed strong when I was weak, so she comforted me by telling me that she would find me on the Air Force Global E-Mail, and we'd stay in touch. All I could do was nod dazedly and let myself be loaded onto the bus that would take me away. I waved to her out the foggy window, and as she waved back I impulsively blew her a kiss. She blew one back, then made a goofy, sexy face which made me laugh despite my tears. Watching her form become smaller as the bus drove away, I realized with an aching heart how much she had come to mean to me over the last few months, and how very much I would miss her.

Shady J
(23)

I sat at the small airport in Kinston, North Carolina with my bags, not exactly sure of what to do next. Nervous, I glanced once again at the rumpled paper in my hand: *SSgt James Slavin will pick you up at baggage claim. Slavin.* What kind of name was Slavin? It sounded unpalatable to my brain, which was strained and finding fault in everything. Would he be tough, like a TI, or dislike me instantly for some reason? My experience of staff sergeants was so varied at that point that I had no idea what to expect. So I sat on top of my duffle bag, which was stuffed full of my carefully rolled clothes, and eyed people as they walked by.

Suddenly a large man in battle dress uniform parted the crowd, and headed in my direction. In reflex, I stood immediately to attention. He was pale, and had a large, flat mouth which looked as if it was stuck in a perpetual grimace. His head was bald and shiny, and he had light blue, wintry eyes. He stopped in front of me.

"Airman Presa, I assume?" he asked in a gravelly voice, looking me quickly up and down.

I nodded. "Yes, Sir!"

"Alright," he said, reaching down to grab my duffle bag, "Let's get the hell out of here." And with that, he hefted the bag on his shoulder as if it were filled with air, and began to walk away. I hurried after him.

As he led me outside, I received my first full view of North Carolina. It was flat, and cold in January, and there were hardly any trees. *Why,* I thought, *has everywhere I've been since joining the Air Force practically no trees?* Perhaps having lived on the west coast my entire life I'd already filled my life's tree quota, and was now doomed to live amongst valleys, swamps and flatlands. I frowned at the thought.

SSgt Slavin led me to a small gray car, threw my bags in the trunk, and we drove off. We were silent at first, but after a minute he cleared his throat and asked, "How was your flight?"

I took a breath- evidently there was no need to be formal. I was glad. "It was good. The last ride was bumpy, and a little scary because of the wind. The whole plane was shaking like crazy. But otherwise it was all pretty easy."

"Good," he said, scratching his bald head. "So," he continued, "I'm SSgt Slavin, and I'll be your supervisor. If you ever have any questions, come to me. You will be staying in the dorms, where all unmarried airman stay- unless you went and got married at tech school?" He turned to look at me briefly.

I shook my head empathically. "No, no I didn't. Sir."

"Okay, good. Makes it easier- you'll be in the dorms. I figure for today, I might take you to in-process some, but first I want to take you by the office so you can see where you'll be working, and meet everybody."

"Okay," I said.

"Everyone's pretty nice at Seymour," he continued, "We call it Shady J, sometimes. It's a busy place to work, since we're in a fighter squadron, but we're a pretty close office. Where are you from?"

"Oregon."

"Ah," he said, turning an eye to me, "You a hippy?"

I smiled a little. "I don't know; I don't think so."

"We don't get many people from Oregon here. Lot's of people from Ohio and New York. How you like it in the Air Force so far?"

I pursed my lips. "I am very grateful to be where I am," I said, "I like having a steady paycheck and a place to sleep. I admit, though, that I'm nervous about doing a job I have never done before."

"Yeah, everyone's like that at first. Tech School doesn't teach you shit. Don't worry, we'll teach you what you need to know. We do have something called CDC's which you'll have to take, which are tests to see if you're able to perform the job, but we'll make sure you are good to go before you take them. You'll get lots of OJT before that happens. Everyone hates the CDCs, but they need to be taken seriously since you can get kicked out if you fail. Do you have your ID?"

I was thrown off. "What?"

"Your ID, your military ID- we have to get on base and everyone needs to show their ID. Get it out and hand it to me."

"Oh, yeah, sorry..." I dug into my coat pocket and pulled it out of my wallet, and gave it to him. He glanced at it.

"This doesn't look like you," he said. "Gotta love them basic training photos. Looks like a constipated mug shot."

I blushed and remained silent as the car pulled up to a large gate with a security post, and an armed guard in BDUs and a beret walked up to driver's window.

"Afternoon," said the guard, taking the proffered IDs.

"Yup," replied SSgt Slavin.

It took only a moment for our IDs to be glanced over and returned, and then we were on our way again. SSgt Slavin handed my ID back to me and I quickly returned the hateful photo back into the depths of my pocket.

The base itself looked more agreeable than what I had seen so far of the rest of North Carolina; there were manicured lawns and tall, green pine trees absolutely everywhere- it even boasted a golf course with a fountain in the center of the base. The buildings were mostly old, red-bricked and cracked, but they didn't have that lifeless feeling that the buildings on Sheppard had, perhaps because everywhere I looked there were people walking in BDUs or civilian clothes. W*alking, not marching.* I smiled.

"It's pretty here," I commented, looking around.

Sgt Slavin snorted. "Yeah, it's decent."

I glanced at him. "You don't like it?"

"It's *decent*. But you will find after being here a while, that for North Carolina, this whole area can be described as the armpit of the state. They sure as hell could have built the base in a better location, if you ask me."

"Are there more trees in North Carolina than what we see here?" I asked.

He tilted his head, unsure. "Trees? Yeah, there are trees, but I mean, nothing to phone home about. It's a pretty state, though, don't get me wrong. There's a beach with islands and stuff on the coast which are great to visit in the summer."

I frowned. "I am a little tired of beaches."

He gave me a weird look. "Who the hell gets tired of the beach?"

I bit my lip. "I just lived near one for a long time, is all."

"I guess I can understand that."

The car made its way around a big bend, and to our right there was a large, paved expanse which I understood to be the flight-line. It was dotted near the road with huge, windowless buildings, each of which had a unique painting over the door.

"Those are the AMU buildings," Sgt Slavin said, slowing the vehicle down to point at them, "The Chiefs, Eagles, Rocketeers, and Lancers. That's where we go to the morning meetings, and talk to the AMU bosses; basically, it's who we work for as analysts. You'll be going there eventually."

I looked at the large buildings and asked, "What is AMU?"

He gave me a dark look. "Didn't they even teach you *that* in tech school? Freakin'... Aircraft Maintenance Unit. Remember it, I ain't telling you again."

I nodded, embarrassed.

He sighed. "Ok, let's go to the office. It's right up here."

"Is it okay that I am in civilian clothes?"

He shrugged. "I don't think anyone will care. If they do just tell them I said it was alright."

"...Okay."

I looked down at myself. I wore my ratty jeans, old tennis shoes, and a big puffy coat with holes under the arms that I had used as a mattress in my tent in Oregon. I hadn't been to a clothing store since I joined, and so all I had was what I had brought with me to MEPS. I started to feel nervous again; I didn't want to look unprofessional when meeting my co-workers, but it looked like I didn't have a choice. I took a deep breath. I needed to calm down, and attempt to look like a cool, composed adult. I looked down at my hands, and clasped them together to forestall any shaking.

We pulled into a large parking lot next to a single story building with a new-looking gazebo out front.

"This is it," Sgt Slavin said, striding towards the glass doors which appeared to be the only entrance. "We share the building with the schedulers, and a bunch of Intel officers, so keep your eye out for them. Salute them, y'know- when you're in uniform. You're not right now so don't worry about it."

"Yes, Sir," I replied.

We stepped into a long hall with open doors on either side, and without a pause he turned to the second on the left, which had a plaque to the left of the door that read 'Maintenance Analysis/Database Management.'

"This is us. C'mon in."

I took another breath to steady myself, and followed him in.

The room was large, but every inch was so packed with desks, cabinets and computers that it looked a lot smaller than it was. There were artistic prints of aircraft and numerous charts and graphs hanging on the wall that meant nothing to me, and a giant row of filing cabinets rose at the center of the room like an island. From my place at the door I could only see one or two people sitting; two young airmen, both three stripes, eyes on me. I started to sweat.

"Hey. Dumbasses," called Sgt Slavin inelegantly, "This is Airman Basic Presa. She'll be starting work with us soon, after she gets in-processed and all that."

Suddenly I found myself surrounded by people; one technical sergeant, three senior airmen and one airman first class- all male, except for one female staff sergeant, who peered up at me with a frown on her face.

"Why isn't she in uniform?" she asked, glowering.

"She just got here, Thea. Just wanted her to see where she'll be working. Nothing official," said Sgt Slavin.

"Still should have worn her uniform," said the female sergeant, looking at him disapprovingly. She turned to me with sharp eyes.

"I'm Sergeant Simmons. Welcome to Shady-J. Next time you come to work, wear your damn uniform."

"Yes, Ma'am. I'm sorry, Ma'am."

She eyed me once, up and down, and then went back to her desk, out of sight.

A tall, slightly overweight TSgt with a pleasant face came forward and grabbed my hand, shook it thoroughly, and said, "I'm Kevin Greeves, so glad to have you here. I'm not really an analyst, I'm a data integrity monitor, but I work with you guys and help out. I've been at Shady for years, so if you ever need anything let me know." He turned and pointed out individuals around the room.

"That's Airman Khadir, Airman Lange, and Airman Han, who we just call Jason; they're all out of the dorms now, but over there in the corner is Airman Kerry; he's still in the dorms, so I'm sure if you need anything he can help you."

"Pshh! Kerry can't even get himself out of bed in the morning- he can't help nobody," scoffed Airman Lange, a short, tan boy in his early twenties with a heavy Jersey accent.

"Shuttup, Lange, goddammit! You're such an asshole." snarled Kerry, a short, overweight Honduran with fierce eyes.

Lange laughed. "Prove me wrong, bro! Come to work on time tomorrow. I dare you. I triple *dog* dare you."

Kerry glared at him, and then turned to me.

"Nice to meet you- you'll hate it here. But if you ignore everything *he* says or does-," he said, indicating a chuckling Lange, "-you'll be alright," and with that he went back to his desk.

Airman Han strode forward and took my hand. I looked at him in awe. He was tall and very muscular; he looked like an Abercrombie & Fitch model.

"Very nice to meet you," he said in a kind, boyish voice, "Don't mind these jokesters, it's great here. I'm Jason, nice to meet you."

"Nice to meet you, too," I replied.

Jason pointed to the last Airman who had not come forward, a handsome middle-eastern looking man in his twenties. "That's Khadir," he said. "He's actually not a terrorist, so don't let his face scare you…"

"Shut the fuck up, man," Khadir said, glaring at him, and then turned back to his work, muttering under his breath, "At least I don't have to explain that I'm not actually a pedophile like you do."

Jason laughed. "Oh, you got me there, buddy! But you know you're just jealous."

I stood there, watching them with my mouth slightly open. It was like watching a play.

Lange, grinning evilly, reached over to Jason's desk and picked up a picture of a pretty girl in her teens, and turned it so that I could see. "Since you're a part of this office, you should know; this is Jason's wife. How old would you say she is?"

"I don't know," I said confusedly.

"This is her when she was *fifteen*. That was like, what, Jason, eight years ago?"

Jason smiled good naturedly. "I like that picture."

"Who keeps a picture of their wife as a kid on their desk? Freakin' pedo. Where are the newer pictures?" asked Lange.

"You won't see no newer picture 'coz she weighs three-hundred pounds and don't look like that no more," piped in Kerry from his desk, turning around with a smirk.

Jason made a face. "Not that much, man. That's pushing it."

Kerry turned back to his desk. "Then take a new picture of her and put that one on your desk."

"Naw, I like this one," he said stubbornly, taking the photo back from Lange and placing it next to his computer.

"Will you guys shut *the fuck up?*" came the irate voice of Sgt Simmons from the other side of the filing cabinets. "Jason, your wife is fucking fat. Khadir, you look like a goddamn terrorist. Everyone get back to work. Jesus *fucking* Christ you guys give me cramps."

Everyone chuckled, seemingly not bothered at all by her outburst, and turned back to their computer screens. Sgt Greeves had already sat down minutes ago and had earphones on. Sgt Slavin had been texting on his cell, but at the sound of Sgt Simmons's voice he stood up, stretched, and said,

"After you in-process you'll be sitting there…" he indicated an empty desk next to Lange, "and he'll probably be training you. Not sure yet. But we'll figure it out, I'm not too worried about it. When you come back we'll give you the whole tour and you'll meet the Superintendent and the Commander. For now, let's get you to your dorm manager and get your room situation settled."

I glanced once behind me as I left the office, and despite the rowdy conversation that had just occurred, everything was quiet except for the sound of typing. I was completely mystified.

My room in the dorms was on the ground floor of a three story building, and it was surprisingly large; it held a bed, a desk and chair, and a sink with a mirror. Towards the back there was a door that led to a bathroom which I shared with the resident on the other side. The carpet, unfortunately, was filthy- it looked as though it had gone through flooding, and been pumped out and dried simply by leaving the window open. It was obvious that it had been continually shampooed in an attempt to mask the mildew smell, and that wasn't working.

Sgt Slavin dropped me off, telling me he would be there in the morning to finish my in-processing. He pointed across a small field to a low, silver building, and told me that's where I would receive my meals. I could obtain three meals a day with my ID card; the meal times would be posted on the door outside. Lastly, he handed me a small map of the base, which outlined the main roads and the locations of the Commissary and the basic exchange, or BX, and the Shoppette, in case I required anything.

"There are base taxis," he said gruffly, "But there's nothing wrong with using your own two legs, in my opinion. It's not that far."

I thanked him, and when he left I shut the door behind him.

Looking around my room, my first thoughts were not complimentary. It was dark, and smelled bad, and when I tried to open the window the screen fell out onto the sidewalk outside. The light bulbs in the room were dim, almost as if they couldn't fight against the miasma of gloom which pervaded the place. I sat down on my bed, and felt that it was very hard, almost like the pallets in basic training. *Someday,* I thought, *I want to own a bed that's as soft as a pillow.* With pillows in mind, I looked around the room, but there was no sign of sheets or a pillow for me to use, though there were some rough blankets thrown haphazardly at the end of the bed. *I guess I'll have to go buy some things*, I thought. I went into the bathroom to see if I needed to buy anything for it, as well; it was very small, containing nothing but a toilet and a standing shower, and if possible, it smelt even worse in there than it did in my room. The grout on the floors and walls were dark gray with held an unhealthy, greenish tinge. I backed out, locking the door behind me.

    I grabbed my room key and the base map that Sgt Slavin had given me, and went outside. It was about mid-afternoon, so most Airman were at work, but a few yards away I could see a few in BDU's smoking cigarettes under a gazebo, eyeing me curiously. Ignoring them, I walked to the dining facility and made a note of the hours, then glanced again at the map. After locating the street I would need to take, I began to walk at a brisk pace, all the while mentally listing all the things I would need to buy to make my dorm room livable: *pillow, sheets, bathroom cleaner, Glade plug-in, Febreeze, rug for the bathroom floor…*

It didn't take long to reach the shopping area, only a few minutes. I hadn't been inside a BX without my uniform before, and I was surprised that it felt just like entering a tiny Target, except half the people shopping there wore BDUs. I grabbed a cart, and started my search for the items I wanted. I quickly realized that the selections were limited, but I didn't care; I took what I felt was the best deal, and then went to check out.

On the way back to my room, my hands laden with my purchases, a car honked twice behind me, and then slowed down as it came abreast of me. Inside were two boys about my age, in uniform, with big grins, their eyes on me.

"Hey pretty lady, need a lift?" asked the driver.

"Where're you going?" asked the other.

"Just to the dorms," I said.

"I can drive you," said the driver, "But only if you go out to dinner with us after."

I frowned. "I don't know who you are."

"And I don't know who you are, either," said the driver, laughing. "That's why we're going to dinner! Come on in, those bags must be heavy."

I shook my head. "No thanks, I'm almost at the dorms, anyway. I appreciate it though."

The driver looked at me strangely, and then he a shrugged. Without another word he drove away at what seemed to me a dangerous speed, his tires screeching on the asphalt.

In my room, I dumped all my items onto my bed, and went into the bathroom and splashed bleach everywhere; on the walls, the floor, the toilet- even a little on the ceiling. The bleach smell was so intense that I couldn't stop coughing, and had to prop the door open with the desk chair to let fresh air in. For the next hour, I scrubbed the floor, walls and ceiling of the bathroom until they were sparkling. I rinsed the bleach with cups of hot water, and watched with pleasure as the grey stains on the grout faded away. After drying it all down with a towel, I left the bathroom and began to clean the sink area and mirror, and then I made my bed. To help mask the smell of the mildewed carpet, I used a Glade plug-in near my headboard, and I also sprayed Febreeze all over the room. I continued to leave the door propped open, with little effect, until it was time to go to the dining hall and get something to eat.

    Before leaving, I looked around at what I had done, and felt proud. It felt more like a room now, and less like a cell. It wasn't that I was not grateful for having a place to stay, no matter what it looked like- it was just that it seemed like the space had been forgotten, let go; it reminded me of the last house I had lived in with my mother, the one I had ruined with my illness. I was trying so hard to move past those days, but everything lately reminded me of them- I had to keep moving forward and hope the keenness of the memories would fade over time.

The dining facility was crowded with people, most of which were in their late teens to early twenties- all dorm residents, people who subsisted entirely on the Air Force 'meal card' and did not receive an extra allowance for food in their paychecks. Standing at the door, I became very shy, because I realized when I rubbed my forehead how sweaty I was, and how much I probably smelled like bleach. A few people turned their heads to glance at me, and then turned away with apparent disinterest. Encouraged by this, I walked behind the lines of people who were waiting for hot food, and looked to see what was on the menu for the day: Spaghetti and meatballs, fried okra, and corn hash. It smelled so delicious that my salivary glands responded sharply, aching with sudden urgency. My stomach growled, and my hand started to tremor slightly.

Just eat, I thought. You're hungry. I tried to recall the last time I had eaten. I had had trail mix while I was at the airport, I remembered. ***That's nothing. Have some spaghetti. It won't kill you.*** I walked to the end of the line, and grabbed a to-go tray... and then, hesitating, I put it back. I was too afraid. The memory of how spaghetti felt while being purged was too clear in my mind. It had always been my favorite food to throw up because it was easy, and light. The thought of consuming all of those carbohydrates, keeping it down and letting it become a part of my body was terrifying to me. With a shake of my head, I turned to the salad bar, determined to eat only lettuce and sunflower seeds.

After gathering my salad, I walked back to my dorm room and ate in silence, telling myself over and over that I was okay, that I had escaped temptation. But I knew that it wasn't over yet. The aroma of hot, wholesome food was in my head, and it filled my senses like a drug. I put my head in my hands, trying to think of something else, anything else- but there was nothing that interested me. I had nothing to cling to.

You want it, said the voice. **Go get it. Just once won't hurt. Come on. Just… go get it.**

My resolution dissolved, and I walked quickly back to the dining hall and got in the hot food line, my legs shaking impatiently. *Just once won't hurt,* I thought. *I won't do it again.* When it was my turn, I told the serving lady in a nervous voice that I wanted large servings of everything; and being a kind, generous woman, she complied. I watched with eager eyes as she filled the big Styrofoam compartment to the rim with spaghetti. It was so full she could hardly close the lid.

"There you re sweetie," said the lady, "I like to see a girl with a good appetite."

"Thank you," I stammered, and scurried away with my shameful prize.

I practically ran back to my room. Once I was hidden from the world, I threw off all pretenses of sanity, and began to devour my meal as if it was the last one I would ever eat. If someone had asked me, just then, how I felt, it would be difficult for me to answer- I felt so many things, but at the same time, I felt nothing. Every feeling I had was shallow, on the surface. In some ways, I felt like I was flying; I could hear my blood rushing in my ears with excitement, but the sensation was tempered with a numbness that spread from my toes to the tip of my esophagus. My mind held no concrete thoughts; my only focus was the next bite, the next swallow of food. There was a small respite from reality as I swallowed, and I gloried in feeling the food slide down my throat. It was the feeling I dreamt of at night, and craved for every minute of the day. As my stomach began to get full, my sadness increased, because I knew it was close to coming to an end- and before I knew it, the spell was broken, and I was sitting in front of an empty container, my face smeared with spaghetti sauce. I groaned; my stomach felt like it was going to rupture. I was in so much pain that I couldn't stand up straight, so, walking like a crabbed old woman, I unlocked the bathroom door. I barely had time to put my head into the toilet before the vomit came, spewing out all over the newly clean floor and walls. When I had gotten rid of all I could with nausea alone, I shoved my fingers down my throat, and used force to coax the rest out. It seemed like ages until I finally sat back onto my heels, my eyes streaming with tears, my lips shaking, vomit smeared across my face and plastering in the strands of my hair against my cheeks.

Slightly stunned by the intensity of what I had just done, I looked dumbly around at the mess I had made- there were orange splatters everywhere. I stifled a sob as it came home to me that I had done it again; I had dropped my guard, let the sickness win, and was once more sitting in the middle of my own abominable mess. I suddenly felt very, very tired; I felt like I could sleep for twenty-four hours without moving. Standing slowly, I went to the sink and washed my face while carefully ignoring my retched image in the mirror. I then grabbed what remained of the bleach, and for the second time that day, I cleaned the bathroom floor and toilet. I also had to replace the toilet roll, because my puke had splashed it to the point where it was unusable. When I was finished, I closed the bathroom door and collapsed, exhausted, on my bed.

I stared at the ceiling through tear blanketed eyelashes and wondered if I would every escape the demon that plagued me. Despite my lack of education, I had never considered myself unintelligent; I knew that bulimia was wrong. It went against everything I believed in. I wanted to be in shape, and in control- bulimia was gluttonous and ungovernable. I dreamed of finding myself attractive when I looked in the mirror, but the more ill I became, the more hideous I found myself. What, then, did my eating disorder have to offer me? The logical answer was, of course, nothing. But if that was the case, then I wouldn't be doing it still, after so many years. It was giving me something that I couldn't get any other way. I fought with my heart, trying to decide what that thing might be. *Adrenaline?* I wasn't sure. Regardless of what kept bringing me back, I knew now that I had opened the gate in a new location, I would have to work very hard to try to close it.

It was getting late, and I had to unpack my uniform and iron it for my in processing the next day, but I was so tired that I could barely move. My limbs felt like lead, and my eyes closed every few seconds without my awareness. *I need to just sit up*, I thought... but it was too late. My body, worn out from the abuse I put it though, was fast asleep.

*

I awoke to a knock on my door. I sat up instantly, my heart pounding in response against my ribcage. Was it time to wake up? I peeked out the window- it was light outside. Had I slept all night? What time was it? I pushed myself off of my bed and opened the door. Sgt Slavin was standing there with his cars keys in his hand. Upon seeing me still in the previous day's clothes, he raised his eyes brows.

"I said seven-thirty. Why aren't you ready?" he asked.

I stood there, gaping at him, before I replied in a panicked voice, "Oh my God. I just- I fell asleep on my bed last night- I slept until just now… I didn't mean to… I'm so sorry." My eyes started to tear up as I became aware of my own wretchedness.

"This is not a good start, you know," Slavin said, crossing his arms. "Why didn't you set your alarm?"

"I didn't mean to fall asleep at all! I-I can get ready in five minutes. Or you can go and I can walk to work. This will never happen again, I promise. I'm so sorry!"

He looked at me with pitying eyes. "Take ten minutes, and clean yourself up- you're meeting the commander this morning. I'll be over there having a cig." He indicated the gazebo where I had seen the airmen smoking the previous night.

"I'll hurry," I said, and shut the door. I can't recall any time in basic where I dressed as quickly as I did that morning. My uniform, of course, was a wrinkly mess, but there was nothing I could do about that; I washed my face and did the best I could with my hair, but without time it was hard to tame it into a professional bun. My face, however, was the worst part of my appearance; my cheeks were puffy from throwing up, my eyes were bloodshot, and my lips were cracked and bleeding from being dehydrated. I spared a few seconds for lip balm and mascara, but it did nothing to improve the overall effect of slovenliness that I gave. With a panicked feeling in my chest, I grabbed my ID, hat, and room key, and ran outside to meet Sgt Slavin, who sat unconcerned in the gazebo, puffing on his second cigarette.

The rest of that day went as horribly as it had started. I was taken around the base and introduced to many people who would become a part of my life at Seymour Johnson; my primary care doctor, my commander, my superintendent- and all I could think was that they were judging me and thinking thoughts like, "She's a mess! Is that vomit I smell?" I spent the whole day in nervous silence, trapped by the terrors of my own mind.

We finished our errands around one o'clock, and Slavin drove me back to the dorms. Before I got out of the car, he said,

"On Monday you start FTAC- the first-term airman center, which is right behind the chow hall there. You'll be there for a week, so it'll be considered your duty location for that time period. I want you to report there *on time* and behave, and all that."

"Yes, Sir," I replied quietly.

"Don't worry about this morning, just don't do it again. And iron your uniform before I see you again."

"Yes, Sir."

"Call me if you need anything, alright?"

"Alright. Thank you, Sir."

I exited the car, and kept my back to him as he drove away.

I went back to my room and collected the trash from my binge the previous night, and went outside to the dumpster and threw it away; I didn't want anything tangible to remind me of what I had done. When I went back inside, I stripped and went into the bathroom, and took a long, hot shower, scrubbing my skin hard to try and strip the smell of vomit off of me. From the other side of the door, in my suite-mate's room, I could hear punk music playing; up until that point I had been unsure if I even had a suite-mate. In one way, I was grateful that I had one- it would make it harder for me to have the privacy needed to binge and purge. At the same time, however, and for the same reason, I was angry. *I'll never have the secrecy I had before I joined*, I thought. And I was irritated, because the punk music blasting through the wall reminded me of Sam, and he was the last person I wanted to think of.

Upon leaving the shower, I crawled under the covers of my bed, naked, letting the heat from the shower turn my body warm and flaccid. With both communicating doors closed, I could barely hear my suitemate's music, and I let my mind drift.

Sgt Slavin had been kind to me; he could have made my day much worse than it was, and I felt grateful to him. I would try not to disappoint him in the future.

Under the covers, I pulled on the extra skin I carried around my stomach, and felt a twinge of anxiety. Was it bigger than it had been yesterday? Was I getting fatter? Maybe I would have to keep purging for a while, just until I lost a few pounds. Then I would stop…

*

Every day after that, regardless of whether I got sick, I made sure that I was awake at five-thirty so that I could shower and walk across the golf course to make it to work by six-thirty. I was never late again after that first day.

If I ever thought for a moment that my new coworkers had been putting on a show for my benefit the day I was introduced to them, I was mistaken; how they had portrayed themselves during my visit was exactly how they were. They were constantly ribbing each other, laughing, and picking fights; I never knew if they were serious or not, if they hated each other, or even if they were best friends. Their jokes were so often beyond my comprehension that most of the time I felt it better to remain silent.

My first few months at Seymour Johnson seemed to fly by. Prue kept her word by finding my e-mail address three days after we had both settled, me at Seymour, and her at Shaw, South Carolina. We wrote to each other frequently, describing our likes and dislikes of our new jobs and co-workers, and if I ever didn't respond quickly enough she called my work phone to make sure I was okay. I could tell it annoyed Sgt Simmons that I received personal calls during duty hours, but for some reason she never stopped me, and there was no way in hell I was going to tell Prue to stop calling.

We also visited each other as often as we could. I was the first to buy a car, a Nissan Sentra, and with my new mobility came a small modicum of confidence. I drove to Shaw twice that first year and stayed with Prue in her own tiny dorm room, and there we would watch movies and act like idiots until late, and in general just pretend we were seventh graders at a slumber party. We would go out for coffee in the morning, and sit at random restaurants in the afternoon, talking for hours- sometimes about tech school, sometimes about our current boyfriends. That was something I always appreciated about Prue; she was very protective of me when it came to men. She insisted on vetting every single man I dated, and I honestly don't recall her ever approving of a single one.

"Eww, Kimmy," she would often say, "What the hell!"

I'd laugh. "You know me, I like them ugly."

"Dammit, it's not the way he looks! Even though what he *looks* like is Squidward from Spongebob Squarepants- but besides that, he won't take care of you. I can tell."

Sometimes I would argue, depending upon the person in question, but it never mattered, because in the end she was always right. She seemed to have a sixth sense about relationships. I tended to date men that treated me like a sex object, something to be used and tossed aside; not a single one of them treated me as a friend and companion. Knowing my inclination to jump into pointless relationships, she even went so far to write every one of my new boyfriends a note, stating, in brief, "If you hurt my Kimmy, I will destroy you and all you care about. Sincerely, Prue."

At work, I was placed under the tutelage of SrA Lange so that I might become the next Database Manager of the Analysis section. Upon hearing this, I instantly gritted my teeth. Lange was a difficult person to get along with. He was loud, and very vain about his looks, and though ostensibly good at his job, it was obvious (to me, anyway), that he got by on his charms, which were certainly not lacking in number. His Boston accent was proclaimed 'adorable' by all females, and he ended every sentence with a joke. He and I had nothing in common whatsoever, so being trained by him was difficult. Sometimes, he would make a joke, and I would think he was being serious- then he would be serious, but because of his inclination to be jocular, I would think he was joking. We were black and white, and in the end I got most of my Database Management training by just taking over the job and finding out my own way to do things.

At the end of a few months, I had gone from slick sleeve (Airman Basic), to one stripe (Airman), and I was looking forward to putting on two stripes and becoming an Airman First Class, and getting a pay raise. I was slowly becoming used to my office and the strange people that populated it. My closest confident was Khadir- or as Lange very un-politically correctly called him, 'the terrorist'- mostly because we sat next to each other and had similar temperaments.

One day, Khadir turned to me and whispered,

"Hey. I think you might have a shot with Lange."

I stuck out my tongue in disgust. "Um, no? I don't want a shot with Lange. Plus, he would never date someone like me. I wear *poly-cotton* blends," I joked, referencing one of Lange's ridiculous dislikes. I was slowly learning how to banter.

"Yeah, you're right, he wouldn't date you," he said jokingly, and I frowned in indignation. "But anyway, you should come out with us tonight. We're going to Cameron's." Cameron's was the one and only dance club in town and therefore was as popular as it was run-down, expensive, and ghetto.

"I don't really dance," I said, "Plus, I'm only twenty."

Khadir waved my argument away. "It doesn't matter. They just stamp your hand if you're under age. You can still come! And you don't have to dance if you don't want to." He leaned forward confidentially. "And if you want, you can pregame at our house before we go. C'mon, it'll be a good time!"

I thought about it. This was the first time I had been invited out by anyone, and though my co-workers seemed like they were inclined to party hard, I was intrigued with the idea of getting along with them better, especially Lange, who irritated the life out of me. Saying 'no' would get me nowhere.

"Okay," I said, deciding. "I'll go. What time should I be at your house?"

"I don't know… eight-thirty? And hey," Khadir dropped his voice to a whisper, "Can you drive Kerry over, too? He doesn't have a car yet. The loser keeps failing his driver's test."

I smiled. "Yeah, I'll bring Kerry."

Kerry, hearing his name, turned to look at us suspiciously. "What? You say my name?"

"Yeah, we said your name, you lazy fuck," Khadir said, "Kim's going to drive you to my house tonight at eight thirty, so be ready."

Kerry relaxed. "Oh. Okay, thanks," he grunted, turning back to his computer, and then suddenly realizing what Khadir had said, he turned back to retort, "And I ain't lazy, you damned terrorist."

Jason, hearing our conversation, pricked up his ears. "You guys going out tonight?"

"Yeah, man. Going to Cameron's. You wanna come?"

Jason sighed tragically. "You know I do, but my wife would never let me. She doesn't even let me drink."

"Fuck that, man! Stand up for yourself! If you want to drink, drink! Quit being such a pussy."

"You don't know what it's like, man."

"You're damn right I don't know what its like," said Khadir.

Jason was silent for a few moments, then said, "Maybe if I told her I was going over to your house to play Madden until late… she might say 'yes' to that."

"And then what, come home wasted?"

"Naw, man, I won't drink," said Jason, "I just want to go out with you guys."

I intervened. "Jason, do you think it's a good idea to lie to your wife about something like this? Why not just tell her the truth?"

Jason stared at me. "You have never met my wife."

"No… but I mean, she can't be that bad."

Jason leaned forward. "You know how you answer the phone all the time, because you're the Database Manager? And sometimes my wife calls and asks for me? Well, whenever you do, she flips out on me, *just* because you're a female answering the phone. She's crazy. Crazy! Thinks I'm cheating on her with everyone in my office, including you, and makes up whole scenarios that never happen. I think she would kill me if she thought I was going out to a bar."

"Jesus," I said.

"So, if I want a night out, she has to think I'm playing Madden at Khadir's. But I need to call and ask, first."

And without another word, Jason got up, pulled his cell-phone out of his cargo pocket, and walked out of the office. Khadir just shook his head.

"Poor guy," he said, "I feel sorry for him. But he dug his own grave."

"Maybe we could invite her out, too?" I suggested, still looking for a different answer.

Khadir stared at me incredulously. "That is the *dumbest* idea I have ever heard. Quit trying to fix Jason's messed up marriage and get back to work so we can get out this shit-hole early, because I need a drink."

*

That night, I dressed as nicely as I could, and spent some extra time on my hair and makeup, but it didn't do much to help my self confidence. My reflection in the mirror looked lumpy and unattractive to me, and, frustrated with trying so hard for little improvement, I wiped off my eyeliner and lipstick and threw my styled hair into a messy pony tail. If I had to be ugly, then I was determined to be ugly on purpose.

I went upstairs to Kerry's room and knocked.

"Just a minute," came his muffled voice from the other side of the door, and I heard the sound of scuffling and large items falling over. After a moment, Kerry emerged with a grocery bag in his hands. "Alright, I'm ready," he said.

"What's in the bag?" I asked.

"Never mind what's in the bag," he said defensively, then, a little softer, "Clothes."

I looked at him. He wore dark jeans with a small tear in them, a long polo shirt, and nice tennis shoes.

"I think you look fine," I said.

"Thanks," he said, "But just wait- those assholes at the club will find something wrong, and won't let me in. It happens every damn time."

"Really?" I asked, looking down at myself. "Am I okay, then? Should I bring something else?"

Kerry didn't even glance a me. "Do you have titties? Then you'll get in," he said roughly.

"That hardly seems fair."

"It ain't. But I'm a five foot two bald Honduran; I'm used to shit not being fair."

"That sucks, Kerry. I'm sorry," I said meaningfully.

"I ain't worried about it," he replied.

It was a fifteen minute drive to Khadir's house, which it turned out was a tall, rickety duplex in a very old neighborhood. When we got to the front door, Kerry let himself in without knocking, and left the door open for me, so I followed.

Inside, I saw Khadir, Lange, and Jason sitting on a couch in front of a television, playing Madden NFL. They all glanced up as we entered and greeted us, but continued to play.

"What the fuck are you guys doing?" asked Kerry.

"What does it look like we're doing, Mexican? We're playing a game," said Lange.

"I ain't a Mexican," said Kerry, "And I can see that you're playing a game. But why, I thought we were going to the club?"

"I'm waiting for my wife to call," replied Jason. "She needs to hear the game in the background. Maybe even a cell phone picture. I don't know. Kim, by the way, if she calls you need to be dead quiet, okay?"

"Okay," I said, looking at him askance.

"When is she gonna call?" asked Kerry.

"Any minute. Grab a beer or something. Wakeman's in the kitchen. Wakeman! Grab Kerry a beer! Kim, you want a beer?"

I shook my head. "No, I'll be the driver for you guys tonight."

Jason nodded. "Cool, cool."

A tall, good-looking black man emerged from the kitchen holding two beers.

"Hey, Marv," said the man in a friendly voice, handing him a beer, "Looking good. Gonna break into the club tonight?"

"Fool, they're gonna take one look at all this sexiness and let me just slide on by," said Kerry, running his hand over his shiny tan scalp. Wakeman laughed.

"Yeah, right man. You're about as sexy as an Oompa Loompa."

Everyone laughed, except for Kerry and me, of course. Wakeman turned to me.

"And who," he asked, with a shark-like smile, "is this lovely young lady?"

"That's Kim," answered Khadir, still engrossed in the game, "the new girl in our office."

"I'm surprised I haven't seen you, then. I'm a scheduler, I work down the hall."

"I keep to myself a lot," I said, "But I'm not really new anymore, I've been here for like six months…"

Suddenly, a twangy, midi-country song became audible, and we all paused for a moment, listening. Jason scrambled to his feet.

"Aww, shit, this is it!" said Jason, grabbing his cell phone, "Kim, shut the hell up!"

"Jason, is that seriously your freaking ringtone?" asked Khadir.

"Shuttup, man!" He flipped his phone open. "Hey, honey. How are… Yeah, yeah, I'm here, we're drinking some coffee and relaxing, it's pretty nice. No, I'm not the Seahawks. Oh yeah, sure, you want to hear?" he held up the phone to the television screen for a moment, "See? Everything's fine. No need to… what? Oh, I don't know. Maybe late. What are you going to- hmm? Oh, no, there are no girls here. Just me, Lange, Khadir, Kerry, and a really tall black man. Yeah, it's just Wakeman. Okay, honey. I love you too. Love you. Bye." And he flipped his phone closed.

"What the royal fuck, dude?" said Lange, staring at him, "You are whipped."

Jason sighed. "I know, but she just gets so jealous, I don't know what to do."

"I'm still on that ringtone, man!" interjected Khadir. "What was that shit, Shania Twain?"

"Tim McGraw and Faith Hill, man!" said Jason. "It's the *shit*. It's me and my wife's wedding song."

"Uh-huh. I'm starting to think I don't really know you, Jason," said Khadir.

"Hey," said Wakeman, "is Thea coming?"

"Yeah, she's waiting on her babysitter."

"Thea?" I asked, "Wait. Sgt Simmons is coming?"

"Her and Khadir are fuck-buddies," said Lange, whereupon Khadir punched him in the shoulder.

I was shocked. "Is that even allowed?"

"No, it isn't, which is why it's a secret," Khadir said, glaring at Lange. "Plus, we're not dating or anything serious, so it's not a big deal."

"I thought she was… y'know, not nice?" I hedged.

"She's actually very nice," said Khadir. "All that other stuff is an act for work. She's really a sweet lady, and a great mom."

"You and your moms, Khadir," said Kerry, "Kamal Khadir: MILF-hunter."

Khadir laughed. "So what if I prefer the moms, okay? They seem to prefer me right back."

Jason suddenly switched off the TV, and turned to us, his eyes bright. "Let's go! I want to hit on some hot bitches tonight!"

"Jason, you know you're still married, right?" I asked in a disapproving tone.

"I won't do anything stupid. I just wanna see if I still got it!" and he went quickly into the kitchen, and called out, "Someone do shots with me before we go!"

Lange jumped up to join him, and Khadir followed. I turned to Kerry. "He said he wasn't going to drink tonight. Should we let him take shots?"

Kerry looked at me. "I've watched this guy suffer for two years; I think he deserves a night out. Plus, it's his decision. When it comes down to it, his shitty marriage is none of our business."

I nodded, but I still felt unsure as I watched three of my co-workers take shots of Fireball at Khadir's small kitchen table. Jason's face had already become very flushed, and his ears were red.

"Alright, let's get out of here. Jason, are we taking your SUV?" asked Wakeman.

"Yeah, man, yeah! Just don't drink in there. Or smoke. Or eat anything… my wife has the nose of a blood-hound. Who's driving? I can still drive, I only took two shots…"

"I'm driving," I said firmly, "just tell me where to go."

Jason laughed a little deliriously. "Kim's driving my car! My wife would love that! Okay. I call bitch!"

"You're a bitch, alright," said Khadir.

"I think you mean 'shot-gun', Jason," said Wakeman.

"Do I? What's 'bitch?'"

"Riding between two people. You wanna squeeze between me and Marv, nice and cozy? The truth comes out tonight."

I climbed in the driver's seat and shut my door, letting them hash it out between themselves. Jason's SUV was a large, fancy Toyota, in pristine condition.

Jason jumped in, with Kerry, Wakeman and Lange getting the back. I turned.

"What about Khadir?" I asked.

"He's waiting for Thea. They'll meet us there," said Kerry.

When we arrived at the club, I was less than impressed with its shabby exterior. It was a single story, run down shack- albeit, a very large shack- and if it weren't for the flashing lights I would have deemed it a drug den. However, it was the only place for forty miles where people could go to drink and dance, so it was very popular. That night, there was a line from the entrance wrapping around the corner, and I expressed my surprise.

"Yeah, this place is a shit-hole," said Kerry.

"And they still won't let you in," said Wakeman.

Kerry glared at him. "They'll let me in tonight, fool. Just you wait and see."

We all stepped out of the SUV, and Lange, who had been wearing a sweatshirt, took it off and tossed it in the back seat. Kerry stared at him incredulously.

"Lange," he said, "What the hell... are you wearing?"

"What? Do you like it?" asked Lange, indicating his shirt. "I just bought it."

"That is the stupidest thing I've ever seen. Wakeman, come look at this."

Wakeman approached from the other side of the SUV. "What?"

"Look what Lange is wearing."

Wakeman looked at Lange's shirt; it was a skin-tight black t-shirt, with a huge, white emblazoned logo that read, 'Armani'.

Wakeman laughed. "What the hell is that, man? Who wears an Armani T-shirt?"

"I like it. I feel it represents who I am."

"Does it? 'Coz I'm pretty sure you're a senior airman who makes the exact same amount a month as I do," said Wakeman. "How much did that shirt set you back? Fifty bucks? Seventy-five?"

"Naw, man, I don't buy cheap shit! I spent two hundred bucks on this bad boy. Feel it! It's *so soft*, bro. It's like a mixture of viscose and cashmere…"

Wakeman backed up, "What the hell man, I ain't gonna feel you up. If you say it's soft, I believe you."

"Hey, there's Khadir and Thea," said Kerry. "Woo, Thea's lookin' fine."

I turned my head in the direction he was looking, and saw Khadir walking towards us with Sgt Simmons, who wore a skin-tight silver dress. With her chestnut hair falling in soft curls on her shoulders, and a smile on her face, I thought she almost looked sweet. I was quickly undeceived.

"Why the fuck are you losers outside?" said Thea irately. "We're going in, it's as cold as a witch's tit out here."

Without another word, we followed her and Khadir to the back of the line, which moved very quickly, and soon we were at the door. Bouncers looked us up and down, and passed each of us through… until they got the Kerry.

"Sorry, man, can't have ripped jeans," said the bouncer.

"You're fucking kidding me," said Kerry.

"I'm not. Sorry, man."

Kerry flushed with anger, but then turned to me. "Kim, give me the keys. I'm gonna go change in the car and come back. I'll meet you inside."

I felt bad for Kerry, so I said, "Are you sure? I can wait for you."

"Just go!" he said, grabbing the keys from my hand and stalking back into the parking lot.

I followed the others inside, showed my ID, received a hand-stamp that showed I was under twenty-one, and was admitted into the club.

My first impressions came to me quickly: loud, crowded, stuffy, smoky. The only light was black-light, and it made everyone and everything around me look strange and alien. Hip-hop music blasted from numerous speakers, making speech nearly impossible. I had temporarily lost sight of my co-workers, but after a moment I spotted Wakeman because he was so tall that he towered over everyone else, sort of like a plant that had received too much sunlight.

"Where's Kerry?" yelled Wakeman over the music.

"He's changing in the car. Bouncers didn't let him in."

Wakeman laughed, his white teeth glowing blue in the light. "Poor Kerry! He never gets a break."

"Will he be okay?" I asked.

"Yeah, he's fine," Wakeman shouted. "He's a big boy."

"Where is everyone?"

"At the bar- except Jason, he took off somewhere. Why don't you go over to the dance floor and check it out? I'm gonna get a drink. I'd get you one, but you know... you're just a baby."

I nodded sarcastically, and then weaved my way through the crowds of scantily clad women and cologne-infused men to a larger area that I assumed was the dance-floor. There were about four or five couples dancing, but most everyone was standing around in a large circle, watching the dancers and sipping drinks.

I scanned the room, searching for Jason, but didn't see him. Maybe he was at the bar, after all. I was about to turn back when the song changed, and all of a sudden the dance floor became alive with sweaty bodies, and I was caught in the middle. I was trying to push my way through when I spotted Jason, drink in hand, bumping and grinding a heavy-set girl who looked to be about eighteen. I rushed over to him.

"Jason!" I said. "C'mon! Let's go to the bar!"

"No way! I have a drink! This is fucking awesome!" He raised his hands over his head and let out a loud, *woop, woop!*

"Jason, you're married!" I yelled, trying to get his attention, which seemed to be everywhere else but on what I was saying.

"Aw, naw. I'm not married tonight!" he slurred, and proceeded, to my horror, to take off his wedding ring, and toss it high into the air behind him. There was no telling where it fell into the crowd, or what corner it rolled into- it was gone.

"Jason, what the hell!" I yelled. "You just threw away your wedding ring!"

"Naw, no I didn't..." he mumbled, and feeling his naked ring-finger, he suddenly stopped and pushed away the girl he was dancing with, a look of utmost terror filling his visage. "Oh Jesus, Kim, I threw- I threw my ring! Oh, Jesus, oh my God...!" he turned to me with a look of desperation. "Kim, you have to help me find it! I'm dead it I don't find it! Oh, my God, what will my wife do? Jesus!"

I grabbed his arm, trying to calm him. "It's okay, Jason, we'll find it. You start looking for it, okay? Look back there; that's where you threw it. I'll go get Khadir and Lange to help."

Jason looked at me gratefully. "Thanks, Kim, you're a bro."

I smiled weakly and went off to fetch help. I saw Wakeman and Lange making their way towards us, but they only howled with laughter when I told them what had happened.

"No fucking way, man!" said Lange. "Wow, he has lost it."

"Can you help us look for his ring?"

"Man, he's the loser who tossed it in the air," said Lange. "If I see it, I'll let you know, but I'm not getting on my hands and knees in this joint."

"Me neither," said Wakeman. "But I'll keep an eye out."

I frowned, disappointed. "Where's Khadir?"

Lange and Wakeman looked at each other. "Uh, Khadir ran into an old girlfriend, so he's with her at the bar."

"Oh. What about Thea?"

"She's in some corner, pissed off."

I left them, and soon found Thea standing near the bathrooms, a half-empty glass of some red drink in her hand.

"Can you fucking believe it?' she asked me, glaring across the room towards the bar. I followed her eyes, and spotted Khadir with his arms around a portly Hispanic girl in cut-off shorts. "He ditched me for Miss Piggy. Well, I hope he suffocates on one of her greasy pork rolls tonight."

"I thought you guys weren't dating?"

She hesitated. "We're not."

"Oh." I turned to the matter at hand, "Jason threw his wedding ring up into the air, and now he can't find it."

"Holy shit, that's freaking hilarious!" she laughed.

"Can you help us find it?"

"No, let him look for it. He should have known better than to do something so idiotic. But then again, it is Jason. Maybe this'll be good for him."

I bit my lip, but said nothing. Thea went back to brooding and sipping her drink, and I went back to the dance floor to find Jason. I expected to find him distraught and crawling on the floor in a desperate search, so I was shocked when I saw him in the middle of the dance floor, bumping and grinding with yet another girl as if he hadn't a care in the world. Furious, I strode right up to Jason and tapped him roughly on the shoulder.

"What about your ring?" I shouted into his ear.

He looked at me with hazy eyes and grinned. "Oh, I found it right away, see?" He held up his hand, and sure enough, there was his wedding ring, in its place as if nothing had happened.

I walked away, frustrated. Was I the only one who cared about anything?- or did I care too much? If I hadn't checked on Jason, would he have let me continue on a pointless search for his ring?

I went to stand in a corner, watching the mass of dancers writhe their bodies against each other like snakes in a pit. I felt like I wanted to leave, but I knew I couldn't, not without leaving everyone without a designated driver; and who knew what would happen to Jason then? I shook my head, angry with myself. Who cared what happened to him?

As I was lost in the thought, someone came up behind me and grabbed me around the waist and put their mouth against my neck. Shocked and frightened, I elbowed the person behind me sharply, and pulled away, turning quickly to look whoever it was in the face. It was a man, tall, muscular, and very drunk; I had never seen him before. I stared at him, my mouth agape. He was chuckling and rubbing his ribs, and didn't seem very affected by my reaction to his groping.

"Damn girl," he said, grinning, "You coulda jus' said 'Naw'."

I backed away, angry and embarrassed. "Don't touch me," I said, and began to walk away swiftly. I turned my head to see if I was being followed, and was relieved to see that I wasn't; the man had shimmied himself towards the dance floor to grind up against some other unsuspecting female. I shivered in disgust. I didn't like Cameron's. I wanted to go home, crawl under the covers, and read a book. But, as it was, I went to go stand next to Sgt Simmons near the bathrooms, and we stood there together for hours waiting for the men to finish whatever the hell it was they thought they were doing.

After that, I never accepted my co-workers invites to go out again- at least, not to go out clubbing.

On Duty
(24)

I loved going in to my office early in the morning and feeling in control, and having people come from different parts of the base just to see me, because only I could help them. I enjoyed, in my limited capacity, being the boss of my own department. Though my knowledge of the vast system I managed was limited in comparison to what it would have to eventually become, my every day tasks were simple for the most part, and what I did not know, I investigated like a detective, and felt an intense thrill of victory at every success. There were times, however, when I would become overwhelmed with anxiety, usually when a customer had been rude to me. When this happened, tears would fill my eyes and I would berate myself for my incapability. Sometimes my co-workers mocked me, telling me to 'man-up' and not to sweat the small stuff, but nothing they said ever made me feel better. Once, Sgt Slavin pulled me aside, and suggested that no one would respect me because I cried at work, and it was viewed as a weakness. Angry despite my embarrassment, I responded, "I think it's actually the brave ones who are able to cry in front of others, and then still continue to work, isn't it?" He looked dubious, but left me alone after that.

Evidently, my enthusiasm for coming into work every morning and the effort I put in every day showed, for I won multiple awards for work excellence in the first three quarters of my coming to Seymour Johnson, all of which I displayed proudly on my desk.

At the end of the day, however, I became the old Kim again- the Kim that I was before I had joined the military. When I walked into the walls of my dorm room, I felt as if I entered into a den of depravity, which I had managed to delude myself for a few hours that I could escape from. *This is my true reality*, I would realize with a heavy heart, as I changed out of my uniform, inhaling the faint scent of vomit from the day before. *How long had it been now? Five years, since I started making myself throwing up?* Once I tried to calculate my monetary loss over that amount of time, but after a certain point, the amount became so ludicrous that I gave it up, no longer wanting to know.

One morning, I went into work and sat down at my desk as usual, said good-morning to Khadir and Jason, and booted up my computer. When I checked my e-mail, I saw, among the usual database manager help queries, a rather official looking message from the Air Force Personnel Center. I opened it, and read it, but I still didn't understand what it was I was looking at. I turned to Khadir.

"Hey, Khadir?" I said, "I got a weird e-mail. Can you tell me what it is, because I have no idea."

He wheeled his chair over, sipping his coffee while he did so, and read over my shoulder. Suddenly, he started to sputter and cough. I looked at him in amazement.

"What is it?" I asked.

"Holy shit, you got an assignment!" he said. "You lucky little bitch!"

"An assignment?" I asked, my heart pounding, "Wait, like, I'm going to a new base? Already? I've only been here a year!"

"I know! What the hell! I've been here for three freaking years! Three!" He slammed his coffee down. "*So* not fair, man. You should log into your Air Force Personnel Account and see where they're sending you; it might actually be a pretty shitty place."

"Shitty, like where, shitty?"

"Like, Minot, North Dakota, Shitty."

I frowned, but quickly logged in, and followed the prompts to where my assignment RIP (Report on Individual Personnel) was listed: (Royal Air Force) RAF Lakenheath, UK.

Khadir slapped me on the back. "Holy cow, man! That's a bomb assignment! Why the hell are they PCS'ing a one-striper? Damn!"

Jason looked over at us. "Kim's leaving?"

"She got as assignment to Lakenheath, man."

"Aw, shit," said Jason, smiling, "Congrats. I'd be jealous if I wasn't getting out soon. But me- I'll be living it up in Florida here in a just a few weeks; my wife in a tiny little bikini, my pecs baking in the sun..."

At that moment, Sgt Slavin walked in with a sleepy looking Kerry, and Khadir told them the news. Sgt Slavin seemed a little surprised, and Kerry looked pissed that he hadn't gotten the RIP.

"I stopped trying to understand why the Air Force does what it does years ago," Sgt Slavin said. "But I will suggest that you don't get too excited yet; it's just an assignment notification RIP, not orders. Nothing is set in stone until you get orders. They can still be canceled."

"Why would they cancel them?" I asked.

Sgt Slavin stretched, and answered with a yawn, "Oh, disciplinary reasons, health reasons. Because it's a Tuesday, or just because they feel like it. Stuff like that."

"I hope they don't cancel mine," I said possessively.

"Well, don't do anything stupid, that might be a good start," replied Sgt Slavin, "And when you get a minute later today, we'll go see the Superintendent and see what you need to do next. When is your report 'no-later-than' date?"

I glanced at screen. "Um, RNLT March 11, 2007."

"Damn, they didn't give you a lot of time, did they? Alright. Well, we'll head over and talk to Aiden in a bit." Aiden was our flight Superintendent; my office was not the best at remembering to use professional nomenclature.

Later that day, I called Prue who was still in South Carolina, and told her the good news. I hadn't been aware that I wanted to go to the UK, but now that it was a real possibility for me, I found that I wanted nothing more in the world. When I told her, Prue squealed with joy, though she quickly tempered it with a sullen, "Well, I guess that means we can't visit each other any more. Thanks a lot, ass."

Sgt Slavin and I went to se the superintendent later that day, and after we were closeted in the office, Senior Master Sergeant Thomas, a.k.a Aiden, cleared his throat, and said:

"Presa, I looked into your assignment, and unfortunately it looks like there is one thing holding you back from PCSing; there's a medical hold on you due to something you answered in a questionnaire, I believe, or maybe because something you told to your primary care doctor. I'm not one-hundred percent on what it is, exactly, so you will have to look into it. I'm sorry, but I can't guarantee that your assignment will still be waiting for you when you get it cleared up. Good assignments go fast." He snapped his fingers for effect.

My mouth pressed into a thin line, and I clenched my fists in my lap. *Of course this happening*, I thought. *Nothing is ever easy for me.*

"Sir, can I go to the hospital now, if I can get them to see me?" I asked, "I don't know what they're worried about, but I'll call and see. I don't remember my saying anything weird."

Slavin spoke up, then: "Well, you know, those health questionnaires that they make everyone fill out every year... they say that, you know, they're just there to help you, and nothing you say on them will ever affect your career, or come back to bite you in the ass. But, the truth is... it *does* bite you in the ass. I lie my damned butt off on those things. Are you depressed? Oh, no, 'course not. Do you drink alcohol more than three times a week? Absolutely not. Do you have homicidal tendencies? Oh, hell no; and et cetera, et cetera. You can do what you want, but I just thought you should know my personal opinion about those damned things, for future reference."

"Thanks, Sgt Slavin," I said, trying to remember the last questionnaire I had filled out. It must have been the one I filled out upon coming to Seymour Johnson... Then it dawned on me; I remembered. There had been a question about depression and anxiety, and I had admitted to suffering negative feelings a couple of times a week. A couple of weeks later, I had received a call from a mental health counselor, asking me to come in. Curious, I had showed up at the appointment, and spoke briefly to a therapist, whom I tried to convince that I had filled out that paperwork right after I had arrived there, and so my answer was solely based on the nerves one can feel after moving. The therapist seemed to accept my statement, and that was that; I had never seen him again. I told Sgt Slavin and Aiden what had happened, and they nodded.

"Yup, that sounds like the good ol' Air Force," said Sgt Slavin. "Go ahead and call Mental Health and see if you can clear it up, and see if you can't keep your assignment."

I thanked them and left the room, ruminating that no matter how bad things got in the future, I would never again discuss my mental health with a military doctor.

*

Though the medical hold took two weeks to clear up, I was lucky enough to keep my assignment, and a few months later I found myself spending my last day at work at Seymour Johnson. I felt a little sad about leaving, but I was mostly excited about what the future held. I didn't feel sentimental about North Carolina and wouldn't even be tempted to glance at it in the review mirror, but I would perhaps feel a few pangs whenever I recalled my co-workers, who with their strange romances and crass humor had entertained me daily. Before I left, they presented me with a small plaque which read, "Give a Woman a Job and She Grows Balls." I grinned when I read it, and gave everyone hugs, despite the ridiculous rule against public displays of affection. I had never been given a gift like that before; something personalized with only me in mind; it meant the world to me.

Our commander also came in briefly to present to me an Achievement Medal for my time at Seymour Johnson, which I thanked Sgt Slavin and Sgt Simmons for, since it was they who wrote up the nomination for me. Medals are something the military holds in very high esteem, so when the commander hung the silver and blue medal on my uniform, I flushed with pride.

But it was soon time to leave, and I said my last good-byes to everyone; to Khadir, the Terrorist; to Lange, the Posh Bostonian; to Jason, the Good Husband; and Kerry, the sleepy Honduran. I also shook hands with grumpy Sgt Simmons, Sgt Slavin, SMSgt Aiden, and Sgt Greeves, and to my surprise they all seemed genuinely sad to see me go.

"Thanks for being so nice to me, you guys," I said as I turned to leave. "I'll miss you."

"Later!" said Khadir, grinning, "Call, or whatever, alright?"

I nodded. "I will. Bye, guys." And with a small wave, I walked out the office door for the last time. I had been at Seymour Johnson barely a year and half.

Over the Pond
(25)

When I left the United States I felt none of the pangs of remorse that some feel when they leave their home country for an untold amount of time. I wasn't leaving close family, for one thing- I wasn't even sure if my dad knew I was leaving the States- and the only friend I claimed was Prue, but I knew that no matter where I went in the world, she would still be there for me, and we would continue to communicate.

The flight took about five hours, and as I descended into that beautiful, almost ephemeral-looking country, covered in mists and delicate shadows, a part of me felt that I was flying back to Oregon. Surely, it resembled it, with its chill in the air and constant drizzle; but I reminded myself that whatever similarities there might be, that's all they were- similarities. What kind of a life I lived in the UK was up to Kim of Now, and not up to the person I had been in the past.

I was introduced to my new office the day I arrived, and as much as I had come to enjoy my old co-workers and their antics, I was pleasantly surprised with the professionalism and easy companionability of my new ones. I found out I would be working mostly with staff sergeants, with the exception of two senior airmen, one of which was named Amy, who quickly made herself friendly.

"What dorms are they going to put you in?" she asked, as my new supervisor, SSgt Dalen, created a new computer log-in ID for me, "I'm in the really old ones across from the soccer field."

I took out a sheet of paper. "I'm in 8110."

Amy made a face. "That's really far away from mine. Oh, well. Until your car gets here, I can drive you to work, and save your legs. It's a bit of a walk to get here, since this office is way out near the flight-line."

"I'd appreciate that a lot!"

Amy smiled, and leaned forward. "I think you'll really like it here. I'll be leaving soon, but everyone here is so nice. I really envy you!"

"You're leaving? Where are you going next?" I asked.

"Moody AFB, Georgia."

"Oh," I said. I knew nothing about Moody, so I wasn't sure if that was a good thing or a bad thing.

"It could have been worse... I could have been sent to Minot, or something."

"That's true."

Amy looked around the office, which consisted of two large rooms, attached at a partition that had been knocked out sometime in the past. She glanced at the back of one of the females I hadn't met, and she seemed to consider something.

"I said everyone here is really nice, and that's true, but I should probably warn you about Whitney," said Amy cagily, her eyes boring a hole into the back of the actively typing woman.

I followed her eyes, and frowned. "What about her?"

"She's sweet, but that girl is *crazy*. Like, legitimately."

"How so?" I asked, doubting her words.

"Well, let's see, how can I explain... really, the best way for you to find out is to spend time with her, but I can give you a few examples. Um...a few weeks ago she said that the reason why black people jump so high is because they have extra bones in their feet... and she swore she had scientific evidence, but when we asked her to show it to us, she 'lost' it. And before that she declared to everyone she was one-hundred percent Hispanic, and was going to purchase land in Brazil to set up roots in her homeland- but Brazil is a Portuguese speaking country; it's not even Hispanic."

I turned to look at the back of the woman who we were discussing, who continued to type, blissfully unaware of what was being said about her. It could still be a joke, or a mistake, I thought. But somehow, looking at her un-brushed, messy head, and seeing her cracked glasses which lay on her desk, I felt that perhaps there was some element of truth in Amy's words, after all.

"Well, she must be good at her job, then," I submitted dubiously.

Amy shook her head slowly, decisively. "Not."

I remained silent, and at that moment Sgt Dalen came over, large and handsome, and said, "So, your user ID is 'PREK'. Isn't it lovely?"

I smiled. "Oh, yes, very lovely, thank you."

"I made it just for you, Keem. Not really- actually the computer generated it, but let's just pretend. You know how to log in, I suppose?"

I nodded. "Yes, Sir."

"Please don't 'Sir' me when it's just us," Sgt Dalen frowned. "Call me 'Super-Fantastic Red Hulk' when we're in the office. It makes me feel like a man."

Amy and I laughed, and he moved away, grinning. For some reason, his banter, though the words themselves might be construed as flirtations, didn't come across as such. He reminded me a big, loveable bear, and I liked him immediately.

"He seems awesome," I said to Amy.

"He is," she said, "He's been my best friend in the office. I'm going to miss him a lot."

"When are you leaving?" I asked.

"In two months; we're also getting a new Master Sergeant to come take charge of the office, as MSgt Meyers- you met him, today- is leaving in a few weeks. And after that, some other people are leaving: Sgt Babick and Sgt Gutierrez."

"Geez," I said, stunned. "Is everyone leaving? Are we getting anyone else to make up for the losses?"

Amy shrugged. "We haven't heard of any besides you and this new Master Sergeant. It's stressing everyone out a bit, because once everyone leaves, it will just be you, Sgt Dalen, Sgt Chassidy, Whitney and the new MSgt to do all of the work- and MSgt's never do any work, so forget that."

I frowned. I didn't mind work, but I also did not like the prospect of carrying unnecessary loads if it could be avoided.

Amy changed the subject. "Hey, there's a party this weekend in my dorm; my friend is throwing a going-away thing for one of his co-workers. Would you like to go? It would be a good way for you to go know some people."

"Sure," I said, "I'd love to go."

"Great! I'll let you know more tonight after I call him. For now I should probably start training you, or something."

I laughed. "I guess so. Or we can ask Whitney if she found proof of those extra bones."

We giggled a little madly, and then set to work.

*

I met Amy at her dorms that Saturday, and she led me upstairs to a common room where we were greeted by music and the smell of barbecuing meat. As we entered the room, a ping-pong ball flew at my face, and I ducked quickly to avoid it. When I looked to see where it had come from, I saw a tall man with the usual Air Force hair cut, laughing loudly at something one his friends had said. He wasn't especially attractive; he had large, blue eyes and a small beak nose, but I was drawn to him; he seemed so alive and in the moment- so very unlike me. He was focused on his friends, seemed to be drinking a lot, and overall appeared to be just having a good time. Amy saw me looking at him, and she smiled and said,

"That's my friend I was telling you about! He's a nice guy. Let me introduce you."

She led me over the table where he was playing beer pong. He was losing horribly, but a keeping good humor about the situation, which impressed me favorably. She touched him on the shoulder and he turned and grinned with uneven, slightly yellowed teeth.

"Amesy-bear!" he said in a deep voice, "You made it!" and he gave her a hug. "And who's this?"

"Nathan, this is Kim; Kim, Nathan," she introduced, "She just got here from Seymour Johnson. This is her second base."

Nathan giggled, his face flushed with liquor. I had never heard a man giggle like that before, and it made me smile. "I always thought, y'know… second base was a good base," he said, leering.

Amy and I laughed, and I said, "Yes, I agree."

"You guys want to play beer pong? You *got* to play beer pong!" he said, excited, "You see, this here is a going away party for our dear friend Scooter, who ships off in a few days for his next base. Say hi, Scooter!" And he indicated a thin, pale boy duck-taped to a chair, with mugs of alcohol also attached with tape to each of his hands. Scooter, who looked a little worse for drink, said 'Hi' vaguely, and then continued to sip from his hand cups.

Nathan turned back to us. "So you have to help us celebrate. Alright?"

"That's why we're here!" said Amy, and as Nathan turned back to his game, we both went over to the refreshment table and poured ourselves a drink.

"He seems nice," I said.

"He *is* nice. He's one of the only guys I could really talk to when I first arrived," said Amy, sipping her drink. "You guys should get along."

"He's also kind of cute," I said, eyeing him.

Amy choked on her drink. "You're kidding! Nathan?"

"What? You don't think he's cute?"

She shook her head vigorously. "Hell to the No! I think you're crazy. Are you already drunk?"

"I don't get drunk anymore. But he wouldn't be interested in me, would he? He hardly looked at me when you introduced us."

Amy stared at me. "You're serious, aren't you? He probably didn't look at you because he thinks he has no chance in hell. You are way out of his league, girl."

I scoffed. "No, I'm not! Plus, I don't believe in 'leagues'. There are just people who are or are not attracted to each other."

Amy sighed. "You are both my friends, so I choose to stay out of whatever may happen. I recues myself."

I smiled, nodded and sipped my drink.

The rest of the night was a blur; Nathan remained surrounded by his friends for most of the night, so I didn't have much a chance to talk to him until after one o'clock, when everyone began to leave. They eventually cut Scooter free of his chair and carried him to his dorm room, where I assume he slept in drunken peace until the next morning. When there were about five of us left, including Nathan, Amy and I, Nathan strode forward and announced,

"I'm starving. Who wants grilled cheeses? And- I need to brag for a moment- I make the best grilled cheese ever tasted by mankind. It's plain ridiculous."

Amy and I were the only ones who agreed to stay and judge his statement for ourselves, and the last of the other guests went home. We sat at his tiny dorm kitchen table and watched him cook the sandwiches. I couldn't help but be a bit judgmental; he didn't do anything special, and he used white bread. When I pointed this out to him, he turned to me with a semi-serious look and said,

"White bread is the bread of the gods."

"I don't know. Would the gods' bread be heavily processed, bleached and fiberless, and prone to cause diabetes?"

"What? Is that what white bread is?" asked Nathan.

"...Yes."

"Then yeah!" he said, slapping my grilled cheese in front of me on a napkin plate. "Eat up! It's the best. I *swear*."

Smiling, I took a small bite; it was good, but I knew I wouldn't be able to finish it without getting sick later, so I picked at it while Amy and Nathan devoured theirs. Nathan finished his and then indicated my uneaten sandwich.

"Are you not hungry?" he asked.

"Oh, not really. I'm on a diet."

"A diet? I don't understand chicks. You guys are always on a diet, or a cleanse or something, even when you weigh like one hundred pounds."

I was flattered despite the fact he had used the word 'chicks' which grated on me. I had felt especially fat that day, and he was calling me thin. All the same, I felt it was my duty to argue. "No, no, I'm not…"

"And you guys always say you're not skinny but you are. I don't understand women. Maybe that's why I'm twenty-two and already divorced," he said.

I looked up at him with interest. "You were married?"

He nodded. "Yup. Married a girl from Tech school. Stupid, right? I tell you what though, I loved that girl a lot, and I was a damn good husband. But she didn't love me; she went and cheated on me when I was deployed."

My heart went out to him, as it always did to those who had been hurt. "That's terrible! It must have been hard."

"You're damn right, it was hard. Happened just a year ago. Worst part about it though is hearing all the 'I told you so's' from my mom back in Ohio," he chuckled.

Amy suddenly stood up and yawned, stretching one arm into the air. "Well, kids, I'm going to hit the hay. I'm exhausted. Why don't you walk Kim home, Nathan? She lives way over in 8110. I was going to do it, but I'm too sleepy."

I looked at Amy in surprise; I had thought she was going to stay out of it. She carefully avoided my gaze.

Nathan nodded. "Yeah, alright; I'd be happy to. Good night, Amesy-bear! See you soon," he gave her a hug, and then turned to me, "You ready? It's pretty late, and I'm pretty drunk, so I better get to bed soon."

"Yeah, I'm ready. Bye, Amy," I said, and we walked out the door and headed toward the soccer field which, which, if we cut across it, would take us directly to my dorm.

It was a cold night, and I shivered; Nathan asked if I wanted his coat, and despite my refusal he took off his large brown jacket and placed it over my shoulders, and I instantly grew warmer.

"Thank you," I said.

"Anything for a lady," he replied jauntily.

We walked on in silence, and then when we reached my room, I thanked him for a fun night, and again for walking me home. He was about to leave, when he turned to me and asked, hesitatingly, "Would it be okay if I stop by sometime? Or call you?"

I smiled myself. *Yes, yes!* "Yes, I'd like that. Amy has my number, so you can ask her for it, if you want. I haven't memorized it yet."

He nodded, and as he left, I shut the door to my room, smiling like an idiot.

*

One of the main problems in the Air Force during the time I was in service, especially during my time at Lakenheath, was lack of man-power, and money. We always needed more people, and not just in my office, but everywhere; people with on-the-job experience, people with solid years behind them. But with the mandated budget cuts hitting the Department of Defense hard- to the sum of over one-hundred billion dollars annually- the Air Force was forced to shrink it's size by a third, and close a quarter of it's bases. As if on cue, the aircraft we maintained began to show their age; they averaged about twenty-five years old per jet. The amount of money the force spent replacing their broken parts would shock and disgust most sane-minded people, and it was discussed repeatedly amongst higher-ups what fleet, if any, should be retired. But in the end, they kept most everything, but retained less people, and less space. Year after year, we overspent our budget, but still lost the personnel we sorely needed to keep the aircraft in the air and our pilots trained for active warfare. That's not to say, we didn't survive, somehow- but it was a tough time of adjustment for everyone, from the commanders having to answer for every dollar, down to the airmen working days on end on the flight-line without much needed rest.

My job was all about saving money; using past information to determine key leading and lagging indicators about aircraft, and somehow turning it into legible, useful information in order to stave off future errors, keep proper supplies ordered, and all that. A lot of what I did was simply turn a lot of shit information into something that officers could read in thirty seconds during a meeting- at least, that's what it felt like I was doing But I didn't mind it. I had an eye for detail and I enjoyed what I did, despite the long hours and the erratic behavior of the manning department of the Air Force, AFPC. They would swell some bases with people in a desperate attempt to satiate their need for personnel, and leave others short-changed for months. For quite a while, RAF Lakenheath was very much the latter; but then, all of a sudden, it became very much the former.

Months had passed, and I had settled into work. Nathan and I had started to date- but we both had an idea it wouldn't last long, as he was due to ship out to Korea any day. Amy was still on base, but she was on leave and didn't come in to the office anymore- two staff sergeants and our section chief had left; a new master sergeant had arrived and taken his place, and we were all less than favorably impressed with him. Some people, when you meet them, you like right away- you just can't help it. But others give you the opposite reaction, and everything they say or do is like nails down the chalkboard. Sgt Resser was nails for me. He was a bald man, of medium height, with hooded eyes and long, curved nose, and everywhere he walked he seemed to thrust his crotch out in front of him like a backwards strutting bird. His voice sounded like he had a permanent bubble stuck in his throat, and he could never let you finish your sentence without emitting some weird noise from it. I couldn't even look at him without becoming annoyed.

One day, while we were all working at our respective computers, Sgt Resser, walked behind us, and in his grating voice, announced, "Office meeting, ladies and gents; come on over to the table."

The six of us who remained complied, and waited for him with bored expressions as he printed out a multi-page document on the printer. I stared at him while it printed, dead-eyed. Why couldn't he have done that before calling us over? He then proceeded to saunter over the join us, but instead of sitting down he lifted his right leg and set it atop a center chair support, like a lazy, bald Captain Morgan. He pretended to read the papers in his hand as he spoke his memorized little speech.

"Well, good news, it looks like they have solved our manning problems. They are sending us seven people in the next few months to fill the gaps of those we will be losing, plus more." He lifted his gaze to us, and I could tell from the gleam in his beady eyes that couldn't wait to drop a bomb on us. "The bad news; they are all coming directly from Tech School."

Sgt Chassidy snorted. "Oh, great! Thanks AFPC!"

Whitney and I looked to Sgt Dalen to see his reaction, since we both viewed him as the real boss, but he just chewed his lower lip, and nodded sagely. I couldn't help but admire his coolness. In the meantime, Sgt Resser was talking:

"For the most part, they are coming staggered; two at once, then about two a month, until they're all here. It's not going to be easy for our NCOs to take on so many new troops at once, so we're really going to rely on our dedicated Airman..." his eyes roved to me and Whitney, "to do most of the training. Do you think you ladies are up to it?"

I shrugged, but Whitney said, "Yes, Sir!"

Resser continued: "I haven't worked out everything yet, but one will be assigned under Sgt Dalen to be trained to be his assistant Database Manager, and the rest will be trained as AMU Analysts, assigned under Sgt Chassidy and Sgt Gates. Two will eventually be changed to Wing Analysts, but that will come later after they've gotten used to the work."

We all watched him in silence, waiting for more. He cleared his throat, and said,

"The first two will be arriving in two weeks; A1C Sean and A1C Manning."

I frowned. "They're just coming from tech school, and they're already A1C's?"

Resser nodded. "They either signed up for six years, or they have some college credits, I suppose."

I grumbled a bit, at that. They would be making as much as I was, and were the same rank as me, even though I had been in service for two and half years, and they were just joining. It didn't feel fair, and I mentioned my feelings out loud.

"If you don't like people coming in with rank the same as you, you should have worked harder before coming in yourself to earn some college credits," said Resser, smirking, and at the moment I wanted nothing more than to throttle him.

The phone rang then, and Sgt Dalen went to answer it, and, deciding unanimously that that meant the meeting was over, we dispersed. We knew that we were being disrespectful to MSgt Resser and his authority, but we found it hard to care; he was a weak leader, and we all sensed in him a streak of pettishness and cruelty that we felt would show itself whenever he was inclined to let it.

Back at my desk, Whitney leaned back in her seat, very pregnant, and sighed.

"Seven new airmen! This'll be fun; especially for *you*," she said with a lopsided smile.

"Why?" I asked.

"Because for some of the time they'll be in training, I'll be off on maternity leave," she said, patting her basketball-shaped stomach. "You'll be the only one left to train them!"

"Oh, good," I said sarcastically, "I can't wait."

*

"What is this Call about, anyway?" I complained one Friday afternoon as I walked in a gaggle with the rest of my office. Most of our new Airmen had arrived, and I tended to walk in front of them like a mother goose. "We have so much crap to do that it's not even funny. It's the end of the month- no one would notice if we didn't show up."

"I think it's a safety call," replied Whitney, adjusting her cockeyed and cracked glasses, "and MSgt Resser would know."

"Yeah, okay, but where the hell is he?" I raged, looking around.

"I think he had to take his dog out for a quick walk and then he's going to catch up with us."

I took a deep breath, trying to calm myself. MSgt Resser had started bringing his miniature something-or-other into work, and keeping it in his office, tied to a coat-rack where it did nothing but whine and piss all day. "That dog. If you can even call it a dog. It's more like a *rat*."

"I think it's cute."

I glared at her. "Traitor."

"Hey, I said it was cute, not that he should be bringing it into work! I think that's wrong," she said.

"It's got to be against the rules."

She shrugged, and touched her very pregnant belly. She was due any day, now. "It probably is. And if that thing poops in his office again the smell is going to make me hurl. Baby doesn't like it."

I looked at her. From the back, or even looking directly on, you couldn't tell she was pregnant. Rail thin, gangly, her stomach was the only large thing about her, so only if she turned to the side it became obvious, sort of like a flounder. As we walked, she took a few deep breaths and sipped her water bottle.

"You okay, Whitney?" I asked.

"Oh," she said, smiling a little, "I'm okay. I didn't get much sleep, and then I was running late this morning because I'm nauseous, and I forgot to brush my hair and teeth, too. I'm feeling a bit all over the place."

Gross, I thought, but out loud I said, "I'm sure you can go back to the office- just wait there for the Airmen to come back and then start training them on the Weekly. Rest until then- I'll tell them you didn't feel well if they ask."

She shook her head, her ratty hair falling in her face. "Naw, I'm ok. Thanks, though."

Still not convinced that she was well enough to stand for so long, I stayed close to her just in case she passed out (which she has been known to do) and we walked a little down the flight line to one of the hangars commonly used for All-Calls. It was crowded with Airmen of all ranks from our squadron, all gossiping, waiting for the commander to arrive.

And so we waited. And waited. Thirty minutes passed. Our gaggle of Airmen started to get restless, and I was in no mood to be a good example.

"Where is the Commander?" I asked finally, exasperated, stretching my legs, "and where the hell is MSgt Resser?"

Whitney just shook her head, still looking green. She sipped her water bottle again.

I couldn't contain my frustration anymore. "We have a shit-ton of work to do, which the commander himself will get pissed if we don't send to him by the end of the day, but he's not letting us work by being half an hour late to his own meeting. We were told to come here by MSgt Resser, who said he'd be right behind us, but where is he? He's taking his dog on an hour long shit. And you're ill and you refuse to go sit down! ARGH!"

"It's okay, Presa, we have to represent Analysis…"

"Give me your water bottle, Whitney."

"Um… why?"

"Because I'm going to dump it out and run around screaming 'her water broke!', and we're getting the hell out of here."

"No way!"

"Give it here, Whitney!"

Whitney bubbled with laughter. "No! You're crazy!"

I turned to scan the crowd and sighed. "Yeah, well, people make me crazy. Ooh, the Commander's coming, Whitney. Here comes his car. Last chance!"

She grabbed her water bottle close to her chest, out of reach. "No!"

"Coward."

And so the meeting commenced, all ten minutes, about safety- safety in the office, on flight line, driving to and from work, and we were dismissed. Inwardly, I seethed, *this was so worth an hour and a half of lost work*! And then I calculated, seven airmen each losing one-point-five hours... *ten-point-five man hours lost*! And there was still no sign of MSgt Resser. The squadron was dismissed, and we all dispersed in our respective directions, the analysts branching off by ourselves. Everyone else, unencumbered by a pregnant woman, headed back to the office at a normal pace, but I stayed back with Whitney, who by this phase of her pregnancy more of a waddler than a walker. I stayed very close to her side, every so often looking over at her green, frowning face with concern. One or twice she belched loudly, and I held my breath so as to not inhale the scent. We were about halfway back to the office and we decided to take a small shortcut through the yard of the small building that was being used by mobility for chemical gear training. At the time, there happened to be a bunch of airmen outside, performing mock cordons, and as they were busily occupied they hardly glanced at us. We were almost out of their lawn, when Whitney abruptly stopped.

"I have to throw up," she announced.

My eyes widened in surprise. "Oh-h, okay, I'm sure we can go inside that building and use their..."

But there was no time for words. Whitney bent as much as she could at the waist and emptied her stomach onto the grass, while directly facing the airmen who were training with their chemical gear. And suddenly, they were all paying attention to us. I will never forget the looks on their faces; disgust, shock, fear, even. I stood there, mortified, as still as a statue. I recall that poor Whitney gave three large, loud, full heaves of vomit, and then stood up, wiped her dribbling chin with the sleeve of her maternity BDU, and announced,

"That's better," and began to walk again, not even sparing a glance at the horrified airmen.

After a moment, and thinking I should probably say something, I waved to them, and said, "Sorry, she's very sick!" and ran after her.

"Whitney!" I said, "That... that was amazing!"

She looked at me strangely. "Really? Why?"

"Because... because you just blew chunks all over their yard, right in front of them, and then walked away like it was no big thing! Did you not see the looks on their faces? You are so bad-ass!"

She smiled a little goofily. "Well, when you're pregnant, if you have to throw up, you have to throw up. And it's not like I can clean it up myself or anything. I can't even bend over."

I laughed. I had always thrown up in secrecy- I had always been mortified at the thought of someone watching me be sick. And though it was still disgusting, no matter how you looked at it, there was still something cathartic about watching this woman spew in front of an audience without an iota of shame.

"I will remember this forever. I feel like you did this just for me, because I was having a crappy day."

Whitney giggled. "You are so weird."

I didn't argue with her.

*

"We have an opportunity coming up," Resser said, looking around the room with vague eyes, "for a deployment for a 2R050."

My heart began to beat loudly. A 2R050 was a five-level; I was a five-level. That meant it would either be me or Whitney, the new mom, and I would just not let the latter happen. As annoying as Whitney could be, I liked her, and I didn't want her to have to leave her kid right after her four week maternity leave ended; it was too soon. Everyone knew the four weeks maternity leave was bull-shit enough without having to deploy right afterwards. Sure, many did it, and did it without complaint, but if it could be avoided I would see that it was. Anyway, Nathan had gone to Korea, and I had no reason to stay. I raised my hand quickly.

"I volunteer. I want to go."

Resser looked at me. "You were next on the docket, anyway. You don't have a choice."

I eyed him stubbornly. "I don't care; I volunteer. I would have volunteered even if I wasn't supposed to go this rotation."

Resser chuckled. "I admire your initiative, Airman Presa. I guess that's why you made senior airman Below-the-Zone. You'll make a great NCO one day."

I remained quiet. I didn't want his praise for my hard work.

He then turned his attention to everyone. "We're going to have to pick up the slack when our little superstar here leaves us, mmkay? You younger airmen are really going to have to step up your game."

The A1Cs stared at him blankly in response.

"Anywho, head on over to mobility when you get a chance, Presa," Resser continued, "And they'll give you all the information you need."

I stood up then, and said, "I have time now, Sir. I've checked everyone's Daily's." I turned to Sgt Dalen. "Can I go to mobility?"

Sgt Dalen looked at me like I was asking to be whipped, but he said, "It's fine with me, but maybe wait until Sgt Resser's done talking, Keem."

But Sgt Resser just smiled with complete self-assurance and said, "That's all I wanted to say for now, thanks. Let us know if you need anything from us to help you prepare, mmkay, Airman Presa?"

I nodded, and grabbed my hat and ID, and left the room.

Mortar and Mettle
(26)

    I stepped off the blue bus into the dark with my green rucksack thrown over my shoulder, my chem-gear balanced in the crook of my elbow, and my M-16, still in its black case, clenched tightly in my left hand. My boots touched down on a sandy, well-packed dust road; on either side stood rows of barbed wire fences and whatever lay behind them was wreathed in shadows. I glanced up and down the road. There were a handful of generator lights, here and there, but otherwise the road was long, dark, and daunting. I turned back to the bus, wondering who else was getting off, but the door suddenly slid shut, the breaks released with a hiss, and the blue giant lumbered away, purring loudly. I stood staring after its tail lights, clutching my belongings in the dark. I was alone in Afghanistan.

I took a deep breath to steady my nerves. *I'm okay*, I thought. *I'm fine. I just need to find... what do I need to find?* I glanced around desperately. I had thought there would be someone to pick me up, or some obvious sign-post to direct me where to go. Had I gotten off at the wrong stop? The directions had said to come here... didn't they? I tried to pull out my instructions but it was so dark I couldn't see, so I turned my head towards the closest generator and began to walk towards it. A few people in strange uniforms passed me, speaking in languages I didn't understand, and I gave them a wide berth as they moved by. I didn't know enough about our allies' officer ranks to know when, or if, I should salute them. I realized with a feeling of panic that I hadn't prepared as much as I should have, and that without a doubt I was going to make a fool out of myself.

Once under the yellow, humming light, I threw my bags down, and sat on top of my duffel bag, and realized all at once how exhausted I was. I had flown for three days straight, almost without sleep; the last flight had been in a crammed, bumpy C-130, so I hadn't managed to even close my eyes while in the air. I stifled a yawn, and took out my directions, and re-read them for the thousandth time.

"...bus will drop you off at destination, second to last stop before exiting North Disney Road."

I had consulted with the bus driver, and he had assured me that this was the correct stop. But where did I go, now? I had been so focused on getting to this point without getting lost- navigating solo through airports in Italy, Kyrgyzstan, and… where the hell else had I flown through?- that now that I was there, I was dumbfounded at what to do next.

Unsure of what to do, my exhaustion and anxiety got the best of me; and there, sitting on my duffle bag in the spotlight of the generator, my eyes began to water. I tried to convince myself it was just the dust in the air, but I knew it wasn't. It was a quiet, pitiful moment; a grown woman on deployment, her tears dropping unhindered onto the collar of her ABU blouse. After a moment I began to wipe my eyes with the back of my hands, rallying, breathing deep, trying to awaken my fatigued mind.

"You alright, Ma'am?" asked a voice from outside the light.

I stood up immediately, alert, trying to see where the voice had come from. A man in Army fatigues stepped closer, eyeing me curiously. I glanced at his rank- three chevrons above three rockers- MSgt. I nodded, relieved beyond words to meet another member of the US military.

"Yes, Sir," I said, "But I'm lost. I just got dropped off here, and I have no idea where I'm going. My directions are badly written."

The MSgt came a little closer. "What unit are you in?"

I shook my head. "They didn't put that on my paperwork, either," I said. "It's my fault for not making sure of it before I left. I thought it would be more obvious where to go once I got here, I guess. But, I work with the F-15E's. Do you know where they're located? That's where I belong."

The MSgt chewed his cheek for a moment, then said, "I know they're somewhere on the other side of the base, but… here, I think it's best if I take you to some of your Air Force buddies. They'll know how to get you over there. Follow me."

"Thank you so much," I said, relieved, picking up my bags.

We walked for a while down the dark road, eventually turning into a small break in one of the barbed fences. The MSgt led me to a small group of men who were sitting on the stairs of a small, ramshackle hut, and I saw with a lift of my heart that they wore Air Force uniforms.

"I found one of yours lost on Disney," said the Army MSgt, "She said she works with F-15's. I was hoping you guys can take it from here, and help get her where she needs to go."

One of the men who had been sitting on the steps stood up, glanced at me, and nodded. "Sure thing, Sir. We actually work right next to those guys. If she wants to take a lift with us here in a few minutes, she'll be right where she needs to be."

The MSgt turned to me. "They'll take care of ya."

I looked up at him, grateful. "Thank you so much, Sir."

"No problem," he said stoically. I watched him go, and sent with him my wishes for his safety.

"So you work with the F-15s?" asked the man who had stood up.

"Yeah."

"We work with A-10's, right next-door. Why they'd leave you high and dry?" he asked.

"I flew out here alone," I replied, "I didn't deploy with my unit, so… I guess they assumed I was smarter than I am and could make my own way. I'm an idiot."

The man chuckled. "Don't worry about it. The first day in this shit-hole is never easy even if you do deploy with everyone. But we'll see that you get where you need to go."

I smiled appreciatively. "I don't know what I would have done without that MSgt leading me to you guys," I said. "I might have sat there all night, crying like a goddamn baby."

"You would have found your way eventually," said the man, "but all the same I'm glad you found us. It's not safe being out here on your own."

I looked at him in surprise. "It's not safe on the base?"

The man shook his head slowly. "It's not safe anywhere around here," he said. Why do you think we carry loaded rifles and pistols everywhere we go? They let local Afghanis work on base, too; you know, the one's who's families we've been exploding?-which if you ask me, is not the best idea in the goddamn world. So anyway, yeah; I suggest you never walk anywhere alone."

I gulped. What had I gotten myself into?

*

I walked with trepidation into the small room. It was just like any other office in the Air Force; it even smelled like coffee and was filled with men. In one corner there sat a person I vaguely recognized as being from my base, and in the other corner, of all the people in the world, sat my old supervisor, SSgt Slavin. I instantly felt as if a huge weight had been lifted off my shoulders. I was in the right place, after all. He looked up at me, his bald head shining in the lamp-light, and he flashed me what for him passed as a smile.

"Hey, Presa," he grumbled, "How ya doin? It's good to see ya."

I wanted to hug him, but as his hand was proffered I settled for that instead. "I'm happy to see you too! It's been a long time."

He nodded. "Yeah, a few years now. How are ya doin'?"

"I'm okay. It was a disaster getting here. I was pretty much just dropped off in the middle of Disney Drive."

"Ouch," he said, not looking sympathetic at all. "But you got here somehow, that's good."

I nodded. "Yeah, a master sergeant helped me out. I haven't slept for three days or more, though, so I'm delirious with exhaustion. I was wondering if someone could help me find where I'm supposed to bunk, so I don't have to keep hefting my clothes around. Plus with these malaria meds… I feel like I might start hallucinating any minute."

Slavin eyed me. "We-ll, I fly out in less than a day. I don't know if you know this but most of your aircraft are already here. I've been doing your work for you- your base was late in delivering you. So if you leave right now and go to sleep you won't have any turnover, and won't know what the hell you're doing when you come back."

My heart sunk. "Mother fucker. Okay. Goddammit." I wiped my eyes, trying to clear the cobwebs. *Work, work, must focus on work. Stop being a wuss.*

Slavin cleared his throat. "How about we train a few hours and see if you need any more info after that? If you're good to go at that point, you can leave with mid-shift. I mean, honestly, there's not an awful lot to it. If you take good notes you should be alright. Anyway, you need to check in officially, and have your weapon loaded, and all that."

I quickly latched on to the idea. "Yes, let's do that. I am just so freaking tired, there was no time to rest at all and they didn't have a bed for me in transit… I'm sorry. I'm rambling. I will be fine tomorrow." I reached into my pack and pulled out my notepad. "Some things I really want to know- How do I get here every day? What are my shift hours? Who is my supervisor? Tell me everything, because I'm a complete blank- no one could tell me anything before I left."

Slavin glanced at me, and bid me to sit next to him. "Your shift starts at six pm, and ends at seven am, but really, you won't get back to your hut until about seven or eight am, due to turnover… so you might go ahead and get used to that now."

"Great," I said darkly, writing that down.

"You'll ride the bus with the maintainers at the stop across from the coffee hut. They'll show it to you when you get dropped off so you know exactly where it is. Make sure you're out there ten minutes before six, alright?"

I nodded.

"As for your supervisor, and where you'll be sleeping and all that…" he said, "I'll take you next door in a few and introduce you to MSgt Evans, and he'll help you out with that, because I ain't got no frickin' idea. This place is a goddamn mess."

I smiled a little. I had missed Sgt Slavin and his blatant honesty.

He turned to his computer, and logged in. "I'll show you a few things to get started- you know, just the basic crap," he said. "So, this is the daily…"

For the next three hours, I was taught how to perform my job at a deployed location, and I was glad to find that it was not much different than it was at any regular base. Afterwards, I was introduced to my supervisor and, after saying goodbye to Sgt Slavin, I was allowed to leave on one of the large blue buses with mid-shift. I was then in-processed properly, given live ammunition for my rifle, and a place to sleep in a B-hut, or 'barracks hut'. The B-hut I was assigned to was just like all the others, being small and wooden and smelling of earth, and housing eight single people in tiny rooms that closely resembled closets. I was lodged in one of the small cubbies nearest the door, and given a pad-lock and key to keep my meager possessions safe. It wasn't much, but at the time it looked like heaven to me. Once left to myself, I undressed quickly, carefully settled my loaded weapon against the wall, and crawled under the rough blankets on my small cot.

This isn't so bad, I thought sleepily, shutting my eyes. *I can do this. I can do this. I can... do... this...*

I fell asleep.

*

I walked alone the road, kicking up small clouds of dust with my boots as I went. It was hot; small beads of sweat trickled down between my breasts and absorbed rapidly into the fibers of my khaki shirt; the bends of my elbows and knees were slick with perspiration. I wished, once again, that the new Air Force uniforms were as desert-friendly as the Army's were. Our ABU's were thick, and didn't breathe- and whereas they might be good for winter environments they were Hell for warm and humid ones. I took a deep breath, and adjusted my M-16 on my aching shoulder. It was a long walk back to the B-huts from the market.

The road itself, named Disney Drive after a casualty of the War on Terror, was approximately eight and a half miles long from tip to tail. From the crowded shopping center to where I rested my head, however, it was only about three miles. I looked at the sun. It was still high in the sky; probably about one or two o'clock. There was no danger of it getting dark any time soon. *I should be fine walking the rest of the way alone*, I thought. *Anyway, what's the worst that can happen when I have my rifle with me?* And if I needed to, I could latch on to a random group of US troops heading in the same direction, but at the moment there were none around; just lots of foreign troops that I couldn't put a nationality to, for the most part.

I had gone to the market in search of the most important items one could buy while on deployment: batteries and soap. At least, that was what was most important to me; I've heard others sing the praises of hot sauce packets, beef jerky, baby wipes, and foot powder. But I was tire of stinking like shitty water, which was the only smell that Bagram Air Field had to offer- shitty, nasty water, with slight undertones of astringent cleanser and mildew. Though I always tried to breathe through my mouth, sometimes I imagined that I could taste the air and grew sick to my stomach. So I endeavored to find the nicest smelling soap I could in an attempt to fend of off the rancid stench of the place. The batteries were just for my portable CD player.

I didn't like going to the shopping center, because there were very few women there, and I always felt like a spectacle. Everywhere I went, I could feel eyes on me, which made the hairs rise on the back of my neck. At deployed locations, General Order 1, or GO-1 was in effect, which meant, among many, many other things- no porn, no sex, and those rules- along with the general rareness of women- made living, breathing females a hot commodity. Strange men would often come up to me and ask me where I worked, what my first name was, or if I was interested in a long distance relationship (before I even knew their name), and when this happened I would remember something that Sgt Simmons had said to me when I was still based at Seymour Johnson: "As a woman in the military, you are either classified as a whore or a bitch." Sgt Simmons was ever wise. And so I would be curt with them, and let them know as plainly as I could that I was not interested in continuing a conversation. It went against my nature to be unfriendly, but in such a place I felt like a piece of bread surrounded by a flock of seagulls; I had to protect myself. I recall one Navy officer, after I told him I was not interested in having lunch with him, stalked away mumbling, "You're not that hot anyway, bitch."

And so, as soon as I could after every market trip, I would begin my trek back to my B-hut, where I would take a nap until my night shift began at eight o'clock.

I walked down the road, the sun beating at the back of my head, sweat dripping down my neck, and I tried to ignore the general strangeness of my surroundings while at the same time keeping an eye out for danger. Frenchmen ran by me in formation, wearing tiny, barely-there shorts. I walked past a broken-down gas pump where a couple of Afghans were arguing loudly in Pashto, and a US Army member stood between them, trying to calm them down with outstretched hands. I walked on. The road itself was busy with cars and trucks and buses, all headed on their own errands to mysterious destinations; once and a while a pick-up truck would pass with Afghans packed knee-to-chest in the bed, so tight they could hardly move. I knew they were welcome on base to work, but they always made me uncomfortable. I learned quickly that the Afghan men in that area loved- or perhaps, especially hated- American women. Wherever I walked, if they were there- lounging near a bathroom after having cleaning it, for example- they would stand up and send a cacophony of kissing and sucking noises after me, shouting foreign words in my direction until I passed out of view. My face would always burn with shame and fear, because what could I do? Who could I tell? I was in a deployed environment. Things were supposed to be harsh. If all I had to deal with was a few harassments, then I was lucky. But it was still degrading, all the same.

As I continued down the road, one such truck, the back packed full of Afghans, began to pass me, and I heard a loud holler. I looked up in shock. Any loud noise had started to bother me, lately, because you never knew what it could be. But this time it was just one of the men on the truck, which had stopped due to traffic. And there, standing up and grabbing his crotch, was the man who had yelled, licking his lips while staring me down. The truck started to pull away again, and the man was forced to sit, laughing, and the rest of the men started to whistle and make kissing noises as the vehicle made its slow way in the same direction I was going, until I stopped walking to let it pass. My face was afire with anger and embarrassment. I looked around to see if anyone else had seen what had happened, but everyone appeared to be going about their business, lost in their own little world. And who could blame them? I waited under a small tree until I couldn't see the truck anymore, and then continued on my way.

*

A week later, my batteries were dead again- I couldn't stop listening to Florence and the Machine on repeat on the long bus-rides to and from work- so I decided to make another trip to the market, this time in my physical training (PT) gear, since I figured I would stop on the way back to work out at an outside gym I had spotted on Disney. So, wearing my long blue shorts and my Air Force grey shirt tucked in at the waist, and shouldering my rifle (because who can exercise without their weapon?) I left my B-hut feeling more comfortable outside than I had in weeks.

Halfway to the marketplace, I received a couple of hollers from the busy road, which I dutifully ignored- but I was stopped in my tracks when a female Navy Captain stopped in front of me, her eyes narrowed.

"What do you think you're doing with your hair, Miss Ponytail?" she asked, her voice angry.

I opened my mouth to answer, but found I couldn't.

"You can't have your hair like that. It was amended in the dress code for Bagram months ago. Fix it."

I nodded, and said, "I-I'm sorry, ma'am, I only read the code that my First Sergeant gave to me, and it said ponytails were still allowed in PT uniform…"

She glared at me. "Well, they're not," she said. "I can talk to your First if you want me to, but for now, correct it."

I shook my head. "No, ma'am, I'll just fix it, and have him check his version of the reg. I'm sure he's just got an old version, is all." I began to fumble with my hair, trying to make a bun with my thick hair and a single hair tie.

She nodded, and began to walk away, leaving me to fiddle stupidly with my hair in the middle of the road. *What the hell was that?* I wondered. *Women can't have ponytails when they run? Are we too goddamned distracting to the men?* I finished my bun, and continued down the road. *Is it for our own safety?* I wondered. *Even if it is, it's wrong that we have to censor ourselves in these ways, when all we want to do is be considered equals. If it was conventional for men to have long hair in the military, like in ancient China, I bet pony tails wouldn't be banned.* For a minute, I let myself hate men. *Can't they stop thinking about sex for five goddamn minutes,* I fumed. *There are more important things in life... like... everything.* But then, I took a deep breath, and calmed down. It wasn't the male species I was mad at. In general, I liked men; it was wrong to lump all of them together into one group. If I did that, what right did I have to feel angry at them for lumping women together about any subject? I shook my head. People were just... people. It just so happened, most of the people that bothered me were men- but it didn't mean Men with a capital M were bad. It meant *some* men were bad, just like some women were.

I made my way to the market, purchased my batteries, and then stopped at the gym to do some running on the treadmill- mostly just to release the tension that had slowly been building in my joints over the last few weeks. When I was done, it was getting late, and the sun was setting; but I wasn't worried. I only had about a mile to walk to reach my B-hut. I re-strapped my rifle to my shoulder and left the gym, sweating profusely, so that my gym shirt suctioned itself to the front and back of my torso.

About midway back, I turned into a forest of B-huts, which were quiet due to it being dinner-time and everyone either working, eating, or resting in preparation for the night-shift. And so it looked like a ghost town as I walked by a row of dumpsters and water bottle pallets; I was tired, and over-heated, my mind occupied on the shower I was planning to take.

As I turned another corner, I ran straight into a small crowd of Afghan men, standing tall in their white, draping shalwar kameez, and a few stepped aside to let me pass, but two stood their ground and smiled at me with broken teeth, and began to smack and lick their lips.

"Excuse me," I said, my face burning. They didn't move.

My heart pounding, I took a few steps to the left, and one of them followed me, blocking my path. I stared at him in disbelief.

Unsure of what to do, I waved my hand in a broad 'shoo' gesture, and they laughed. After a quick interchange with each other in their language, the man standing in my way stood aside to let me pass. I quickly walked by them, and as I did so they sent their kisses and lip suckings after me. I turned cautiously after a few steps, and saw with horror that they were following me closely. I panicked, and I started to jog. Though in shock at their behavior, I knew in the back of my mind that most likely around the corner of the next hut there would probably be a bunch of military men standing around, and so there was no reason to over-react. But when I turned the corner, there was no one there; only a small alley leading to a dead end. With a feeling of fear rising in my gut, I turned back, and I walked into the group of men again, who were still making their disgusting noises. I began to shake, and held my M-16 strap tightly, ready to maneuver it forward if they came any closer.

Suddenly, a couple of Army corporals appeared as if out of nowhere, crossing out, talking quietly, and the Afghans walked in the other direction, disappearing as if they had never been there. Breathing erratically, I jogged up behind the corporals, and asked them in a quavering voice if I could walk with them, because some Afghans had started to follow me and might have meant to hurt me. They looked at each other as if I were a child telling them I had seen the bogeyman.

"Of course you can walk with us, Ma'am- we can even walk you wherever you're going if you want," said one. "But I'm sure the Afghanis didn't mean any harm. They just have different- um, ways of behaving than we do."

I bit my lip, glancing around to see if I could catch sight of one of the men who had followed me, but I could see no one. How would I recognize them if I saw them again? How could I tell anyone about what had happened, when I couldn't differentiate one Afghan in Pashtun dress from another? What was the point? My eyes started to water, but I held back them with all my self-control, refusing wanting to give in. Maybe they were right; maybe I was over-reacting. Maybe I was just a coward.

"I would appreciate it if you'd walk this way a bit, until we reach the area where my B-hut is," I said in a hushed voice, and they quickly acquiesced, possibly sensing my discomfort. I thanked them when they left me outside my door, but they didn't see that before I went inside, I walked in two large circles around my hut, and then went in and out of the female restroom twice before I was sure that I wasn't being followed.

*

The alarm was going off again, and as quickly as I could, I grabbed my weapon and gear, and, throwing on my helmet, I ran through the door towards the nearest bunker. I wasn't alone; everywhere I looked, there were other Airmen, swarming, yelling, giving directions to those who needed them.

"Presa!" yelled a MSgt from behind me, "Where the hell you going? Don't go towards the explosions, you idiot! Out the *front* door!"

I wheeled around, and realized with misgiving that everyone was running in the direction opposite of where I was headed, and without another moment of hesitation I followed the crowd out the front exit and ran as low to the ground as I could, holding on to the top of my unbuckled helmet until I made it into the safety of the bunker.

I sat down deep inside, breathing hard, and turned with wide eyes to look out the opening. The alarm was still going off- repetitive, and penetrating. I listened with strained ears for any sound outside of the norm… and I didn't have to wait long. Explosions and shots echoed in the distance. I tensed up, and grasped my rifle tighter. The radios of a few of my superiors became alive with barely intelligible speech, and I drew closer to the one I knew best, MSgt Wilks, so that I could find out what was happening.

"What's going on?" I asked in a quiet voice.

"Mortar attacks again," he said grimly. "I just hope they miss the goddamn ammo dump this time. And I suppose there's a big truck missing on base with 'a strange looking Afghan driving it', so we have to keep a look out, because who knows what it's filled with. Now, how the hell are we supposed to know what a strange looking Afghan looks like? They all look the same." He rubbed his face with the back of his hand, his eyes searching the dark outside the bunker for signs of movement. "Son of a bitch. I hate this shit."

I melted back into the shelter, listening as the gunshots filled the air. It's odd, how when you're at home, fireworks remind you of gunshots, but when you're deployed, gunshots remind you of fireworks. I tried not to imagine people being killed by those fireworks. I closed my eyes, wishing everyone well.

The radios buzzed to life again, and this time the ranking officer had to give a account of those who were present in his bunker. After that was done. The lot of us sat pushed against the back of our little cave, waiting for the all-clear.

"You know what this is about, don't you?" asked one of the airmen who worked closely with the pilots, "They were telling us this shit might happen, and look- it's happening."

"What is it about?" I asked.

The airman leaned toward me, "A few days ago, one of our aircraft was out flyin', doin' our business- and all of a sudden we started to get shot at, or so we thought. So we did what we had to do, y'know- we ganked 'em. Turns out, though, they weren't shootin' at us after all- it was just a wedding party, shootin' in the air, celebratin' as they was deliverin' the bride to her husband's house. We killed a wedding party for nothing. This is their retribution."

I looked at him sadly. There was nothing I could say.

"They're usually pissed off at us for other stuff, like us killing their goats and whatnot- we always pay 'em for that, way more than what they're worth- but I think this was one of the last straws, y'know," he continued. "Us dyin', them dyin', for reasons havin' nothing to do with terrorism. Damn shame."

I brought my knees to my chest and wrapped my arms around them. It *was* a damn shame. I felt bad for the wedding party, and those who had survived it- how angry they must be. *I would be mad, too,* I thought. *I might even want to fight back.*

We sat there for hours, listening to sporadic gunfire and explosions- and then the all-clear was called over the radio, and we exited the bunker sleepily, and went back to our work stations to try to focus on what we had been doing before the alarm went off. It was hard, though. *One of those mortars could have hit our building. We could have died.* But there was no point in thinking about that. I sat down at my computer and booted it up again, waiting with glazed eyes for the log-in screen to appear.

*

Fourteen hours. I had been at work for fourteen hours, and before that I hadn't slept, because I had been so plagued with nightmares that my body couldn't relax. One dream had been so realistic- thousands of spiders had started to crawl through the ends of my fingertips and out my nostrils and mouth- that I couldn't stop shaking afterwards and had given up on sleep altogether. I knew bad dreams were a side effect of the malaria medication that we were all forced to take, and there was nothing special about them- but there was something horrific to me about being sent to a strange country where you're assisting in the death of it's natives, and then at night, when you're supposed to be free of horrors, you are welcomed by sci-fi level nightmares.

The fourteenth hour arrived, and I shut down my computer, yawned, and stretched. I could tell by the number of voices in the hall outside my office that everyone was preparing to leave, finally- who knows why they had been late, this time- and with bleary eyes I walked to the gun-rack and shouldered my M-16, and walked through the crowd of airmen in the hallway towards the bus parked out front. I climbed in and found a spot near the back, and laid my head in the crook between the window and the seat, shut my eyes, and let my mind wander.

Everyone's deployment is different from everyone else's. Mine was different from the airman who sat next to me, even though we worked in the same squadron, and had the same bosses. It was different, because we were different people, and our functions in our unit varied greatly. My function was to sit on my ass and spit out numbers for the people in charge so that they could make command decisions. Most of the people in my squadron's function, however, was to the fix the jets and get them into the air as soon as possible, so that they could respond to emergency calls from the Marines and the Army, and potentially save their lives. I had always felt pride that I had a small part in getting the jets into the air, but had always wondered what it would be like to be out there on the flight line, side-by-side with my brothers and sisters, covered in hydraulic fluid and sweating from exertion.

On my seat in the bus, I smiled to myself, remembering earlier that week when I had approached a technical specialist, and asked him to take me around the flight line. As a parson who had worked with the aircraft for over twenty years, he felt a bit like a proud father towards them, and was more than happy to show off his babies. And once out there, I had stayed out there all day. I took off my ABU blouse, and walked around hatless. I helped service jet fuel start bottles, learned how to marshal aircraft, and was even needed once for my 'small hands' to reach a tight spot in the belly of the jet to retrieve a wayward item. I loved it out there, every minute of it. It was the same world as mine, but faster, more raw- much closer to the pulse of what was going on in the Middle East. That was why I had joined the military, after all- to be in the middle of it all. To feel like I was a part of things. And out there, sweating in the sun and helping where I could, I did feel like I made a difference, in my own small way. And when I couldn't help, I watched, and learned, and respected. And when the alert jets were needed due to an emergency call, I was present when the pilots and the weapons system officers ran from the hangar, climbed up the side of the aircraft and readied the engines as the canopies closed around them, and without hesitation, took off into the sky in an evasive pattern to avoid attacks. I watched them, breathless, my hands clasped together, wishing them well. The men and women who had worked on the aircraft to ensure it was flyable and safe for the pilot watched them take off with hope in their eyes, and in some cases, nervousness and frustration that they weren't able to get something completed on the jet that they had wanted to. All we could do was pray for their safe return.

At some point in my reflections, I had drifted off to sleep, and I jerked awake as the bus lumbered to a stop with a hiss. I looked around me, blinking a few times. The bus was crowded with exhausted airmen, and a few that had fallen asleep woke up as well when the bus came to a stop. It was dark outside, still, it being very early in the morning, but the sun would be up soon- but for the time being, we could barely see anything outside of the windows.

"Where are we?" one senior airman yawned to the bus driver, a staff sergeant with black hair and a shaving waver.

"Just north of Disney," answered the sergeant. "There's a line of buses in front- you all could get out and walk if you wanted to, you're close enough to the stop. But I see people lining up on the road up there. I think they're gonna announce…"

Just then, a loud speaker, barely intelligible, instructed all personnel to line up along Disney Road for a fallen comrade ceremony. A lump rose in my throat- it seemed we had to do this almost everyday, now- a few people behind me moaned.

"I'm so damn tired," said one airman, "I'm glad we're close to the huts. I just want to pass the fuck out."

"Do you think if we run we can make it to the B-huts before they come by?" asked another.

"Maybe afterwards we can play poker for bit," suggested another.

Everyone stood up quickly, grabbed their items and quickly began to leave the bus. I stared at them in horror. I impulsively grabbed one of them by the sleeve as they passed.

"What do you think you're doing?" I asked, pissed. "These people *died*. If you died for your country, would you want people running to their room to avoid paying their respects to your body?"

The airman who I had caught shook himself loose. "I pay my respects every day," he said, "I work my ass off, and I'm exhausted. Chill out, Presa."

I let them all go, staring after them with smoldering eyes. I couldn't believe what I was seeing. My fellow servicemen, whom I was usually so proud of, were running away like children trying to avoid a responsibility. With my lips set into a thin line, I stood up, gathered by rifle and bag, and got off the bus. I glanced around, and saw a long line of people of all nationalities, military branches and ranks standing in long lines on both sides of Disney road, facing inward. I took a couple of short, deep breaths, and then found a spot for myself- and I stood there with everyone, in silence, all of us waiting to show our deep appreciation for those who had given their all for their country.

In a few minutes, heartrending music began to play as a line of flag draped caskets made its way north along the road. As they approached, everyone standing along the road came to attention, and saluted in unison. The bodies passed by me closely, and with such slow deliberation, that if I had reached out I could have touched them. I saw at once that they were not United States casualties, but French ones, but that didn't make them any less terrible. If anything, it only solidified for me the fact that we were not in this war alone. It was easy to forget that, sometimes- much of the US tended to keep itself in a bubble and focus only on itself. But we had allies. And those allies' troops had mothers and fathers and brothers and sisters who would miss and mourn their deaths just as much as any American would miss a member of their own family. My eyes followed the caskets- there were so many. Frenchmen walked solemnly by the side of the cars, eyes slightly downcast, berets slightly askew. I shivered despite the warmth of the early morning. Death was passing me by, so close that its fingers caressed my soul.

When the caskets passed, everyone dropped their salutes and began to disperse; but for a while I stood there, despite how tired I was, thinking about the airmen on the bus who had made a mad dash to their B-huts in order to avoid paying their respects. I was glad that I had not followed their example. I was glad that despite my many failures, I had not given in to the temptation of an extra half hour of sleep. After all, it was the least I could do to remain awake in the presence of those who would never, and could never, open their eyes again.

*

An e-mail from SrA Presa at Bagram AB, to her co-workers at RAF Lakenheath, UK, March, 2008

I became aware the other morning, for the first time, of the difference between a soldier and a warrior.

When one considers these two words; soldier, warrior; one might consider them to be the same. For certain, they are often used in the same context for the same means; but I do not feel they are equal despite their similarity. One of my experiences while deployed made me feel most keenly that I belonged to one group as opposed to the other though in fact many would say I am either both or none. Let me explain.

When I joined the Air Force in 2005, I was bluntly told it would be a watered down version of the US Army. I had been told a lot of things about the Air Force and the military in general that were lies, stretches, or half-truths, but in the end I didn't really pay much attention. I didn't have much going for me back home, with a GED, no money for college, and a family life that left something to be desired. I knew I had to do something important, something for myself, or I would be stuck in a place in my life that I did not want to be.

I was proud when I swore in. I had worked as hard as I could to get where I was, standing in front of a giant American flag and promising my loyalty and devotion to it and the country it represented. I was proud, but even so it was pride to my self, not to the United States. Growing up in today's skewed society it can sometimes be hard to appreciate your country when you have no perception of life being any other way. And believe me, there are few better ways to get a grander view on things than joining the military.

The first time I was called an Airman was the fifth week of basic training, but I now admit that I didn't feel like one. I didn't know what it meant to be an Airman. On graduation day, I was more nervous about leaving for Technical training and learning my job than focusing on what it meant to be where I was, or the history of the ceremonies I participated in. A few years later at RAF Lakenheath I was called a Warrior for the first time in my awareness, though perhaps I had been named so before. But... Warrior? I knew I did my job to the best of my ability, but I didn't feel like a warrior, with my desk and hot coffee and shiny boots. In a short span of years, I had come from a quiet civilian existence to taking on these two titles: Airman and Warrior, and yet still they remained ambiguous and in the background to everyday life.

I am now deployed to Bagram, Afghanistan. I have succeeded in my career thus far, and my life has grown into something I could only have dreamed of before. Yet, I had felt lacking whenever I watched news on the war, or read an article about our nation's losses. I needed to know for myself what it was like. I wanted to feel that I actually had served the country that has brought me so much, and to that same extent, serve others. I have now seen the reverberations of war from a much closers distance and I swear I have grown from it. Though I am nowhere near the immediate danger levels of many, I still have been taken out of my cubicle and shown a darker and more real side to it all. Afghanistan is a war torn country and I eagerly listen to stories from brave men and women who daily leave the relative safety of Bagram to experience it first-hand. I am amazed, impressed, and humbled with everything I have learned. I also believe that I have finally found my place in the grand scheme of things. When I hear a member of the Army recount to me their feelings of awe and thankfulness every time they hear an F-15 fly overhead, it moves me beyond words. I am here for them, for their safety and their benefit, and I will never belittle myself or others by wondering 'why?' again.

The hardest things we have to come to terms with is our own mortality. We are faced with it here at the ever-increasing amount of fallen comrade ceremonies, sometimes up to four times a week. There are so many that it is distressingly easy to get complacent about them. It is both a blessing and a curse that we as humans can adjust to any situation and our sense of 'norm' can be displaced with a new one. I understand this, but at the same time I feel that the death of a fellow service member, be they national or foreign, is a very important exemption.

I was riding the bus back to my camp one early morning after a long shift and before the start of a fallen comrade ceremony. It is well known that is you hear the ceremony announcement that will be in appropriate dress and fall out to attend. I was tired after my shift, but all the same I was still prepared to show my respect to those that had died. We were almost to our destination when I became aware of the conversation around me, and I will never forget the words I heard, or the anger I felt. A group of individuals were saying how relieved they were that they were back at camp so that they didn't have to attend 'that *curse word* fallen comrade ceremony' and how they would wait in their B-huts 'until it was over and then meet to play poker.' I was so angry. I still am angry, even writing it down now. How could anyone be so selfish and thoughtless? I asked a few people around me, still shocked, if they were going to bed instead of attending. They stared blankly at me as if I were mental. I reiterated that someone had indeed died, and why didn't they feel the need to go? Once again I was met with blank stares.

I am old enough to have learned that if someone doesn't care about something, no one can make them, but I am too young and stubborn to stop trying. I did what I could at the time to convince them that paying respects was the right thing to do, if not for the fallen, then for their families. If everyone didn't attend the ceremony because of superficial excuses (tired, hungry, etc.) then the road would be empty of people when the flag-draped caskets passed by. It is a heart-wrenching scene to imagine. But in the end, no one from that bus came with me. I tried to lead by example, but it was an example no one there cared for.

I regret today that I didn't speak more convincingly to those on that bus, and maybe that is why I feel compelled to write this.

Though members of the Army are always called soldiers, the dictionary classifies a Soldier as one who is engaged in military service. Therefore, in reality, we are all soldiers: Army, Marine, Air Force, Navy, and all Guard and Reserve. But a Warrior is described as a person who shows or has shown great vigor, courage, or aggressiveness. So, at the end of the day when Retreat plays, we are all of us soldiers, but not all are Warriors. No one can thrust the title of Warrior upon you and make it be true. You must feel deep in yourself that you are, indeed, worthy of it.

So here I sit at my desk, with my coffee and boots and that hardly seen a scuff, and I am a Warrior still.

Very Respectfully,

SrA Presa

*

The airplane descended peacefully into England, and for the first time in months I felt the tension in my heart release. I was home, and I would never see Afghanistan again. I looked out the small window and once again marveled how green England was, how *alive*. It was so different from the simple pallet of the Middle East. I felt bad for those who would never be able to experience the sweet, verdant coolness of a land like this. Sighing, I settled back into my seat and closed my eyes, waiting to land.

This time, I wasn't flying alone- my unit and I were coming home together after a long, successful mission. It was much, much easier traveling with a large group that knew what they were doing; from Turkey we had simply boarded a commercial airplane which was going to fly directly to RAF Lakenheath. From there, we would be escorted to a hangar, where all of our friends and families eagerly awaited us.

When we landed, the men and women in the airplane cheered, and a few even high-fived- one said 'God Bless the Queen'. Really, I'm sure no one knew what they were saying- it just felt so goddamn good to be home.

In the hangar, we were surrounded by people in uniform, saluting, shaking hands- spouses in all forms of dress ran up to their husbands and jumped into their arms, and little children started crying as they saw the parent they had been worried about for long, and missing for months.

I glanced around, my heart lifted from the spectacle around me- and I realized with a pang that there was no one there to greet me. I had no husband, or children, or dear friends who had been upset at my absence. I pursed my lips and looked down at my boots, trying not to feel bad for myself- after all, I had made it. I had deployed for my country. I should be proud.

"Presa," said a man's voice behind me, and I turned to see MSgt Resser striding towards me, his hand extended.

"Sgt Resser," I said, surprised. I grasped his hand and shook it firmly.

"It's great to have you back," he said, slapping me a few times on the shoulder. "We all missed you- the office is just not the same without you, you know. Things are just a mess. Anyway, how are you doing?"

For some reason, tears came to my eyes. Sgt Resser, out of everyone, had come to see me. The guy who could not possibly fail to know how I felt about him had come to check up on me. I didn't care if it was his duty or not, because at that moment I was just so relieved not to be the only person without someone there to welcome her back.

"I'm doing well, Sir," I said, and wondered, after a moment of reflection, if it was the truth or not.

And Then There Were Two
(27)

I opened my eyes, and my gaze hit the ceiling like two gunshots. Same lamp with one bulb burned out; same fan bedecked with dust; same familiar water spots. Nothing new, nothing of interest; and worst of all, I was still alone, alone, alone. Another day, isolated and insatiable.

It was the weekend, and I had nowhere to go. I had no friends. Amy was gone, Nathan was in Korea for a year, and who knows where he would go, after that; we had a date set that night to talk, but that wasn't for another ten hours. I felt awful; I was so dehydrated from throwing up the past few days that my lips were cracked and bleeding, and my face was puffy and irritated. My body was bloated as well, so much so that my clothes didn't fit, so I wore nothing but baggy sweatpants which were splattered with the previous day's vomit. I knew I smelled terrible, but when I considered showering, I couldn't help but wonder: what's the point? Who am I going to go see? Who am I trying to impress? I would clean myself and immediately become filthy again; for I knew that even if I tried to sleep all day, or read in bed, or distract myself in any other way, it didn't matter; I would eventually give in to my insatiable hunger and seek food. And then I would feel guilty, no matter the amount I took in, because I was a fat, ugly monster, and someone like me deserved to starve. Those thoughts would cause me to overeat, and when I came up for air I would realize that I had binged over a week's worth of calories. Horrified at myself and defeated, I would stick my worthless head into the toilet and throw up everything my stomach contained, knowing all the while that there was no way to become as empty as I truly wanted to be.

And so for the moment, I laid in bed, staring at the ceiling, knowing my fate, dreading it, but at the same time accepting it. How long had it been at that point, since my bulimia had begin? Six years? It felt like so much longer. I could no longer remember a time where it wasn't a part of my life. How had I coped with stress before? As a relatively healthy child, I had coped by eating. As a sick child, I coped by eating, and then throwing up. What a fine line it was between the two. What had caused me to tip over the edge, I wondered. Not that it mattered anymore; I couldn't ask for help in order to analyze it. After all, hadn't I seen at Seymour Johnson what happened to the career of those who visited mental health? I would have been blocked from PCSing, from advancing my career, if I hadn't lied my way out of it. What kind of incentive was that for someone to seek the care they needed? No matter what happened to my mind, or my body, I could not lose the Air Force. It was the only family I had. It was the only thing I was good at. What did I have, outside of the military? A dad and a sister I didn't talk to, who possibly still thought of me with trepidation and a vague sense of horror? No; I would not seek help. My illness was a secret that I would keep, somehow; even from those I considered to be trustworthy.

But I did not pretend to myself that I wasn't ill. I was aware of its oily, snaky fingers weaving its way through my mind every second. Sometimes I could fight it by slapping myself savagely in the face, or taking large doses of Nyquil and falling asleep, but those were only brief reprieves. At some point, I would eat; I would eat, and the beast inside of me would rear its head, and in its soft, hollow voice would begin to chant, ***You know it's time, now. It's time, it's time.*** I felt powerless against such a creature, which, though shapeless and colorless, ruled my entire world.

My mind drifted to Nathan. How did I feel about him, anyway? We were dating, but we hardly knew anything about one another. I found him to be vaguely annoying when we spoke to each other, but my intense need for human companionship, and his sense of romance, kept me coming back for more. Our relationship vaguely reminded me of the one Sam and I had shared, though whenever my mind drifted in that direction I was quick to shake myself and think of other things. The only subjects Nathan and I talked about were little, nonsensical couple-ish things; he would say how much he missed me, how beautiful I was, and what we would do together if he were there, and it always sounded so heavenly that I hardly noticed that our conversations held no real substance.

"If I was there, we'd go out to dinner," he would say, "I'd open the car door for you, and kiss you, and then take you dancing, and we'd dance all night."

My heart would swell, because I wanted that so badly; to be with someone, to be wanted like that, to be out in public and to dance and feel free in my body. It was a fantasy very far away from my daily reality, and every time we talked I closed my eyes and daydreamed until it felt real. If the conversation did drift to other subjects, as it sometimes did, I began to realize how little we had in common; he was religious, I was not. He had different views on certain subjects that I felt didn't fit well with mine. I told him as much during one our late night conversations, but he dismissed my worries.

"A lot of couples are opposites," he would say, "and that's why they stay together so long; it brings spice to the relationship."

Very often I would stay up late, sick from binging and purging, waiting for him log-on to a computer in Korea so that I could talk to him; but he would oversleep and stand me up. When this happened I felt unaccountable rage at him. Didn't he know I relied on him for my sanity? If he had just told me he was too tired to make it that night, I could have taken Nyquil and passed out instead of sitting up for hours waiting for him only to feel abandoned. It happened so often that I started to hate him as much as I relied on his presence in my life to be a reminder that somewhere in the world, someone wanted me.

One day I received an e-mail from Prue. I hadn't heard from her in a very long time, and I almost cried as I read the long message, filled with her witticisms and curses. She was doing well, she said; she had started dating a guy named Owen who she insisted I would like, and they were getting serious. She also mentioned that she had run into an old acquaintance of ours recently, Tom, and as they were talking he had not stopped mentioning me and how beautiful he thought I had been in Tech school. Did I remember Tom? He was a scheduler that went to classes down the hall from us at school, and though he didn't talk to us much, he was very cute and funny. It seemed that he was actually based in Lakenheath but had been on stateside assignment for past few months. He would be returning to the UK in a few days and was interested in meeting up with me. I wrote back to tell her I remembered Tom very well, I would love to see him again, and that I hoped she and Owen were very happy and that he was treating her well- and that if he wasn't I would punch him in the jugular.

That night, I wrote Nathan a long message telling him that I didn't think we should date anymore. I told him we didn't have enough in common, that I didn't feel committed to him. The parallels with my old relationship with Sam were becoming too obvious. And, like Sam, Nathan refused to accept my opinion our situation; he believed that it was my illness talking, and that I actually held no opinions of my own.

"You're just so depressed right now you feel like you can't let anyone in," he wrote. "I'll be here for you no matter what. Even if you just call me your friend for now, I'm here, though you know I want more."

I was filled with guilt. He had helped keep my sadness at bay for many nights over the past few weeks, and I was repaying him by telling him I didn't want to be with him anymore. Worse still, I wasn't strong enough to bring my point home to him in such a way that he understood there was no going back. Perhaps it was because I was afraid of burning my bridges with him. All I had ever done was burn bridges, and if there was an option to maintain a friendship with this man, however tentative, then why shouldn't I take it? I tried not to consider what this endeavor might do to him and his feelings; and anyway, I didn't consider myself powerful enough to cause emotions that were capable of greatly harming anyone.

I continued to speak to Nathan every night that week, and to my shame I let him tell me that he loved me before we parted. Sometimes he wouldn't log off until I said it back; and though I did, I would caveat it with the words, 'as a friend,' but his ears seemed to be closed to anything but what he wanted to hear.

In the back of my mind, I was thinking of Tom, and how much I looked forward to seeing him again.

*

Looking back, I should have known. I should have stopped myself. But I was such a self-absorbed, attention seeking lost soul, that when affection was dangled in front of me I felt powerless to resist it. Thus it was that when I met Tom again, we began a playful flirtation, and after a few days, began to date. I liked him a lot; he was funny, and smart, and our sense of humors played well off each other. I felt then that I really needed to smile, and when I was around him, I was smiling all the time. It felt a bit strange at first to hang around him because he was so attractive- not usually my type- but I made an exception for him because he was so fun, and free, and that enticed me.

Though we often went out to dinner and small get-togethers with his friends, we had never expressed our attraction for one another. I was afraid to tell him that I cared, anyway, since he was due to PCS in three weeks to a base in Florida. What was the point of getting a relationship with a guy that was leaving? I had learned from my short time with Nathan that long distance relationships were not for me. But something in Tom's eyes every time he looked at me made me nervous, and a part of me wanted to kiss him every time I saw him. So, like a reckless teenager, I stayed behind enemy lines and flirted, piteously waving my little white flag.

One night, before we were scheduled to go to the movie theater, I stopped by his room to pick him up. We had gone out earlier that evening with our co-workers and drank quite a bit of alcohol- perhaps too much. I certainly drank more around Tom than I ever did otherwise, despite my personal vow to never drink to drunkenness again- but he had that 'fuck it all' effect on me that always swept me away, since I had very little attitude of my own to keep me planted. So I was pretty wobbly and fuzzy-brained when I knocked on his door that night, wondering if I even really wanted to go see the movie or if I should just get my drunk-ass to bed. After a couple of beats, Tom opened the door, shirtless and wearing soft pajama pants that left nothing to the imagination. He was tan and well-muscled, and the shallow part of me gulped as my eyes devoured his body.

"Hey, I was hoping maybe we can just stay in?" he asked, moving into his room, which was tidy and smelled like cinnamon. "I'm kind of drunk- plus I don't really want to see everyone else. I just want to spend time with you."

I was quiet for a minute. He sat on his bed, and bid me to sit- I did. He leaned back on one arm and turned to me. I knew what was coming.

"I really like you, Kim," he said. "I've never gotten along with anyone as well I get along with you. We fit, you know. I want us to be together, even after I leave."

I opened my mouth a few times to start speaking, and failed. Finally after a moment I was able to clear my throat and respond.

"Tom, I don't feel that way," I said, "and I'm in this weird limbo relationship with this guy in Korea. I-I'm not sure what to do."

He grabbed my hands and deep into my eyes. "I know you care about me," he said, "We have so much in common. All you have to do is say the word and I'm yours. Forever."

My heart was pounding. I was so confused. I cared about him, and was wildly attracted, but I wasn't ready to let go of Nathan's friendship. He was flying to visit me from Korea in just a few weeks, despite the fact that I had strung him along for months, telling him I still wasn't sure how I felt about him. And now I was considering my feelings for another man. How could I do that to Nathan? What kind of a horrible person was I?

"Tom," I said, pushing his hands away gently, "I really care about you, but I care about Nathan too, in a way. That's not right. It's disgusting. You both should just leave me alone."

Tom looked at me sadly, but shook his head. "No, I know I'm the right one for you."

I eyed him. "That's what Nathan says."

He came closer, and pressed his body against mine. "Kim," he said, "I know what it's like to be sad," he whispered, "and to be alone. We are so good together; I don't feel any of those things with you. And you're so beautiful. I've never seen someone so beautiful. Please. Be with me." He reached his hand up to my cheek and stroked it, running his fingers through my hair. I shivered.

Lifting my face to his, I said, "I want to be with you but it's not the right thing to do," I said, breathing into his face.

"You want to be with me. That's all I needed to hear," he whispered. And he leaned in to kiss me, softly, passionately, and I gave in to him completely.

*

Why wasn't he answering his cell-phone? I felt tears of rage build behind my eyes. Was this really happening to me again? My e-mails remained unanswered, my instant messages unchecked. I stalked his social media, only to discover that after a few days of his arriving in Florida he had started to date a thin blonde who had a penchant for partying in short skirts. I didn't want to believe what was happening, but there was no way for me to deny it: I had been played. Tom was gone.

I abused my body horridly over the next few weeks; I hardly ate or drank anything, and when I did I threw it up immediately. I repulsed myself so much that I even purged the coffee I drank in the morning. I couldn't stand to have anything in my stomach. I was forced to go the ER many times for saline drips, always mystifying the nurses as to why I was so dehydrated and ill.

Nathan kept writing to me, telling me how his days were going, and mentioning that he was excited to come visit me on his mid-tour. Nathan's kindness was like fingernails down a chalkboard. I didn't understand why he kept bothering with me. I had told him, after that night, that Tom and I had slept together, but I did not tell him that we also admitted we had feelings for each other and endeavored to start a relationship. I had thought that my sleeping with another man would push him away for good, but the fact that Tom and I were inebriated when it happened made it seem almost blameless to him. I was too cowardly and ashamed to tell him the blunt truth. But as the time drew nearer for Nathan to fly back to the UK to see me, I felt that he needed to know everything, no matter how I felt.

One night when he called as usual, I broke down crying, and told him everything.

"Nathan," I said. "You know how Tom and I slept together? Well, we kept sleeping together, after I told you, and we weren't drunk those other times. I really liked him. I thought we had a really great connection, but he used me; he lied to me. You needed to know that, okay? And I'm sorry I hurt you. You can hate me now."

The other end of the line was silent for a while, then,

"Are you fucking serious? You cheated on me?"

"No! I mean, I don't know, maybe. I broke up with you weeks ago, but we just kept pretending like we were in a relationship, almost, without saying we were; we've been talking almost every night and saying how much we care about each other. It's so confusing; I don't know what we are. But either way what I did was wrong, I should have told you the truth right away of what was going on between Tom and me, because I knew how you felt. I'm sorry. I'm so sorry. I was afraid of losing you as a friend and now I'm going to lose you anyway."

"Is it over? Between you and Tom?" asked Nathan, his voice thick with emotion.

"Yes, he used me and left me. So you can be happy that I got what I deserve, at least."

Nathan was silent again for a moment. "Kim," he said finally, "I'm very hurt- I can't express to you how hurt I am. But listen to me... you will never lose me. I'm your friend. Okay? And I'm always going to be here for you."

I sniffled, unable to process what I was hearing. What did I feel? Relief? Disappointment? After everything I had done to him, why was he still holding on to me? Why wasn't he slamming down the receiver, cursing my name, and telling all of his friends what waste of time I was?

"Why are you doing this?" I asked, "Why are you being so nice to me? I don't deserve it."

"I just care about you, Kim- so much," he said. "And I think you need someone to be there for you. I think I can be that guy. I just need you to let me *be* that guy."

"I don't know."

"Kim," he said, his voice serious, "Marry me, and I will make sure that you never feel alone again. I'll take care of you. I love you with all of my heart; I have since the night we went walking, and looked up at the stars together. Do you remember? You're meant to be my wife."

"I'm afraid."

"Don't be afraid. I'm committing myself, my *soul* to you." His voice was passionate, and I thought I heard the ring of sincerity in every word. My heart began to pound; he was serious. "Do you love me?"

"I love you," I said, surprising myself considerably, because it didn't feel like a lie. "I just don't know if we're right for each other…"

"You love me, or you don't love me," he said. "Do you love me?"

I hesitated. I had hurt this man so much, had led him on, went behind his back with another man, and deceived him. If I said no, I might lose him forever, even as a friend. Was I ready for that?

"I do love you," I responded.

"Will you marry me?"

"Yes…I'll marry you."

And thus, at twenty-one, I became engaged to a man I had known for four months, and had seen in person only a handful of times.

*

We decided to get married at a local registrar's office at Bury St. Edmunds, a sort of medieval market town about half an hour away from the base, and to this day I don't know how I had the guts to go through with the ceremony. After he flew in from Korea, I quickly realized that the fragments of his personality that I had disliked while he was away became intolerable to me now that he was near. He showed no interest in my illness, though I brought it up frequently in hopes of support and comfort; he seemed to think it would fade away once we got married, that it was just a passing phase. Additionally, he had gained weight while he was in Korea, which made him sweat all of the time, which I found repulsive despite my attempts to pretend otherwise. His teeth were yellow and brown, and he had dry flakes falling from his ears due to a skin condition. He talked about sports constantly, which I found boring; he always wanted to go out and drink with friends, which was exhausting and anxiety inducing to me who was more content to stay at home, watch a movie, and fall asleep by eleven. After my experience with Tom, I had truly gotten all alcohol I wanted in my life, this time. I wanted no part of it, and I told Nathan so- but even if we did end up staying in, he still drank himself the point of inebriation, which I could never understand. He simply seemed unable to remove himself from it.

My co-workers detested him, since he was always rude and drunk whenever he was around them. Sgt Dalen pulled me aside after I announced my intent to marry Nathan, and he urged me to think long and hard about my decision make sure I was making the right choice. As embarrassed as I was by Nathan and his behavior in public, and as much as I felt at odds with him at home, I still felt like I owed him for treating him so badly with Tom. He was the only man- besides Sam- who had seen the ugly side of me and still wanted to stay. He loved me; I was the one with the problems. So while I thanked Sgt Dalen for caring about me enough to confront me with his concern, when the day came, I married Nathan in a simple ceremony, wearing a blue skirt and white button up, and became his lawful wife.

Nathan remained for a few days after the wedding, but then was forced to go back to Korea to finish his one year tour there. One part of me was grateful, because it gave us more time to get to know each other from afar and discuss the issues that had arisen when he visited. But for some reason, our problems kept getting swept under the rug. Neither of us wanted to fight; we both went right back to that dream-land we had both lived in when we had started dating by imagining how great things would be, what our house would look like, what we would do on our weekends together; such was the extent of our conversations.

About the same time I married, Prue married her boyfriend, Owen, in a secret ceremony so they could relocate to a new base together. I tried to be critical of Owen, as she had always been critical of the men in my life, but they seemed to get along so well, and he appeared to love her so passionately, that I felt I had nothing to worry about. They eventually got married in a 'real' ceremony after they both got assigned to Tinker AFB, Oklahoma, and I wanted dreadfully to make it to her wedding to be her maid of honor, but at that time my work would not allow me the time off to travel. We were both upset that I missed it, but that didn't stop us from chatting about the wedding, and I looked over the photos of the event a million times. She was a stunning bride, and Owen made a handsome groom. I was glad for her, but also a bit jealous.

Thus it was that when it came time for my husbands return to the UK, I had almost forgotten all of my irritations with him and I awaited his coming with open arms. And truly, we had a very happy homecoming; I had picked out a small cottage for us in a village about twenty minutes from the base, and he carried me through the threshold like a new bride, and we made passionate love on our bedroom floor since we hadn't purchased a bed yet. Looking into his eyes, I told myself that I loved him, and that whatever misgivings I had had before, they were ridiculous- now that he was home, and we were together, everything would be okay.

Over time, we filled our tiny home with furniture, and since my paycheck covered all of the household bills, the entirety of his check went into paying off my credit cards and then into our savings account. I had never felt so stable, or so safe, in all my life.

For a few months, things went smoothly. And then I started to notice things about my husband that didn't feel right to me.

I was always the first to go to bed, and he would stay up later; but once in a while I would come downstairs and he would quickly close all internet browsers. At first, because of my experience with Sam, I suspected porn, but I quickly realized that he was chatting with women he had been very close with before our marriage. I asked him to stop hiding his behavior, and chat with them openly if he had nothing to hide. He demurred, and insisted that what he was saying to them was none of my business.

I had felt jealousy before, but this was something new to me. These were real women. I felt a surge of rage that frightened me.

"What are you saying to these 'old friends' of yours that I can't see?" I asked him.

"Just talking about the old days," he shrugged.

"Why do you always close out all of the windows when I come downstairs?"

"I don't know. Calm down."

"It just seems really shady, Nate." I said.

He glared at me. "Shady, like what you did with Tom, shady? Oh, don't worry. *I'm* not a cheater."

I held my breath. "I haven't so much as looked at another man since I became engaged and then married to you, and you know it."

"I don't *know* it."

"Well, I haven't! And I don't want my husband downstairs at one o'clock every morning chatting with strange girls, and refusing to let me know what they're talking about, okay?"

"Fine," he said, shutting down the computer. "Just shut me out from the world, then. Keep me in a box and take me out when you want me."

"I don't want to shut you out from anything, I just want us to be open and honest with each other, and what you're doing isn't helping."

"Gotcha," and without looking back, he went upstairs to bed.

*

After that, everything between us was strained. All of the problems that had risen between us on his mid-tour came back; the sweating, the hygiene, the drinking; except now it was one hundred times worse, because we couldn't escape each other. I endeavored to discuss my issues with him, but being of a very defensive frame of mind, Nathan never seemed to take my suggestions well, no matter how gently I approached the matter. Once, while drunk, he punched the wall because I dared to suggest that he perhaps had drank too much alcohol. Frustrated and emotional, I dropped the subject.

Our marriage was headed down a dark path, and I didn't know what to do. In the beginning just being around him had been enough to suppress my bulimia, but now I was finding ways to do it behind his back. After dinner, I would sneak up to the bathroom adjacent to our bedroom and purge there in secrecy; sometimes I would be gone for an hour, but he never questioned where I was, or seemed to notice my depressive behavior afterwards, my red eyes or puffed-up cheeks. I went to him one day, crying, begging him to go with me to go to couple's therapy. I felt like I was at the end of my rope, because I no longer saw a future for us. He was drinking himself into a buzz every day after work, and he didn't seem to realize- or when I told him, care- that I was killing myself. He simply stared at me as if I were crazy.

"You're the one that needs therapy," he said in a demeaning tone, "I don't need to see any quack doctor. Quit trying to paint me like I'm an alcoholic, or a bad husband. When your problem gets under control, our problems will go away. That's all there is to it."

It was about a week after that conversation that my breasts became extremely tender, and with a feeling of trepidation I drove to the store and bought a home pregnancy test. When I got home from work, I went upstairs to the bathroom and took the test- and there it was: two blue lines. I was pregnant.

My first feeling was one of joy, quickly followed by fear. A baby meant I was going to be connected to Nathan for the rest of my life, whether I wanted to be or not. I knew he would be happy that I was pregnant; I wasn't worried about that. He had said many times that he wanted to have a big family, and that he loved children. I was the one who always said I wanted to wait until I was thirty-five. But there I was, twenty-two and pregnant despite my birth control pills, despite all the trauma I had put my body through the last seven years; here was proof I was a functioning woman.

I knew Nathan was downstairs on the couch, so, holding onto the test, I descended the stairs slowly, and then stopped in front of him. He took a sip of his Strongbow, and looked at me curiously.

"What's wrong?" he asked.

I couldn't hold back my smile as I said, "Look," and I handed the test to him.

He reached out and looked at for a moment, and then a slow smile spread across his face.

"Is this for real?" he asked, looking at me.

"Yeah," I said. "I'm pregnant. I have to get the real test done at the hospital to be sure, but... yeah. We're going to have a baby."

"That's awesome, Babe," he said, crushing me into his chest. I was so happy in that moment that I felt like crying. I believed then, that despite how things had been going between us, we would find a way to patch things up, if not for our own sakes, then for the baby's. It's funny that despite everything I had been through up to the point I still didn't know that that wasn't how the world works.

*

For the first few weeks of my pregnancy, I harbored hopes that the baby inside of me would somehow curtail my depression. I was quickly undeceived. I gained weight quickly during the first trimester, and though I knew most of it was fluid, I still felt distressed about my looks and I found it hard to focus on work. Additionally, I was constantly nauseous, and I found out that I was one of the two percent of women to be diagnosed with Hyperemesis gravidarum, which is a pregnancy complication where the feeling of severe illness that most women felt in the first trimester remains for the entire duration of the pregnancy.

The Air Force, unfortunately, did not know what to do with me in this situation, since it was so rare. Everyday, I woke up, threw up; ate a little, went to work, threw up, and then most days was sent to the ER to receive IV fluids, as my workplace did 'not have the authority' to send me home to rest without a doctor's note. Where I had gained weight in the beginning of my pregnancy, I failed to gain any more for the rest, despite the child growing inside of me. It was an extended nightmare for me, who wanted to be an upstanding airman, but could not lift my head at work without the world spinning. Most of the males in my office seemed embarrassed by my condition, and told me frankly they did not know how to deal with it, which did not make matters easier. Sgt Dalen just felt bad for me, and was sorry he couldn't help more. If I was unable to make it to a meeting, Sgt Resser sometimes would announce to the others in attendance, 'Airman Presa cannot make it today, as she is vomiting her guts out due to pregnancy.' It was a horrific few months that I could only stare with eager eyes on the calendar for the end of.

 Nathan and I managed to float along in our marriage during the pregnancy by never delving an inch below the surface. When I became ill at work, like a dutiful husband he would drive me home, and I would sleep for hours until he returned, whereupon he would begin to drink and play video games. I would often sit by him while he played in an attempt to feel close to him, or I would read; but more often than not I would bring out a pad of paper and draw, and reminisce on the hours my sister and I used to spend together at the kitchen table.

I had written to my sister and my father after I found out I was pregnant, and I had gotten a few brief words of congratulations in reply- but other than that, I had heard nothing. I hadn't expected more than that, really; we had stopped all forms of communication years ago, and I hadn't been an attentive aunt to my nephew Mason, so there was no reason to expect such behavior from my sister towards my own child. It didn't sadden me; I only wondered abstractly what it would have been like to have been born into a normal, non-depressive nuclear family unit.

Conversely, when I told Prue I was expecting, she sang out with joy, and promised to shower her with presents and love from afar. "I just know it'll be a girl, because girls are the best and you deserve the best!" she gushed in one of our phone conversations, "Do you think she'd like blocks? Ooh, I found an awesome shirt that says 'I Love Boobies.' I can buy her that, and one in your size, so you guys can be twins *laughter*. Or maybe I should buy it in a onesie? Onesies are so cute! Oh, she's gonna be such a cute little jellybean! I can't wait to meet her! I'm shedding tears of joy, Kimmy!"

Talking to Prue always made me feel better, despite my floundering marriage, shitty work environment and constant nausea. And despite my family's lack of involvement in my pregnancy, I realized that they didn't matter, because in their place I had Prue, my adopted sister, and she was all I needed.

Something that every senior airman must do upon reaching a certain time-in-grade is take a test to see if they are fit for the next rank of staff sergeant. My time to test, unfortunately, fell upon the first quarter of my pregnancy, when I was vomiting at least three times a day and could hardly drive myself around. I knew, walking into the testing building, with bile rising up in my throat, that I was not going to do well; but I stubbornly sat down at my designated desk and waited for the world to stop spinning.

The test proctors at the front of the room gave all the testers present a five minute warning, and let us know that once the test had begin we would not be allowed to leave the room for any reason, not even to use the restroom. Upon hearing this, I stood up quickly, and walked as with swift feet down the hall to a little bathroom. Once there, I put my head into the toilet, and threw up for all I was worth. *Get it all out now*, I encouraged myself. *Hurry, hurry.* When I finished, I stood up, flushed the toilet, and washed my face thoroughly, but a quick glance in the mirror told me I still looked like a woman who had just been thoroughly sick. One part of me thought this humorous; I actually had a valid excuse to look sick at this point in my life.

When I re-entered the room, I asked the proctor if I could keep a trashcan by my side in case I needed to throw up during the test, and with wide eyes the he nodded and indicated a small can for me to take. Pleased, I sat down at my desk, and soon began the examination, half sure of my complete failure, and half full of hope.

I didn't end up using the trashcan, though when I returned it at the end of the test, the proctor looked at it in mild disgust, as if I had tainted the trash somehow. Though I assured him I didn't use it, he still looked a little uneasy around me, as if I might projectile vomit at his face at any moment; so I did him a favor and left as soon as possible.

A few months later, the list of those who had been selected to become staff sergeants was released; and much to my surprise, my name was on the list. My heart swelled with pride. I had done it! I had dragged my exhausted, ill body from the coast of Oregon, and made something of myself. Sure; I was, at the moment, an exhausted and ill pregnant lady, but what of it? I would soon be Staff Sergeant Presa, and I had earned it all by myself. No one would ever be able to take that away from me.

<u>Norah</u>
(28)

My baby, Norah Katherine, was born on November 12, 2009.

I don't know why I chose the name Norah; many people have asked me, Did you name her after Nora Jones, the famous singer? No, I have to tell them, I didn't. I read the name once in an Agatha Christie book, and fell in love with it- and when I found out I was pregnant, I remembered it. It was as simple as that. I always knew, in the back of my mind, that if I did have a child that its name would be a literary one of some sort, and it never mattered to me if the name was from some grand old classic or a paperback mystery, as long as it was from a book that had brought me joy and comfort when I needed it.

Her middle name was Katherine- my mother's name. It was something that I had pondered over for a very long time. I did not feel sentimental about many things in my life- perhaps I just lacked the proper juices in my brain, or something- but I recognized that other people were sentimental, and that perhaps later on in life I would become so, as well. When I was thinking about names, I recalled that in my mother's suicide letter that she had mentioned she would like one of my or my sister's children to be named after her. The turbulent memories of the last few years of my mothers life kept me from making the decision until the last moment; was it right to name my child after a woman who had committed suicide?

What changed my mind, in the end, was recalling that my mother, before she had lost herself to depression, had lived her entire life for my sister and me. She had been born to be a mother. She had loved us, had taken care of us when we were sick, made our school lunches; she had mothered us tenderly, and for as long as her depression allowed her to. I didn't doubt that if she had gotten the help she needed, she would still be alive to shower my daughter with the same love and affection that she had bestowed upon my sister and me.

And so, with no further misgivings, I named my daughter Norah Katherine, and after a short conversation with Nathan, I gave her his last name, despite the fact that I had kept my own after our marriage.

"If she wants to be unconventional like Mommy and keep her own name," I told him with a smile, "She can choose to do so when she's older."

When I was allowed to take her home from hospital, I was given four weeks of maternity leave before I would be forced to go back to work. Though I was filled with anxiety due to the shape and condition of my post-natal body, and suffered from lack of sleep, I still felt happy, because I had discovered in the face of my child what true love was.

I recall one snowy day in December; I had just gotten home from taking Norah on a walk around the parish, and I was worried that she had a wet diaper, and had felt cold on the way. I looked down at her face, and felt my stress melt away as if it had never been there. She had such round cheeks, pink from the outside chill, and soft almond eyes that gazed up into mine, curious, and non-judgmental. I felt as if I could get lost in those eyes forever. I lifted her into my arms and rubbed my nose gently against hers. She giggled.

"No-rah," I said softly, "Baby No-rah."

I picked up a soft pink blanket and sat down gently in my rocking chair. I wrapped her up carefully, placed her head in the crook of my arm, and started to sing to her one of the few songs I knew all the words to: Baby Mine, from Dumbo, the same song my mother had sung to me. She seemed to like it just as much as I had; she stared into my face with awe, especially at my mouth, watching as my lips formed the words. My heart swelled inside my chest. I loved her; I had never felt love like that before. I wanted to be with her always. I wanted to see every smile and wipe away every tear. How quickly this little being had entered my life and become my reason for living! Gazing into her mellow eyes, I wondered, *Was this what my mother felt for me? Was this what she felt in her heart when she held me close to her chest, and rocked me to sleep?* I liked to think so.

*

Nathan threw his hands into the air and said, "Don't give any of that feminist bullshit!"

I stood up, my face flushed with rage.

"It's not bullshit! Its how I feel! If you cared about me you would respect that!"

Nathan shook his head, pissed. "I have an ex-wife who won't give me back my name, and a wife that won't take it. I look like a huge ass-hole. If you cared about me you would respect how I feel about that."

"I asked you how you felt about me keeping my name when we got married, and you supported me!"

"You pushed me into it," he said, glaring at me.

"No, I didn't! Oh my God. That's beside the point of what is bothering me about what you just said. Do you support women keeping their own last name or not?"

He hesitated. "I think it separates the family and it's a bit disrespectful, don't you? Like my name isn't good enough?"

I looked at him, aghast. "Did you even listen to me when I told you about how I felt about this, about women being treated as property, about being expected to take up their husband's name, when it is unthinkable that the husband should take up theirs? You said, 'Yeah, I totally understand, Babe' and that was that. You didn't say a damn thing about feeling disrespected."

"Well, I do," he said, stubbornly, sitting back into the couch.

I put my hands on my head; it had suddenly begun to throb terribly. "I don't know how to fix this."

Nathan stared at me in silence, waiting. I looked up.

"I'm so tired of fighting with you, you know? Why do we always fight?"

Now it was his turn to put his hands on his head in frustration. "Jesus, don't do this again! How many times do we have to do this?"

"Until it stops! We don't fit together, Nate! We are night and day. You party, I don't. You are religious, I'm not. I'm sick, you ignore it. I have told you repeatedly I am not happy, but you refuse to go to counseling with me. I'm at the end of my rope, here."

He glared at me. "Don't make this out to be my fault."

"I don't mean to... I mean, think about it. We are constantly at odds. Don't you deserve someone who appreciates you, as you are now? Don't I deserve someone who likes me as I am?"

"Oh, so I get it. You want a divorce," he said bitingly.

"Isn't that what we've been circling around these last few months?" I asked, my eyes starting to water.

"I haven't thought so. I think you are just too eager to give up. If you loved me, you wouldn't give up. Do you love me, or not?"

I hesitated, afraid of sharing the truth which burned inside of me. "I love you as the father of our daughter, but no, I don't love you like I should love a husband."

He hadn't expected that, and he sat there, stunned. He started to get angry again.

"Kim… are you serious? Are you fucking kidding me? After everything I have done for you? Everything we have been through together, you just want to get up and go? And what about Norah, how the fuck do you think she will feel growing up in a broken family? Would you do that to our kid? Think about someone besides yourself for once!"

"I *am* thinking about her! I've told you before I will not stay in a marriage that doesn't make me happy. My parents did it for twenty years, and I saw it all, and hated it. I don't want that for Norah. She needs to see her parents in a happy, loving relationship, even if it means it's not with each other. Children learn what love is from watching their parents, and believe me she would not learn a damn thing from watching *us*. Lots of people get divorced; it's not the end of the world."

Nathan gazed at me with stormy, resentful eyes.

"You are really going to do this, aren't you?" he said quietly.

"Yes. I am. I've decided."

"You know I'm going on a goddamn deployment in two days, right? Why are you doing this now?"

I bit my lip, and let the tears fall. "I don't know! I can't stand it anymore. I can't lie to you when you're gone, and write you e-mails telling you how much I love you and miss you. I'm not good at pretending."

He laughed mockingly. "Oh-ho. You're wrong there, Kim. I think you are ve-ry good at pretending."

I swallowed. He was right; I was. But I hadn't meant to, in this case. I didn't know how to respond.

He stood up from the couch and began to pace slowly around the room. "If you do this, you're on your own again, you know."

"I know."

He looked at me. "I love you."

I turned away, ashamed. "I think you love the role of being a husband more than you love me, Nate."

He rubbed his temples in frustration. "I need to get the hell out of here. I'll be back… sometime. Take care of *our* daughter, okay?"

"Of course I will."

He paused at the front door, and said, "You know, I was really starting to think we had created a household together, where at the end of the day you settle in, take off your boots and really feel like you're home, you know? But now… now I can't stand being in this place for a single goddamn second." And then he left.

*

When Nathan left for his deployment, I became filled with guilt and self-doubt. Was I doing the right thing? Would I regret it later? Could I even make it on my own, with a child to take care of? I became irritable at my job and looked forward to coming home each day so that I could stretch out on my couch and stare for a while into oblivion.

One night, lonely for a sympathetic ear, I decided that I desperately had to speak to someone. I had put Norah to bed and was sitting on my couch, and the silence began to disturb me because it reminded me of old days when all there was, was silence. After a moment of contemplation, I picked up the house phone and dialed my sister's number. I hadn't spoken to her for a while; it would be nice to catch up.

"Hello?" came Rachel's voice from three thousand miles away.

"Hi Rach, it's Kim," I said.

"Kimbo!" she said. "How are you?"

"Good, how are you?"

"Oh, busy! How's Norah? I'm can't believe you're a mom! Is it weird?"

I laughed. "Not really. I fell into the groove pretty easily, I think. How are your boys?"

"Loud, demanding, and hungry," she said.

"Little cuties," I said, and a moment of hesitation, continued: "So... I'm calling because I'm getting a divorce."

"Oh, Kim, I'm sorry. What happened?"

"It's complicated. We just don't work well together. I don't love him like I should. There are other reasons, but that's the gist of it."

"Aw. What's going to happen with Norah?"

"She's going to live with me," I said, "and she'll visit her dad as much as possible. I want her to know him."

"That's good."

"Yeah."

We were silent for a moment, and then Rachel said,

"I was going to call, or write you soon... but- you know how I've always hated sounds and stuff, right?"

I pursed my lips. *How can I possibly forget?* "Yeah."

"Well... It turns out there's a name for it. I wanted to tell you, to let you know that I wasn't just being an asshole all those years when we were kids. It's an actual disorder called Misophonia. A lot of people have it in differing degrees, but mine is very bad, apparently. Sound transmits as rage, or fear. It alerts the 'fight-or-flight' impulse, or something."

"Wow. Is there a way to cure it?"

"It is a new diagnosis, so doctors are still figuring it all out. But I think there are therapy sessions you can attend to train your brain into believing that certain irritating sounds are actually soothing. But no, there's no magic pill, or anything."

"What about my feet? You always hated my feet. Those weren't a noise."

"Misophonia can also transmit to some physical items, as well," Rachel said.

I was quiet then, thinking over the information I had just received. Just like that, the mystery was solved. For fifteen years of my life I had lived in silence because my sister had violently detested noise, and I had never known the reason. Whenever I thought about it, which was often, I had believed it was because I was annoying, and loud, and unlovable, and far as my feet went, I had always just assumed they were hideous. But such was not the case, after all. My sister had just been suffering from something that no one, not even herself, had understood. I took a deep breath. I wasn't quite sure how I felt. Despite knowing the facts, I still felt bitter when I recalled those years of her screaming at me when all I was doing was trying to breathe, or eat, or simply exist- yet...

"Rachel," I said suddenly, "I'm glad you found out what's going on. Hopefully there's something out there that can make things easier for you."

"Thanks, Kim," she said. "And... I'm sorry I was such a crappy sister. I didn't know what was going in my head."

I bit my lip, restraining the urge to laugh and say, 'Damn right, you were a crappy sister! Where were you when I needed you?' But I knew that wasn't fair. It hadn't been her job to baby me. She wasn't my mother. She had her own life, her own troubles. And after all, I definitely hadn't been there for her every time she needed me.

"It's okay, Rach," I said. "I'm just glad we're getting along better now."

"Me too," she said, and then began to talk about her new comic book project. We talked for three hours that night.

By the Horns
(29)

By the time my divorce was finalized, my tour at Lakenheath was over. It had passed very quickly, it seemed, and though I was nervous about where I might be sent next, I tried to keep an open mind. All the same, it was a bit of a shock when I found out I was assigned back stateside, to Nebraska. I don't think I had ever given the mid-west more than a passing thought in my life, but I was grateful for the move because it made visiting Prue possible again. But before I could relocate, my career had advanced to the stage where I was obligated to go back to Sheppard AFB, Texas, to attend the next level of learning for my career field. This *really* excited me, because Sheppard was only two hours away from Tinker AFB, where Prue was stationed with her husband.

I e-mailed her right away, and we planned it all out: I would attend school during the week, and every Friday she would drive and pick me up (since I would be there without a car), and we would spend the whole weekend together doing whatever we wanted. This would go on for about a month and a half, until I would be forced to move on to Nebraska. As Nathan was deployed, I sent Norah to her paternal grandmother's house in Ohio, and then continued on to Texas. Sheppard was just as I remembered it- utterly dead looking- but this time arriving there felt like coming home.

School was negligible in my memory compared to weekends with my friend. We went dancing and karaoking, watched a rodeo, went shopping without caring how much money we spent, went to a firing range, rode go-carts, went rock climbing; every single thing we did was magnificent because we both felt spontaneous and free in each other's company. As much as I enjoyed my time with her, there were moments where I couldn't help feeling a bit jealous. Everything seemed perfect in Prue's life. She had a brand new house and a good-looking husband that doted on her. I hadn't a notion anything was wrong until one night, after the rodeo, Prue and I sat down outside, exhausted from laughing. The bull, though safely on the other side of the fence, had kept running up to us, carrying with it a whirlwind of dust which had left us covered with dirt from hair to torso. Eventually we calmed down and just sat together looking at the stars, happy.

"You know," Prue said abruptly, "I don't think I've ever had this much fun here, and I mean that. I never get to go out and do stuff like this."

I was surprised. "Really? Why not?"

"Owen… gets jealous sometimes. Of like, everything," she said, playing with her wedding ring, "It gets to the point where he doesn't want me to go do anything without him because he doesn't trust me. I've done more fun things with you in these three weekends than I've done with him in our entire marriage."

"Prue, I had no idea. I thought you guys were this perfect couple. So he gets jealous? What does he do?"

She pouted her lip. "Oh, he just gets really mad if a guy looks at me, or if he thinks I look at a guy. He's just a dumbass. He didn't even want you to stay with us on the weekends, because he was jealous of you, too, but I talked him into it."

"I'm sorry if I caused problems," I said, sobered by my friend's unhappiness. "I don't have to come back next weekend."

She turned and gave me a serious look, "Yes, you do, because you are *my* friend, it's my house too, dangit, and I want to see you."

I smiled, inwardly relieved. "I want to see you too. But don't let me cause friction between you, or anything."

She snorted. "It wouldn't be you that caused friction! He's- he's just an idiot."

"I never would have known. I thought you guys were happy, and getting along great…"

She looked at her ring again and shook her head slowly. "No, we're far from 'getting along great'. But I don't want to talk about it right now." She turned and gave me her usual smile, her gray eyes sparkling again. "I'm just glad you're here, Kimmy! I've missed you so much."

For the remainder of my visits, she and Owen seemed to play the part of a normal, attentive couple, at least whenever I was around. Owen was courteous to me, opened my door, and was always polite and charming. If it hadn't been for Prue telling me that he had jealousy problems, which I never saw first-hand, I would have liked him just fine. I tried bringing up the subject of Prue's unhappiness once or twice before I left for Nebraska, but she never felt like talking about it; she would brush it off with a comment like, "Men are just stupid," or "I was tipsy when I said that." Though I was a little worried about her, I knew she could take care of herself; hadn't she, after all, taken care of me for so long? So I left her with a lingering embrace and a big smile; I even hugged Owen.

"Take care of her," I told him meaningfully, squeezing his shoulder.

Owen smirked, and, peering over at Prue, said he would do his best.

*

Instant Message Conversations Between Prue and Kimberly, August 4- November 9, 2011

Prue, August 4: Hey Kimmy love. Don't know how to say this.. But I'm getting divorced.. Not really my choice but he keeps blaming me and telling me its my fault.. I just don't know what to do. But he is being very difficult.. Grrrr it's so frustrating. How did you do it????

Kimberly, August 5: *PRUE! I can't believe it; not going to try a separation first? :(May I ask what he's blaming you for? Maybe I can help a teensy bit but I don't know how I did it. You don't go through divorce easily. It may break you down for a while, but cling to the person you are and keep thinking about what you want out of life, and you will eventually start climbing there. If it's meant to end between you guys, then end it as quickly as you can and move on with grace. I love you and please write back! Also, if you are sick of going over the details of things, you don't have to. I'll still be here if you want to :) <3*

Prue, August 5: *Thanks Kimmy love! That's why I love you. He blames us getting divorced on me, and said I didn't try hard enough or care. I volunteered for this deployment to kind of separate us and see how we feel at the end. But he has been freaking out on me since I got back. We have been having issues for a year and a half. I found some messages between him and some chick last year when we PCS'd to Tinker and she even sent him naked/sexy photos of herself. Since then it's all been down hill. I wanted to leave him then, but he convinced me not to. And it got really bad when his Grandpa died in April. He was really close to him and he just became very angry, and started gearing it toward me. Two weeks ago he was talking about how he has been working on his anger issues, etc., and I brought up the point that I noticed... that ever since his grandpa passed away he has been very angry and taking it out on me. He snapped and told me not to blame my problems on his grandpa's death. And then he decided not to talk to me until yesterday when he told me he sent me divorce paperwork two weeks ago and now he is trying to leave me with the house and everything even though I told him I wont be able to afford it. He told me he didn't care. So I am just trying to focus on being happy etc. I really need a vacation after this.. I miss you Kimmy love. Thanks for listening to me ramble...*

Prue, August 5: *Kimmy he just told me that if we don't stay together he will call it an "early end to everything"... Dude. This is out of control. He just came from mental health. They said he is borderline suicidal and he has to check in with them often. I don't know what to do at this point.*

Kimberly, August 5: *What the! Men sometimes, right?! Sorry... I do take this very seriously, because I want him and you to be okay, individually, that is. If he can't open up to you that is not your fault and there is little you can do about that; that is all about him. I am glad he is going to mental health and I hope he takes that opportunity to talk about how he is feeling. Does he have a few days of leave where he can go visit his family? Friends he is close with? Even just two days (physically) with someone you are close with helps a lot. And for what it's worth, you not trying hard enough or not caring about your relationship is bull-hockey. You are the kindest and most caring friend, and I can't see you treating a marriage to any lesser degree than that. I hope he is well, but don't you dare let him bring you down! (Sorry for MY rant; I don't like it when men try to lay things at doorsteps without first being willing or able to work them through!) <3 CHIN UP! Love love.*

Prue, August 5: *OH Kimberly. I love you so much. Thank you for all of this, it helps so much. I am just ready to be myself again ya know? I love your rants!!! They are amazing. =) I just want to get through all of this as quickly as possible so I can move on with.. well.. Me.*

Kimberly, August 21: *Hello Lovely! Are you and Owen ok again? I see he's being mushy on Facebook.*

Prue, August 22: *Uh yeah no. Now he doesn't want to get divorced. Too late buddy, ya already changed my mind. He keeps posting mushy shit in hopes that he will make me fall in love with him again. At this point I can't stand him. Is that normal? I always go back to him but this time I'm going to stand my ground. How are you and the munchkin?*

Kimberly, August 23: *I felt the same way about my ex when I decided I wanted a divorce. I suppose 'disgust' is a good word for it... maybe it's a self-protection thing. Like, you still like some memories and stuff but they're just that... good memories. I'm glad you are standing your ground, Prue! It is very empowering and I think once everything is settled you will enjoy life exactly as you want and deserve! :D I am doing ok... rough time moving and shit. Norah is doing well! Wonderful girl. Miss you :(*

Prue, August 24: *Yes Empowering is a great word for it! LOL. I feel better already. Like a huge weight has been lifted. Well this way I can come see you whenever I want! LOL. Miss you Kimmmmay love!*

Kimberly, September 1: *I miss you :(*

Kimberly, October 30: *Hi Prueee! Just writin' to let you know I was thinking of you and missing you and how are ya? :D Are things with the hubby still crazy? Let me know if you need to get away and I'll come steal you for a weekend somewhere!*

Prue, October 31: *I miss your face!!!! Well... hubby is sleeping in another room and I am going to file for divorce in the next couple of weeks. I woke up the other night and he was lying in bed next to me and I had to kick him out. I locked the door but he managed to unlock it.. ugh. So creepy. I had to put a chair under the handle before I go to sleep. I'm heading to Cali on the 8th till the 25th with my family but any time after that would be AMAZING. LOL I miss you!!!!!!!!!*

Prue, November 5: *Why is asshole talking to you??*

Kimberly, November 6: *I posted that I wasn't doing anything for Thanksgiving, and he sent me a PM suggesting I come down to see you that weekend! Not a bad idea, so I didn't tell him to blow me. Will you be free that weekend?? :D If the weather is drivable maybe I can come down there or fly!*

Prue, November 6: *Well I'm staying at a friend's house because he flipped out after we got into an argument and tried to kill himself by putting the toaster in the bath tub today. My supervision fears for my safety and wanted me to leave the house. We got into a tussle when I tried to get the toaster from him and pushed me. Oh hell no. sigh. Just ready to be done.*

Kimberly, November 7: *What the fuck! I know u can take care of yourself but that kind of nonsense is draining no matter how strong you are. He needs to get some sense knocked into him! Grr, what a messed up fucktard! His ass should be the one staying out of the house. Sorry but I really hate anyone messing with my family (which I consider you). Please let me know if I can do anything, anytime, and I'll be there with a hug or a hack saw. <3*

Prue, November 7: *Aww thanks Kimmy! Nicest thing anyone has ever said. Lol. He is in a mental health facility for now and may be released tomorrow. I took the liberty of getting all the paperwork done today and took it to him during visiting hours.. he was upset that I would do it then but I told him it was the safest place for me to tell him. Lol. He kept saying he loved me etc. Blah. But I'm gonna have to get him served when I get back.*

Kimberly, November 9: *You should find a creative way to serve him the papers... like get a waitress to put them in a menu, haha. I cant wait until this is all over for you and you can enjoy being single and happy!*

Prue, November 9: *Lol!! I know right! Maybe put it in a tube in his Crown or Jack Daniels bottle since he enjoys drinking so much these days. Ugh! I just wanna be alone in my casa with my puppy.*

Dollars to Doughnuts
(30)

    I closed Skype, blowing kisses to my daughter as I did so. Only when her small, cupid-like face faded from view did I let the pent-up tears fall, and allow the sob that had been frozen in my throat escape. I missed Norah- I missed her so, so much- I wanted to clasp her in my arms, to snuggle her little warm body against mine. She was my everything.

    Despite my pain at her absence, I felt that what I was doing was morally correct thing to do, letting her visit her father more than the legal agreement stated before she entered kindergarten. It wasn't like he was violent, or a bad father- he was a decent dad, and I wanted her to know him and have a relationship with him, perhaps in a way that I never had a relationship with mine. Plus, Nathan had never let me forget that I was the one who had wanted the divorce; I was the one who split our family apart, and made our daughter live apart from her father, or her mother at different times of the year, respectively. I felt a large burden of guilt, at that; I had caused the rift in my daughter's life. I was the one that made her travel back and forth every year, always making her wonder what bedroom she would be sleeping in next.

    "That's hilarious," Nathan would growl, during the times I asked for child support, "You divorce me, take my daughter, and when you let me have her, you still ask for money. It's just plain, fucking hilarious."

Overcome with guilt, I stopped asking for child support when Norah with her father, usually four to six months out of the year. Thought it made things difficult financially, I knew that it would eventually stop when she came of school age, and I looked forward to the day when she would start kindergarten with an eager heart, both for her sake, and for mine.

I started work at Offutt, Air Force Base, Nebraska, only a few days after I settled there, and I sensed immediately that it was going to be a very different experience than I what I had become used to at my previous bases. For one, I was the only Analyst and Database Manager in the entire unit; in fact, in the entire squadron. There were others with my job title located on the other side of the base, but we had nothing to do with each other; I was to work alone. I also was not going to be working with F-15's for the first time in my career, and that left a small hollow in my heart; I had come to love those breakable, loud-as-hell jets, especially since my deployment with them.

Additionally, my security clearance was to be upgraded to Top Secret, so that I could work with the Intelligence Squadron on any issues that may arise in their database. Though I felt up the challenge of working a more difficult job in a higher security, solo environment, I felt isolated. I would no longer have my crazy, fun-loving co-workers to talk to during the slow hours of the day; and now, I would be in a windowless, secure building, where cell-phone and visitors were not allowed. It seemed that my new assignment had been specifically created to make a person feel separated from the world.

At the end of the work-day, I would come home, and very often I would turn to bulimia to push my thoughts away, and then fall into a dreamless sleep. I would do my best not to think about my daughter, my ex-husband- anything that made me *feel*. Sometimes I would stop at the grocery store on the way home from work, and begin to binge while I drove, trying desperately to keep my depressive thoughts at bay. And, in a sick way, it worked; it had always worked. My every day was a thoughtless, bulimic blur, until Sunday, when I was able to Skype with my daughter and I felt alive again. *Three more months; two more months*, I would count down in my mind, *and she'll be with Mommy again.*

It was the day before Thanksgiving, and I had just completed an especially painful binge and purge where my throat had bled copiously all over the linoleum floor, and I was lying down on my bed sobbing, hating myself.

If only I had someone to spend time with, I wished; someone to go do things with, to be a true friend. Prue lived too far away to visit often, unfortunately; and though I had been asked out on a few dates by members of my new unit, I had sworn never to date another member of the Air Force ever again. I was not a drinker, or a partier, or even much of a socializer; so how could I, a proverbial hermit, meet someone new?

I dragged my laptop onto my bed, and while lying on my aching stomach I researched on-line dating. Finding that there was only a small fee involved, I tossed caution to the wind and I signed up on Match.com, and spent most of the night writing a long, detailed profile for myself. I describe myself as quiet, but goofy; shy, but after I came to know someone well, I could be very talkative and outspoken. I was looking for someone mature, who had the capacity to learn to love my daughter; someone who had layers, who had already been past the first turbulent forays of youth. The site gave an option to list your preference of age-range, and after considering it, I chose to exclusively look for men who were five to ten years older than I was. I didn't want a younger man; in fact, I felt that five years my senior was almost too young for what I was looking for in a mate.

After I was done creating my profile, I made it 'live' and then fell into a deep sleep, slightly nervous, but also satisfied that I was taking a decisive step towards my own happiness.

I awoke the next day to over fifty messages and 'winks' from men. Winks were basically an alert letting you know that someone thought you were attractive. I stared at the number dumbly, and then moved my cursor around the site, reading my messages, perusing profiles, investigating these strangers who seemed to be interested in me. And, after an hour, I had to admit that I was not overly impressed.

I knew that I was not much of a prize; I was ill, and half-crazy; I was divorced and had a child who would always come first in my life. But the profiles of the men I looked at didn't seem to be men at all, but a bunch of boys looking for sex. I noticed a pattern right away; most of the profile pictures were 'selfies' taken at a party of some sort, and among their biographies there was, without fail, the comment that they were 'laid-back' and liked to 'hang-out' with friends. It got the point in my investigations that the moment I saw those words I closed that tab with that persons profile on it, counting them as unoriginal. I had spent a lot of time on my profile, and actually told everyone something about myself. I wanted the same altruism from the man I dated. I was done playing around. Being 'laid-back' told me nothing- it was a cop-out.

Thanksgiving night I was awake until one-o'clock on the morning, and frustrated with the offers of dates I had received, I decided to do my own search. *Why wait for the men to come to me?* Obviously, the women were the minority on those type of sites, so it made more sense to become the hunter instead of the hunted. Deciding this to be a wise move, I performed the search for my older man-of-the-world, half-wondering as I did so how I would recognize him when I saw him.

Despite my doubts, when I saw a man with brown eyes and a salt-and-pepper beard, holding his son in his profile picture, I felt as if some part of me knew him already. I had never considered myself attracted to beards before, but I liked his; I liked that it was flecked with silver, and that it wasn't overly groomed- it looked casual, and sexy- and for me, that was saying a lot. It wasn't often that I found myself physically attracted to *anyone*. I clicked on his profile, and began to read eagerly.

He told a lot about himself in his biography. His name was Scott; he was thirty-five years old and taught mathematics at a local university, something he had always had a talent and a passion for. He was divorced, with two children. He admitted that he was partially to blame for the split, but he was ready to move on. He was a bit of a nerd, who enjoyed video games and sports, but he was not a neglectful partner because of them; he had learned his lesson. I became enthralled with this man while I read about him; with his honesty, his devotion to his kids, his self-depreciation. I stared at his photos for a few minutes, gazing into his dark eyes. He was almost exactly ten years older than I was, and to me, that felt perfect. His kids were beautiful, a boy and a girl, the girl about Norah's age. *Maybe they could be friends.* With only a moment of hesitation, I clicked the 'wink' button. I closed my browser after that, a little embarrassed, wondering if he would be weirded out that a twenty-five year old was trying to hit on him.

*

Our First Date, as written by Scott Tichenor

    The path to my first date with Kimberly starts with my move to Nebraska from Illinois. I had taken a visiting professorship at Doane College in a little town called Crete. The job seemed like a good opportunity for me to distance myself from my previous life and get my feet on the ground after a life-shaking divorce. I had just left graduate school without finishing my dissertation, so I figured it would be a good way to cocoon and finish things. That was the idea, anyway. It turns out that being eight hours away from your nearest family and apart from your children lends itself to depression rather than productivity. I found my brain focused on loneliness rather than mathematics.

    I had been on-and-off dating sites since it had become clear that my divorce from my partner of seventeen years was imminent. The 'on' times were frustrating, while the 'off' times were depressing. Through the entire process I don't believe I was quite ready to move on; I tended to pour my soul out almost instantly, which most women see as a red flag. Hey, I hadn't dated for... well, ever, really.

I had given up online dating when Thanksgiving rolled around that year. My children were going to be with their mother in Illinois, and so I stayed in Nebraska. Out of pity, perhaps, one of my colleagues invited me to have Thanksgiving with him and his family, and I ended up having a wonderful time and ate some great food. During the meal, looking around at my co-worker's family and seeing his happiness, I had a moment; a true 'I'm finally ready to move on' moment. After I made my departure I headed back to my office at Doane, and created an online dating profile.

As a thirty-five year old man in the Middle-of-Nowhere, Nebraska, I started searching through profiles. I must have sent about twenty messages that night, excitedly trying to find someone with similar interests and goals. Despite the fact that I received exactly zero responses from the messages I sent that evening, my third go around with internet dating was not destined to last long.

Friday November 25th at 10:56 AM, I received a 'wink'. At the time, I was in my office trying to work on my thesis to distract myself from the dating world, but the wink drew me in. Why would this amazing looking woman, a decade younger than me, wink at me? I'd been drawn in by fake accounts before. This can't be real, I thought to myself. I mean, geez, look at these pictures. I spent quite a while soaking in her account. She sounded so cool, and such a good fit for me. Our profiles were mirror images in many ways. It seemed too good to be true.

I needed to convince myself she was real. I sent her a message asking her to text chat, and before I knew it, less than twenty-four hours since I had joined the site, I was talking with Kimberly. I had not seen her in my searches the previous night because she was just a little outside the distance limit I had set for my own search; but it didn't matter. She found me. There were so many little factors that led us to that moment in time, that if either of us had been a little off from our paths we might have missed each other completely. I am so thankful everything worked the way it did, so that she chanced to read my profile.

I don't remember how the chat went because I was nervous, but I'm sure we started out with the basics. Eventually, we began to make plans for a face-to-face date. Kimberly was busy that weekend volunteering for charity and wanted to push it off to the next, and for so many reasons I felt that I could not let that happen. Surely I would have died that week with anticipation. I also still had to see her and hear her voice before I would believe she was truly real. She acquiesced, and suggested that we go out to dinner after she was done ringing a bell for the Salvation Army on Saturday.

I don't remember what I did during the day on Saturday, but I know I tried very hard not to think about the upcoming date. I had resolved not to be a needy puppy and just have a good time, focus on seeing if I wanted a second date and not messing things up if I did. It was an hour drive to reach Kimberly's house, and during the long drive my anxiety had betrayed me and I was sweating profusely. I remember stopping at a gas station to dry my overly damp armpits with some toilet paper. After I was freshened up, I drove to her house and ended up showing up a tad early, but as her response to the doorbell was prompt and pleasant, I guess she was ready a little early, too.

It was newly dark outside and the porch light was on. Her hair momentarily distracted me as the lighting made it look blonder than the dark brown it was in reality. She was wearing a long dark coat, and in the light she glowed softly; she looked like the woman of my dreams.

I offered to drive but she refused. She wanted to show off her new car and GPS. I don't find myself in the passenger seat often, and this was by far my all-time favorite trip as a passenger in a car. Kimberly's driving prowess was not up to her usual standard as we missed turn after turn, with GPS berating us with new directions each time. She was so embarrassed, but I enjoyed myself the entire time.

We eventually arrived in downtown Omaha and parked at a public lot near the restaurant she had picked out, called M's Pub. It was only a tad cold outside but it was enough of an excuse for her to put her arm in mine during the walk from the car to the restaurant.

We were seated at a square table in the middle of the room and were seated next to each other. We began with simple first date type conversation topics, which led me pretty quickly to realize that we had quite a bit in common. The moment that stands out to me as pivotal is when the conversation turned to video games. As we each started listing off games we liked, Kimberly mentioned my favorite game of all time, Final Fantasy VII. At that point, the date went beyond just being a good date and I often think that's when I fell in love with her. As Kimberly was finished with her falafel and I had devoured my curry chicken (I was actually going to order the falafel before she did...) we moved on from the restaurant and the date took another turn.

We walked around the block to a small coffee shop; it was more like a stand in front of a bank or hotel so there wasn't much in the way of seating. We each ordered a drink and then sat in big, puffy chairs by the door. At that point the conversation became deeper. I started to pour out my soul in exactly the way I promised myself I wouldn't. To my utter amazement, Kimberly didn't flinch and followed me right into the depths where first date conversations do not belong. We showed each other our damage and neither of us shied away from the other. I appreciated her candor and ability for real conversation. It was so refreshing to be able to speak of real emotions and feelings. I remember feeling so free and happy in that coffee shop. I was able to be myself while out having fun with an intelligent and beautiful young woman.

I was buzzing the whole drive back to her house where my car was parked. I was hoping beyond hope that she would ask me in, and Kimberly didn't miss a beat; when we arrived, she invited me in right away. I was so relieved. We sat down on her couch about a cushion away from each other and the conversation turned to our possible immediate future. I expressed my desire to see her again to which she was immediately amenable.

"I believe I would like to kiss you," I said in a soft, playful tone. And with her consent I leaned across the couch and gave her a gentle kiss on the lips. The excitement that had been building all night started to make my legs shake. Passion could easily have led to more, but I wouldn't let it. Despite my shaking legs, I was determined, absolutely determined, that this would not be a one night stand. I wanted- no, needed, to see her again.

So, after making plans for a date the very next day, I forced myself to go towards the door and then walk out of it. My brain was in a frenzy the entire drive home. Once or twice, while driving, I shouted with excitement, reveling in the feeling that I had finally found the one.

*

Scott and I lay in my bed, my head resting on his bare chest. The house was silent- early summer light streamed through the open window and settled delicately on the subtle silver highlights of his hair. I looked up at him adoringly as he lie there, relaxing; he sighed once, and began to stroke my arm lazily, sending small shivers of ecstasy through my body. I was in Heaven. Scott was unbelievable; I thought men like him didn't exist. He was kind, and honest, and smart- and I was attracted to him. It was a new feeling for me, to want someone- I had not honestly wanted anyone for a very long time- and suddenly I had the embodiment of everything I could ever desire lying there, half asleep in my bed.

Abruptly, I wondered if he would still care for me if he knew everything- if he knew what a mess I was. A small feeling of panic began to grow inside my chest. He was such a wonderful person- what right did I have to ruin his life with my illness, my madness? I bit my lip, almost drawing blood. It didn't matter if I thought he was fantastic if he thought I was a monster.

I reached my arm up, and stroked the side of his face softly. His eyes popped open, and he looked down at me and smiled.

"I have to tell you something," I said nervously.

"Okay."

"And after I tell you, if you want to run away, or just quietly leave, please don't feel guilty for it. I understand."

"Um…okay?"

I took a deep breath. "I've been bulimic for over ten years. It's pretty disgusting, and it really affects my health, mentally and physically."

Scott was quiet for a moment. "Bulimia is the one where you- you throw up, right?"

I smiled weakly despite myself. He was so innocent in some ways. "Yes, that's the one where you throw up."

"Are you okay?" he asked, concern in his voice as he reached down to envelope my small hand in his larger one. Tears filled my eyes but I refused to let them fall.

"Yeah, I mean... no. I've been doing it for so long I don't know how to stop. It's an addiction, and people can end up dying from it. And it makes me crazy, sometimes- it has helped ruin my past relationships, it makes me so crazy. So, I just wanted you to know what you'd be getting yourself into before you decide to keep me, or anything."

Scott nestled a little closer. "I've already decided to keep you."

"You don't know what it's like, though! I eat masses, just tons of food- thousands upon thousands of calories, and then I stick my finger down my throat to get rid of it. Do you want to be around me, knowing that I do that? It's gross. Worse than gross."

"Well, you're right that don't know much about it," he said slowly, "But I'm going to learn everything I can, so that I can be here to support you. I would like to help."

I shook my head. "I should just let you go now and save you a lot of trouble. You're probably trying to think of a way out right now, but you're too nice..."

"Maybe you should let *me* decide if I want to take on any 'trouble' or not," he said sternly. "If you want to break up with me, do it- but don't do it because of what *you think* I am thinking- that's ridiculous. Only I know what I'm thinking, and what I'm thinking is- I love you, and I want to be here with you."

The tears I had been holding on to began to release themselves, and I turned my body into his, until we were practically lying nose to nose.

"I love you too," I sniffled. "But five years from now, when you're miserable and hating me, don't say I didn't warn you."

"I appreciate the warning," Scott said, "But I think we'll be just fine. I'm here for you until you don't want me around anymore."

"Of course I want you!" I cried, burying my face into his arms. "Jesus. What the Hell did I do in life to deserve such a wonderful guy like you?"

Scott patted the back of my hair, and whispered, almost to himself, "And what did I ever do to deserve a wonderful woman like you?"

And he kissed me to seal the deal.

Behavioral Commonwealth
(31)

"Hello, Sgt Presa," said Captain Yates, "How are you today?"

I fiddled absently with the bottom of my uniform blouse, my eyes on my boots. "I'm okay. I mean, I got sick yesterday, but I'm okay."

Captain Yates sat up straighter in his seat. "When you say you 'got sick...'"

I looked at him. "I binged and purged, on purpose. That's what I mean."

"I see." He jotted something down in his notebook.

"Why do you think you did that?" he asked, continuing his interrogation.

I thought for a moment, and then replied, "I had a normal day at work. I woke up, stared at myself in the mirror, and cried a little bit because I felt ugly. At work, I listened to some of my fellow airmen talk about their sex lives, which grossed me out a little, but it was nothing I'm not used to. All guys talk about are sex and food and movies. I didn't eat anything all day because I was afraid I'd throw up at work. And when I came home, I ate everything in the house because I was starving and I just... I don't know. Is there a point to asking me why I did it? If I knew why I did it, I guess I wouldn't do it anymore. Right?"

He wrote this down in his book, chewing on his bottom lip.

"You said you looked in the mirror, and felt ugly. Do you feel that way often?"

I eyed him. "Well, look at me. I'm hideous. If I ever don't feel ugly it's because I forget for a while… but I always remember, eventually. There are mirrors everywhere."

"I think you see yourself in something like a fun-house mirror, Sergeant Presa," said Yates, "In a way that no one around you sees you. It's very common for people with eating disorders to see themselves through distorted vision."

"That's what nice people say- and it's definitely what a therapist would say to an ugly person in order to heal her. So thanks," I said, looking at my feet again.

"You have a lot of red marks, on your nose, and chin. What are they from? It looks a little like you fell?"

I shook my head. "I pick my face a lot," I explained. "When I look in the mirror. It's not all the time, but when I feel really… fat, and unattractive. I pick it until it bleeds and looks all nasty, like this-" I indicated my nose, which was flaked and sore in many spots- "It takes forever to heal."

"Does it hurt?"

"Yeah. Quite a bit."

"You mentioned you didn't eat anything while you were at work. Is that a normal thing for you- to skip meals?"

"All the time."

"Do you think that has something to do with you overeating at the end of the day?"

"Probably," I said, "But I have also eaten throughout the day, and felt so fat at the end of it that I threw up everything I've eaten the last few hours. This is just my latest pattern. I really try not to get sick at work. There's always the chance I'll get caught."

He pursed his lips. "Why did you come to see me today?" he asked. "How do you see me helping you, or yourself improving?"

I raised my eyes to his, and against my will they began to grow moist. I blinked a few times, and cleared my throat to answer.

"I don't know what you can do for me," I said, "I have studied bulimia and eating disorders for years, and as far as facts go, I know a lot. I know it's stupid, and dangerous, and I'm familiar with a lot of the theories about how it begins, and why it continues. But despite that, years later, here I am, still clinging to it, and I don't know why."

I turned my face to stare out the window, and continued. "I've been called lazy, and an idiot, and worse, for being bulimic, but I don't *feel* like those things. The truth is, it's hard being like this. You know what's easier than being a bulimic? Just about everything else in the world. For some reason, I haven't died yet... and it's been *years*. I've tried to quit more times than I can remember at this point. But I have a daughter, now, and...she's two years old. I love her more than anything, and I want to be there for her- I want to be able to be a good role model for her. It's hard enough growing up a girl without a mom that's- that's crazy."

I looked at him again. "I came here because I'm near the end of a very, very long rope. If you can't help me somehow, then I really don't know what I'll do."

Yates nodded, writing in his book, once in a while looking up at me with kind eyes.

"My boyfriend helped give me the courage to come here," I admitted, "Because he was worried about me. I fought with him for a while, because I'm afraid that the Air Force will kick me out." I paused. "Are you going to kick me out?"

He cocked his head to the side, thinking. "Eating disorders are usually something you get medical boarded for, which often leads to discharge," he said. "But if we fix this, we may be able to stop that from happening. But I can't lie- it might happen. But the main thing is for you to get better, and for that, I need you to work with me. Will you work with me?"

"I will work with you," I said, "But I can't promise my bulimia will be as compliant."

He frowned, took note of this in his book, and then set it aside.

"How would you feel about a day-program?" he asked.

I paused, letting that sink in; that was a new one.

"What do you mean by 'day program'?" I asked suspiciously.

He leaned back in his seat, explaining, "There in a place downtown called OMNI Behavioral Health, and they do treatment for eating disorders at one of their branch offices. I've looked into it before, with another patient, but so far I haven't sent anyone. Basically, you spend half the day at receiving therapy at their offices, and they would also help you with your nutrition; and then after lunch they would release you to work. So, at least up until then, you will have eaten well, and received some care for your bulimia during the morning."

"What about work?" I asked.

"The way I see it, the time you will miss at work getting better is less than you would miss in the long run if you remain ill," he said convincingly. "You need to focus on your health right now, Sergeant Presa. So…what do you think? What if I send you to meet with the psychologist there, and she can talk to you for a bit, and then we see how you feel about the program?"

"What would we tell my boss, though?" I asked, feeling slightly panicky. I didn't want anyone at work to know- the males at work would never respect me again.

"I would have to tell your First Sergeant, and maybe your Superintendent," said the Captain, "But no one else would need to know anything; it's no one else's business. And as far the exact details, they would remain solely between us."

I sat silently for a minute, contemplating how I would handle a day program. My mind went back to the eating disorder clinic in LA, and how I had been forced to eat everything on my plate; but back then, I had been watched constantly, and so the option of purging in secrecy had been removed. But now, I would be released after a half day- with a full stomach. The thought made my insides twist.

"I can at least meet with the therapist," I said slowly, still unsure.

"Great," said the Yates, standing up and extending his hand. "I'll set it up and give you a call." We shook hands, and as he ushered me out his office door, he said, "Have a good day, Sergeant Presa. See you soon."

I waved goodbye dumbly, and walked down the clinic's hallway, wishing I had never come in the first place.

*

"I don't want to go," I told Scott, burying my face into his shoulder, "They make me eat so much food, and the girls there are awful. It's obvious that they don't like me."

Scott reached out an arm and caressed my back tenderly.

"They're idiots," he said softly, "But remember, you're not going there for them. You're going there for you."

I pulled back, looked him in the eyes. "But what about the food? They stuff me until I can't breathe! And then we sit there for hours, not moving, and then... I have to leave to go to work. It's awful. I've done nothing but cry and freak out the last few times I've been released, and people at work are creeped out by me. I can't handle having all that food inside of me."

"I know, I know," Scott said, hugging me. "Maybe give it another few days, before going to the Captain to tell him it's not for you? He made it pretty clear it's the only local place that deals with eating disorders. And you need help."

"I know! But why does that mean I have to settle for this place? Why can't I choose somewhere that fits *me*, instead of a place that is only *central* to me?" I asked, tears streaming down my cheeks and soaking his shirt.

Scott sighed, and kissed the top of my head. "I don't know, honey," he said. "The Air Force is confusing to me. I don't understand how they are willing to treat alcoholics and such, but drag their feet over helping someone like you, who has done so well in her career, and threaten to kick you out."

"Don't even get me started on that!" I raged suddenly, "The Air Force is all about alcohol- alcohol at graduations! At parties! At award celebrations! It's an *acceptable* disease. But if you check an illness outside of that box, you're a waste of taxpayer's money. Oh God. I'm a waste of taxpayer's money." I buried my head on his shoulder again.

"Shh, it's okay," Scott said, "Let me drive you, alright? I don't have to go Doane until later today. I'll take you to OMNI, and then pick you up after lunch. We can spend a few minutes together, then, and later you can drive yourself to work when you're ready. Would that help at all? Even a little?"

I looked up into his brown eyes, and couldn't help but smile at him despite my tears. I leaned into him, and kissed his lips soundly, nuzzling his nose gently as I did so.

"You're the love of my life," I said quietly, kissing him again. "Thank you for caring about me so much, even though I'm a disgusting mess."

Scott smiled gently. "You're not disgusting, even if you are a mess. I only wish I could do more for you. I love you, Kim."

I hugged him tightly. "I love you, too," I whispered.

*

Breakfast at OMNI was wretched; you were required to make your own breakfast according to your nutritionist's specifications, and that morning I had two servings of fruit, a bowl of protein cereal, orange juice, and a soy yogurt. It was too much for me, and I ate it slowly, sadly, and let a few tears slide unchecked into my cereal bowl. Though I felt unfortunate, I knew some of the other girls had it tougher than I did, and I tried to be sensitive to how they felt- but it was difficult to care when facing what I perceived to be a impossibly large mass of food.

There were five other girls in the program with me, and all were anorexic as opposed to bulimic. There are many who tend to lump all eating disorders together, and though I can see where one might be tempted to do so, I wish they wouldn't, because all eating disorders have differences. I don't think it speaks for all of the recovering anorexics I was with in that program, but I know for a fact at least some were appalled at my rounder body shape, and horrified by the fact that I binged. Likewise, I was put off by their visibly protruding bones, their colostomy bags, and how- despite their active treatment- they all vocally wished they were skinnier. Though I knew it was just their illness talking, it was still disconcerting to hear it from someone who looked like they might blow away in a light breeze. It was there that I realized that though I wanted to be slender, I did not want to resemble a skeleton- because who knows when I would ever be happy with my body? With the anorexic mentality, I would have to die before I ever felt thin enough. I was learning that how much a person weighed, by itself, could not give or take away happiness.

Unfortunately, I was foolish enough to mention my feelings during a group therapy session one day. The girls, who already didn't see me as a part of their group, became angry.

"I used to think I wanted to become very thin," I said to the group counselor. "But I think, maybe, I just want to be lean, and healthy, somehow. Mostly healthy. I don't know how some people do it, but I want to learn. I don't want to be… just bones."

One of the girls in the group, an ex-model, stood up in a rage.

"Oh, so you think you're better than everyone here?" she spat, "Because you can stand to have fat on your body? Well, get over yourself! You saying all that shit just make us feel badly about ourselves."

"I-I'm sorry," I said, extremely flustered, "I didn't mean to offend anyone. I wasn't talking about any of you. I'm just trying to get what I can out of this session. But none of my comments were directed at any of you, I promise."

"Well, you come across as a stuck-up, self-righteous bitch," said the girl, "and we would all like it if you kept your mouth shut from now on, yeah?"

I turned to the counselor for help, who simply nodded and said, "You're both allowed to express your feelings, but in this case I have to side with Kim. I don't think she meant any harm…"

"Bull-shit! And I've got more to say to this bitch. She's always going on about her daughter, when she knows perfectly well that I can't have kids…"

I stood up then, unable to handle anymore. I ran through the entryway, grabbed my coat, and with tears blurring my vision I exited the building, refusing to look back.

*

Captain Yates stared at me blankly. "You… left. Just like that?"

I nodded, still upset. After leaving OMNI, I had called Scott to come pick me up, and he had driven me straight to Yates' office. I didn't want to get in trouble for not being at the clinic all morning, but he needed to know what had happened, and how I truly felt about that program.

He sighed. "Kim, you can't just walk out of a program that the Air Force is paying for- that you *agreed* to," he said.

"It's not for me," I told him, my voice pleading, "That half-day program- it's set up for someone further along the line of recovery, or for anorexics. I've told you all this before. Please believe me; I need something else."

"Many people feel like this when they first enter treatment, but given time…"

"No!" I said, angry at last. "Listen! Just because I'm bulimic doesn't mean I don't know doesn't work for me. Stuffing me full of food in the morning and setting me loose in the afternoon to puke up won't help me get better. Keeping me closeted with a bunch of anorexics who hate me won't make me feel better about myself. Why don't you believe me?" Tears fell from my eyes. "I need something else! I'll keep saying it until it happens! Please!"

Yates looked frustrated, but then took a deep breath and leaned forward, looking at his hands. "And what do you suggest we do?" he asked calmly.

"I… I don't know. Maybe send me to an inpatient facility somewhere," I ventured, grasping at straws. "Would the Air Force do that?"

He shook his head. "I seriously doubt it…"

"Would you ask?" I begged him, "Before you say no?"

He gazed at me silently, and then nodded, his eyes full of pity.

"If I do this, and it works out, and you go- you need to stay there until the very end, until they discharge you," he said.

I gulped, "I'd stay."

"I really hope so. Alright, look- you need to do some research if you want me to look into this. Find some inpatient facilities that look like they would suit you, and send me the links; I'll see what I can do. I don't promise anything, but... I will try."

I thanked him and walked a bit unsteadily out the door, my hands trembling. What was I doing? Did I really want to go back to an inpatient facility... to be in someone else's complete control? I thought of my daughter, and Scott, and I realized that if I wanted to live, if I wanted to be a part of their lives for decades to come, that I had no choice. For them, for myself, I had to act. Something had to change, to alter my life from its current path, or the only future that awaited me was my death.

Down at the Lodge
(32)

As I was led into the lodge, I was confronted by the curious eyes of the other residents. I tried to calmly return their gazes, but I was too nervous, and ended up rushing with a burning face to follow the nurse towards a tiny office where a couple of women wearing white sat behind glass, watching with hawk eyes everything that happened outside. She bid me to sit on a couch placed outside the room, and I complied, trying to avoid the relentless, inquisitive glances that besieged me.

"Just sit there, Hon, while I go get the doctor," said the nurse politely, and disappeared down the hallway, leaving me to the wolves.

I was immediately approached by a tall girl with black hair, about twenty years of age. She sat down with her eyes roving over me as I were a piece of meat, and asked,

"So, what are you in for?"

I was immediately discomfited. There was no way that was a polite question to ask someone who had just arrived. I buttoned my lips, refusing to answer.

"Well," continued my questioner, "I'm here because I have PTSD. No one has secrets around here, so you might as well get used to it. I'm Erika; what's your name?"

Shocked, I replied, "Kim."

"Nice to have you here, Kim. Willow is a good place. I bet you'll be my room mate, since one of mine just left- well, she ran away, but I don't think she's coming back."

"She *ran* away?"

She nodded. "Yep! She was here on court order and wanted to get out really bad, so she left! She got caught, of course, but I'm pretty sure they're taking her somewhere else now because they hauled her away in a cop car. So, where are you from?"

I looked at her. She was more than just tall- she was a proverbial giantess, with long, black hair and hard brown eyes. She had the feel of the country about her, and that along with the bluff, honest manner, she seemed almost Amazonian. "I flew in from Nebraska, but I'm not from there, really. I'm in the Air Force. They sent me here because I'm- um, bulimic."

Erika looked pleased. "I knew it. I could tell it was an eating disorder, because you're a stick figure."

I frowned, recalling the girls I had seen at OMNI. "No, I'm really not."

"Yeah, okay. That's what they all say, Stick."

The nurse returned then with a doctor in a white lab coat, and he stepped forward and offered me his hand.

"Miss Presa, it's a pleasure to meet you. I'm Doctor Golblum, one of the doctors here at Willow. If you'll follow me?"

We went down a short, immaculately clean hallway, and went into an office that looked just like any other doctor's office, except that it was securely padlocked on the outside. Once inside I was ordered to disrobe behind a screen and don a hospital gown. My blood pressure was taken, my heart beat registered, temperature taken, and lastly I was asked to step on a scale so that my height and weight could be measured.

"We will be checking your weight a few times a week," said the nurse to me, "but you are not allowed to know your weight, or ask about it at any time. Every time you step on the scale your back will be the numbers so you won't see a thing, and we'll let you know when you can step off."

"Is this so I don't obsess over how much weight I gain while I'm getting healthier?"

The nurse gave me a disapproving look. "Being obsessed with numbers is what got you here. This helps stop the cycle. Okay?"

I nodded slowly, and backed up onto the scale.

After we were finished I sat down on a small chair and watched Doctor Golblum as he looked through multiple charts which I could only assume were mine.

"Looks like you're on anti-depression medication and anti-seizure," he said. "How does that seem to be working for you?"

"I think it's working okay. I don't know. I'm tired all the time."

"Have you had any seizures? Shaking?"

I shook my head. "No seizures. I'm not shaking as much as I used to."

"Thoughts of harming yourself?"

"Not... for a long time. No."

"Thoughts of harming others?"

I smiled. "Well, there was this one time with my old boss..."

The doctor stared at me, his pen poised.

"I'm-I'm just joking. No, I've never wanted to hurt someone else."

The doctor nodded, not amused.

"Well, I think for the time being I'll keep you on your current medication until I see a need to change it. That sounds alright?"

I nodded.

He wrote something down on my chart and handed it to the nurse, and then stepped forward and said, "I'll do a quick examination just to check if everything is alright, and then we'll get one of the orderlies to get you settled into your room, alright?"

"Okay."

The examination was routine, and soon I was dressed again and the nurse led me back to the common area, where many girls were gathered; some were knitting on the couch where Erika and I had sat, while others colored with crayons in children's coloring books around a small table. Everyone was quiet and seemed to be waiting for something.

"Okay, Hon, Miss Trish, one of our BHS's, will take you from here," said the nurse, and a small blonde woman emerged from the office with a huge smile on her face.

"Hi Kimberly! Welcome to Willow! I'm Trish, one of the Behavioral Health Specialists here, or BHS's, for short. We have all your personal items in our office there, we're just going through it all to make sure theirs no contraband in there- like razors or any liquid containing alcohol. Once we're done, we'll give it back to you and you can put everything in your room, okay? Until then, I can show you where you'll be sleeping, if you'll follow me."

I followed her down another hallway, a longer one than the one I had followed the nurse down earlier. She stopped in front of a large, tan door, knocked twice and shouted, 'BHS!' and opened it without waiting for an answer. Inside there were four twin-sized beds, as well as two large dressers, two armoires, and one vanity. The only person present was Erika, who lay akimbo on the bed placed in front of the sole window. She sat up as we entered.

"Erika," said Trish, "This is Kim, you're new roommate. What... when did you switch beds?"

"As soon as Betty ran away. I didn't want to sleep right next to the door anymore. You hear *everything*."

Trish put her hands on her hips and looked angry. "You're not supposed to switch beds without our consent. We have all the residents mapped out so we know who's who."

"Well, can you 'map it out' so I'm at the window now?" Erika said, "I've been here longer and I think I deserve a good night's sleep for once."

Trish sighed. "Fine, but no more moving around. That is your new spot for better or for worse. Kim, this is your bed," she said, indicating a bed whose headboard was inches away from the door. "It's not the best spot, but we have earplugs if you need it."

"You'll need it," interjected Erika. "One of our other roommates snores real bad."

"Thanks, Erika," said Trish coldly, ushering me out and leading me back to the office.

"She seems, um, tough," I said, looking for something to say.

"She is, but she's alright," said Trish. "I bet after a day or two you guys will be good friends."

I grunted in assent, and watched through the glass of the office as two orderlies dug through my suitcase, reading the labels on my bottles of shampoo searching for that dangerous and forbidden ingredient, 'alcohol'.

"Well, since they might take a while in there, why don't I go ahead and give you your Willow binder, which you'll use for the entire time you are here, goodness knows how long that will be. It has a lot of good information in it; it tells you what your schedule will be like, what the rules are, and a lot of other good stuff. In the next day or so, you will be meeting with a dietician to figure out what your meal plan is, and also your psychiatrist. Until then, you'll pretty much just be settling in, learning how things work, and your meals will be eaten in the lodge with one of the orderlies- you won't be going to the dining facility yet, not until you talk to your dietician."

"Will I have to eat snacks?" I asked, trying to look like I didn't care.

"I don't know," said Trish, "All of that is up to your dietician. For now, why don't you sit on the couch and read through the handbook? I'm sure it will answer a lot of your questions. Now would be a good time to do it since your stuff is being looked through and most of the girls are in sessions."

I took the binder from her; it was just like any other binder, filled with about thirty pages or so. I sat down on the couch and opened it to the first page which read, 'Welcome to Willow Lodge, Timberline Knolls.' I turned to the next page, the table of contents. Rules and information, pages three-five. I found the page and began to read. The guidelines seemed very strict, but clear. Every minute of every day was mapped out- even free time. There were designated smoking breaks, but only four, and I wondered how the smokers in the lodge felt about that.

Mail was delivered daily to all residents, which made me glad that I had left word with Scott to send Prue my address so she could write to me, since I couldn't think of anyone else I wanted to hear from while I was in the recovery.

There were three phases of living at Timberline; Phase One, called 'Coming In,' was where I currently was, which meant I had very few privileges. I could not go outside except with the staff to walk from one location to another; I could not use a cell phone or a laptop, or receive visitors without explicit permission from my treatment team. If all went well, over time, and with the consent of my medical team, I could advance to phase two, called 'Looking In,' where I would be able to go out on 'passes' to areas such as Target, Barnes & Noble, and also use my I-Pod, if I had one. Phase three was called 'Looking Out', and was rewarded once a resident's treatment team felt someone was getting ready to be discharged. The individual was given a white hat and allowed to take walks unsupervised, and even given day-passes where they could leave the compound by themselves for a certain amount of hours.

Meals would be eaten with my lodge at the dining hall, and my menu would depend on whether I was on a meal plain to gain weight, lose weight, or maintain it. If I was on a meal plan to lose weight I would be expected to eat everything on my plate, or be forced to drink cans of Ensure to equal the amount of calories I had failed to consume.

Upon reading this, I gulped in fear. I didn't think I would be put on a meal plan to gain weight; the last time I had weighed myself I was one hundred and thirty-two pounds, and according the Air Force, on a five-foot-eight frame that was not underweight. But this place seemed strict, and I didn't know what the dietician would decide. Turning the page, I kept reading, skipping the parts I found to be irrelevant to myself.

Exercise was prohibited except as allowed by the medical team. There were groups that had elements of physical activity in them, such as yoga and dance movement- but a person had to be green-lighted before being able to attend. If found to be physically and mentally stable enough, one might be allowed to run on a treadmill twice a week for twenty minutes, and no faster than six miles per hour. I frowned at this. If that was all I exercised, how would I pass my PT test when I was discharged? I closed the binder, contemplating.

I had fought hard to enter Timberline Knolls. I had found the closest, highest rated facility I could find, brought it to the attention of Captain Yates, and pleaded my case to him; and he had, to my astonished delight, agreed, and persevered, and now here I was, sitting on the couch in the very facility I had dreamed of being admitted to, feeling terrified. I knew that if I went into my new psychologist's office, when they assigned me one, and told them I threw up nearly every day and felt completely out of control, that I would be put on a meal plan where I would be forced to eat everything on my plate. And worse, I would most likely not be able to take part in yoga classes, or use the treadmill, because of the bulimic's tendency to try to burn off excess calories through exercise. In my mind, I would become fatter, and when I got out of Timberline Knolls, I would hate myself even more, and I would relapse twice as bad as I was when I entered.

I knew I had a choice. I had been lying about the extent of my disorder my whole life. When I begged my Captain Yates to send me to Chicago, I had intended to open my heart, tell only the truth, and let all of my demons free in hopes of becoming free, myself. But face-to-face with the reality of how that could happen, I was backpedaling. So what, if I withheld some elements of the truth? How much did they really know, anyway, from Nebraska? Had he sent over good notes? What could I get away with, here?

I began to feel a little sad; I knew I could get away with lying, and that disturbed me. Why was I like that, always frantically trying to control everything? Could I let it go, even for just a few months? But the idea of being force-fed and being compelled to remain still like a veal calf-like state was too terrifying to me, and I knew I would lie. What remained was to decide how much I would lie, and find out how much I could get away with.

After a few minutes of sitting in silence, a group of girls came into the common area, as if a class had just been released, and they eyed me curiously. A few came up to speak to me a few questions about myself, and I was pleased to find they were less blunt than Erika had been. I learned the women there were admitted for many different reasons; some for eating disorders, some for trauma- others for alcoholism and drug use. Their ages varied widely, as well, from nineteen to fifty-five.

"I heard that one woman escaped recently," I commented to a portly, ginger haired woman about my age, "I thought being here was voluntary?"

The woman shrugged. "We are all here for different things and under different circumstances. Some are court ordered, like she was. But yeah, while you are here, what groups you attend are your decision. If you fail to go, it's on you."

"So, hypothetically, I can just lie in bed all day?" I asked, shocked.

She nodded. "Yes, but then you don't get to use the phone, or get any privileges, and you don't get better. It's a waste of money to whoever is paying for you. And if you're court ordered you don't get credit for being here."

"That's... amazing."

"I like it, because once and a while I get to sleep until noon. It's not a big deal if you do everything they say most of the time, and go to most of your groups. It can get boring sometimes. But other time, things get crazy!"

An emaciated brown haired girl next to her agreed. "*So* crazy! Like when Cayley smuggled in meth? That was nuts!"

My jaw dropped. "Meth?"

"Yeah! No one knew how she got a hold of it. It was awful because we were locked up in our rooms for hours while they were dealing with her. Apparently, it gave her super-tweaker strength, because she was going ape-shit, kicking and biting the BHS'. They couldn't hold her down. They ended up calling the cops."

"Holy crap."

The red haired girl giggled. "You'll see stuff like that here, sometimes. People will all of a sudden freak out. You'll be talking to a girl one minute who seems completely normal, and then the next she is trying to climb the wall, or cut open her veins with a broken spoon."

At that moment a BHS came out from the office and yelled, "Four-thirty group! Get to where you got to be, ladies."

The red haired girl turned to me. "What group are you in?"

"I'm not sure, they haven't told me. I'm still waiting for them to go through my stuff and I need to see the dietician."

"Oh. Well, why don't you come with me to Nutrition? Most people go there anyway, and you'll get to see the dietician."

"Shouldn't I wait here for the BHS…?"

"Naw, don't worry about it. There are only so many places you can go. She'll find you. It's not like you'll get in trouble or anything."

I grabbed my binder and followed her to a corner of the lodge which housed a large room behind glass windows. There weren't many chairs, but there were a ton of bean-bags, and every one of them was filled with girls. Some were lying on their stomachs on the floor filling out a grid-type sheet.

"What are they doing, uh… what's your name again?" I asked my new friend.

"Raina," she said, sitting on the ground, "They're filling out their weekly menus. You don't fill one out yet, just wait for the dietician. There she is."

A small, dark haired woman entered, and without glancing at or greeting anyone, she sat in a chair placed in the center of the room.

"Anyone have any menus for me?" she asked, opening her binder.

A few girls stood and handed their sheets of paper to her, and then sat back down, but most kept on writing.

"Anyone need any new sheets?" the dietician asked.

I raised my hand. "I'm new, we haven't met," I said.

She looked at me, expressionless. "Then you don't need a sheet yet. We're going to talk after we're done here."

I put my hand down. "Oh. Okay."

The dietician turned to the group. "Does anyone have any questions about the menu?"

A couple of girls raised their hands, and the woman asked, "Is this about if the lasagna for Thursday's dinner can be substituted for a Vegan option? Because the answer is yes, it can, they just didn't print it on the menu."

A couple of hands went down, but one girl asked, "What is the vegan option?"

The woman consulted her notes, and answered, "Eggplant lasagna."

The girl frowned. "I don't like eggplant."

"Are you vegan? I didn't know you were vegan"

"Today's my first day."

The dietician looked at her, and wrote something down in her binder. "We'll talk in a bit, Sherry, yeah? Keep Thursday dinner blank for now and we'll figure something out." She looked around for more hands, but there was only one. "Carrie, are you going to ask about Nutella?"

Carrie, a pretty brown-haired girl with freckles, put her hand down and answered in a serious tone, as if she were addressing Congress. "Yes. I have been asking for weeks and I feel like my voice has not been heard."

The dietician sighed deeply. "I have put in the request and that's all I can do, Carrie."

"Other girls have put in stranger requests and have gotten what they wanted."

"That's because their requests have had to do with dietary restrictions."

Carrie pouted. "I'm going to ask next week, you know, and the week after that. You can't keep me silent; I'm paying out the ass to be here; *I'm paying your salary*, and I want my freaking Nutella."

"Go ahead and keep asking and I will keep giving you the same answer: that I will put in a request, and that's all I can do."

I had watched the entire interchange with a blank face, but I was inwardly amused; here was society in microcosm. Women of all ages and from all ranks of life were forced to live together and function as one body. It reminded me a little of the Air Force, except everyone here was slightly crazier, and had vaginas. They woke up together, ate meals together, watched members of their group fall to pieces together- it was highly interesting, and I felt like I could sit there forever and just watch them interact. I knew at some point I would forced to become a part of that body, but in the meantime, I was content to sit on the sidelines and evaluate.

The group lasted about twenty minutes, and we were dismissed to free time until dinner at six o'clock. Many of the girls went to their rooms, while others went to the common area to recommence knitting or coloring.

"Do a lot of girls knit here? I didn't think knitting was such a big thing." I asked Raina, watching as one girl tore apart her work in frustration.

"Most of us knit!" she said energetically. "It's a great way to pass the time. A lot of us come in not knowing how, but by the time we leave we're able to make just about anything- sweaters, hats, little booties. Just wait. You'll be a knitter, too."

Inwardly, I vowed that I would not.

Trish, the BHS, came out of the office and called, "Kim, we have your luggage here. Let's bring it to your room so you can unpack."

She rolled my suitcase to my room, and once we were inside she heaved it onto my bed with a grunt, and unzipped the bag leaving it open wide. She glanced over at the bed near the window, where Erika was still laying, ignoring us.

"Your drawers are right there, the top two. Half the closet should be empty for you... yes, it is. Good. Go ahead and empty your luggage and let me know when you're done, and I'll take it away."

When she left, I turned to the bureau and opened the drawers, and started to refold my clothes and put them in. Suddenly I heard a voice behind me, saying,

"Yup- stick figure. I couldn't fit your pants over my darn ankle if I tried."

I jumped, turning quickly. Erika stood near my bed and was holding up a pair of my jeans in front of her face, scrutinizing the size. "Size twenty-seven? What the heck? I think I wore that in like, second grade."

I flushed crimson, and reached out for my pants. "They're not that small," I said, ripping them from her hands, and shoving them in the drawer, "And please don't touch my stuff. I don't know you."

Erika walked back to her bed and sat down, eyes on me, her head tilted to the side. "Okay, geez. I was just playing. Are you sensitive or something?"

"No, I'm not sensitive! It's just that we're all here for different stuff, and maybe you can keep your opinions to yourself? You don't know anything about me."

"You're right; all I know is that you're from Nebraska and that you're *really* sensitive."

I glared at her. "You're not very nice, are you?"

"I'm nice," she said, lying back on her bed. "You don't know me either."

I paused, a retort on the tip of my tongue, but instead of saying anything I'd regret I sat down on my bed and took a deep breath.

"Let's start over. We're room-mates, so let's not argue on the first day. I'm Kim, I'm in the Air Force. I'm a single mother and I have bulimia. I'm here to stop hating my body, and I would appreciate it if comments about my size were kept to a minimum. Better yet, don't make them. Please."

Erika's eyes softened a little, and she replied, "Okay, no problem."

"Thanks."

"Don't you want to know about me?" she asked suddenly.

"Sure," I said.

"I'm nineteen; I grew up on a farm in Maine. I'm here because my piece of shit cousin raped me."

"That's- that's the most horrible thing I have ever heard."

"Yeah, it's awful," she said, almost nonchalantly.

"What... I mean, can I ask how old you were when- when he-?"

She looked at me. "Twelve years old, up until last month."

I was shocked into silence. The horrors of what this girl must have gone through settled into my soul, and stayed there. Every bit of antagonism I felt towards her dissipated in an instant. I wanted to take her in my arms and hug her, and tell her it would get better- but as an outsider, a stranger, I didn't know if it ever would.

"I don't know what to say," I said quietly.

"There's nothing you *can* say, that's what sucks about rape. And there are girls here who have been through a lot worse, believe me. That's what being here has taught me so far."

"I'm sorry I was rude to you," I said.

She shrugged. "It's okay, I was probably rude too. I'm like that sometimes. I guess I'm more used to being around cows than people. Cows don't care if you're a little rough."

I smiled a little. "I went cow tipping once. It didn't work out how we wanted."

Erika looked at me as if I slapped her. "People that do that should be shot! Harassing poor animals. It's animal abuse, that's what it is."

"We didn't actually do it. The cows woke up."

"Good! You can kill a cow like that, you know, if you do somehow manage to knock him over. They weigh a ton."

"I didn't know that. Did your parents own a farm, or something?"

She nodded. "Yeah. I actually have an Associate's in Dairy Farming. I'm thinking about making it a career."

I smiled at the thought of this big, strong Amazon milking cows. "I didn't know there were degrees for farming. I thought it was a generational, pass-down-the knowledge type of thing."

She scoffed. "Yeah, right, as if that would be enough. Dairy farming is a highly technical business, especially nowadays." She reached under bed and started to put on her boots, which to my eyes looked to be about a size eleven. "What do you do in the Air Force?"

"I analyze aircraft. Numbers and charts. That's the easiest way to explain it."

"Sounds… not very interesting, sorry."

I laughed. "It's not really. But I'm good at it."

She stood up. "I'm going to go out to the milieu to wait until dinner, want to come with me? I'll introduce you to some of the other girls. We can bring your suitcase back to the office too."

"Sounds good; thanks."

As I walked next to her down the hallway, I became aware of two things: one, she was at least four inches taller than me. Two, I felt weirdly maternal towards her, and I was only twenty-five years old. We had barely spoken, but what we had said to each other carried more weight than the number of words implied.

We turned in my suitcase at the office and then Erika took me around, pointing out what she felt to be the key features of the lodge; the tiny room which contained the treadmill, the offices at the far end of the hall which was where individual therapy was held; the two large group rooms where, depending on the time of day, group sessions such as Sexuality, Body Image, Spirituality, and many others were held. Erika also took me boldly up to a few other women, and introduced me to them. Faces and names escape me now, but I recall that one and all were kind, and seemed pleased that I appeared to be a resident that would not cause much trouble.

"Most of us don't like drama," said Erika, "There's so much of it already."

"What kind of drama?" I asked.

"Well, girls telling on each other, saying they're doing things they shouldn't- Jumping jacks in the shower, barfing in the bedroom. Talking shit. Sneaking extra cigarettes. I don't know, the list goes on. A bunch of women together is never a good thing, in my opinion."

"I was with a bunch of women in basic training," I said, "It was hard, and we fought a lot about stupid crap, but after a while we seemed to get along alright."

"I'm pretty sure the girls in your basic training weren't going through severe withdrawal symptoms, or taking methadone."

I bit my lip. "No. They weren't."

She smiled an odd little smile. "And therein lies the difference!"

By the time the tour was over it was dinner time, and many girls had congregated by the front door, waiting to be escorted to the dining hall. A few girls in white baseball hats, gaudily decorated with glitter, had left a few minutes before to walk on their own to the dining facility, as was their right as Phase Threes. Erika introduced me to a few more residents, and then said, "See you after dinner. You have to eat on-lodge for three days just in case you try to run off, or drown yourself in the lake. After that you can sit with me in the dining hall. They have pretty good food there."

A BHS with red, cropped hair named Amelia came out of the office and called, "Let's go eat, ladies!" and, unlocking the front doors, led the group out.

Looking around, I saw that I was not alone, but three other girls were with me. One was sitting on the couch, and looked very angry. Another was sitting on a large chair in a corner of the room, knitting, and the last was leaning against the wall like me.

"This is bull-shit!" yelled the irate girl on the couch, slamming her hands down, "Just because I didn't finish that goddamn motherfucking sandwich I get in trouble. I hate this motherfucking, piece-of-shit place!"

The girl on the chair kept knitting placidly, but commented, "This isn't the first time you refused to eat something Amy. What was wrong with the sandwich?"

Amy glared at her. "It had mayonnaise on it. I don't EAT mayonnaise. I told them a thousand times, but they keep putting it on my goddamn sandwiches. If they want me to have a fat they need to give it to me some other way. But they don't LISTEN."

"Tell your psychologist."

Amy threw her hands up into the air, exasperated. "I did! And she said I had to trust my team! But I don't, I don't trust them! Because they don't even listen to me when I say I don't like mayonnaise!"

A male BHS came in the front door with a large white bag, and looked around. "Four of you?" he asked. "Amy, Whitney, Sara, and... one not on the menu?" he asked, looking at me. We all nodded. "Okay, let's go to the kitchen and eat; I'm hungry today."

We made our way to the kitchen which was located only few feet away from the office, and we sat down around a large wooden table.

"I'm Mike, your BHS for this meal," he said, introducing himself to me as he passed out everyone's dinner. "Since you're not on the menu yet, we give you the basic stuff. You can get a drink from the fridge in here, we have water and juice and all that."

"Do I have to eat it all?" I asked nervously.

"No, you don't- not until we hear from your dietician. But I suggest you eat until you're no longer hungry and feel comfortable."

"Mike!" yelled Amy from her side of the table, "What the fuck is this? Is this a joke?"

"What's a joke?"

"My goddamn chicken sandwich. It has mayonnaise on it," Amy breathed, positively livid. She held up the offending sandwich like it had caused her personal harm. "I don't eat mayonnaise!"

Mike sat down in front of his own meal and looked at a clipboard which had a list of everyone's menus on it. "This says specifically, 'Amy- chicken sandwich with lettuce, tomato, mayo.' Lisa, your dietician, penciled it in."

"What?!" Amy screamed, standing up.

Mike gazed at her calmly. "Sit down, Amy. If you want to go and talk about this we can, but you need to take a deep breath and think about how the way you're acting is affecting yourself and others."

Amy did not sit down- instead, she hefted the Styrofoam carton containing her dinner, and with a scream of rage, she hurled it across the kitchen where it exploded on the wall, and then proceeded to run out of the room, sobbing. No one at the table moved.

Mike sighed then, and stood up and walked over to the office. He talked briefly to one of the other BHS' inside, who nodded in response. Then Mike came back, sat down, and began eating.

"Sorry about that," he said.

Sara, the girl who had been knitting, said, "She's terrified of sauces. She keeps trying to lie and say she doesn't like how they taste, but everyone knows she just doesn't want to eat them."

Mike chewed his food thoughtfully. "Yeah, well, we'll deal with it. No more talk about food while we're eating, okay? Want to play a game?"

No one answered. "Okay," Mike said, "I guess not today."

After we were all done (I had eaten half of my chicken sandwich and all of my peas), Mike announced it was time for food and feelings, or 'FAF'.

"I'll go first," said Mike. "My food was tasty. I liked the chicken sandwich, except that I wish it was spicy because that's my favorite kind. I had a piece of apple pie which tasted like it was from McDonalds, which to me, that's actually a good thing. I feel satiated and content with what I ate." He then turned to Sara. "Sara?"

Sara seemed to think about it for a moment, and then replied, "I had the gumbo and it was kind of gross, because I'm used to my parents' gumbo and no one makes it better than them. I didn't have dessert today. I feel happy with what I ate."

It was Whitney's turn; she was a pale, fragile looking girl, and was looking down at her empty plate with sullen, tired eyes. "My sandwich was horrible," she whispered. "The peas were horrible, the fruit was horrible. I feel sick, fat, and over-full."

"I'm sorry you feel that way, Whitney," said Mike, writing down a few words on his clipboard. "How about you, Kim?"

I sat up a little straighter. "Um… my food was good, I haven't eaten a chicken sandwich for a really long time, so it was kind of nice. I feel… fine, I guess."

"Okay. Well, clean up and you guys are free to go until the rest of the girls get back. What do you guys have going on tonight?" He asked Sara.

"Kendall's going to tell her story," replied Sara, "So I'm going to go to that. I guess other people have AL-ANON, or something. I didn't really pay attention to the schedule today."

"Yeah, that's why you keep having to eat down here with me," said Mike, "You should go to all of your groups so that you don't get in trouble."

Sara shrugged. "I get sleepy."

"We all get sleepy, but that doesn't mean sleeping is the best thing for you."

She stretched, smiling lazily. "It sure *feels* like it's good for me."

Mike chuckled, and said, "Alright, get out of here, guys."

"My knitting is calling to me!" Sara said, prancing out the door. Whitney and I tossed our containers in the trash and followed her.

The rest of the lodge didn't return for another half an hour, and I learned that most of the girls were going to their twelve-step meetings, and those that remained were staying to listen to a fellow lodger tell her personal story of how she ended up in treatment. Many were already congregated in the big group room where we had been earlier with the dietician, so I followed suit and settled onto the ground with my legs crossed, and waited.

After a few minutes, a small, slender girl with dramatic eye makeup and cropped hair entered and drew a seat to the center the room. She held in her hands a few sheets of paper, and she shuffled them with quivering fingers. The room quieted respectfully.

"For those of you who don't know me, I'm Kendall," said the girl in a soft, piping voice, "And it's my turn to tell you my story. I had to write it all down, because... well, I'm not good at public speaking or anything, and I didn't want to forget anything. But I'm just going to go ahead and start now, so..."

Kendall cleared her throat, and began to read, "I'm from Idaho, and I grew up with my mom and dad in a normal house, I suppose, with my little brother, Rob. We had a small organic farm that we all worked on. I don't remember a whole lot before I was eight years old, but I remember Rob. He was three when I was eight, and I was always babysitting him; he was my little buddy. My mom and dad loved him very much, but I never got jealous of him because he was the youngest, or anything, like some older kids do, you know?

When Rob was almost four, my dad took us up on one of our tractors. I was supposed to watch him, you know, but I wasn't- I was looking out at the field. I heard him scream, all of a sudden, this really loud, scared scream- and when I looked, I saw that he'd fallen off the side of the tractor... and I saw his head get crushed by the wheel. It looked like- like a watermelon. I don't know how else to say it."

I stared at Kendall in shock. One would have never guessed that such a small, lovely girl harbored such a tragedy in her soul.

"My parents never got over it," she continued, reading, "They got a divorce, and after a while my mother remarried and had another baby, my brother Edward, who I love very much. My mom and dad still don't talk to each other, and I've been in therapy since I was eight. When I got older I started to act out and skip my sessions, and began using meth. I started to have sex in order to support it- it didn't matter who the people were as long as they paid. When I didn't make enough money doing that, I did live sex shows..."

She looked up at us, placing her papers in her lap. Her eyes were misty. "I really don't know what else to say," she said. "I've been using for five years now, and my mom sent me here last month to get clean. I hate it here. I miss my boyfriend back home but I know when I see him again I'll just go back to the drugs, since he's my dealer. But I miss him so much it hurts," she put a hand to her heart, and a tear fell from her eye, "I'm just so conflicted, I guess. I want to be clean but I don't want to be alone. And I don't want to do the shows anymore."

My own eyes began to water as I listened to this wonderful, beautiful girl; I felt that I understood her. Though our stories were very different, I felt as if we were the same in many ways. Addiction was like that; it made you desire what drove you away from what you needed the most; it made you fear the unknown, and forsake everything that could possibly bring you back to reason.

"But that's all I wanted to say," she said, standing up, "I just felt that it would be good for me to share my story. Sorry it was so short. I'd like to go now."

After a short pause, we all applauded weakly, and began to disburse. I watched as Kendall left the room, and as she did so, she crumbled up the papers she had read from and tossed them into the trash.

*

I entered the small office, and a small blonde woman with dimples rose to greet me, her hand extended.

"Kimberly? Hi, I'm Karen Edwards, nice to meet you. I'll be your primary mental health counselor here at Willow."

"Nice to meet you," I replied, sitting.

She held a manila folder up to her face, and slipped a pair of small silver glasses down the bridge of her nose.

"I looked over your notes from your last therapist, so I know a little bit about why you're here. Would you like to talk about it with me?"

"Sure."

"You're currently diagnosed with bulimia nervosa, and general anxiety disorder. Does that sound correct to you?"

I nodded, starting to feel a little uneasy.

"Since this is our first time meeting, I would like to hear from you about what you think is going on. I know what your doctor said- I have that right here. But I want to know what *you* think. That's what I'm interested in right now. And it will help me get to know you, and you to get to know me."

I took a deep breath. "I'm not a fan of re-telling everything."

She tilted her head a little, and smiled gently. "You can just lay back and close your eyes, if you want. You can pretend I'm not here. Or you can start telling me anything you want to tell me. I'll just listen, and we can see what happens."

I started to pick at my fingernails, nervous. What was she up to? What did she expect me to talk about?

"I throw up sometimes," I said slowly, thinking I should start with the obvious. But even that didn't feel right. "I throw up a lot. All the time."

Karen nodded, an interested look on her face, but said nothing.

"I think I've been doing it for… ten years now. I don't know, exactly."

"Mm, so you started in your teens, then."

"Mm-hm. Around the time my mom moved out, when she and my dad divorced."

She sat there, looking at me. Waiting.

"I don't know how to explain anything, I'm sorry," I said suddenly.

"You're doing great, Kimberly," Karen said. "Say what you want to, or even just sit there and think for a bit. We have a whole hour for just you and me."

I sat back against the couch, thinking. After a minute, I began to talk, refusing to rationalize why I chose to say what I did.

"My sister had something wrong with her when we were little. Her hearing- she couldn't stand the sound of chewing, or breathing, or clicking, or walking, or- anything. She told me recently that it's called Misophonia, and it's a real disorder- but growing up we never knew. My house was always quiet, except when the TV was on. I hated it. I walked around the house like a geisha because I was afraid she would hear me and get mad. Now, I could probably walk through a bunch of dried of leaves and no one would know I was there, I can walk so quietly. My mom never really stood up for me about it- I guess she felt bad for Rachel- that's my sister- because she really seemed to be suffering."

I looked down at my hands, and continued to pick at my nails.

"I really loved Rachel, but she was crazy emotional. She hated me ninety-five percent of the time, but then the other five percent she would sit and draw with me at the table, because she's a really good artist, or we'd play a video game, because we're nerds. But we were never really close, because I made sounds, and my feet wiggled, and it made her angry to look at them."

"It seems to me that your sister had some problems of her own, growing up," commented Karen softly.

"I guess she did. Yeah," I said. "We were both overweight, too, and she was always a bit bigger than I was. My mom used to say she was jealous of me, but I never believed her, because I was jealous of *her*." *I was?*

"Why were you jealous of her?"

"I don't know. Maybe... well, she was stronger than I was, I guess. She had her opinions about stuff, and had likes and dislikes. I just tagged along with whatever she liked or did, and told myself I liked it, too. Not that I didn't like them, exactly... but... I don't know how to explain it."

"Try."

"Well, for example, we used to watch Japanese Anime together, and I liked it, I did. But I watched it because *she* liked it, and I wanted to be close to her. I read comics because she liked them. I drew because she liked to draw. I read books that she had read because I wanted to know what kind of stories she enjoyed. I played video games even though they scared me sometimes because she wanted me to play them. But when- when she left, when she moved out, after my mom died- I realized..." My eyes began to water.

"What did you realize?"

"That- I didn't have a favorite color. I didn't have a favorite song, or movie, or television show. I only had the things that my sister had left me, but because she was gone they didn't interest me anymore. I didn't know who I was. I had nothing but- my bulimia."

Karen continued to watch me with soulful eyes, and after a moment, she said, "That sounds like a very lonely place to find yourself."

I bit my lip. "I guess it was. My dad was gone all the time, working, or out at bars, drinking and partying. Sometimes he brought the bar home with him. I was fifteen, and I'd be like, 'Dad, who are these people?' and he'd say, 'I have no idea!' It scared me. The men there scared me. I asked my dad, one time, why the old men looked at me even though I was a kid, and he said that the first thing all guys do is see 'sexy', and only after they check out the ass and tits on a woman do they consider if she's age appropriate or not." *I'd almost forgotten that conversation*, I thought. *I'd like to forget it, now*

"I feel like I'm rambling," I said to Karen, "I just don't know where to start, I guess."

"Rambling is good for you," she replied, "It shakes loose a lot of stuff you didn't know was inside of you, and needs to get out. Ramble all you you'd like."

"But I don't want it to get out!" I cried, shocked at my own fierceness, "I can't stand to hear myself talk about it. I can't stand to even think about it. It sucks. It all sucks."

"I'm sure it does suck. And that's why it needs to come out," she said softly.

I turned my head, tears streaming down my cheeks. I felt like I was butterfly being held down by pins, fluttering desperately, trying to escape. I only had to push a little bit harder, and then I could be free-

"I hate myself," I said then, sobbing. "I'm annoying. I even think it's annoying that I hate myself. And I'm hideous. It's fucking hopeless."

"Nothing is hopeless, Kimberly."

My lips quivered, and I sniffled. Karen handed me a box of tissues, and I blew my nose. I took a couple of breaths, and then said in a small, child-like voice, "Can I stop... after doing it for so long?"

Karen leaned forward. "Look at me."

I looked.

"*Yes.*"

And I believed her.

*

"Your session is cancelled today," said Tish, walking up to my briskly. I put down the Agatha Christie novel I had been reading, and frowned. "Karen is being held up, but she'll reschedule with you as soon as she can, okay?"

"So, do I just get free time?" I asked.

"You could, or you could go to one of the electives going on right now... let me see what they are." Tish hefted a binder up to her face and read for a moment. "It looks like there's Body Image or Relationship Addiction," she said. "I can get someone to take you to either one. What do you think?"

I hesitated. I had been to the body image elective that week, and I hated it with a passion. Not that it wasn't helpful- it was- but I felt I could only deal with so much of it in such a short time. As far as relationship addiction, I knew nothing about it, and though I felt it didn't apply to me or my life, I thought perhaps I could still learn something from it.

"I'll go to Relationship Addiction," I said, standing.

"Alright." Tish looked at her wristwatch. "They should just be getting started, so I'll go ahead and walk you over there really quick. Come on."

In a few moments, I found myself in a small room that I had never been in before with eight women I had never seen, all of whom were seated in a small circle. They looked up as I entered the room, and one of them waved me in. I assumed it was the counselor.

"Come on in, grab a seat," she said, indicating a spot next to her. I sat.

The woman turned back to the circle. "Alright. Where were we? Right; Crystal- you were talking about how you knew early on that your husband was bad for you, but for some reason you found yourself going back to him. That's really common for women who are addicted to being in relationships- though every individual has a different experience, there are similarities. The majority of us are filled with insecurity, and use our significant others as proofs that we are worthy of living. We are often perfectionists, and feel that we have to be at a certain standard before we can ever truly deserve to be loved. We quickly become attached to a lover, instead of being attracted, because we become afraid of losing them more than we are happy to be with them.

"Crystal, as far as you knowing your husband was bad for you- him being an alcoholic, an issue you said your mother had struggled with- that is another commonality found is women like us. We tend to latch on to those that symbolically represent our parents. We also are magnetically attracted to needy people, as they are less likely to leave us."

Crystal, a thin blonde woman in her fifties, nodded from her position on the ground, and sniffled. "It's so sad, to have it all laid out like that," she said. "You think you're the only one, you know- but you're not. It's just- it's hard to hear it when you're climbing towards sixty. I wish I had come here a lot sooner." She wiped at her eyes. "I knew he was all wrong, ever since we got married at eighteen. He'd go to the bar every night and spend all our money, and then come home pissed and hitting me for no reason. But I kept thinking he'd get better; he would be so apologetic afterwards, you know. I thought he needed me. He even told me once he would kill himself if I left him." Tears flowed down her wrinkled cheeks, and one of the other women handed her a box of tissues.

The group therapist cleared her throat.

"You- and everyone here- are not meant to be the punching bags and caregivers to our lovers," she said. "That is not how a healthy relationship is built. Crystal, I am glad you found the strength to be here, right now, at *this* moment. I think it's an amazing step forward to your growth, and to living a full, happy life."

The circle nodded, and I did as well. I was by that time very affected with what was going on around me.

"What are some reasons, do you think, that women sometimes stay in relationships that they know are not healthy for them?" inquired the therapist.

"Financials," answered one woman. "I raised our kids for twenty years, and when I finally got the balls to leave him, I didn't have any skills to make it on my own."

"Insecurity," said another, "If you leave him, what if you can't find someone else?"

"Some you're are afraid of change, maybe?" suggested a tall woman with red hair.

"Because you think you owe them for something," I said, surprising myself.

"All of those are absolutely true. The financial element is a definite factor with many women staying in relationships long past the time they become aware that they are, in fact, unhealthy. Even in this day and age, thirteen percent of married couples live in a husband-as-breadwinner environment, and that's not including those who are living together unmarried. Though it is a personal choice how one chooses to live, such a situation can exacerbate the difficulty if the relationship becomes harmful, or even abusive."

"My husband wouldn't let me get a job," said Crystal tearfully, "He said it would make him like feel less of a man if he couldn't take care of me."

"Tell me this, since we're talking about abusive relationships. Why don't more women go and get help?"

We were silent for a moment, thinking.

"I wanted to leave my boyfriend, because he used me for money all the time, yelled at me, cheated on me. But I didn't leave, or tell anybody, because I was really embarrassed about it. I'd moved out from my sister's house and told her I didn't need her help, and then I met Paul, and I didn't want anyone to know it wasn't working out. That I had messed up again."

"If he was cheating on you and treating you like shit, it doesn't sound like you were the one messing anything up," said one of the women in the circle.

"Yeah… but I never was a good listener. He had problems and I never listened like I should have."

"It still doesn't give him the right to treat you like that," insisted the other woman.

"No one has the right to rule over another person's body or emotions," intervened the therapist, "Though, being human, we are constantly entangled with one another, and it can get confusing when you are separated from the rest of the world, and depressed, and you are in a position where the only person you have to turn to is him. I think a lot of times, women don't even know they're in a harmful relationship; they delude themselves into believing that what they have is normal. One of the common traits in women with addictive behaviors in relationships is that they never ask for their needs to be met- if they are even aware of them to begin with. That is not to say they don't feel angry or upset- but they are so patient in their relationships that anger takes a long time to show its face. And when it does, it can be explosive, or implosive, releasing itself as physical violence, or addictive behaviors such as gambling, alcoholism- the list goes on."

As the counselor continued to talk, my mind began to bend inward. Was I addicted to relationships? It wasn't that I believed I had ever been in an abusive one- but I had certainly clung to affairs that I knew didn't make me happy- men that were needy, and needed to 'fixed' somehow. I had even dated people simply because I didn't wanted to be alone, and had sex with them not because of any pleasure I would receive, but because it was the price of being in an adult relationship. Sex was just a thing to be endured.

I leaned forward and put my head in my hands, the voice of the therapist droning on in the background. I felt as if a light had been switched on in my skull. I had stayed with Sam for so many years because I felt that I owed him for taking me in, and had performed sexual acts I was not ready for because it had been expected of me. While I was with him, I had not experienced a single orgasm- in fact, I had been so obsessed about being compared to the women in his porn films that I had done everything in my power to make our sex life all about him, instead of about *us*. And of course, I had given him money- thousands and thousand of dollars over the years from my own earnings as well as my father's. I had done all of that, despite the fact that after a few months of knowing him, I could barely stand the sight of him.

I sat up straight again, and sighed. Well, it was good I was aware of it, now. I thought of Scott, and I wondered with a quiver of fear if I was stepping into the same pattern again, only with a different man… but then I shook my head- no. Scott was different. He was someone I had chosen for myself, not someone who had fallen across my lap. He was compassionate, and caring, and I was attracted to who he was now, instead of who he could be after he was 'fixed'. Thinking of him made me miss him so much that tears almost came to my eyes, but I was determined to hold them back. I wanted to learn all I could about relationship addiction, so that I would not bring any doubt or bitterness into our love life.

"How does someone overcome relationship addiction?" I asked the therapist during a small lull in conversation. I was aware that it was slightly off-topic from what they had been discussing, and a few of the women looked at me curiously. But I was never very good in group therapy sessions. I ignored them.

"Well, the biggest step you can take is to become aware of the roles you've played in the romantic relationships you've had throughout your life. Have you found yourself consistently playing the role of a parent instead of a lover? Do you tend to attach yourself to one type of person? Have your needs been met, or unmet? Is there a pattern there? As you learn who you have been in past relationships, you can begin to see more clearly when choosing new relationships- even friendships- and decide if they remind you of dysfunctional ones from the past. Awareness is key- and so is learning to *take time*. Get to know people before giving them your confidence or your heart. Surround yourself with individuals that make you feel good about yourself."

I settled back into my chair, thinking of Scott, and Norah- and I smiled. Nothing in the entire world made me feel better than they did.

*

I turned abruptly, and used my elbow to punch the foam cylinder, smashing it backwards towards the ground. With another quick movement, I rotated my torso, and with my gloved hand reached out and punched with all of my strength. Though it made less of an impact, I still felt satisfied. I continued to advance with a series of small jabs and hooks, beads of my sweat flying through the air and streaming down my arms and legs.

I was in a battle. Onlookers might see a woman attacking a free-standing punching bag, but that wasn't who I was fighting. In my mind was a kaleidoscopic vision of everyone and everything that had frustrated me and hurt me in my life- the disappointment, the grief, the broken hearts- it was all there. One moment I would see before me the face of one of the Afghan men that had so frightened me on deployment, and the next I would see my sister, telling me she to be quiet, or to cover my bare feet. Sometimes I saw an image of myself, weak and pathetic, and I attacked then, too.

I was in the tiny, one-treadmill gym at Timberline Knolls. I was one of the few girls allowed to attend twice a week, due to my not being an over-exerciser or underweight, and when I had seen the punching bag in the corner I determined that I would try something new. And after picking up the gloves, I had never put them down.

The BHS's who always babysat us sat nearby, coffee in their hands, and they'd watched me and make comments when I made especially big hits that sent the sand-weighted bag horizontal to the floor.

"It's like watching 'Enough'" said one of them once, staring at me with a little awe.

Whenever I came back from those gym sessions, I wanted to do nothing but sleep. I felt more emotionally spent than I had ever felt before in my life. But when you're in residential, your day is full- and after a shower, it was time for the next session.

The brute physicality of the gym contrasted greatly with the deep soul searching of the other sessions. I was able to choose what weekly schedule, to a point- I attended sessions such as body image, art therapy, nutrition, yoga, self defense, grief and loss- and I learned something valuable from each and every one of them. I attended multiple NRA, AA, and AL-ANON meetings as well, to learn everything I could from them, as well. I also continued to have my individual therapy sessions, and also group therapy sessions, which I began to treasure, since that's when I felt the least alone. I had not, after all, been put 'on the menu', so to speak, which meant that I did not have to eat everything on my plate when I sat down to meals. This took some of the stress off of me, since I didn't feel any pressure to eat a certain amount of food- though I found myself not worrying about what I ate at all, and usually ate until I felt satiated without any feelings of guilt.

I sat down to every meal with Erika. After our initial misunderstanding, we had become good friends, and were often together. At night, I braided her hair- she had taught me how- and she braided mine, and I let her borrow my headbands and larger T-shirts anytime she wanted. I liked her free, bluff manner, and I think in return she liked to shock me. She made me laugh very often- in some ways she reminded me of Prue, but it was undeniable that Erika was her own person, through and through.

Sometimes we would have no much fun talking and laughing that I would forget why we were there, and then something would happen to remind me that my friend had lived through a nightmare. Though she remained upbeat most of the time, and mostly kept her feelings secreted in her diary, a couple of times she couldn't help it- her trauma came back to claim her.

It was a part of the rule of Timberline that you were there to focus on your own recovery, period. It could interrupt your own progress if you delved too deeply into someone else's issues, and overall, I agreed. I didn't think much of it until Erika ran into our room one day, sweating, and sat down roughly on her bed. Her eyes were focused to pin-points, and she was trembling all over. Without saying a word, she lifted her knees to her chest, put her hands on her head and began to whimper, and began to rock herself, trying to self-sooth. I had seen it before; she was having a flashback.

I ran out of the room quickly to the BHS station to ask for a nurse, but they were all occupied.

"But Erika needs one of those shots they give her to make her rest!" I said, angry.

"She will be okay until a nurse is free; it won't be that long. You should get to your next session, Kimberly."

I shook my head. "I'm not leaving Erika alone when she's like that."

The BHS frowned at me. "You need to focus on your own recovery."

"I'm not leaving her."

"You will get a mark-down if don't follow the rules," she threatened.

"I don't care," I said, and I ran to the kitchen, opened the freezer, and grabbed a frozen orange and brought it back to Erika. Sitting quietly near her, I touched the top of her hand gently with the orange.

"Here's an orange," I whispered. "I'll stay with you until a nurse comes if that's okay."

Tears soaked Erika's eyes as she grabbed the orange, and began to roll it up and down her arm erratically. But she didn't answer; she couldn't. I just stayed near her, at the edge of her vision, so that she knew she wasn't alone.

After about five minutes, the BHS and a flustered looking nurse came in, shot in hand. The BHS walked directly up to me, and with an angry face ordered me to leave the room.

I stood up leisurely, turned to the suffering Erika, and said, "The nurse is here, Erika. I'm going to session now. I'll see you when you wake up." And with that, I marched out of the room, not feeling an ounce of regret.

Twenty-One Guns
(33)

Two months later, midnight, I was released from treatment. I couldn't wait to see my daughter and my boyfriend again, and to tell Prue about my experiences and thank her for always being there for me. I had learned in Timberline Knolls to always let people know you love them, and how much they mean to you, and to not take friendship for granted; I was determined never to take Prue for granted ever again.

Though leaving the security of Timberline was frightening, I felt like I had the strength to step up and become a whole person. I had a plan of attack- continue to eat well, exercise moderately, and see my therapist and dietician. I had my support, Scott, to turn to when times got tough. While still in treatment, as the intensity of my addiction faded, I began to realize that I still sincerely enjoyed drawing- I had forgotten that while lost in the all-consuming cycle of binging and purging. Though I had no wish to become a comic artist like Rachel, I bought new pencils and Bristol paper and spent many joyful hours sketching, using my hobby as a weapon to keep my demons at bay. Despite my looming past and tentative future, I felt positive and healthy- prepared for anything.

The morning after I was released, the cell phone which I had left behind began to chime repeatedly. When I checked it, there were multiple messages from acquaintances asking me 'What happened? Did you need anything? Where are you now?' No one had known I was at the clinic but Scott, Prue and my work; my instincts began to warn me that something awful had happened. With panic rising in my chest, I called one of my former co-workers and asked her what was going on... and with a breaking voice, she told me.

The night before, at midnight- the *hour* I was released from treatment- Prue had been sorting clothes in her bedroom. She had recently been awarded the house in the divorce, and had been busy making it her own and packing away Owen's remaining items. Unbeknownst to her, Owen had crept into the home, made his way down the hallway and to the bedroom- and while her back was turned, he shot his ex-wife through her heart... and then proceeded to turn the weapon on himself.

When I heard those damning words, the phone fell from my hands. *It can't be true!* I quickly went to Prue's Facebook page, which she was on everyday almost religiously. No recent posts. I went to Google. If there had been a crime like that, it would be all over the news...! My heart stopped. There, at the beginning of the search results, was a photo of Prue and Owen at their wedding, blissful and smiling, and above it, the hateful title "Airman Murdered in Home by Husband."

"NO!" I screamed, slamming my hands down on the computer desk multiple times; the air reverberated with the aftershocks. "NO NO NO NO NO! YOU BASTARD!" I crumpled to the ground, shaking uncontrollably, my body unable to process what had happened. The girl who had stormed her way into my heart seven years ago, not even bothering to remove her shoes, was dead. *Everything is vile, everything*! I raged inwardly. *What's the point of it all?* I found myself hyperventilating: I couldn't breathe. I wiped my tears and snot on the carpet to clear my airways but they kept replenishing themselves. Taking gasping breaths, I crawled to where I couldn't see the computer screen anymore, and called Scott's message service, where I could only repeat over and over again that Prue was dead, that she had been killed. After I hung up, I lay there on my back, trying to breathe, trying to process what had happened, but couldn't. My best friend was dead. An amazing, bright and glorious light had gone out in the world, and I didn't want to be there anymore.

"Prue," I sobbed, covering my face with my arms as hot tears ran down my cheeks, "I'm so sorry I wasn't there. I'm so sorry. I love you, I love you."

By the time Scott got home and found me on the floor of my bedroom, the sobbing had stopped, and he found me staring blankly at the ceiling, barely aware of passing time.

"Honey, what happened?" he asked, coming immediately to my side and taking my hand.

I blinked, and new tears melted down the side of my face. "Prue was shot by her ex-husband, and then he killed himself. It happened last night."

He squeezed my hand. "Oh, my God. I'm so sorry, honey," he said. "That's…"

Unable to discourse any further, I rolled to my side, cradling myself, and cried as if my heart would break.

It's funny how time passes either quickly or extremely slowly when one is in the thralls of grief. For me, the two days after Prue' death sped by; the details of those days escape me to this day. I recall nothing; the next thing I remember, Scott and I were in driving to Oklahoma for her funeral. I did a lot of staring at nothing during the drive, and Scott did a lot of hand holding. My mind was still reeling from the intense sorrow I felt; I was constantly exhausted, and couldn't force myself to eat. I tried to keep my mind blank, but it was difficult. Whenever I thought of Prue' and my last visit together, tears burst unchecked from my eyes, and Scott had to pass me a tissue in order for me to realize I was crying again.

"You know," I said, interrupting one long silence, "She was always looking out for me and my relationships. But here she has one big one, and the bastard ends up killing her. There's something terribly sad about that, you know?"

"Yes," said Scott, "It's very sad." He gave my hand a squeeze. "I wish I could have met her. She and I talked a little on Facebook. The last words she wrote to me are, 'tell Kim I love and miss her sweet face.' And she thanked me for keeping her updated while you were in the hospital."

"She was such a good person," I said, rubbing my eyes, "I don't understand how this could have been allowed to happen. Who gave that asshole a gun? He was on suicide watch and had a restraining order, for God's sake. He was in therapy for depression and who knows what else, but what do they do? 'Oh, hello, Sir, I see you have homicidal and suicidal ideations but lack a suitable weapon, how may we provide you with one?' *Fuck* gun laws in this country."

Scott could only nod soberly.

As we drove into Oklahoma City, I was assaulted by memories of our last visit together, and I eagerly pointed out a few locations as we passed them.

"That's where we ate lunch before we went rock climbing." "That's where we sat and Prue ate a giant chili dog in three bites. *Three* bites, can you believe it?" "There's where she bought me a 'peartini' which she meant to share with me, but I ended up drinking all by myself, because I'm such a pig."

Soon, however, we entered the base, and made our way to church where her funeral was being held. I could see by the rows of cars in the parking lot that it was crowded, and I became nervous. This was the first funeral I had ever been to, and it was my best friend's. Scott kissed the side of my face, put his arm around me, and led me inside.

The rooms and pews were full everywhere we went, and I started to tremble. Somewhere, in here, lie Prue's body, and I would get to see her one more time. I didn't know how I would react. As we entered the main part of the chapel, I saw members of her family standing around, and dozens of Airmen conversing in subdued tones. I turned, searching, and there, at the back of the room was a small enclave where Prue' body lay. I couldn't see her from where I stood, but I could see the casket, and her childhood best friend crying quietly beside it.

"There she is," I whispered, taking deep breaths to calm myself. I started to move forward, and each step felt as if I were walking in a dream.

And there she was, looking impossibly tiny, and all decked out in her Air Force blues. Her face didn't look like her face- ever inch of it was covered with makeup. In life, Prue never wore makeup like that; maybe a little mascara and lip gloss, but that was it. Someone had made a caricature of my girl. But those were all details that I absorbed in a moment. It was still my Prue.

"I'm here," I told her, my voice cracking, "They've put a lot of make up on you, haven't they? I bet you would have smacked someone for that. But it's okay. You're still beautiful." I gently took her hand- it was so small, cold and frail. I stroked the top of her fingers, remembering all the times she had punched me playfully in the shoulder, or tried to tickle me to force to smile. Next to her casket, her childhood friend gazed at me through her tears, and smiled sadly, as if to say, *Isn't this a farce? The most alive person in every room has become the first of us to die.* I smiled back as much as I could muster, and then leaned forward to give Prue a kiss on the cheek.

"I love you," I whispered. "I will always love you. Thank you for being my only friend."

I stepped back, and Scott began to lead me away, but I couldn't take my eyes off of her. I couldn't believe this would be the last time I would ever see her again. Even if we had gone months without hearing from one another, I had never doubted for an instant that Prue was out there, caring about me, and that we inevitably would see each other again. But now that was lost. She wouldn't be seeing anyone again.

"Good-bye," I breathed lovingly, longingly, as I was led out of sight.

Upon returning to the main room, I was invited to sit with her family for the duration of the funeral, and was given a long-stemmed red rose to hold, bereft of thorns. The service itself was very emotional as the speakers included all of her brothers and sisters, and her father, whom I had never met. Everyone told stories about Prue; about her strong nature, about her humor, and even her cantankerousness. It was all a part of the girl we loved, so every word made us smile and remember.

Eventually, words gave out, and a prayer was given. The majority of the mourners were dismissed, and as they filed out the casket was sealed and pall-bearers began readying themselves to carry it to the hearse which would drive Prue to her final resting place. As I was being treated as a member of the family, I was led with the rest of her loved ones outside so we could witness the final trip that Prue would ever take.

It was cold outside, and I clung to Scott's arm and my red rose like they were all I had left in the world. I must have caused him pain, holding him like that, but he never uttered a word of complaint. I started to feel a little sick as the pall-bearers came out of the chapel carrying Prue's casket, and as the bagpipes started playing I grew positively nauseas. *This is unreal*, I thought, watching the casket make its slow way towards the hearse. *Prue is in there*. I had seen many flag-draped caskets in my career, but I had never thought I'd see one containing the body of some one I loved.

And suddenly, gunshots. I jumped and buried my face deeply into Scott's shoulder, terrified. I had forgotten the military tradition of the twenty-one gun salute. I knew that military funerals honor their fallen comrades by shooting rifles into the air, but I had been unprepared for it. *She was killed by a gun three day ago!* I thought brokenly. *And they're shooting rifles into the air! I would be happy if I never heard a gunshot again!* I twitched after each volley, unable to control the reflex, and new tears emerged after each report. By the time it was over, I was freezing, shivering, and exhausted. I felt like every muscle in my body was tense, and I couldn't stop eyeing the Honor Guard and their rifles. Suddenly, a man I hadn't seen before was playing Taps on his bugle, and the hearse which contained my best friend began to pull away. I took a few staggering steps forward, not quite yet able to let her go…but it was too late. She was gone, but the bugle kept playing, solemn and heartrending. How many times, at the end of long school days, had we heard that song? It had meant absolutely nothing to me then. But, standing there and clutching my thornless rose to my chest- I still have that rose, to this day- I understood it. It meant The End.

**

A post on Kimberly's Facebook wall from Prue, February 2011.

Dearest Kimberly,

Oh how I miss your sweet gorgeous face, white girl 80's dance moves (to include the sprinkler, lawn mower and your variation of Cameron Diaz' dance moves from Charlie's Angels) and of course those "mental photograph" trips to Starbucks. I will never forget the way you held my rope at Rock town or handled that pool stick at club rodeo. What two friends can every say that they had to spit up dirt together at a rodeo?? Mmmm that's right... these ones. *wink* Lego store and mani-pedi trips will never be the same without you. I also love how you held that Glock 38, you meant business, Ma'am! You know you are my favorite tech-school friend/sister, especially after you picked the lock in a billeting bathroom so I wouldn't have to pee in the sink.
Miss you already, Kimmy!

-Prue

***

I knew when Captain Yates called me in on a day that was outside of our scheduled appointment that he had bad news for me. It was only a week after Prue's funeral, and I wasn't doing very well. I had eaten hardly anything, and everything I had managed to consume had been purged- I felt completely unable to keep anything in my stomach. After three months free from bulimia, I had let it back into my life in order to help me cope. I had no notion of how to get rid of it again. I felt defeated.

It was with hollow eyes and dry, cracked lips than I entered the captain's office. I greeted him perfunctorily and sat down on his couch, waiting.

"I know things are hard, from the loss of your friend," he began softly, "and with leaving treatment so recently… I can't imagine how you must be feeling, even with my training. But I have called you in to talk to you about your career in the Air Force. Do you feel able to talk about it, right now?"

I gazed at him blankly, and nodded.

He took a breath. "You are being taken before the medical board," he said, "for bulimia and anxiety. We both knew it was a possibility, remember, but it seems they want to go ahead and see if… well, if you are to be discharged."

I only stared out the window as if I wasn't listening. He continued:

"I don't want you to panic. It takes months; sometimes over a year for these things to go through. There are examinations that must occur, and paperwork that a lot of different people at different people levels have to sign- bureaucracy, you know- so that holds things up quite a bit. But- and I need you to know this- I have researched the retention rate of airmen with eating disorders after they have been medical boarded, and I'm sorry to say it is very close to zero percent."

"So," I said slowly, my mouth feeling as if it was full of sand, "My eating disorder takes another thing away from me. It's my fault, though. That's what I get for asking for help."

I stood as if I wanted to go, but Yates stopped me. "I don't want you to think that asking for help was a bad thing," he pressed, and I could see in his eyes that he felt dreadful. "You were trying to get better. That's never, ever a bad thing. And you learned a lot of useful things at Timberline Knolls, didn't you?"

I nodded dumbly. Yes, I had learned a lot- and had missed out on being there for my friend when she needed me the most. I turned to leave.

"Let me know when I need to sign papers, or whatever else they need me to do. I won't fight the medical board," I said, and left him staring after me with apologetic eyes.

Sepsis and a Wedding

My sister and I had not spoken more than a handful times in the previous few years- she hadn't even been aware that I was in residential treatment- and when we had communicated, it had mostly been over social networking sites like Facebook. As far as I knew, she hadn't even been aware that I was in residential treatment. Her star in the comic book world continued to climb, and as a busy, self-employed person living in Maine with two children and a husband, she had little time for herself, and even less time to write or call anyone for casual conversations. But I was okay with it, because I felt that she and I had an understanding. We cared for each other, but not in a needy, grasping way- we didn't need birthday or Christmas presents from each other, because we both knew we were short on cash, and that presents didn't matter. The long-distance sister-acquaintance relationship we had established just seemed to work for us.

That is, it worked until the day I received a message from her husband, Roy, saying that Rachel was in the hospital with sepsis and that there was a large possibility that the worst could happen. My big sister could die.

Upon reading his message, I began to shake violently. My heart just couldn't stand anymore strain. I couldn't lose my sister; not after losing Prue, not after losing the Air Force, not after *everything*. I called her husband's phone multiple times, and when he failed to answer, I texted him, desperately inquiring what hospital Rachel was at, asking if I could fly out and be with her, if I could come and watch their sons so that *he* could be with her and not have to worry about the boys. I received no answer for hours, and, panicking, I called up all the hospitals in their area, looking for my sister, only to be shot down at every turn. Eventually, I slammed down the receiver for good, and buried my face in my hands, defeated. I couldn't find her. She could have entered the hospital in an assumed name, for all I knew. My sister was going to die and I wasn't going to be there for her. Just like Prue.

Eventually, Roy did text me back, stating that he had asked Rachel if she wanted me to fly to Maine to be with her, but she had said, 'No.' I was stunned at this response. *No?* Roy thanked me profusely for being so kind and wanting to help, and assured me that he would call and let me know if anything happened. *If anything happened.* My heart grew cold, and a lump rose in my throat. They were treating me as if I were a stranger. I began to shake with rage and torment; I could hear my heart beating in my skull. *What the fuck, what the fuck, what the fuck.*

My mind flashed back to when my sister and I had still lived together, right after our mom had left for California and it had just been Rachel and I home alone every night as our dad went to work. I remembered with such clarity the night that she was awoken me with her cries of pain, and I had confused them at first with cries of pleasure, and tried to ignore them; and later I had been so relieved that I hadn't. I dreaded to imagine what would have happened to her if I hadn't been there to call 911; would she have gotten cancer? Would she have died? I shivered at the thought.

But that was a long time ago. I hadn't been there for her in years. Besides cheering on her career from the sidelines, what kind of a sister was I? I was so self-centered, always absorbed with my own problems. What about Rachel's life, Rachel's problems? She had been through so much, without any support from *her* family. Maybe she was right to not let me in.

Weeks passed, and I received no word about my sister. I tried to keep her in the back of my mind and focus on the events in my own life, lest I go insane; I texted Roy periodically but he hardly responded. Meanwhile, things were happening quicker with medical board than I had anticipated; despite what Captain Yates had said about it taking a long time for them to make a decision, it only took a short while for them to make a decision about me. I was to be honorably discharged. I only had to pick a date, and then I would be released into the world as a free civilian. My military career was officially dead.

After learning this, feeling dazed and lonely, I went onto social media, and discovered through a public statement that my sister's life had been out of danger for some time, and that she was at home with her family to continue her recovery. I felt numb when I read the news; relieved, of course, but mostly numb. I had assumed since I had heard no bad news from Roy that she had been doing better, but as I had heard no good news, either, it had been difficult to be completely sure. *This must be how the family members of celebrities feel*, I thought dispassionately.

Scott and I, during that time, were forced to make some quick decisions regarding our future together. We decided, after much discussion, that after I was discharged we would move to Illinois, where his children lived with his ex-wife, so that we could be a part of their lives. He would be moving a few months before me, since he was due to start his new teaching job before I'd be able to leave the Air Force. The thought of being separated from him even for a few months was torture to me. I had found the man of my heart after years of disillusionment with other men, and in the pattern of my life he was being taken away from me soon after we were brought together. But he wanted to assure me that I was his and that he was mine; and so in the restaurant where we had had our first date, he proposed to me, and on a glorious summer day in July, with Norah and I dressed in gleaming white, he made me his wife. To this day, I can't recall a decision I've made that has had a more positive impact of my life than the one I made to marry Scott.

And somehow, I knew that Prue was watching us, cheering me on with all her heart.

Land of Lincoln
(35)

I was separated from the Air Force on December twenty-eighth, 2012. Having believed for years that I could never live a successful life outside of the military, I became determined to prove myself wrong. Scott and I had moved to a small town in Illinois called Bloomington, and rented a cheap apartment close to his job at the community college. It was not for either of us an ideal situation, but we did what we could to make it work. I tried not to tell myself that it was a step backwards from where I had been, but sometimes, when the cheap toilets malfunctioned, when our noisy neighbors kept me awake at night, and when we couldn't afford groceries, I became brooding and depressed. Norah, upon coming home to the apartment for the first time, looked around with critical eyes and said, "Daddy's house is way nicer- his has *two* floors." Though I tried to turn her comment into a lesson in humility, inside I felt a twinge of guilt, feeling that I had failed my daughter. I hadn't been able to keep my career in the Air Force, had taken her away from the nice neighborhood we lived in, and brought her here, to a high-crime area filled with people we didn't know that for some reason had the cops called on them every other day.

We struggled to find money to pay for Scott's child support and care every month, but we both agreed that despite that, we wanted to have his children over as often as his ex-wife would allow so that they would feel secure that their father was a part of their lives. As a consequence, however, we went broke every month trying to pay for food and for the extra space in our apartment. But we never considered seeing the kids less. The more time I spent with his son and daughter, the more I grew to love them and see them as my own. I knew I would only ever be their step-mother, but I didn't care- I wanted to be the best step-mother I could be, and I spoiled them with affection where I couldn't spoil them with toys, or clothes, or any other material thing. Norah and Scott's daughter Chloe became best friends, and over time, they became as close as two real sisters could ever wish to be, and watching them play together made my heart glow with a long-forgotten joy.

Despite our beautiful family, I felt like a failure for being kicked out of the Air Force; I was constantly depressed, and so riddled with anxiety that some days I couldn't raise my head from my pillow. My husband worked full-time to keep my spirits up, always telling me that it didn't matter to him what I ended up doing with my life; as long as it made me happy he would be there to support me. It was due to his constant love and patience that I finally brought myself to come to terms with reality, and began to consider what my options were: I could try to find a job, but that wouldn't change the fact that I was a nervous wreck, and what's more, the type of jobs I could get wouldn't bring in much income- hardly enough to cover the cost of the childcare I'd need for Norah. My other option, the one I was most leaning toward, was to become a university student. If I managed to get into school, I would be fulfilling the dream of a much younger Kim, who had been heartbroken when her father told her that he wouldn't help pay for college; and if I graduated, I'd be the first member of my family to obtain a college degree. Additionally, I would be able to receive student loans, and use the Yellow Ribbon program to help keep my family afloat financially, however barely.

And so, three months after being discharged from the Air Force, I enrolled in Bradley University as a Social Work major, and for the first time in ten years, I walked through the threshold of a learning institution as a full-fledged student.

I immediately fell in love with many aspects of school, though I had a hard time acclimating to my new role and environment. It was difficult for me to go out in public in civilian clothes everyday, since I had worn a uniform most days of the week for eight years. It was something so simple, wearing jeans and a top- but I had not worn them regularly for so long that sometimes I would have panic attacks while dressing, and lay prone on the ground, hyperventilating, and not come back to myself hours. It was also strange being the eldest in every class, and I felt frustrated, at times, with the naïveté that some of the other students showed in subjects such as homelessness and diversity. I tried to remind myself that Bradley was a private college, and as such, was largely populated with the children of well-to-do families who had not as yet seen very much of the world. But when discussions arose in class such as whether gay families should be able to adopt, or if the homeless should receive free access to healthcare, I found myself having to close my ears lest I get into a pointless argument with an eighteen year old.

"I honestly think that when people are poor, it's their own fault," I recall one white, young female student saying during one such discussion. "I mean, all they have to do is work, right, and everything will get better for them? Even if it's at Taco Bell. But they're lazy, and most are on drugs, and that's why they don't work."

On that instance, I had been unable to keep my mouth shut, unfortunately, and I had turned to her with fire in my eyes. The girl had reared back, possibly afraid that I might eat her.

"If you really think that, why are you a social work major?" I asked angrily.

"I want to help kids," said the girl stubbornly.

I glared at her. "I seriously doubt you could help them with that biased and shitty attitude you have," I seethed, only to be brought to peace by our professor, who skillfully took over the conversation before we started slapping at one other.

Many of my classes were like that, and I'm afraid I never made myself popular. If anything, I became closer to my professors than to any of my fellow students; I especially grew fond of my Diversity teacher, Professor Oreke, who, having grown up in Jordan and immigrated to the United Stated, had great insight as to what it really meant to grow up in a diverse environment, and knew how important inclusion and variety in the classroom and corporate worlds was to the health of a community.

I had never considered myself liberal before leaving the Air Force; I had never aligned myself to any group. I was just me, with my own preferences and my personal dislikes. I knew, when I thought about it, that I wanted more strict gun-laws in our country; I knew I wanted equality for everyone despite their race, gender, or sexual preference- but I never spoke up about it. Though I hated to admit it to myself, I felt afraid to ostracize myself from the other half of society that felt differently than I did. My time at Bradley changed that. I learned that I was allowed to have an opinion, and to say it out loud, and if anyone chose not to associate with me for it than it was not my problem- it was theirs.

Of course, one should have tact when voicing one's opinion, because everyone's opinion has merit; but tact was something I lacked. I recall one of the first times I volunteered at a local soup kitchen, as a way of breaking the ice between volunteers we went around the room and stated one like and one dislike we each had. By that time, I had already become irritated with some of the self-congratulatory volunteerism and fierce conservatism I had witnessed, and so when my turn came around, I cleared my throat, and said,

"I like gay rights, and I dislike the views of conservative republicans."

I pursed my lips as I was booed and hissed, but I felt a little proud of myself; all the other answers that had been given had been nonsense such as "I'm afraid of lightning and I enjoy flowers," so I knew I had thrown a curve-ball by saying what I did. But I didn't care. Those were my real likes and dislikes, not some fake fluff to spit out just to be considered socially acceptable. After everyone had had a turn, a few members of the congregation came up to me to shake my hand and congratulate me on my boldness. One woman even said,

"Thank you for that! I almost cheered! This bunch of cadavers needs to hear that stuff! If my husband was here he would have stood up and applauded you!"

I smiled happily. Maybe there was some merit to speaking you mind, after all, if it helped others find the bravery to speak theirs.

*

I looked down at my phone, surprised; my sister was calling me. She hadn't called for a long time- I actually couldn't remember the last time we had spoken. Certainly not since she had recovered from sepsis. I hesitated a moment, and then brought the phone to my ear, pushed the button.

"Rach?" I asked.

"Hey," said my sister, "I hope I'm not calling at a bad time. I have just a few minutes and wanted to talk a little."

"Yeah, no, that's great. I have time. I'm just sitting at home right now," I said.

"How's Norah?"

"She's doing good. Being crazy, as usual."

"I've seen her photos on Facebook. She looks just like you when you were little."

"Yeah, she looks a bit like me. She has a lot of her dad in her too, though. How's the comic biz?"

She sighed. "Busy as hell. But it's going really well. I have some amazing projects lined up, thankfully, but sometimes I wish I could just have a vacation."

"Yeah, I know what you mean. Probably to a lesser degree, though."

Silence for a moment, and then, "Roy… told me that when I was in the hospital, you offered to come see me."

My heart started to pound. "Yeah, I did. I actually called all the hospitals in your area, looking for you. I was going to fly out there, despite what you said."

"That's the thing," Rachel said, "*I wanted you to come.* When he asked me if I wanted you, I was really, really high on pain medication- I don't even remember him asking me that, actually. But the point is, of course I would have wanted you to come. We could have really used your help with the boys, and everything. It was super sweet of you to offer to fly over. I wanted to say sorry for-for that."

My lips began to quiver. "It's just… you're about all the family I got, Rach," I said, my voice breaking, "Of course if you're dying I have to be there. It got… really close, didn't it?"

"Yes. It did," she admitted.

"But you wanted me to come? You were only high?" I asked.

"Yes."

"So, the next time you're almost dead, I'm going to go to wherever you are, no matter what the Hell you say, okay?" I said with tears falling from my eyes, but a smile on my face.

Rachel laughed. "I hope I don't almost die again! Twice in a lifetime is quite enough for me, thank you."

I sniffled. "I love you, Rach."

"I love you too, Kimbo," said my sister, and with those words my heart became so bright it could have lit up the world.

*

I looked at Scott, and saw without him having to say a word that he had bad news. I hardly needed to guess, but I did anyway:

"We don't have enough for rent, do we?" I asked, my eyes sad.

Scott shook his head. "We are four hundred short. It's my fault; I forgot that I had two child care checks out. I thought they had been cashed a while ago…"

I put my hand on his arm, comforting him. "It was an accident. We'll figure something out."

He sighed. "We will have to ask my parents for help again."

I hung my head, frowning. His parents had been helping us with hundreds of dollars almost every month since I had left the Air Force. At this point, it was getting ridiculous. But Scott's paycheck, despite him being a brilliant professor and a breath away from a doctorate, only paid for his child support and care, and a fifth of the rent. Everything else had to come from my Yellow Ribbon Program, or his parents.

"I wish we didn't have to," I said quietly, leaning into him. "It's because I don't have a job. They must hate me."

Scott put his arms around me. "They love you," he said. "We're just in a shitty position right now, and they understand. We'll climb out of it somehow."

I pulled away. "I can drop out of school," I offered.

"Hon... we already looked into that. There's not a job you can get that will pay enough to make up for child care, and is also something that you can do everyday without hating yourself. No- stay in college. It does help out, after all- at least a little."

Despite what he said, I kept the idea of quitting school in the back of my mind for the next few weeks. In the meantime, I did everything I could to try and save money; I stopped buying food for myself, and ate only protein bars that I hoarded in my backpack. I bought everything second-hand for Norah, and when her dad complained when she visited him that her clothes were 'garbage', I forced myself to keep my mouth shut instead of argue. If he wanted her to have everything new and nice he could start paying child support regularly, I raged silently.

One day while I was out jogging, I received a call on my cell from an unfamiliar number. I took a few deep gasps in an attempt to normalize my breathing, and then answered.

"Hello?" I said.

"Hi, is this Kimberly?" said a man's voice.

"This is she," I replied.

"Hi, this is Ralph from Tops Casting. We met a while back; I remember you because you were in the Air Force at one point, right? I'm a Vet, too, so I remember stuff like that. Anyway, I was wondering if you might be interested in some work as a stand-in on a TV show here in Chicago."

I paused for a moment, letting that sink in. I had met Ralph when I had gone, on a whim, to a casting call looking for military extras. I had desperately needed the money, and considered it to be a one-time thing; I in no way imagined I would actually leave an impression.

"Um, yeah, I'm interested," I said finally, still nonplussed. What else could I say? When someone wants you to work on a TV show you don't say 'no'.

"Why- I mean, what TV show?" I asked.

"The show's a spin-off of Dick Wolf's Chicago Fire, called Chicago PD. Starts filming here in two weeks or so. When I met the actress I want you to stand in for I thought to myself, 'where have I seen her face before?' and then I finally remembered you; you guys could seriously be twins. The actress' name is Marina Squerciati."

"That's… that's amazing," I said. I hadn't heard of Marina Squerciati before, but I knew I would look her up at soon as I got home. "How much work would I get?"

"Pretty damn regular. Five to six days a week, eight to twelve hour days. A hundred and twenty dollars per eight hours, with time and a half after that."

My jaw dropped. "Wow." *We would be able to pay rent!*

"So, you in, then? Can I put you down as Marina's stand-in?"

"Uh, yeah, please do! Thank you."

"No problem. Us Vets gotta look out for each other. I'll give you a call in a few days to let you know when to head up here to take some pre-lim pics and whatnot. Sound good?"

"Yes!"

"Great! Thanks so much Kim. Talk to you soon. Bye."

He hung up, and I stood there, gaping at the phone in silence.

Well, I thought, stunned, *I guess I should let my school know I won't be showing up this semester.*

<u>Second Team</u>

(36)

I stood shivering in my four layers of clothing, blinded by the multiple lights shining into my face. Once a while, one would move, and spare my eye-sight for a second, but then it would come back quickly, usually just as glaring as before.

"Hey, Kim can you take the second position, please?" asked the camera man, looking through his lens into my face. I nodded and stepped to the second blue line on the ground which represented the actress' second position.

The snow had stopped for the moment, but it was still well below freezing. Though the actors were safe and warm in their trailers, the crew, and stand-ins such as myself, were stuck outside in the cold setting up each shot. As the focal point for the camera, I had taken my beanie off, and was standing stock-still and bareheaded, waiting for the gaffers to set up their lighting so the actress wouldn't have to stand for too long in the chill temperature. I tried not to be bitter about it, but at that moment, with my teeth chattering and my nose running, I found it difficult. At that point, I had been at work for eleven hours, all of which had been filmed outside. The sun had gone down long ago, and I was tired. My joints were aching. Thinking of the actors, warm and probably drinking tea, sent waves of envy through me.

"Okay, thanks, Kim," said the camera man, and he turned to say, "Ready for First Team."

And all of a sudden the air came alive with voices echoing the cry of 'First Team!' I shivered again, shoved on my cap, and shuffled my feet in the snow until I saw Marina walk towards me, muffled in her Canadian Goose parka. She smiled when she saw me. I don't know why people said we looked like twins; she was one-hundred times more gorgeous than I was.

"Hi, Kim," she said kindly. "Thanks."

I nodded, and moved out of the way as she took my spot. I moved behind the camera equipment to watch as the scene was shot; it took only ten minutes, and then Marina was whisked back to warmth. I had stood for forty-five minutes in that position to help set up the shot.

"Second Team!" the air echoed in a cacophony of voices. I ran quickly forward, yanking off my hat again.

The camera man glanced at me, and pointed to the same blue line I had stood on before. "Can you stand there again, please? We're turning it around. Same scene, different angle."

I bit my lip, but took my place on the blue line, and remained still for another forty-five minutes.

At the end of the day, and at the end of every day, I drove almost an hour to my friend's house where I stayed during the week, because unfortunately I lived too far away from Chicago to stay home during filming. I had no time during the week for anything except to shower, sleep for six hours, wake up, and go back to work, five times in a row, until it was the weekend and I could drive home and spend a day or two with my family. I was constantly exhausted, and ate little except what I took from the crafty stand. I missed my husband and my kids terribly, but I had no time whatsoever to speak to them during my long work hours. Though I was bringing in enough money to pay our bills, I felt as if my spirit was being pummeled.

That was not to say that I didn't like my job, because in a strange way, I really did. I enjoyed the lights, the camera, and the rush of filming scene after scene. I enjoyed feeling like I was a part of something, in a way I hadn't felt since I had first joined the Air Force nine years previously. The film business was never something I had envisioned for myself, but the more I contemplated it, the more I believed that it had definite possibilities for someone like me, who was so right-brained it was almost considered a handicap in the real world.

But, because I was away from my family, and because I wasn't eating well, I was morose and lethargic at work, and though I took my job seriously, I began to pine for a week off to spend with my kids.

We were filming in a train station late one night, when one of the production assistants rushed up to me, and said frantically, "Kim, we need you to wear Sophia's clothes."

I turned to him, surprised. "What?"

"We need you to photo double. Come on, come on, wardrobe trailer. Go. Go!"

I turned and jogged down the street outside the station until I reached the trailer, and when I climbed in, two women looked me up and down quickly, and threw a pair of pants, a shirt, and boots at me.

"Put 'em on, quick," said one of the ladies.

I complied, only to find that I could barely button up the pants. I glanced at the size: size twenty-seven. *Dammit.* That was my pre-TK size.

"Is… is there a bigger size?" I asked.

The women looked at me as if I had two heads. "Girl, there ain't no bigger size! If you don't fit what the actress wears, then you shit outta luck," answered on of them, grabbing the front of the pants and pulling the clasps shut with impossibly strong arms. I held my breath- it was so tight I could hardly move.

"Alright, put on the boots and jacket," demanded the other woman, tossing an elegant green coat at me that probably cost more than my month's rent, "And get out there, they need you ASAP."

I acquiesced, and began to comically to bend at the waist in an attempt pull on the military-style marauder boots. The women, after watching for a few seconds, became frustrated with my incompetence and started to tie the laces for me, and then spun me around, slipped the jacket over my shoulders, and pushed me unceremoniously out the door of the trailer into the night.

Though I had always disliked my size, I had never been so aware of it as I was then, stuffed into jeans that were too small for me and standing as still as I could in front of the camera, pretending to be a woman I wasn't. I had always known that 'Hollywood' sizes were small, but actually being forced to wear them and feel how they didn't suit your body was an especially wretched feeling. Luckily, I was able to wear the big green coat during all the scenes that night, so in a way I had a suit of armor protecting me from the harsh eye of the lens. But afterwards, when the shooting was over, I looked at my body in the dressing trailer mirror with the coat off, and gasped when I saw love handles spilling over the side of the pants. Yes, I was a healthier weight than I used to be. I didn't throw up half as much as I used to. But now I was fat. I tore off Sophia's clothes with rage, wondering why they had hired me at all.

I worked as a stand-in and photo double for Chicago PD for most of season one. But in the end, my brain got in the way; I hated the way I looked and cried often. I missed my kids and husband. I was tired and my various medications didn't help; one of the main side effects of all three was 'drowsiness'. And so, two months before the end of the season, I went home to my family, and I slept for about a week before I was able to move around again.

Just going off of how things ended with Chicago PD, one might believe that I decided to give up the idea of being in front of a camera. But in this case, one would be wrong. After I was rested and had spent time with my family, I realized that I still wanted in. I liked the work, I really did- but being away from my support was not good for me- my body or my mental health. I needed to find a balance between career and home that worked for who I was; even if it didn't fit into the realm of normalcy. In an attempt to slowly dip my feet back into the business, I worked a few (very brief) stand-in jobs for films such as Jupiter Ascending, and the TV shows Shameless and Supernatural. Additionally, I managed to use the weapon knowledge that I had gained in the Air Force to do stunt work for the feature film Divergent. I became proud of the things I had done, and most of all, I liked that I was able to come home to my family afterwards.

A part of me realized that what I was doing was desensitizing myself; if I constantly put myself out there, then being in the public eye wouldn't frighten me so much. And it was with that mentality that I got my first modeling job, with the hair company KMS California, to walk the catwalk in Chicago.

I was very unsure of myself. I was a healthy BMI, and not very tall (I'm barely 5'8"). What was I doing on a catwalk? When I thought of models, I thought of very thin women such as Kate Moss, and that most certainly was not me. Remembering my melt-down in the trailer while filming Chicago PD, I became extremely anxious. My fear only amplified when the woman choosing my wardrobe suggested that I perform squats in order to tighten my thighs. But as I buttoned up a hideous pair of black and white pants (because my thighs were 'too large' for a skirt), I began to get angry.

Why should I have to tighten my thighs in order to fit into someone else's idea of beauty? Weren't most women larger, and healthy, and still happy? Why was it only very skinny women who should be represented on a catwalk when they made up such a small percentage of the world? Maybe it was a good thing that I was going to be on stage. I thought of my daughter, Norah, and how she would grow up knowing that her mother had walked in front of hundreds of people, looking beautiful at a *healthy weight for her body.* I tried to imagine my own mother doing what I was going to do, and I chuckled to myself. She never would have done that; I don't know what life would have been like for me if she had. And though I still had a complicated relationship with my appearance… I was learning. I had made my body a priority. I had been through a lot of counseling by that time, and had unconditional support in Scott. I could challenge myself.

And so, somehow, I became a model. After KMS California, I was hired to do a few print ads, fashion shows, and hair shows- and I actually enjoyed it. I was aware, all the time, that I was usually the largest model present, but for some reason they kept casting me, and I used that as proof that I belonged there. I was healthy, and I was strong, because despite that fact that I wanted to run and hide the minute I entered a crowded room or auditorium, I somehow managed to stride gracefully onto the catwalk with my held high. Once in a while during a show, I would smile and look around at the audience, and think to myself,

Hi, everyone. It's me, the fat kid from school. Eat your damn hearts out.

Not Really the End
(37)

I ran up behind Norah, laughing like a Disney villain. Her long golden hair was trailing behind her in the wind, and there were leaves sticking out every which way from it from when she had gone rolling in the leaf pile. We were visiting my in-laws, and every fall they made a great, big leaf pile for all of their grandchildren to play in, and Norah was obsessed. When I caught up with her, I lifted her in my arms, swung her around, and kissed her apple cheeks. She giggled.

"Mommy, stop! You're tickling my face!" she shouted, smiling up at me with bright hazel eyes.

"Maybe I should *bite* you instead, my pretty!" I threatened, opening my mouth wide.

"Noooo!" she shrieked, running away again. I watched her go, but this time I didn't chase her; Scott was walking towards me with a gentle smile on his face. I met him and slipped my arms around his waist, and held him close.

"I just want to say for the millionth time," I said, "that I'm glad Norah starts kindergarten next week. I can't handle being away from her for six months again. And it's not good for her, either. I realize that, now."

Scott kissed me on the forehead, and we watched as his daughter Chloe ran up to take over the chasing of Norah, and suddenly they were in a full-blown game of tag.

"You were just trying to be fair," he said. "But I'm glad it's over, too. And Chloe is glad to have her sister back. She missed her like crazy."

I rested my head on Scott's shoulder, thinking.

"When she goes to school, I don't know what I'm going to do during the day," I said.

"You're going to do whatever the Hell you want to do," said Scott, grinning. "You are going to practice 'self-care'. You learned that at TK, right? You should actually do it for once."

I frowned. "What if I get sick every day, and spend a lot of money…"

"You won't. But if you do get sick sometimes, I'll be there to help, and you'll have your therapist, too, and you'll pick yourself up again and start over, because that's what you do. That's what you've always done."

I sighed, watching as our kids rolled on the grass. They looked so cute together. I was so happy Norah had a sister she could be close to while growing up. It was what I had always wanted to happen between Rachel and I. It was the way Prue and I had been.

"You have more faith in me than I do," I said.

"I love you," said Scott. "And I believe in you."

I smiled up at him, his words reverberating in my heart. "I love you too."

Afterword

I'm not sure how the idea to write a book about my life first emerged in my brain; perhaps the thought has always been there, in the background, waiting for the right time to make itself a reality. There were times, over the years, when I would write bits and pieces of my life-story in a journal, only to give up on the endeavor a day or two later, because I found it too emotionally draining and difficult. And it is; it's *difficult* reviewing your own life, analyzing the decisions and failures of your past as if you were a voiceless observer in your own mind. One might wonder whether if is ever a good idea to go over your past with a fine-toothed comb like I chose to- and I certainly wouldn't argue with those who are against it. While writing my book, I hated myself. I hated the little girl that I used to be, the desperate, helpless teenager that I grew into, and the opinionated, selfish young woman that I became.

What hurts, sometimes, is that that in many ways I still am that person; I see it in my every day life, the way I sometimes hide myself from my family because I feel overwhelmed with responsibility; the way I thrust my views onto others and refuse to hear theirs; the way I hate to admit I'm wrong in any argument. While I have matured in many ways, I still feel like a child in others.

But despite this, for months I worked dedicatedly, writing chapter after chapter of my story, sometimes dragging them out like demons in an exorcism, and other times letting them flow like melting snow in spring. I grew obsessed with finishing my novel, and sometimes I worked through the night, only looking up from my computer when the sun was rising over the trees outside of my house. I became tired, and sometimes had glaring migraines that laid me out for days; and at one point, I started to believe that all my writing was killing me… until my husband mentioned to me an interesting point about my writing that I hadn't realized.

I had gotten dressed to leave the house to go write at a coffee shop, but before I left, I suddenly felt a wave of exhaustion. What was the point of me getting all of that stuff out, anyway? It would probably never be published, and even if it was, no one would find my weird, disjointed life interesting. Plus, every time I wrote, my husband Scott had to keep charge of the household, to make sure everything kept running for the kids' sake, and I felt guilty. Unsure of myself, I expressed my feelings to him, and I mentioned that I might quit writing for a while.

"No, you're not going to stop writing," said my husband, his eyes soft and sweet, but stern. "I want you to keep going. I think it's good for you."

"How is it good for me?" I complained, leaning back onto our couch, tired. "All I do is neglect you and the kids. And I'm so exhausted all of the time…"

Scott hesitated, and then held my hand in his. "Honey, do you recall the last time you got sick?"

I remained still for a minute, thinking. No, I couldn't remember.

"It's been a few weeks, honey," said Scott, "And when you did it then, it had been weeks before that. This- what you're doing- I don't say it's easy for you, but something about is good for you. All of the energy you used to spend on you illness has transferred itself to this. It's like... catharsis for you."

A small thrill went down my spine. He was right; it was strange how I hadn't even noticed I wasn't purging much anymore. I had been so occupied with completing my book that I had somehow managed to silence the bulimia, which for fourteen years had reigned supreme in my mind, always demanding, never forgiving. I couldn't even remember the last time I had heard the deriding, oily voice of my disorder.

"I noticed it a while ago, but I didn't want to jinx it," continued Scott. "But I thought you should know, now, since you are thinking about stopping. But please don't stop, honey."

My eyes became misty, and I leaned into my husband, my head snuggled on his chest. "I won't stop," I promised. "Not until I'm done."

And only then did I understand
It is (the cat)—and every creature like him—
Who can teach us how to praise—purring
In their own language,
Wreathing themselves in the living fire.

Excerpt from *Wild Gratitude*, written by Edward Hirsch

Made in the USA
Charleston, SC
15 April 2016